Growing Apart

Growing Apart

Religious Reflection on the Rise of Economic Inequality

Special Issue Editors

Kate Ward
Kenneth Himes

MDPI • Basel • Beijing • Wuhan • Barcelona • Belgrade

MDPI

Special Issue Editors

Kate Ward
Marquette University
USA

Kenneth Himes
Boston College
USA

Editorial Office
MDPI
St. Alban-Anlage 66
4052 Basel, Switzerland

This is a reprint of articles from the Special Issue published online in the open access journal *Religions* (ISSN 2077-1444) in 2017 (available at: https://www.mdpi.com/journal/religions/special_issues/economic_inequality)

For citation purposes, cite each article independently as indicated on the article page online and as indicated below:

LastName, A.A.; LastName, B.B.; LastName, C.C. Article Title. *Journal Name* **Year**, *Article Number*, Page Range.

ISBN 978-3-03842-577-9 (Pbk)
ISBN 978-3-03842-578-6 (PDF)

Contents

About the Special Issue Editors

Kate Ward is Assistant Professor of Theological Ethics at Marquette University. Her research focuses on economic ethics, virtue ethics, and ethical method. She has published articles on wealth, virtue, and economic inequality in journals including Theological Studies, Journal of Religious Ethics, Heythrop Journal, and Journal of the Society of Christian Ethics (forthcoming). She is completing a monograph exploring the impact of wealth, poverty and inequality on the pursuit of virtue. Dr. Ward holds a Ph.D. in Christian ethics from Boston College, an M.Div. with concentration in Bible from Catholic Theological Union, and an A.B. in psychology with honors from Harvard College. She and her husband, Matthew Filipowicz, live in the Riverwest neighborhood in Milwaukee.

Kenneth Himes, OFM (Ph.D., Duke University; M.A., Washington Theological Union; A.B., Siena College) is Professor of Christian Ethics at Boston College. His research and writing focus on ethical issues in war and peacebuilding, the development of Catholic social teaching, and the role of religion in American public life, as well as fundamental moral theology. Dr. Himes is the author of Targeted Killing and the Ethics of Drone Warfare (Rowman and Littlefield, 2016); Christianity and the Political Order: Conflict, Cooptation, and Cooperation (Orbis, 2013); Responses to 101 Questions on Catholic Social Teaching (Paulist, 2013; first published 2001; Polish edition published in 2005; Indian edition published 2008); and Fullness of Faith: The Public Significance of Theology (Paulist, 1993; co-authored with Michael J. Himes; Chinese edition published in 2014.) The second edition of his highly regarded edited volume, Modern Catholic Social Teaching: Commentaries and Interpretations, was published in 2017 by Georgetown University Press.

religions

MDPI

Editorial

Introduction to This Issue

Kenneth Himes [1,*] and Kate Ward [2]

[1] Theology Department, Boston College, Chestnut Hill, MA 02467, USA
[2] Theology Department, Marquette University, Milwaukee, WI 53233, USA; katharine.ward@marquette.edu
*   Correspondence: kenneth.himes@bc.edu

Academic Editor: Philip Goodchild
Received: 27 March 2017; Accepted: 4 April 2017; Published: 6 April 2017

Only a few decades ago, the neoconservative writer Irving Kristol could dismiss economic inequality as a social problem (Kristol 1980). To his mind, there was little empirical evidence demonstrating that inequality was a significant issue. Today, we have a substantial amount of empirical data that reveals economic inequality as an important element in a number of realms—politics, education, health, social cohesion, and law, not to mention ethical concerns about solidarity, the common good, and human dignity. In short, economic inequality matters.

With that in mind, the Jesuit Institute at Boston College funded a year-long faculty seminar that would examine economic inequality from a variety of academic perspectives. The seminar began in the fall of 2015 and concluded in the spring of 2016. Throughout that period, a group of faculty representing various schools and departments within the university met regularly to read how different academic disciplines looked at economic inequality and discuss the insights that one discipline's perspective might enrich another's way of studying inequality.[1]

The faculty seminar at Boston College led to the decision to host a conference that would present some of the work done by the seminar members. Further, it was decided to invite student papers on the topic as well. In April of 2016 the two-day conference, "Growing Apart: the rise of inequality" "was held on the Boston College campus. In addition to concurrent sessions in which the seminar faculty and student presenters gave papers, there were plenary sessions with invited scholars. Many of the papers presented over the course of those two days have been revised and are published in this issue of *Religions*.

The Interdisciplinary nature of the seminar and conference explains the presence of authors and topics that may not ordinarily appear in a journal such as *Religions*. Although the guest editors of this issue are both trained in Christian ethics and a number of the other papers included here are by theologians based in the academy, we felt it important to include several papers that illustrate how scholars in economics, law, sociology, education, political science, philosophy, and social work address the topic of economic inequality. While each of these scholars used methods and resources specific to their fields, the conference was open to the general public and so speakers aimed their papers at a general audience that allowed non-specialists to benefit. In revising the conference papers for publication in this issue, the editors asked all the authors to keep in mind that readers of *Religions* may be well read in other academic fields but expertise is generally located in areas of theology, religious studies, and textual criticism. We believe the essays presented in part one of this issue provide helpful and wise insights from a diverse set of perspectives that can assist those who approach economic inequality from the vantage points of theology and religious studies.

---

[1] The seminar members were well aware that there are different ways to speak about economic inequality, including but not limited to inequality of wealth, income, and life outcome. Since all these measures were deemed relevant to our shared concerns, the members addressed all of them, attempting to make clear distinctions as necessary for clarity.

By including contributions from writers representing other academic disciplines, this issue of *Religions* helps us understand why economic inequality deserves more attention from religious thinkers, particularly those who bring a normative stance to an issue that touches upon justice, human rights, and the meaning of a good society.

Economic inequality, particularly in the areas of income and wealth, has been steadily expanding in the United States. This reality is a concern for other nations as well. Yet, the topic of inequality was largely ignored by academic economists until recently. And many of those involved with public policy also downplayed the centrality of economic inequality as a societal concern until its reality and influence became impossible to ignore. Perhaps this was due to the fact that for many social theorists wealth distribution was a minor issue compared to economic growth, since the belief was either "a rising tide would lift all boats" or "trickle-down economics" would eventually, but surely, benefit those worst off. Frequent recourse was made to the argument that an expanding pie makes redistribution easier than reallocating shares of an existing pie that was not growing. As confidence in those claims has waned, the issue of economic inequality has gained more serious attention.

In part one of this issue, there are essays by scholars representing the social sciences and law. The initial essay by the sociologist Victor Tan Chen provides an account of how inequality is experienced in one specific setting, long-term unemployed automotive workers. His account provides a vivid description of the impact of economic inequality upon individuals and their communities, as well as providing insight into the difficulties involved in overcoming inequality.

The second essay by Tiziana Dearing offers lessons drawn from the field of social work about income inequality and how that reality, in turn, challenges social work to develop innovative services that might address the challenges presented by income inequality.

In the third essay, political scientists Kay Schlozman, Henry Brady and Sidney Verba discusses recent research on how economic inequality undercuts important practices of democratic politics. Their essay also reveals the negative spiral in which U.S. politics now finds itself, where economic inequality skews political life and where political power is employed to further deepen economic inequalities.

Mary Walsh and Maria Theodorakakis, a professor of education and a graduate student in the field respectively, look at the evidence that economic inequality is harming children's health and brain development that, in turn, limits academic achievement and intellectual growth. They also relate the story of new educational programs and policies that hold the promise of mitigating some of the harms of economic inequality as it affects the education of children.

Another pairing of professor and graduate student, Joseph Quinn and Kevin Cahill, has produced the fifth essay in part one of the issue. These economists examine two of the most commonly cited and employed methods for alleviating economic disadvantage, namely the Earned Income Tax Credit (EITC) and Minimum Wage laws. Their economic analysis points out the strengths and weaknesses of each strategy for countering economic inequality.

Finally, Frank Garcia, a professor of law, broadens the setting for considering economic inequality by examining the impact that international trade law has on the increase or decrease of such inequality. At a time when international trade has been broadly attacked as a cause of inequality, while others have defended trade as a remedy for inequality, the analysis of trade law is a timely essay.

With part two of the issue the essays move into areas more familiar to readers of this journal. Two philosophical essays begin this section of the issue. Micah Lott provides a brief essay that seeks to clarify just what is meant by claims, often heard during the past election year, that the system is "broken" or "fixed" in such a way that the rich will only get richer while others will suffer. His essay also presses for clarity about what exactly it is that we are discussing when we talk about an economic system.

The other philosophical essay is a longer reflection on the issue of whether inequality is actually harmful to those at the top of the economic pyramid. Dustin Crummett considers various arguments that great wealth, or having too much, hinders human well-being. Might efforts to overcome substantial economic inequality actually benefit those commonly seen as the beneficiaries of inequality?

The next essay, written by Stephen Leccese, provides a history lesson about an earlier era of grave economic inequality. The Gilded Age, a period roughly extending from the end of the American Civil War to the end of the nineteenth century, has been cited as the closest parallel to our present age of economic inequality. What emerged from that period was the birth of a new approach to economics championed by a group of scholars who broke with much of classical economic theory and who saw the goal of the field of economics as serving the public good.

One of the thinkers influenced by the "new economics" emerging out of the Gilded Age was the Catholic social theorist and advocate, Msgr. John Ryan. In the essay by Kenneth Himes, Ryan's lifelong campaign for a living wage is acknowledged, but the question is posed as to whether resources in modern Catholic social teaching might be put to creating a limit on wealth and not only establishing a minimal income.

Joyce Konigsburg evaluates the contemporary situation of living wage arguments from the perspective of Catholic social thought and economics. She evaluates risks and benefits of living wage proposals for employers and the dignity of workers and deems they are a socially sustainable form of redress to inequality.

Another scholar of Christian ethics, Kate Ward, analyzes the views of Pope Francis and how he discusses inequality. It is suggested that Francis provides an approach to inequality that is closely linked to a virtue ethic response shaped by the Jesuit understanding of the virtue of hospitality. The resonance of that approach with feminist treatments of inequality is also analyzed.

Finally, two more essays by scholars of Christian ethics broaden the discussion of economic inequality by situating it in an international perspective. James O'Sullivan writes about how economic inequality has been treated from the perspective of various global initiatives that have set goals for lessening inequality. His analysis of "global goal setting" strategies is informed by contemporary human rights theory and approaches to human development.

The concluding essay, by the distinguished Indian moral theologian Shaji George Kochuthara, provides an examination of economic inequality within the contexts of a globalization dominated by neo-liberal economics as well as the impact of such thinking on nations such as India. In response, fashioning an alternative economic model that employs the insights of Catholic social teaching leads to a strategy that underscores solidarity as the key element in battling against inequality.

This rich collection of essays offers readers a set of scholarly reflections on what is one of the crucial social evils of our time, the huge and growing gap between "haves" and "have nots." Because the problem is so complex and beyond the competence of any one discipline to adequately address, the approach to be taken must be inter-disciplinary. A modern university is ideally suited to bring together participants in conversations, which provoke insights that can motivate, clarify, and guide action toward remedying the ills associated with economic inequality. The guest editors of this volume wish to express our gratitude to the Jesuit Institute at Boston College for its support in hosting such conversations. And we thank the editors of *Religions* for inviting us to share some of the ideas that emerged from our seminar and conference.

Conflicts of Interest: The authors declare no conflict of interest.

Reference

Kristol, Irving. 1980. *Some Personal Reflections on Economic Well-Being and Income Distribution*. Washington: National Bureau of Economic Research.

religions

MDPI

Essay

An Economy of Grace

Victor Tan Chen

Department of Sociology, Virginia Commonwealth University, Richmond, VA 23284, USA; vchen@vcu.edu

Academic Editors: Kate Ward and Kenneth Himes
Received: 31 October 2016; Accepted: 15 March 2017; Published: 18 March 2017

Abstract: This essay is adapted from a plenary talk the author gave at the "Growing Apart: The Implications of Economic Inequality" interdisciplinary conference at Boston College on 9 April 2016, as well as portions of his book *Cut Loose: Jobless and Hopeless in an Unfair Economy*, a sociological ethnography based on interviews and observations of unemployed autoworkers in Detroit, Michigan, and Windsor, Canada, during and after the Great Recession. The essay discusses four themes from this research. First, it provides a sociological understanding of how long-term unemployment and economic inequality are experienced by today's less advantaged workers. Second, it illustrates how social policy can improve their circumstances. Third, it examines the limits of policy, and how dealing with inequality also requires changing the broader culture. Fourth, it makes the case for one possible approach to bring about that cultural change: a morality of grace.

Keywords: unemployment; inequality; morality; grace; blue-collar; white-collar; meritocracy; education; family structure; labor markets

---

1. Introduction

In this essay, I discuss four themes from my book *Cut Loose: Jobless and Hopeless in an Unfair Economy* [1]. First, using two of the profiles from my book, I provide a sociological understanding of how long-term unemployment and economic inequality are experienced by today's less advantaged workers. Second, I describe some of my findings about how social policy can improve their circumstances. Third, I examine the limits of policy, and how dealing with inequality also requires us to change the broader culture. And finally, I make the case for one possible approach to bring about that cultural change—what I call a 'morality of grace'.

I started my book in the fall of 2008, when the financial crisis struck. It may be hard to remember how frightening that time was, when the economy seemed to be collapsing, and even companies as iconic as General Motors were on the verge of liquidation. At the height of the economic crisis, 15 million Americans were out of work. Four out of ten of these workers went through long-term unemployment—that is, being without a job for more than six months. As for American autoworkers, their industry had just gone through another wave of downsizing, but over the span of the recession the layoffs intensified. Auto industry employment shrank from 1 million jobs to 600,000 [2].

I decided I wanted to go to Detroit and understand what was happening to the men and women who were losing their jobs. The auto industry and autoworkers are central to the American story. This is the industry that helped make America an industrial powerhouse. These are the jobs that helped build a strong middle class in the years after World War II. Employees had powerful unions, high pay, good benefits, job security—even if they did not have a college degree.

Over the last several decades, though, the economy and culture have moved in the exact opposite direction. According to tax data collected by Thomas Piketty and others, the top 10 percent of earners now take in half the country's income. The wealthiest 10 percent own three-quarters of its wealth. We have not seen this level of inequality since the time of *The Great Gatsby* [3].

Meanwhile, the middle class is being hollowed out. The nonpartisan Pew Research Center recently reported that the size of the middle class—defined by a consistent income range across generations—has fallen from 61 percent of households in 1971, to 50 percent in 2015 ([4], p. 5). Eight years out of the recession, unemployment is significantly down and there is steady job growth. But millions of Americans continue to be left behind. A quarter of today's unemployed have been out of work for six months or more—a rate almost as high as what was experienced during the peak of the recession in the 1980s [5]. Many people who want to work aren't even counted as unemployed because they have given up on finding a job. The labor participation rate—the share of people who are either working or looking for work—is at its lowest level since the 1970s [2]. Since the recession, wages have grown slowly. The typical American family makes less than it did in 1999 ([6], p. 7). Two-thirds of Americans say they are anxious about their financial situation [7], and a majority say they would have a difficult time paying a $1,000 bill from an accident or other unexpected expense [8].

We have come a long way from the well-paid, secure jobs that American autoworkers used to enjoy. To use another auto-related symbol, one could say that our new economic reality is represented, in its most extreme form, by the Uber driver: no benefits, no job security, hustling every day to make a living. But this is not just a problem for blue-collar workers. It's also a problem for white-collar workers, who are increasingly seeing their good jobs outsourced, automated and contracted away. Today, hospitals send radiology scans to doctors in India to analyze [9]. Lawyers have their document reviews handled by computer programs [10]. As for us, we have to look no farther than our own academic departments: more than half of all faculty now hold part-time appointments [11].

I wanted to understand how these broad economic changes were affecting individuals, families, and communities. Thus, at the tail end of the Great Recession and after, I spent time in Detroit and Windsor, Ontario, which is right across the Detroit River. My goal was to compare how people experienced long-term unemployment in the United States and Canada. I also wanted to compare apples to apples: I looked at the same kinds of workers, working at the same kinds of plants, for the same companies in the same industry. The idea was to focus on the policies and cultures on either side of the border, and examine how and why they made a difference. I ended up doing interviews with former autoworkers at two Chrysler engine plants in Detroit and Trenton, Michigan, and two Ford engine plants in Windsor, Ontario. I also interviewed workers at factories that supply auto parts to GM, Ford, and Chrysler. Thanks to outsourcing, these parts suppliers now employ many more people than the Big Three do, although at lower wages, and with fewer benefits and protections [12].

2. The Impact of Unemployment

What impact did unemployment have on the workers and families I studied? Here is a passage from my book regarding one of the unemployed workers I became acquainted with. The statistics on unemployment and its economic impact are important, but as a sociologist my goal is to get beyond those numbers and provide a sense of its social and personal impact:

> John Hope lost his job in 2009. For fourteen years he had worked at a car plant near Detroit, heaving truck bumpers onto the practiced balance of his lean, muscled arms and machine-polishing away the wounds in the rough steel, readying them for immersion in a chemical bath that would gild each piece with a thin layer of luminous chrome. It was a work of magic, conjured up in a foul, fume-drenched cavern, an industrial alchemy that transformed masses of cheap base metals into things of beauty and value.

> John, fifty-five, excelled at the work. Every day on the job meant handling metal and machinery that could, with a moment's indecision, crush or maim him. He took pride in the strength required to hold the bumpers without tipping over, and the skill needed to buff each piece precisely, so that every hairline nick or abrasion disappeared, the chemical sheen wrapped perfectly across the smooth steel, and the bumpers arrived at the end of the line looking like lustrous silver jewelry. "If I ain't doing it good, you're going to lose the money", notes John in his Alabama drawl.

His Southern roots linger in that whirling, excitable, workingman's voice, but his job—and the pride, status, and paycheck that came with it—long ago separated him from a personal history of vicious rural poverty. Deserted by young parents when he was just a baby, raised by a grandmother who had to abandon him a decade later when she went blind, John learned to fend for himself. For a time he and his older brother slept in vacant houses and cast-aside cars, on porches and forest floors . . .

[In the seventies,] the lure of Detroit's auto plants, with their union-won wages, took hold of his imagination. John followed a cousin up there [and] took a job at a plant in Highland Park . . . For over a decade John saw his income rise steadily . . . It was enough to support his family of four, enough to buy a red-brick ranch house in the city, enough to give his daughter and son video games, clothes, and other trappings of a middle-class American childhood. It was enough for John to look back and feel pride in what he—an abandoned child, a once-homeless boy, son of the dirt-poor South—had accomplished.

Then the Great Recession hit . . . As America's automakers fell, the damage spread to the plants that supplied them . . . His company decided to ship all the work to one of its larger factories, to cut costs. More than a hundred workers at his plant were terminated, John included . . .

Now it is the middle of winter, and John is feeling the loss of income hard . . . When I visit on a frigid day in January, two stove burners have been left fired up, providing heat. The furnace is shut off because John doesn't have $1000 to repair it . . .

"You're used to working, and getting what you want", he says. "When you're not working, it's like being in jail, but you have to get your own food." He slaps his knee and shrieks with laughter. It is the way he deals with adversity—with a smile and a devil-may-care quip. Ask him how he copes, and he will flash a wide grin. "I feel good. I got a great sense of humor." Ask him about his job search and he'll say things will work out. "As long as you believe, you're going to be all right", John says . . .

But as the conversation goes on, the certainty starts to unravel, the defensive smiles recede. "I'll be back to work soon", he insists—but then adds, after a pause: "It can be stressful." . . .

The job was more than a job. "To me it's real bad", he says slowly, forcing out each syllable, "because the thing about my job—man, it makes me think—my job was like my mother and father to me." Quietly, John starts to sob. He wipes the tears on the denim collar of his button-down shirt, rubs his eyes gently with his fingers. "It's all I had, you know", he goes on. "I worked hard because I had no mother and father. I was cut loose. I hate to think about them . . . When you growing up young, your mother and father, they take care of you. And I ain't never had that . . . All my life I depended on my job as my mother and father. If I could only make it every day, I know I'm all right." ([1], pp. 1–4)

As research has found, long-term unemployment hits people with a psychological blow that is comparable to divorce and the death of a loved one [13,14]. Work is so central to who we are. "What do you do?" is one of the first things we ask someone when we meet them. Work gives us a sense of our importance, of our contribution. It provides a routine, a structure, a deep meaning to our lives.

Let me provide one other example of the emotional toll that unemployment can take—here, not just on individuals, but on entire families. Royce is an American and a former parts worker (all of the names of the respondents quoted in this essay are pseudonyms, per Institutional Review Board requirements). He, his wife and four kids live outside Detroit, in a nice suburban house. When Royce lost his job, he sunk into a depression. "I wasn't feeling that I was doing my part", he says ([1], p. 208).

The loss of his breadwinner status also created tensions in his marriage. His wife, Elena, has a job at a property management office. After years of being a stay-at-home mom, she is hungry for success.

"I'm … big on my position in the company", she says. "Because that's just how I am. Wanting to look good, wanting to feel good" ([1], p. 146). But Elena's success means she has less patience for Royce's failures. When they argue, which is often these days, Elena will yell, "This is my house! I pay all the bills! I put all the food in the house!" ([1], p. 118).

And yet, several months after Royce lost his job, Elena ended up losing her job, too. "It's a lot of emotion dealing with this, and it's just as hard as the loss of the income", she says. The family's finances have become desperate. Their gas was recently shut off. They owe huge amounts of interest on a recent payday loan, and the bill collector keeps knocking. For extra cash, Royce ended up pawning his wedding ring. The fights have gotten worse, too—sometimes, they escalate to the point that Elena starts slapping Royce. "I will try to knock him out, and knock him out the door", she tells me. During their yelling matches, their five-year-old son cowers in a corner of the living room, crying ([1], p. 119).

3. Policy

Royce and Elena's story reminds us how wounding and destructive unemployment can be to one's health and one's relationships with partners and children. And yet, even in these intimate areas of domestic life, a stronger social safety net can make a difference. In Canada, I found, universal health care and generous job retraining programs made it easier to cope with long-term unemployment. Support for working families, especially single parents with children, went a long way to help the kinds of households usually hit hardest by unemployment. Finally, the government there gave Canadian companies rules of the road so that they could do right by their employees. When every company is required to pay severance, for instance, companies who try to take the high road are not at such a competitive disadvantage.

So, how did these differences in policy play out in concrete terms? Here is one example: Kirsten is an American and a former Chrysler worker. She is divorced and a mother of two young children. During the recession, Kirsten decided to take a buyout and leave Chrysler. In part, it was because her relationship with her fiancé had become abusive. Matters boiled over early one morning, after Kirsten came home right after her Chrysler shift, and her fiancé demanded sex. Kirsten refused. Her fiancé started slapping and strangling her in front of their two young kids. Their son called the police, and her fiancé fled. Kirsten went to work at the engine plant the very next day, with black-and-blue bruises all over her face. Kirsten says she took a Chrysler buyout to get away from that abusive relationship. But she misjudged how tough the job market would be. "I didn't know that times were so hard", she says ([1], p. 124).

Unable to find work, Kirsten is now delinquent on her mortgage and credit card payments and considering bankruptcy. She is deeply depressed and recently started taking an antidepressant for the first time in her life. "When I was working at Chrysler, I had nothing like that to worry about", she says ([1], p. 125).

On the Canadian side of the border, unemployment tended to be less severe for single parents, and stronger policies appeared to play a role in this. Alice is a Canadian and former Ford worker. In many ways she is a mirror image of Kirsten. She, too, is a divorced mother of two. She, too, went through an abusive relationship. At one point, Alice's alcoholic husband broke her nose and blackened her eyes. The next day, she showed up at the plant. Like Kirsten, Alice couldn't afford to miss work. Ultimately, the high wages Alice earned at the plant were her ticket out. After she left her husband, she continued to work midnight shifts and raised her two young kids by herself. As I heard often among my women respondents, these good jobs at the plant gave them and their children independence and protection in a sometimes violent world.

Alice took the buyout and left Ford during the recession. Life since then has not been easy. She is deep in debt, with tens of thousands of dollars in personal loans and unpaid credit card balances. But overall, Alice is optimistic. She is attending college to become a nurse, with her tuition fully paid by a provincial retraining program. Even though her unemployment insurance has ended, Alice receives other benefits from the government. She gets a monthly living stipend through her retraining program. She also receives a child tax benefit every month and a sales-tax refund every three months. "It's going the right way", she says of her future ([1], p. 142).

4. Limits to Policy

The tough experience of being unemployed in Canada is improved in meaningful ways thanks to these government benefits. That said, *enacting* good policies is not enough. For one thing, policies that are good on paper aren't necessarily implemented so well. There are budget shortfalls. There are sluggish and inefficient bureaucracies. The situation has become worse in recent decades. In both America and Canada, in-person services have increasingly been replaced by call centers and websites. Government services have increasingly been outsourced to private firms, or just left underfunded and overburdened.

Take Ken, one of the American parts workers I became acquainted with. His wife left him after he lost his job. Ken has become depressed and he sometimes has thoughts of suicide. He recently started taking antidepressants that a primary care physician gave him. Ken hasn't been able to see a therapist or psychiatrist and he can't afford insurance. Ken tried applying for Michigan's Medicaid program for childless adults—he was told they had no funding left and weren't accepting new enrollees. So Ken went to the state job center and asked about counseling. He was told there was a two-month wait. "You can commit suicide tomorrow", he says. Desperate, Ken decided to start going to a church for group therapy. The only sessions available, though, are for Narcotics Anonymous. Ken doesn't have a drug problem, but he starts attending anyways. "They'll talk to anybody", he says. "They'll let anybody in" ([1], p. 159).

As Ken has learned, governments frequently do not have the funding or staff to fulfill the promises of their social policies. So Ken relies on himself, mowing lawns for cash and hustling every other way he can. "I'm strong", he says. "I'll make it. I'll be alright. I'm not going to let nothing get to me . . . I'm not ready to check out" ([1], p. 160).

Beyond these problems with implementation, there is another reason we need to go further than a narrow focus on enacting good policies. As important as this work is, it is painfully clear that the hard-hitting measures needed to deal in any long-term way with inequality cannot be sustained in this current political climate. There needs to be a change in the broader culture as well, a culture that ultimately determines what policies are even possible.

This is another reason that I chose to study autoworkers. They represent not just the old economy, but also an older culture of solidarity that we have forsaken. With their strong unions, they championed an all-for-one, one-for-all attitude—one that said, "Let's lift up everyone at the same time." In Washington, labor unions like the United Auto Workers led the charge for higher minimum wages, health care, and civil rights. People forget that Walter Reuther, the president of the UAW, literally stood beside Dr. Martin Luther King Jr. while he made the "I Have a Dream" speech during the March on Washington. Back then, a social contract existed between many workers and their employers. Workers toiled away with the expectation that their corporate mothers and fathers would take care of them. Companies made good on those promises, and even big business respected the power of labor. In words that are shocking today, in the 1940s the president of the US Chamber of Commerce, the country's largest business lobby, said: "Collective bargaining is a part of the democratic process" ([15], p. 21).

As late as the seventies, American CEOs in major companies earned just thirty times more than the average worker, according to the Economic Policy Institute. Huge disparities of pay between executives and workers were seen as unseemly back then. But today, the social norms at top have changed. The gap between CEO and worker pay is about 300-to-1 [16]. Meanwhile, union membership is a third of what it once was [2,5]. Whether you approve or disapprove of unions, it is clear that they have long served as a countervailing power. In the postwar period especially, they checked and balanced the influence of corporations. They promoted pro-worker policies, and perhaps more importantly, they evangelized egalitarian norms throughout society.

With that culture and those institutions in place, it is not surprising that the federal government responded in a robust fashion after the Great Depression to deal with unemployment and support struggling families. But today, in the wake of the Great Recession, political leaders have been less willing to pursue substantial policies to lift up ordinary workers. In fact, across the globe, countries that once provided generously for the unemployed and underemployed have dramatically curtailed their benefits. In Canada, that retrenchment happened during the nineties—under a center-left government [17].

The workers I spoke to were realistic: they knew they could no longer rely on weak institutions to bail them out. Consider Tom, a Canadian and former Ford worker. After his unemployment ran out, Tom went on welfare. But the help the government gives is both insufficient and humiliating, he says. As for unions, they were once important. But "you're at a point where you have to give something back", he says. "And now everybody's saying, 'The union is doing this, the union is doing that.' No, they're not. The company is deciding what they're gonna do'" ([1], p. 165).

Without anyone or anything to rely on, Tom focuses on schemes to get under-the-table cash. Anything else is a daydream. "When a thousand people band together it makes a difference, but just by myself, no", he says. "They're gonna tell me what to do anyhow, so let's go along with it. Don't make waves." But Tom's inability to turn to institutions means he has no choice but to look to his personal initiative—and his personal failure to seize that initiative. Tom complains about the unfairness of it all, but at the end of the day, when he's alone with his thoughts in the home he's about to lose, he is the one he rips into. "I should be able to find employment", he says. "I couldn't even get a fucking job at a worm farm" ([1], p. 200).

In the absence of strong unions and interventionist governments, what is left for today's workers is a go-it-alone perspective of self-reliance—this idea that, "I get an education, I work hard and get the skills I need, and I become successful." Yet this individualistic viewpoint makes the experience of long-term unemployment all the more wounding. Many of my workers felt like—as they put it—"losers". And yet being a worthy person in our society is all about being a winner—as some politicians like to remind us.

This culture of winning and losing affected my respondents' personal relationships in noticeable ways. What I heard among some of the families I interviewed is that people do not care for marrying, or staying with, a so-called loser or a "scrub". And it goes beyond these working-class households: today, the college-educated marry each other in much greater numbers than in past generations [18]. To a growing extent, as psychologists have found, marriage is about "self-expansion"—about a partner who helps you grow and succeed—and less about loyalty and commitment [19].

This view is part of a broader culture in America, what I call *meritocratic morality*. This is a belief system that upholds the virtues of self-reliance, willpower, and individualism. The idea of the American Dream captures this viewpoint, though its values have spread throughout the world. According to meritocratic morality, success depends, and should depend, on your own efforts and abilities. This individualistic ideology even seemed to influence some of the autoworkers I interviewed—again, a class that has benefitted enormously from unions and their culture of solidarity.

Paul is a former union steward. Nevertheless, he has a meritocratic, common-sense view of what autoworkers deserve to make. "You got factory workers that didn't have a fifth-grade education, right, living next door to doctors and lawyers . . . in $600,000 houses", he says. "Here's a guy that says, 'I'm a doctor and I spent . . . $100,000 dollars . . . for an education, for me to get this doctor degree', and you got a guy that moved out here that can't speak plain English—he still barbequing on the front porch. You know, it's like this has got to cease" ([1], p. 214). Blue-collar workers like Paul have internalized the belief that they don't deserve a very high standard of living. And it's because they don't possess the kind of merit that's now appreciated in this labor market and in this culture.

Of course, there is a fundamental contradiction here. Even as this culture of judgment wins over ordinary workers like Paul, or at least forces them to defend themselves against its criticisms, these same rules of meritocracy don't apply to the very top levels of the economy. Groups of elite workers—professionals, managers, financial workers—continue to wall themselves off from competition [20]. They still organize collectively, through lobbying, credentialing, licensing and other strategies. But ordinary workers no longer have the same ability to do so, because unions have declined and government steps in less often on their behalf. What we confront in our new economy is what I call a *stunted meritocracy*. It is meritocracy for you, but not for me.

The obvious answer to this problem would be to enact policies that would bring about equal opportunity—in other words, reform the system to make sure the intelligent and industrious rise to the top. But even if we lived in a society where ability was judged perfectly, in which the rigged rules of this economic game were made fair, a stunted meritocracy would eventually emerge. This is because meritocracy and equal opportunity are distinct concepts. Meritocracy is a system where the talented and hard-working advance. Equal opportunity means that we each have an equal chance at developing those talents and moving up.

As political scientist James Fishkin has argued, this distinction leads to fundamental tensions in any society that strives to achieve equal opportunity [21]. Fishkin notes that societies distribute wealth and status on three grounds (see Figure 1). According to the principle of merit, qualifications for positions should be evaluated fairly. According to the principle of equal life chances, the likelihood of a child's later success should not depend on arbitrary traits like gender, race, and family background. And according to the principle of family autonomy, parents should be free to shape their children's development. The problem, Fishkin argues, is that these three principles are inherently at odds. Choosing any two of them rules out the third. If we want equal life chances for all, we have to prevent parents early on from giving their children a leg up in the meritocratic race, or otherwise impose remedies later in life, such as various forms of redistribution and affirmative action, that will weaken the link between a person's merit and their reward. If we want meritocracy, we have to find ways to diminish this transmission of advantage from generation to generation, or otherwise accept the fact that opportunities will not be equal.

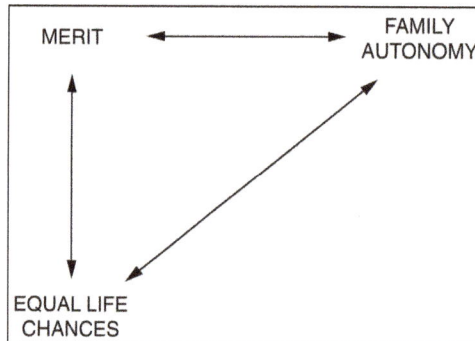

Figure 1. According to James Fishkin, when two assumptions about equal opportunity (the principle of merit and equality of life chances) are combined with a third assumption (autonomy of the family), "a pattern of difficult choices emerges", whereby "commitment to any two of these assumptions rules out the third" ([21], p. 5).

In the real world, access to a good education is drastically unequal. The best predictor of how much education and income you receive is your parents' education and income. Even at age three, there are large gaps in the test scores of the children of high school graduates and the children of college graduates, and those gaps persist into high school [22]. But Fishkin's argument is that the inequality we see is more fundamental than this: even in a perfect meritocracy with quality education for all, elite workers can still prepare their children in superior ways.

I want to emphasize that meritocracy has many positive consequences. Its spurs individuals to greater achievement, and countries to greater prosperity. But today, this mentality is being taken too far. While personal responsibility is vital, our economy has become excessively individualistic and unforgiving. It no longer has patience for the notions of loyalty and community that once tempered our relentless pursuit of happiness. A hypercompetitive and status-obsessed culture, in turn, leads to the judgment of less successful people as lazy, uneducated, and incompetent. If they don't have the markers of merit—education, marketable skills, a good job—then they are less than worthy—as workers, or as marriage partners. As some politicians put it, they are also less-than-worthy citizens—"takers" living off government, rather than "makers" who create jobs, innovate, and make this country great.

For elites, meritocratic morality can take the extreme form of a "greed is good" ideology, one that rejects altruism and slave morality altogether, in favor of the no-holds-barred egoism of the free market, in which self-interest is praised almost as a form of compassion. And yet meritocratic morality is far from just a secular phenomenon. Truly, our modern-day Pharisees can be found in the pulpits and marketplaces alike, judging other people zealously and expecting purity and perfection in all areas. For the unemployed, this perspective contributes to a poisonous self-blame. Sociologist Michael Young, who coined the term "meritocracy", actually saw it in this negative light: as a social order that would raise up the talented and leave the untalented to blame themselves for their failure [23].

In this sense, meritocracy is a jealous god, bearing manna in one hand and a sword in the other. Those who succeed are praised as men and women of ability and worth, and held up as examples, however anecdotal, that everyone can make it in America. Those who fail are scorned as losers, whose low status is all the more painful because it is deserved.

In my book, I define meritocratic morality in opposition to three other kinds of moral thinking about advancement in society and the distribution of economic rewards: egalitarian morality, fraternal morality, and grace morality. As Figure 2 illustrates, I have adapted three of these moral perspectives from the theories of James Fishkin. (Note: wherever words are listed between the four major principles in the diagram below, they identify qualities shared by the two perspectives connected by arrows. For instance, both meritocratic morality and fraternal morality are characterized by competition.)

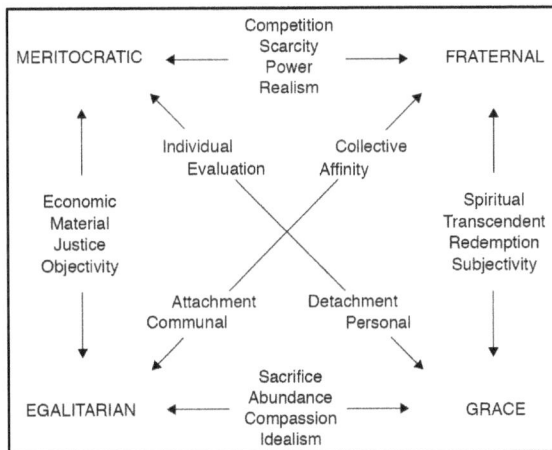

Figure 2. The key characteristics of four opposing moral perspectives that determine opportunities and outcomes within society ([1], p. 24).

Egalitarian morality seeks economic justice for the collective. Today's egalitarians in Europe and North America tend to be more moderate than the ideologues of communism. Rather than equal outcomes, they focus on equal opportunity—a fair shot at the game of life. And yet, just like the proponents of extreme meritocracy, they behold the world with an economic lens focused on each gain or loss.

Fraternal morality is the morality of the tribe. It restrains the behavior of the individual, prioritizing the interests of the collective rather than their own. In return, the individual finds spiritual gain: the transcendent joy and dignity of joining a larger whole. The word fraternal refers to masculine brotherhood, and that is something I want to emphasize, for there is also a dark side to fraternalism: its exclusion, and its chauvinism.

The fourth kind of moral code is what I call the morality of grace. I am not religious, but I take inspiration in the Christian concept of grace—this idea that everyone is saved by God's grace, not just the deserving. This view has a long tradition in American thought, going back all the way to the Puritans [24]. I feel it best captures the antithesis of the meritocratic ideology. It is a spiritual perspective of nonjudgment and abundance, as opposed to an economic perspective of measurement and scarcity.

In my book, I focus on three reasons that the ideology of meritocratic morality may be growing stronger relative to other moral viewpoints. The first reason is the decline of unions throughout the industrialized world, and the demise of left ideologies that, however flawed they were, provided an alternative language of class consciousness and worker dignity.

Second, the nature of merit has changed, in ways that put blue-collar workers at a disadvantage and debase their self-worth. Before, they could point to the backbreaking work they did on the assembly line to justify their high wages. Hard work still matters—but what my workers called smart work matters more. "It used to be you come up and say, 'Okay, I've got a strong back,' and all that", says one of my workers. "Strong back don't mean shit. You gotta have dedication and you've gotta have some kind of smartness, or something" ([1], p. 49). In the modern, postindustrial economy, the focus of merit is more on entrepreneurialism, independence and intelligence, rather than just a strong work ethic. To get a job lower down in the labor market, these sorts of things matter less. And yet the bar of sophistication here is also rising, not just in terms of credentials, but also the presentation of self—the slick résumé, the cheerful personality, the spotless personal record [25].

A third factor bringing about ideological change over time is what I call the new technology of meritocracy. The criteria for judging merit have expanded greatly, thanks to the growing technical capacity to quantify ability and performance [26]. Work today is less about making a living and more about managing a career [27]. At its extreme, it's about building a personal brand that encompasses all aspects of your life, each one measured and evaluated [28]. And yet the expansion of metrics means the expansion of evidence that proves workers like mine—the less educated, the less advantaged—to be inferior.

5. Grace

I think we need a return to some sort of balance—a healthier and saner way of looking at life. In my book, I make the case for a morality of grace that can complement and deepen our pursuit of egalitarianism. A perspective of grace refuses to divide the world into camps of deserving and undeserving, as those on both the right and left are wont to do. I see it as an antidote to our hypercompetitive and hyperjudgmental society, where we're always being evaluated and judged: from standardized tests in school, to job performance reviews at work, and especially in the job search, where every mistake we've ever made is captured by Google.

Unlike meritocratic morality, grace rejects our obsession with measuring and judging the worth of people, and excusing nothing. But unlike egalitarianism, it also rejects the categories of right and wrong, just and unjust. It offers neither retribution nor restitution, but rather forgiveness.

President Obama gave voice to this idea of grace in his eulogy last year for one of the victims of the Charleston church shooting, the Rev. Clementa Pinckney. In praising the parishioners who welcomed their killer into their Bible study, and the victims' family members who forgave him in court, Obama invoked grace—the "free and benevolent favor of God", as he called it—bestowed to the sinful and saintly alike. "Grace is not earned", he said. "Grace is not merited. It's not something we deserve" [29].

It is worth emphasizing here that the morality of grace is not synonymous with organized religion, which often loses its way in the pursuit of temporal power. Furthermore, the concept of grace can be seen in many other religions—from Buddhism's call to accept suffering with equanimity, to the Tao Te Ching's admonishment to treat the good and bad alike with kindness, to the Upanishad's focus on the eternal and infinite nature of reality.

We can see the idea of grace in secular writings as well, from the abstract theories of the philosopher Martin Heidegger to the humanism of the astronomer Carl Sagan. Sagan wrote eloquently about these themes in his book *Pale Blue Dot*, which was inspired by Voyager 1's photograph of Earth as a tiny blue speck against the vast blackness of space. Amid the competition and cruelty of human civilization, Sagan wrote, this image underscored the "folly of human conceits" and our responsibility to "deal more kindly with one another" [30].

On the most basic level, we see a model for what grace means in our closest personal relationships. If we often choose our friends and lovers based on merit—their intelligence or thoughtfulness or compatibility—with time we come to love their idiosyncrasies and foibles, holding them close just as the boy in the old childhood tale loved his frayed velveteen rabbit.

What does grace have to do with the economy? It helps us recognize that our society possesses enough wealth to provide for all. It allows us to part gladly with our hard-won treasure in order to pull others up, even if those we help are not the most deserving. It gives us the open-mindedness to question whether always being, or hiring, the best and brightest should be our chief goal.

While the unemployed workers I talked to didn't use the word "grace", they spoke about it in other ways. A former Ford worker told me he is worried for his kids and their future because the intensity of competition is becoming more and more toxic everywhere in society. "You hear students [say] it's all right to cheat because . . . I needed the A to get that job I need", he says. Being successful in business, too, is about doing "whatever you can do for the bottom line". And yet he knows there is more to life than this. He wants his kids to learn decency and happiness, things that wealth and fame ultimately cannot provide. Likewise, a union official told me she isn't sure that *anyone*—corporate executives, certainly, but her autoworkers as well—really need the life of material comfort and plenty they aspire to have. You can be happy with much less, she points out.

Taking up a perspective of grace is important because the prevailing culture of judgment worsens our society's growing inequalities. It stands squarely in the way of any serious and sustained effort to deal with the economy's deep-rooted, structural problems. We dismiss redistribution as "class warfare", the work of envy and resentment. We fixate on the so-called culture of poverty that prevents people from pulling themselves up, rather than the culture of prosperity that blinds us, the more fortunate, to the hurdles others face. Egalitarian morality finds it difficult to overcome these objections, in part because it, like meritocratic morality, has a fundamentally economic perspective. It measures and judges in the opposite direction—but it measures and judges nonetheless. With a focus on the material and quantifiable, the redistribution of your own wealth is by definition a sacrifice.

Unlike egalitarianism, a morality of grace downplays the importance of material circumstances. Under this perspective, individuals give up their wealth and power—not for the sake of redistribution per se, but because these possessions and positions are not significant when viewed from a broader vantage point. In turn, a morality of grace can open up political possibilities for the sorts of measures that would help middle-class families. It resonates across partisan lines, connecting with the thinking of secular feminist scholars who call for an economy that prioritizes care work, and yet also with the principles of evangelical Christian activists deeply concerned about poverty [31]. In fact, the Rev. David Platt, a prominent evangelical Christian leader, has made one of the most powerful cases for grace, decrying America's culture of competition, materialism, and single-minded self-improvement.

"While the goal of the American dream is to make much of us, the goal of the gospel is to make much of God", Platt writes ([32], pp. 46–47).

For his part, Pope Francis has not given up on the American Dream—but he has recast it. As he suggested in his 2015 address to Congress, the American Dream is not about materialist excess, but spiritual striving [33]. It is not about success, but fulfillment. In his apostolic exhortation a year later, Pope Francis also spoke to the idea of grace, calling for the Church to be more welcoming and less judgmental toward those who stray from doctrine [34].

In fact, a morality of grace is most needed not among the poor, but among the powerful—those who judge from up high, secluded in their literal and figurative gated communities. A genuine commitment to this viewpoint makes the rich more tolerant of taxes to pay for social programs, for example. It gives corporate leaders greater respect for workers' rights and government regulations, measures they fiercely resist when they see profit as their sole aim. The presence of these sorts of policies, in turn, creates new social norms about what is, and what is not, acceptable behavior. As for the economy's discouraged and desperate, taking up a perspective of grace means more in the way of solace, self-worth, and perhaps even employment, as society recognizes that economic efficiency is not the end but the means to a fulfilled life [35]. Social movements must take the lead, as they did in previous historical periods, to inspire the public and bring about this cultural change—and policies that make labor organizing and other forms of grassroots activism easier, and reduce the influence of money in politics, will make it more likely they will succeed.

In other words, there can be a virtuous circle at work here. Strong policies can help bring about a perspective of grace. If you don't have to scramble to undercut your corporate competitors—if you don't have to struggle to survive on low wages—you can think about the big picture. And grace, in turn, can make these policies more possible and sustainable. When we are not obsessed with comparing ourselves with others, when we are not intent on blaming others for their failures, we can deal more kindly with one another. We can deal more kindly with ourselves. Grace is a forgiving God.

Acknowledgments: Funding for the research and writing described in this essay was provided by the National Science Foundation, the American Sociological Association, the Harvard Joblessness and Urban Poverty Research Program, the Harvard Multidisciplinary Program in Inequality and Social Policy, the Harvard Weatherhead Center for International Affairs, the Institute for Research on Labor and Employment, the Berkeley Center for Culture, Organizations, and Politics, the Berkeley Canadian Studies Program, and Virginia Commonwealth University's College of Humanities and Sciences. I would also like to thank the two anonymous peer reviewers for their thoughtful and helpful feedback.

Conflicts of Interest: The author declares no conflict of interest. The founding sponsors had no role in the design of the study; in the collection, analyses, or interpretation of data; in the writing of the manuscript, and in the decision to publish the results.

References

1. Victor Tan Chen. *Cut Loose: Jobless and Hopeless in an Unfair Economy*. Oakland: University of California Press, 2015.
2. "US Bureau of Labor Statistics. " Available online: www.bls.gov (accessed on 30 October 2016).
3. Thomas Piketty. *Capital in the Twenty-First Century*. Cambridge: Harvard University Press, 2014.
4. Pew Research Center. *The American Middle Class Is Losing Ground*. Washington: Pew Research Center, 2015.
5. Victor Tan Chen. "Charts and Data." Available online: https://victortanchen.com/charts-and-data (accessed on 30 October 2016).
6. Bernadette D. Proctor, Jessica L. Semega, and Melissa A. Kollar. *Income and Poverty in the United States: 2015*. US Census Bureau, Current Population Reports, P60-256(RV). Washington: US Government Printing Office, 2016.
7. Dave Shaw. "The Economy's Improving, But Americans' Economic Anxiety Persists." *Marketplace*, 14 March 2016. Available online: http://www.marketplace.org/2016/03/11/economy/anxiety-index/economys-improving-americans-economic-anxiety-persists (accessed on 13 March 2017).

8.   Kimberly Adams. "Where to Turn When There's Nowhere to Turn." *Marketplace*, 17 March 2016. Available online: http://www.marketplace.org/2016/03/16/your-money/anxiety-index/where-turn-when-theres-nowhere-turn (accessed on 13 March 2017).

9.   Andrew Pollack. "Who's Reading Your X-ray." *New York Times*, 16 November 2003. Available online: http://www.nytimes.com/2003/11/16/business/who-s-reading-your-x-ray.html (accessed on 13 March 2017).

10.   John Markoff. "Armies of Expensive Lawyers, Replaced by Cheaper Software." *New York Times*, 4 March 2011. Available online: http://www.nytimes.com/2011/03/05/science/05legal.html (accessed on 13 March 2017).

11.   John W. Curtis. *Trends in Faculty Employment Status, 1975–2011*. Washington: American Association of University Professors, 2013. Available online: https://www.aaup.org/sites/default/files/FacultyTrends.pdf (accessed on 13 March 2017).

12.   Center for Automotive Research. *Contribution of the Automotive Industry to the Economies of All Fifty States and the United States*. Ann Arbor: Center for Automotive Research, 2010.

13.   Richard E. Lucas, Andrew E. Clark, Yannis Georgellis, and Ed Diener. "Unemployment Alters the Set Point for Life Satisfaction." *Psychological Science* 15 (2004): 8–13. [CrossRef] [PubMed]

14.   Richard E. Lucas. "Time Does Not Heal All Wounds: A Longitudinal Study of Reaction and Adaptation to Divorce." *Psychological Science* 16 (2005): 945–50. [CrossRef] [PubMed]

15.   Frank Levy, and Peter Temin. *Inequality and Institutions in 20th Century America*. Working Paper No. 13106. Cambridge: National Bureau of Economic Research, 2007.

16.   Lawrence Mishel, and Alyssa Davis. *CEO Pay Continues to Rise as Typical Workers Are Paid Less*. Issue Brief #380. Washington: Economic Policy Institute, 2014.

17.   Keith Banting, and John Myles, eds. *Inequality and the Fading of Redistributive Politics*. Vancouver: University of British Columbia Press, 2013.

18.   Andrew J. Cherlin. *Labor's Love Lost: The Rise and Fall of the Working-Class Family in America*. New York: Russell Sage Foundation, 2014.

19.   Arthur Aron, Tracy McLaughlin-Volpe, Debra Mashek, Gary Lewandowski, Stephen C. Wright, and Elaine N. Aron. "Including Others in the Self." *European Review of Social Psychology* 15 (2004): 101–32. [CrossRef]

20.   Jacob S. Hacker, and Paul Pierson. *Winner-Take-All Politics: How Washington Made the Rich Richer—And Turned Its Back on the Middle Class*. New York: Simon & Schuster, 2010.

21.   James S. Fishkin. *Justice, Equal Opportunity, and the Family*. New Haven: Yale University Press, 1983.

22.   James J. Heckman. *The American Family in Black and White: A Post-Racial Strategy for Improving Skills to Promote Equality*. Discussion Paper No. 5495. Bonn: Institute for the Study of Labor, 2011.

23.   Michael Young. *The Rise of the Meritocracy*. New Brunswick: Transaction, 2011.

24.   Alan Heimert, and Andrew Delbanco, eds. *The Puritans in America: A Narrative Anthology*. Cambridge: Harvard University Press, 1985.

25.   Ofer Sharone. *Flawed System/Flawed Self: Job Searching and Unemployment Experiences*. Chicago: University of Chicago Press, 2014.

26.   Victor Tan Chen. "Living in an Extreme Meritocracy Is Exhausting." *The Atlantic*, 26 October 2016. Available online: https://www.theatlantic.com/business/archive/2016/10/extreme-meritocracy/505358 (accessed on 13 March 2017).

27.   Carrie M. Lane. *A Company of One: Insecurity, Independence, and the New World of White-Collar Unemployment*. Ithaca: ILR Press, 2011.

28.   Steven P. Vallas, and Emily R. Cummins. "Personal Branding and Identity Norms in the Popular Business Press: Enterprise Culture in an Age of Precarity." *Organization Studies* 36 (2015): 293–319. [CrossRef]

29.   Barack Obama. "Remarks by the President in Eulogy for the Honorable Reverend Clementa Pinckney." 26 June 2015. Available online: https://www.whitehouse.gov/the-press-office/2015/06/26/remarks-president-eulogy-honorable-reverend-clementa-pinckney (accessed on 13 March 2017).

30.   Carl Sagan. *Pale Blue Dot: A Vision of the Human Future in Space*. New York: Random House, 1994.

31.   Sabine O'Hara. "Everything Needs Care: Toward a Contexts-Based Economy." In *Counting on Marilyn Waring: New Advances in Feminist Economics*. Edited by Margunn Bjørnholt and Alisa McKay. Bradford: Demeter Press, 2014.

32.   David Platt. *Radical: Taking Back Your Faith from the American Dream*. Colorado Springs: Multnomah, 2010.

33. Jorge Mario Bergoglio. "Address of the Holy Father." 24 September 2015. Available online: https://w2.vatican.va/content/francesco/en/speeches/2015/september/documents/papa-francesco_20150924_usa-us-congress.html (accessed on 13 March 2017).

34. Jorge Mario Bergoglio. "Post-Synodal Apostolic Exhortation Amoris Lætitia of the Holy Father Francis." 2016. Available online: https://w2.vatican.va/content/francesco/en/apost_exhortations/documents/papa-francesco_esortazione-ap_20160319_amoris-laetitia.html (accessed on 13 March 2017).

35. Victor Tan Chen. "The Spiritual Crisis of the Modern Economy." *The Atlantic*, 21 December 2016. Available online: https://www.theatlantic.com/business/archive/1857/11/spiritual-crisis-modern-economy/511067 (accessed on 13 March 2017).

religions

MDPI

Article

Social Services, Social Justice, and Social Innovations: Lessons for Addressing Income Inequality

Tiziana C. Dearing

Boston College School of Social Work, Chestnut Hill, MA 02461, USA; dearing@bc.edu; Tel.: +1-617-552-1605

Academic Editors: Kate Ward and Kenneth Himes
Received: 8 February 2017; Accepted: 2 May 2017; Published: 10 May 2017

Abstract: This paper first explores three lessons about income inequality that have emerged in cross-disciplinary study. Second, it relates those lessons to ethical practices in social work and social services, and other ethics of social justice. Third, it briefly examines sample innovations in social services that hold promise for addressing the three lessons of the income inequality described. Finally, the paper offers reflections on a potential path forward in a quest to mitigate the harm of persistent income inequality and create more equitable systems for those experiencing it.

Keywords: income inequality; social justice; social services; social innovation

1. Three Lessons about Income Inequality

This paper is the product of seminar-based interdisciplinary study on income inequality. The author reviewed key literature on income inequality from the fields of law, economics, philosophy, theology, social work, education, and business, guided by scholars in each field. An examination of literature across these disciplines raised a set of lessons relevant to the practice of social services and advocacy as they relate to addressing income inequality—pursuits common to social workers and human service managers. Programmatic and advocacy interventions, however, may not be designed with the interplay of these three lessons in mind, thus reducing their likelihood of having a sustainable impact on the challenge of income inequality.

Therefore, this paper has three goals: (1) to articulate the three lessons observed; (2) to relate those lessons to the ethical practice of social work and social service management; and (3) to examine current innovations in practice that may hold promise for addressing income inequality given the complex nature of the problem as highlighted herein.

The data are strong regarding the tenacity and negative impacts of income inequality. This paper accepts those findings as accurate and seeks to report them sufficiently for later consideration of how social services, social justice ethics, and social innovations can help address them. The three lessons include that (a) lower-income voices are suppressed in the political process; (b) the economic mobility "ladder" is missing some rungs; and (c) fiscal and educational policies and practices that used to help address or mitigate income inequality are losing their potency. These three lessons paint a picture of the potential for an enduring income inequality that social service providers and others with a strong social justice ethic must address, using new methods and approaches.

1.1. Lesson 1: Lower-Income Voices Are Suppressed in the Political Process

The field of political science offers evidence that lower-income voices are suppressed in the public and participatory spheres. This suppression plays out in at least three ways, each closely related. The first two are presented convincingly by Schlozman et al. (2012) in *The Unheavenly Chorus: Unequal Political Voice and the Broken Promise of American Democracy*.

The first of those two is the observation that political participation consistently varies by income, with those who have higher levels of socio-economic status (SES) engaging more actively and regularly. Schlozman et al. (2012) use data from the Pew Internet and American Life Survey to demonstrate not only that increases in SES equate with political participation, but also that type of participation varies by SES quintile, with higher quintiles increasingly engaging, using money through donations. From a social work perspective, where community organizing is a valued tradition, it is particularly disheartening to learn that one of the few political activities in which higher SES did not matter was political protest—disheartening because, as Schlozman et al. (2012) note, "the fact that there is so little variation across the SES quintiles for an act that is often characterized as the 'weapon of the weak' is itself noteworthy" (Schlozman et al. 2012, p. 124).

Second, and related, organized political participation favors the interests of those in higher income brackets. Schlozman et al. (2012) present a hierarchy of political activity—from protest, to working on a campaign, to giving money to a campaign—that correlates with SES; participation in all three especially correlates with increases in income. Not only do the policy interests of the more active not necessarily align with the less active, e.g., preference for means-tested programs in which the less active disproportionately participate, but money can also hold particular sway in affecting public policy disputes. They write, "Given how unequal our bank accounts are, to allow cash gifts or preferments to public officials . . . is to place citizens on a very unequal footing when it comes to potential political influence" (Schlozman et al. 2012, p. 270). Gilens and Page (2014) present complementary findings regarding the influence of economic elites in public policy outcomes. Using a "tentative and preliminary" (Schlozman et al. 2012, p. 564) statistical model, they demonstrate that, "The estimated impact of average citizens' preferences," are non-significant ("near zero"), while "economic elites are estimated to have a quite substantial, highly significant, independent impact on policy" (Schlozman et al. 2012, p. 572).

Third, elected officials pay more attention to the preferences of higher-income constituents, regardless of the political activism, engagement or contact between the elected official and lower-income constituents. This may be difficult to accept for egalitarians, who might hope that political action can counterbalance income influence in a democratic society. Nevertheless, Larry Bartels documents this reality in his book, *Unequal Democracy: The Political Economy of the New Gilded Age* (Bartels 2008). After giving a nod to a 1995 work by Verba, Schlozman, and Brady where they note, "inequalities in activity are likely to be associated with inequalities in governmental responsiveness" (Bartels 2008, p. 253), Bartels describes an analysis he did of US Senators in the 1980s and 1990s, in which he found the following:

> . . . views of constituents in the upper third of the income distribution received about 50% more weight than those in the middle third . . . . Meanwhile, the views of constituents in the bottom third of the income distribution received no weight at all. Far from being 'considered as political equals,' they were entirely unconsidered in the policy-making process. (Bartels 2008, pp. 253–54)

Granted, Bartels considered the responsiveness of elected officials thirty years ago. Given the U.S. Supreme Court's findings in Citizens United vs. FEC in 2010, however, combined with increasing rates of income inequality in the United States (Zimmermann and Ritzen 2016) and the ever-increasing cost of getting elected[1], it would be reasonable to assume not only that disparities in the power of political voice based on income have not shrunk since then but, instead, they have grown. As U.S. Senator John

---

[1] In 2014, a group of reporters from *Time* combined data from the Federal Election Commission with other sources to create an interactive calculator and set of maps demonstrating how the costs of elections at various levels in the US had changed over time. Their summary finding for the article was that the cost of running for a U.S. Congress seat rose 555% from 1984 to 2012 (Sherer et al. 2014).

McCain quipped after the Citizens United verdict, "If money is free speech, then the wealthiest people in America are those that get to speak the most freely" (Haberman 2014).

These three findings—that lower-income individuals are less politically active, that political activity favors the interests of those in higher income brackets, and that elected officials pay more attention to the interests of people in higher income brackets—suggest that lower-income voices are, for practical purposes, suppressed in the political process and public policy spheres and, therefore, at a disadvantage to address public policies contributing to, or exacerbating, income equality. This is a crucial lesson for social workers and social service providers. While the practice of community organizing has been much maligned since President Obama—a former community organizer—first ran for the office[2], it is core to the tradition of social work. Indeed, there have been decades in which social work has been nearly synonymous with organizing around poverty and inequality (Specht and Courtney 1995). In addition, social and human services agencies that focus on public policy will frequently seek to organize their constituents to voice favor for or protest against specific public policy measures in the hopes of affecting, for example, local and state budget priorities.

This trend of income disparity suppressing political voice has implications for the ability to foment public policy changes on behalf of people on the wrong side of income inequality. What happens when no amount of organizing elevates the voices of the poor? What is the response within social work and the social services to a political system so unbalanced that those at the bottom of the income ladder have no effective political recourse to change that position, and yet, unless they change that position, they have no political recourse? As Schlozman et al. (2012) note, "If you're not at the table, you're on the menu" (Schlozman et al. 2012, p. 309).

1.2. Lesson 2: The Mobility Ladder Is Missing Some Rungs

The second important lesson comes from the intersection of economics and sociology. Combining what economics demonstrates about family outcomes with what sociology demonstrates about opportunity and social connections, it becomes clear that while America may pride itself on being a place where upward mobility is possible for anyone, the mobility ladder is missing some rungs. Three key findings raised in interdisciplinary study of income inequality contribute to this aggregate lesson: the difficulty of moving up income quintiles; the existence of what Robert Putnam calls the "youth opportunity gap" (Putnam 2015); and the impact of place on future outcomes.

First, research from the field of economics demonstrates the suppression of upward mobility across income quintiles. U.S. Census data clearly show that the share of total income is disproportionately concentrated among higher earners in the U.S., even though they represent a small percentage of the overall population (Elwell 2014). Elwell explains that the top income quintile holds more than 50% of the nation's total income, leaving the four quintiles below to share the other 50% (Elwell 2014, Summary). Not surprisingly, the four remaining quintiles do not share that remainder evenly. Those in the lowest income quintile receive only 3.2% of total household income (Elwell 2014, p. 3). They hold little income in terms of personal earnings, but also relatively little income in terms of share of the overall pie. Corak (2013) then shows that it is more difficult for people in the lower income quintiles to move to the higher income quintiles over time.

Income inequality exacerbates that problem. Chetty et al. (2014) show that areas of the U.S. with higher levels of economic mobility for low-income families are those that start with less income inequality, and vice versa. On the whole, however, the U.S. is trending toward more income inequality since the 1970s, not less (Atkinson 2015). This bodes poorly for the future prospects of those at the bottom end of the income ladder in general.

---

2   Alaska governor and vice-presidential candidate Sarah Palin and Rudy Giuliani, former Mayor of New York City, both made speeches on Day 3 of the 2008 Republican National Convention in which they specifically disparaged candidate Obama's background as a community organizer. (Palin 2008; Giuliani 2008).

It is useful to note here that the US is also trending toward more *wealth* inequality, as are other Western economies. Piketty's *Capital in the Twenty-First Century* (Piketty 2014) argues that slower economic growth leads to the increasing importance of capital for financial prosperity. That, in turn, leads to an "accelerating" wealth gap as those with capital can invest it for further asset growth, whereas those without cannot. Further, the nongovernmental organization Oxfam's annual study of inequality demonstrated that, in 2016, 62 people owned as much wealth as another 3.5 billion (Oxfam 2016). Race exacerbates the wealth gap, with whites in the United States holding six times as much wealth as black or Hispanic individuals in 2010 (McKernan et al. 2013).

Second, a lesson from sociology demonstrates that gaps in income can lead to gaps in future opportunity. In his recent bestseller, *Our Kids* (Putnam 2015), sociologist Robert Putnam continues his longtime study of social capital and its influence on individuals in America. Here, however, he directs that look at social capital to consider (a) its impact on opportunities for children; and (b) how its existence, access to it, and use of it have changed. Putnam finds that social networks, in essence, have an amplifying effect on other factors driving inequality, ultimately putting affluent families even further ahead in the game. Putnam refers to this as the "youth opportunity gap" (Putnam 2015, p. 207). Recently, other researchers have begun to sing a similar theme, expressing concerns about "opportunity hoarding" among higher-income families (Lyken-Segosebe and Hinz 2015).

In addition to the role economic and social capital factors play in opportunity, one must consider the role of place itself. The idea that "your zip code should not determine your future" has become widely embraced in nonprofit work and policy circles. Economists Chetty and Hendren's (2015) work on the "childhood exposure effect" undergirds the point. In their research, they found that low-income children (defined at the 25th percentile of income distribution) who lived in neighborhoods that were worse environments for children—as indicated by factors like violent crime, income inequality, segregation, and quality of schools—experienced a negative impact on their future upward mobility. When a low-income child moved from a neighborhood with a less supportive environment to a more supportive one, that child's adult upward mobility improved, and the improvement got larger the younger the child was at the time of moving. Where a child grows up has at least some level of predictive effect on future outcomes (see the essay by Walsh/Theodorakakis).

Sociologist Robert Sampson sounded this theme a few years before Chetty and Hendren's findings on the childhood exposure effect. In *Great American City* (Sampson 2012), he advanced the concept of "enduring neighborhood inequality," showing how certain neighborhoods in Chicago demonstrated an impact on the opportunities and outcomes of youth, even when controlling for a variety of other factors. Sampson writes, "neighborhoods are not merely … empty vessels determined by 'bigger' external forces, but are important determinants of the quantity and quality of human behavior in their own right" (Sampson 2012, p. 22).

Missing rungs in the economic mobility ladder matter for any practical approach to income inequality, and the social services are no exception. Consider a suite of interventions typical to social service agencies. A low-income youth receives support to stay in school. That youth is part of a mentoring program, receives nutrition support through school meals, and snacks in an after-school program in which the youth participates regularly. Assume, further, that each of these programs uses models supported by evaluation, and that each is rooted in research on the impact of factors like hunger, social isolation, the lack of role models, and poor use of out-of-school time on child outcomes.

What if each program is successful in helping keep the youth enfranchised, focused, performing academically, away from the criminal justice system, etc.? Nevertheless: (a) the youth's neighborhood still can suppress his outcomes with statistical significance; (b) the youth's range of economic mobility is limited by geography of birth; and (c) there is a concomitant, "suite of opportunities" that remains outside the youth's grasp despite overcoming these other barriers to success. If that is the case, then interventions focused on the individual must happen within the context of concerted efforts to produce massive structural changes at the neighborhood, regional, state, and federal levels. In the field of social work, this is considered part of "macro" practice (Netting et al. 2012). In human and social services it means advocacy, legislative action, and systems change work. It is worth noting, however, that social service agencies struggle mightily to raise annual budgets, putting pressure on them to emphasize direct service work where outputs and outcomes may be more easily demonstrated, rather than to engage in indirect, systems-change work, such as advocacy or public awareness.

1.3. Lesson 3: What Worked In the Past Does Not Work Now, or Is Existentially Threatened

The third key lesson comes from a set of findings in the fields of education, public policy—specifically, fiscal policy—and law. Each finding represents trends with disparate impact on already marginalized populations. These trends call those engaged in social work and social services to enter the fray on policy discussions more traditionally in the wheelhouse of other disciplines or practices. Together, the findings show that mechanisms that used to help resolve income inequality no longer do so effectively (in the case of education), or are existentially threatened (in the case of social welfare spending). The findings include: the existence of an income achievement gap; the dampening of education as an equalizer; and the suppressive impact of global fiscal policy on national spending (for more on this last point, see the essay by Garcia).

To begin, researchers in education have demonstrated that there is an "income achievement gap," and that said gap has begun to outstrip the racial educational achievement gap (Reardon 2011). Primary school education drove up living standards and intergenerational mobility between 1900 and 1970 (Duncan and Murnane 2014), but a black-white gap in academic achievement has persisted for decades (Reardon 2011) and has been a focus of educational policy discussions and nonprofit work on racial justice. In an edited volume on the growth of inequality for children in the U.S., however, Reardon (2011) explains that an *income* achievement gap has been growing steadily, likely for more than half a century, and that it is "now more than twice as large as the black-white achievement gap" (Reardon 2011, p. 93). Childhood socio-economic status, therefore, has disproportionate impact on educational achievement. The lesson goes on to demonstrate that educational achievement has disproportionate impact on future earnings and opportunities.

The emerging salience of the income achievement gap does not make the black-white achievement gap less notable or important. Indeed, one could argue it raises the stakes on the black-white achievement gap even higher, given the racial dimensions of childhood poverty in the United States. Black children in America, for example, are more than twice as likely to experience poverty during childhood compared with white children, and seven times more likely to experience persistent poverty (Ratcliffe and McKernan 2010).

The income achievement gap data combines with other data about education to help demonstrate that what used to work to resolve income inequality does not work as well any more. Namely, the education solution to modest beginnings is no longer a powerful one, at least for some. In their 2014 book, Duncan and Murnane argue that schools no longer hold the promise they once did to become income and opportunity equalizers. They write:

> macroeconomic forces that have driven a widening wedge between the incomes of affluent families and those of poor and working-class families have also made it much more difficult for schools to help children from low-income families acquire the skills they need to compete in today's economy. (Duncan and Murnane 2014, p. 2)

One key culprit is the emergence of personal computing and computing technology in general. First, it drove the need for a more highly educated workforce. Then, it helped facilitate shrinking the world, allowing for outsourcing of work to lower-wage markets. That, in turn, tightened the correlation between educational attainment and earnings (Duncan and Murnane 2014).

The correlation between educational attainment and earnings is, however, now being called into question. In February 2016, the Brookings Institute, a Washington D.C. think tank, released one of its regular "Social Mobility Memos," entitled, "A college degree is worth less if you are raised poor" (Hershbein 2016). It showed that the impact of a bachelor's degree on adult earnings was muted by lower socioeconomic status when starting the degree program. In other words, the poorer one is before getting the degree, the less positive impact that degree will have on one's lifetime earnings, despite the fact that the degree costs the same. So, while educational attainment and earnings are ever more tightly correlated, and earnings are a way to close the income inequality gap, the promise of education producing earnings that can close that gap is weaker for low-income students. Education is no great equalizer if it has unequal impact, rooted in inequality at the point of entry.

That, in turn, leads to data about global macroeconomic policy and its influence on national fiscal policy that might address persistent income inequality. The income inequality troubles of individual American families happen against a backdrop of international investment, commerce, and trade. Here, the disciplines of law and public policy enter; specifically, the emergence of international economic law as a result of globalization. In a piece also produced from the income inequality, seminar, legal scholar Frank Garcia (2017) echoes Duncan and Murnane, noting that foreign investment exacerbates domestic income inequality, "outbound by facilitating transfer of low-skill jobs from developed countries, increasing returns to capital; and inbound in developing countries by increasing the skill premium." At the same time, he notes that the global economy supports tax avoidance, which in turn suppresses revenues available to invest in social welfare in national budgets. The system, then, supports growth at the upper end while suppressing investment in fiscal policies to support the lower end of the economic spectrum.

How do we know that reductions in policies such as social welfare spending affect the ability to mitigate income inequality? In mid-2016, the McKinsey Global Institute released a study of six developed economies[3], showing that, on average, 65%–70% of households were in income segments with flat or declining market incomes (defined as wages and income from capital) between 2005 and 2014 (Dobbs et al. 2016). The data suggest that up to 80% of income groups might not advance in market income over the next decade.

In terms of *disposable* income over that same period, however, results varied dramatically. In the United States, while more than 80% of households were within income brackets for whom incomes either stagnated or fell, fewer than two percent of those households experienced loss or stagnation in their disposable incomes. Indeed, most households experienced a small *gain* in disposable income over that time period. The United States shared this distinction with Sweden, known for the strength of its social welfare policies. The report's authors ascribe the strength in disposable income in the US, despite the weakness of market income growth, to fiscal policy around transfer payments and taxes. "In the United States," they note, "net transfers in 2005–14 turned a four percentage point decline in median market income into a one-point gain in disposable income" (Dobbs et al. 2016, p. 14). Taxes and transfers can, in their words, play a "decisive role in limiting or reversing the decline of market incomes" (Dobbs et al. 2016, p. 16). In other words, the ability of the national budget to provide tax relief and financial assistance to those experiencing income inequality is necessary in order to help combat that inequality. Dobbs et al. (2016) also reflect Frank Garcia (2017) argument about macro pressures on the national budget, and the resulting likelihood that the US will not be able sustain this taxes-and-transfers approach to relieving income stagnation over time (for more on the significance of such tax and transfer policies see the essay by Quinn/Cahill).

Leaders of domestic social services agencies would be unlikely to see global fiscal policy as their purview when seeking to redress the effects of persistent income inequality. Instead, education continues to be a core national strategy for trying to close income and achievement gaps. One need look no further than the passage of No Child Left Behind in 2002 or the emergence of the Common Core initiative, backed by the Bill and Melinda Gates Foundation, for evidence. Further, the GuideStar database (GuideStar 2016) lists nearly 60,000 charities focused on elementary and secondary education

---

[3]   The comparison included Italy, the United States of America, the United Kingdom, the Netherlands, France and Sweden and was based on 2014 or latest available data.

alone in the US. Nevertheless, this multidisciplinary study of income inequality suggests that (a) those seeking to address domestic income inequality through social services increasingly will have to understand and engage in questions of global macroeconomic forces; and (b) pursuing educational attainment for low-income children will be increasingly insufficient to address persistent disparities without other, simultaneous efforts to address systems issues, such as opportunity hoarding or the quality of technical education provided within schools.

To review, the preceding section has discussed three core lessons about the tenacity of income inequality resulting from interdisciplinary study of the issue. They include: (1) lower-income voices are suppressed in the political process; (2) the mobility ladder is missing some rungs; and (3) what worked in the past does not work now, or is existentially threatened. The combination of these three lessons arguably constitutes a definitive moment in income inequality in the United States, especially for those on the wrong end of it. Income inequality effectively mutes political voice and influence for those at the lower end of the income scale. Mobility up that income scale is badly broken. The byproducts of income inequality—such as where one lives and whom one knows—have their own suppressive effects. Tools that used to help equalize disparities, like public primary education and a college degree, have lost at least some of their equalizing power. Simultaneously, global trends in fiscal policy gut national budgets, depress spending for social welfare, drive jobs that helped move people up the income ladder for generations out of the country, and create new elites whose voices will then disproportionately be heard in the halls of political power. It represents a brutally efficient cycle in which those about whom the discipline of social work cares, and to whom social service leaders dedicate their work, fare the worst and have the least chance of faring better.

2. What Social Work and Social Service Ethics Have to Say in Response

This section briefly examines what the professional ethics of social work and social services can offer in addressing the lessons of income inequality just described. The ethics discussed here then manifest in the social innovations offered in the next section.

2.1. Social Work Ethics

Social work and social services are not synonymous. According to the National Association of Social Workers (NASW) Center for Workforce Studies and Social Work Practice, (a) social services and human services can be treated synonymously; (b) social and human services focus on well-being at the individual, family, and community levels; and (c) social workers can occupy a broad range of direct service and administrative roles within social and human service agencies (NASW 2011). Nevertheless, the *NASW Code of Ethics* states the primary mission of social work as, "to enhance human well-being and help meet the basic human needs of all people, with particular attention to the needs and empowerment of people who are vulnerable, oppressed, and living in poverty" (NASW 2008, Preamble). Given the expressed overlap between the social work mission and the work of social services, therefore, it is reasonable to turn to social work's professional code of ethics for guidance.

In its Preamble, the *NASW Code of Ethics* lays out a set of principles necessary for the ethical practice of social work (NASW 2008). These principles guide professional behavior for the social worker (Netting et al. 2012), and arguably reflect the professional practice of delivering social services. The code offers six core values of social work, which include service, social justice, dignity, and worth of the person, importance of human relationships, integrity, and competence (NASW 2008, Preamble). Of particular note for this paper are social justice, dignity and worth of the person, and the importance of human relationships.

Regarding social justice, according to Netting et al. in their textbook on macro social work, "Ideally, social justice is achieved when there is a fair distribution of society's resources and benefits so that every individual receives a deserved portion. Social work is in the business of distributing and redistributing resources" (Netting et al. 2012, p. 13). Social service approaches to just resource distribution vary tremendously. Indeed, philosophers have labored long and hard to formulate persuasive interpretations of justice as applied to the question of income inequality, with particular emphasis on the influential work of political philosopher John Rawls. Nevertheless, note the NASW emphasis on redistribution. This emphasis suggests specific priorities in response to the lessons just discussed, including, but not limited to, questions of opportunity hoarding and federal transfer payment policies.

Regarding the dignity and worth of the person, Netting et al. explain this value is often referred to as "self-determination" (Netting et al. 2012, p. 14). The language of self-determination is used by a number of disciplines, including international law, political science, education, and psychology, to name a few. Perhaps a definition borrowed from public health ethics would be useful in this instance. For this, the author turned to a book review exploring a work on the public health ethic of social justice written by Powers and Faden (Silva 2013). Silva summarizes self-determination as including personal choice, and then quotes Powers and Faden, citing the ability to " ... guarantee individuals a degree of protection against the interference by the state or one's fellow citizens in their choices and actions" (Silva 2013, p. 35). This definition identifies the conflict effectively. What happens when the state does not interfere with choices and actions, but social and formal systems stymie the expected results of those actions? For example, if a low-income individual chooses to pursue higher education in order to earn better wages, but a complex set of systems suppresses those future wages, even if the actor makes all the "right" choices and actions? From a social services perspective, the combination of commitment to the dignity and worth of the individual, with the priority of self-sufficiency and the ability to achieve desired levels of well-being, arguably calls for a concerted effort to correct such interference.

Lastly, consider the importance of human relationships. Netting et al. suggest that a commitment to the importance of human relationships calls for inclusion of those who are marginalized in the change process (Netting et al. 2012, p. 14). Such an argument follows closely on the heels of the concept of self-determination, as they note, and suggests that a proper social services response to the hindrances of self-determination will, by definition, place those struggling for self-determination at the core of any pursuit of a solution. "At the core" means not only in the focus of the work, but also in the definition and execution of that work.

2.2. Solidarity

Before exploring some innovations in social and human services that deploy these ethics in ways promising for addressing the challenges of income inequality, one additional social justice ethic has something to say about the lessons learned—solidarity. During the income inequality seminar that led to this paper, the group explored readings offered by a representative from theology. These works explored religious ethics and what they offer to an analysis of the causes of and responses to today's income inequality, from a variety of religious perspectives. Across the traditions, several advocate the principle of solidarity as a core ethic in addressing the impact of income inequality on lower income Americans.

In his paper exploring a Buddhist-Christian dialog on income inequality, Joerg Rieger advocates for the idea of "deep solidarity" (Rieger 2013). He defines the concept by explaining, "while solidarity has often been taken to mean a commitment ... to support others who are considered to be worse off, deep solidarity starts with the understanding that many of us find ourselves in the same boat" (Rieger 2013, p. 158). In her exploration of an "ethics of accountability," Mary Elizabeth Hobgood asserts, "Solidarity means working together to claim a fair share of power in a class structure that impoverishes some, privileges others, and damages everyone" (Hobgood 2009, p. 108). Lastly, in her discussion of Catholic social teaching and inequality, Mary Jo Bane argues that solidarity "implies that it is both appropriate and necessary for government at various levels to take responsibility when families, communities and the private sector cannot or will not" address income inequality effectively and sufficiently (Bane 2014, p. 397). Common across these claims are two ideas: first, that a commitment to human relationships calls the individual to take and/or cause action on income inequality; and second, that the experience of income inequality is a shared one, and a damaging one, for all—even those benefitting from it.

These ethics of social justice—originating both from the professional practice of social services and from religious traditions regarding social justice—suggest a course of action for those seeking guidance on whether and how to address the three lessons learned about the tenacity of income inequality. They suggest (a) that action is necessary in order to correct the imbalances created by sustained income inequality; (b) that action can and should be toward enabling people to self-determine, both in the ability to attempt self-sufficiency and prosperity and in the ability to achieve said self-sufficiency and prosperity with some level of equity in the potential outcomes from those attempts; (c) that approaches to righting imbalances and fostering equity in complex social systems should, as much as possible, be driven by those experiencing the inequity themselves; and (d) that the persistence of income inequality is, ultimately, morally damaging to all those who participate in the unequal system, regardless of one's position within that system.

2.3. Sample Innovations in Social Services

Since 2000, the country—and, indeed, the world—has experienced two recessions, including the Great Recession of the late 2000s. The impacts on low- and middle-income families have persisted, as evidenced by the trends reported in the McKinsey Global Institute study of stagnating wages (Dobbs et al. 2016).

This section offers a glimpse of two social service approaches that have emerged since 2000 that offer potential responses to the lessons identified in the first section, in ways consistent with the ethics presented in the second section. These approaches also embrace, either intentionally or indirectly, the idea of "intersectionality," a theory in sociology that recognizes the interplay between social identities and oppression—that, for example, race and class form "intersecting oppressions" that must be dealt with as such (Jones et al. n.d.).

Boston Rising, a now defunct antipoverty fund focused on the Grove Hall neighborhood of Boston, embraced a belief in the intersectionality of race, place, and poverty, the value of choice, and control for those experiencing poverty, and the idea that the generational cycle of poverty can be broken in a particular neighborhood as a result of sustained, collaborative effort.[4] Believing in intersectionality, and recognizing the complexity of intergenerational poverty in a low-income, historically African American neighborhood, Boston Rising sought a simple framework for its investments that would, ultimately, make headway against this intractable problem. After more than two years of studying best practices from other organizations, as well as the work of scholars and leading practitioners on poverty and inequality, Boston Rising determined that poverty could be disrupted in a given neighborhood by creating three conditions: (1) an education that leads to employment; (2) employment that facilitates building assets over time; and (3) social connections that can be leveraged for problem solving along the way (Boston Rising n.d.).[5] While Boston Rising ultimately was closed after its lead donor redirected his philanthropy (Abraham 2013), during its short life it received awards and recognition as an innovative approach to philanthropy with an ambitious mission.

The missing rungs on the income mobility ladder, failure of education to support people in jobs and asset accumulation, the role of income and social connections in creating economic opportunity, and downward pressure on spending to support income stability for low-income Americans, suggest that the Boston Rising approach was, indeed, oriented properly. That orientation also included approaches that (a) believe individuals, families and communities want to solve problems for themselves and chart their own paths; (b) build on an individual, family or community's own strengths

---

[4] The paper's author was the first CEO of Boston Rising. As the organization is now defunct, there is limited public material available for citation. The description of Boston Rising's approach, therefore, comes predominantly from the author's own account, coupled with citations for support where available.

[5] For evidence of these three pillars, see the areas of specialization as reported for Boston Rising in its LinkedIn profile.

and assets[6]; (c) foster both "bonding" and "bridging" social capital, thus stretching the concept of community and emphasizing cross-class and cross-place solidarity; and (d) believe in and promote the principle of subsidiarity, which, when translated into social service terms means that the acts of policy making and program design should be kept as local as is possible and reasonable (Brendan 2006). Those approaches correspond directly to the ethics outlined in the previous section.

When Boston Rising closed, its remaining resources were redirected to an initiative the organization had studied extensively during its own formation, Family Independence Initiative, or FII (Abraham 2013). Founded by Mauricio Lim Miller, who won a MacArthur Fellowship for his work (MacArthur Fellows Program 2012), FII is rooted in "intrinsic motivation to determine [one's] own path," and a belief in self-determination (Moore 2014). FII Evaluator Melanie Moore describes their work as "Helping families by doing nothing for them" (Moore 2014, p. 6). Lim Miller had worked as a social worker running an acclaimed, traditional community development agency for decades with results he found unsatisfying (Stuhldreher and O'Brien 2011). When then-mayor of San Francisco, Jerry Brown, challenged Lim Miller to figure out how to approach anti-poverty work differently, Lim Miller realized he had no idea how to do that, but that thousands of families like his own immigrant mother had, in fact, figured it out (The Boston Foundation 2016). He then designed an approach that supports self-organized groups of families with financial incentives and data tracking capabilities to set their own financial, educational, and personal family goals, and track their progress over time (Stuhldreher and O'Brien 2011). Families set their own agendas around things like employment, home ownership, higher education, savings, and health, and use their own social networks and social capital to engage in problem solving. For example, families seeking homeownership might find someone in the community who can teach them the steps to improving their credit ratings. FII recruits a limited number of families in a location to participate, and then families reach out to their own social networks to grow the circle and the results. Those results are striking. Between 2010 and 2013, for example, FII in Boston, MA, went from 35 to 600 participating families, but only recruited the initial 35 directly. In 2013, average family savings rose 210%, household debt went down an average of 37%, and 73% of children who attended school improved their grades. The percentage of people who felt they had someone they could "count on" for problem solving (consider this the proxy for social connections) went from 27 to 91 (The Boston Foundation 2016).

For purposes of brevity, this paper offers glimpses into two social service innovations that seek to address the more pernicious aspects of income inequality while deploying social justice ethics in doing so. Another example that merits further investigation is LIFT, a national organization that uses volunteers to help families facing crises resulting from poverty as they pursue goals they define for themselves. In resemblance to Boston Rising, which learned from LIFT, volunteers help members focus on personal development (parallel to education), social capital (social connections), and financial wellbeing (assets) (LIFT 2016b). According to LIFT's 2015 annual report, the agency helped members recover $7.8 million in wages (LIFT 2016a, p. 6) and obtain nearly $2 million in public benefits and housing (LIFT 2016a, p. 23). While undoubtedly more examples exist, these effectively capture the intersection between innovations in social services and the approaches suggested by social justice and professional ethics.

3. Potential Path Forward

The innovations described in the previous section begin to address the intersectionality of income inequality, its tenacity, and some of the barriers and failures laid out in the three lessons about it—specifically, access to education, pursuit of economic well-being, and access to opportunities afforded by social capital. In addition, Boston Rising took a place-based approach, specifically in an attempt to address neighborhood and childhood exposure effects. Part of a path forward, then, in

---

[6]   In social services, this approach is widely defined as "strengths based" programming.

the quest to mitigate the harm of persistent income inequality and create more equitable systems for those experiencing it would be to advance more approaches like those described just now, as well as others that embrace social justice, self-determination and the importance of human relationships in their work, and that tackle educational, economic and social capital factors.

Family Independence Initiative would be the first to say, however, that a tremendous amount of work remains to be done beyond what approaches like it and LIFT can accomplish on their own. In a blog for FII, Lim Miller explores what U.S. Census data say about a family's ability to stay out of poverty, having left it. He notes that 30% of families leaving poverty cycle back below the poverty line within three years (Lim Miller 2015). He goes on to fault federal fiscal policy for this cycle, asserting, "Benefits are provided when you enter poverty, and when you are wealthy" (Lim Miller 2015), but not as one leaves poverty and attempts to jump the missing rungs in the mobility ladder. Lim Miller's ultimate point is that federal policy is the result of a failure to believe that people in poverty can leave it, and are willing and trying hard to do so.

Given the missing rungs in the mobility ladder, it seems clear that fiscal policy in the US must address both the need for average people to build assets, as well as the existing gross disparities in asset accumulation by race. In a study of data from the 2007 Study of Consumer Finances, Chang found that "Single black and Hispanic women have a median wealth of $100 and $120 respectively; the median for single white women is $41,500" (Chang 2010, p. 3). Asset ownership has a compounding effect over time, as these data suggest. Yet social welfare policies tend to penalize low-income families for accumulating assets—benefits shrink as savings increase. In addition, policies to compound assets—for example, the mortgage tax credit—do not kick in until families already have achieved sustainable incomes (Lim Miller 2015). Such fiscal policy might be effective if the beliefs were true that people on the wrong side of income inequality are not interested in, or capable of, changing their lots. In that case, fiscal policy would provide necessary supports for the poor in order to sustain them, and then make fiscal investments in those who have achieved some level of stability because they will be most capable of prospering and continuing to be upwardly mobile.

FII's work demonstrates the fault in that logic, however. Indeed, rectifying the racial wealth gap, countering opportunity hoarding, restoring the benefits of education more broadly to the American workforce—all require part of the path forward to be innovating not in practice, but in principle. To fight the tenacity of American income inequality, the next wave of social innovation will have to include innovations in belief. More specifically, the fight will require a broader embrace of solidarity.

In this case, solidarity refers to beliefs that (a) income inequality is a shared experience; (b) income inequality inflicts collective damage, due to the interconnected nature of humans and the human economy; and (c) it is necessary to prioritize policies that will rectify the worst effects of it while seeking to right the systems that perpetuate it. The 2016 American presidential election cycle arguably demonstrated that segments of the population not only understand but also are quite exercised about these beliefs. The McKinsey Global Institute study showed that income stagnation disproportionately affects young people and the less well educated (Dobbs et al. 2016). Polling during the political primaries demonstrated that the two main presidential candidates most widely considered disruptive of the status quo—Republican nominee Donald Trump and Democratic candidate Bernie Sanders—performed disproportionately well with lower-income and less well-educated voters, and with young people, respectively (Thompson 2016; CIRCLE 2016). Both candidates ran on platforms focused on marginalization of low- and middle-income families and on the disproportionate wealth and power of upper-income America.

Neither Trump's nor Sanders' approaches, however, represented a true embrace of solidarity. For the U.S. to achieve solidarity around income inequality, two additional things must happen. First, those currently benefitting from pernicious income inequality must decide it is unacceptable and damaging, even for them in the long run. Second, in seeing income inequality as a shared experience, people must decide to pursue a collective response. Awareness of the shared experience of income inequality must drive policy and political action toward a sense of community and common cause, rather than driving people on either side of the opportunity gap further apart. Otherwise, the interests of those at the top of the ladder will favor keeping the system as it is, and will continue disproportionately to find their way into public policy.

Unfortunately, as of this writing, the 2016 election cycle represented not a coming together, but a pulling apart. Reasonable people will disagree about the viability of those up and down the mobility ladder coming together in common cause and shared experience to rectify the structural economic and social injustices that give income inequality its staying power. Nevertheless, it must happen if people of good will want to make sustainable change for those being left behind.

Conflicts of Interest: The author declares no conflicts of interest.

References

Abraham, Yvonne. 2013. Rising and falling. *The Boston Globe*, June 9. Available online: https://www.bostonglobe.com/metro/2013/06/08/rising-and-falling/6xTtnkeTj0frxJyxFPIpvJ/story.html (accessed on 27 July 2016).

Atkinson, Anthony B. 2015. Setting the scene. In *Inequality: What Can Be Done?* Cambridge: Harvard University Press.

Bane, Mary Jo. 2014. Catholic social teachings, American politics and inequality. *Journal of Catholic Social Thought* 11: 391–404. [CrossRef]

Bartels, Larry M. 2008. Economic inequality and political representation. In *Unequal Democracy: The Political Economy of the New Gilded Age*. New York: Russell Sage Foundation, pp. 253–54.

The Boston Foundation. 2016. Family Independence Initiative-Boston. The Giving Common: An Initiative of the Boston Foundation. Available online: http://givingcommon.guidestar.org/FullPDF.aspx?OrgId=1124934 (accessed on 26 July 2016).

Boston Rising. n.d. LinkedIn Profile. Available online: https://www.linkedin.com/company/boston-rising (accessed on 25 July 2016).

Brendan, Mary Ann. 2006. Social Work for Social Justice: Strengthening Social Work Practice through the Integration of Catholic Social Teaching. Paper presented at the NACSW Convention on "A Vital Christian Presence in Social Work", Philadelphia, PA, USA, October 2006. Available online: http://www.nacsw.org/Publications/Proceedings2006/BrendenMASocialWorkforSocialJusticeE.pdf (accessed on 26 July 2016).

Chang, Mariko. 2010. *Lifting as We Climb: Women of Color, Wealth, and America's Future. Economic Security and Opportunity for Communities of Color*. Oakland: Insight Center for Community Economic Development. Available online: http://ww1.insightcced.org/uploads/CRWG/LiftingAsWeClimb-WomenWealth-Report-InsightCenter-Spring2010.pdf (accessed on 28 July 2016).

Chetty, Raj, Nathaniel Hendren, Patrick Kline, and Emmanuel Saez. 2014. Where is the land of opportunity? The geography of intergenerational mobility in the United States. *Quarterly Journal of Economics* 129: 1553–623. [CrossRef]

Chetty, Raj, and Nathaniel Hendren. 2015. The impacts of neighborhoods on intergenerational mobility: Childhood exposure effects and county-level estimates. *Harvard University and NBER*. Available online: http://scholar.harvard.edu/files/hendren/files/nbhds_paper.pdf (accessed on 26 July 2016).

CIRCLE. 2016. Total Youth Votes in the 2016 Primaries and Caucuses. The Center for Information and Research on Civic Learning and Engagement. Available online: http://civicyouth.org/total-youth-votes-in-2016-primaries-and-caucuses/?cat_id=405 (accessed on 27 July 2016).

Corak, Miles. 2013. Income inequality, equality of opportunity, and intergenerational mobility. *Journal of Economic Perspectives* 27: 79–102. [CrossRef]

GuideStar. 2016. Directory of Charities and Nonprofit Organizations. Available online: https://www.guidestar.org/nonprofit-directory/education-research/elementary-secondary/1.aspx (accessed on 25 July 2016).

Dobbs, Richard, Anu Madgavkar, James Manyika, Jonathan Woetzel, Jacques Bughin, Eric Labaye, and Pranav Kashyap. 2016. Poorer than Their Parents? A New Perspective in Income Inequality. McKinsey Global Institute. McKinsey and Company. Available online: http://www.mckinsey.com/global-themes/employment-and-growth/poorer-than-their-parents-a-new-perspective-on-income-inequality (accessed on 26 July 2016).

Duncan, Greg J., and Richard J. Murnane. 2014. *Restoring Opportunity: The Crisis of Inequality and the Challenge for American Education.* Cambridge: Harvard Education Press; New York: The Russell Sage Foundation.

Gilens, Martin, and Benjamin I. Page. 2014. Testing theories of American politics: Elites, interest groups, and average citizens. *Perspectives on Politics* 12: 564–81. [CrossRef]

Elwell, Craig K. 2014. The distribution of household income and the middle class. *Congressional Research Service*, March 10. Available online: https://fas.org/sgp/crs/misc/RS20811.pdf (accessed on 26 July 2016).

Garcia, Frank J. 2017. Globalization, Inequality and International Economic Law. *Religions* 8: 78. [CrossRef]

Giuliani, Rudy. 2008. Republican National Convention. *CSPAN.* Available online: https://www.c-span.org/video/?280790-1/2008-republican-convention-day-3 (accessed on 27 April 2017).

Haberman, Clyde. 2014. The cost of campaigns. *The New York Times*, October 19. Available online: http://www.nytimes.com/2014/10/20/us/the-cost-of-campaigns.html?_r=0 (accessed on 27 July 2016).

Hershbein, Brad. 2016. A college degree is worth less if you are raised poor. *Brookings Social Mobility Memos*, February 19. Available online: http://www.brookings.edu/blogs/social-mobility-memos/posts/2016/02/19-college-degree-worth-less-raised-poor-hershbein (accessed on 26 July 2016).

Hobgood, Mary Elizabeth. 2009. An economic ethics of right relationship. In *Dismantling Privilege: An Ethics of Accountability.* Cleveland: Pilgrim Press, pp. 66–110.

Jones, Katherine Castiello, Joya Misra, and K. McCurley. n.d. Intersectionality in sociology. Sociologists for Women in Society. Available online: https://www.socwomen.org/wp-content/uploads/swsfactsheet_intersectionality.pdf (accessed on 25 July 2016).

LIFT. 2016a. Creating a Better Way: LIFT FY2015 Annual Report. Available online: http://www.joomag.com/magazine/lift-annual-report-2015-creating-a-better-way/0002899001447875829?short (accessed on 26 July 2014).

LIFT. 2016b. The LIFT Solution. Available online: http://www.liftcommunities.org/why-lift/the-solution/ (accessed on 14 July 2016).

Lim Miller, M. 2015. The Poverty Line—A False Target. *Family Independence Initiative.* Available online: http://www.fii.org/blog/the-poverty-line-a-false-target/ (accessed on 26 July 2016).

Lyken-Segosebe, Dawn, and Serena E. Hinz. 2015. The politics of parental involvement: How opportunity hoarding and prying shape educational opportunity. *Peabody Journal of Education* 90 (1): 93–112. [CrossRef] [PubMed]

MacArthur Fellows Program. 2012. MacArthur Fellows/meet the class of 2012. *MacArthur Foundation.* Available online: https://www.macfound.org/fellows/871/ (accessed on 26 July 2016).

McKernan, Signe-Mary, Caroline Ratcliffe, C. Eugene Steuerle, and Sisi Zhang. 2013. *Less than Equal: Racial Disparities in Wealth Accumulation (Urban Institute Research Brief).* Washington: The Urban Institute.

Moore, Melanie. 2014. Unleashing Intrinsic Motivation through Social Signaling, Feedback Loops, and Access to Resources: Support from Social Science Research for FII's Approach to Poverty Alleviation. *Family Independence Initiative*, January 3. Available online: https://www.google.com/url?sa=t&rct=j&q=&esrc=s&source=web&cd=2&cad=rja&uact=8&ved=0ahUKEwihnMfAgpDOAhVCziYKHbYLDxIQFgglMAE&url=http%3A%2F%2Fwww.fii.org%2Fstudies-and-papers%2Funleashing-intrinsic-motivation-through-social-signaling-feedback-loops-and-access-to-resources%2F&usg=AFQjCNFWQpPV7hS2dJUWtKdm3OaOJx9c5A&sig2=PQDeKu7PO9Q91kGQBC7EnQ (accessed on 27 July 2016).

NASW Center for Workforce Studies, and Social Work Practice. 2011. Social Workers in Social Service Agencies: Occupational Profile. *National Association of Social Workers.* Available online: http://workforce.socialworkers.org/studies/profiles/Social%20Services.pdf (accessed on 27 July 2016).

National Association of Social Workers. 2008. Code of Ethics of the National Association of Social Workers. Available online: https://www.socialworkers.org/pubs/code/code.asp (accessed on 26 July 2016).

Netting, F. Ellen, Peter M. Kettner, Steve L. McMurtry, and M. Lori Thomas. 2012. *Social Work Macro Practice*, 5th ed. Upper Saddle River: Pearson.

Oxfam. 2016. An Economy for the 1%: How Privilege and Power in the Economy Drive Extreme Inequality and How This Can Be Stopped. Available online: https://www.oxfam.org/sites/www.oxfam.org/files/file_attachments/bp210-economy-one-percent-tax-havens-180116-en_0.pdf (accessed on 27 April 2017).

Palin, Sarah. 2008. Republican national convention. *CSPAN.* Available online: https://www.c-span.org/video/?280790-1/2008-republican-convention-day-3 (accessed on 27 April 2017).

Piketty, Thomas. 2014. *Capital in the Twenty-First Century*. Cambridge: The Belknap Press of Harvard University Press.

Putnam, Robert D. 2015. *Our Kids*. New York: Simon and Schuster.

Ratcliffe, Caroline, and Signe-Mary McKernan. 2010. Childhood poverty persistence: Facts and consequences. *The Urban Institute*, June 14. Available online: http://www.urban.org/sites/default/files/alfresco/publication-pdfs/412126-Childhood-Poverty-Persistence-Facts-and-Consequences.PDF (accessed on 26 July 2016).

Reardon, Sean F. 2011. The widening academic achievement gap between the rich and the poor: New evidence and possible explanations. In *Whither Opportunity? Rising Inequality, Schools and Children's Life Chances*. Edited by Greg J. Duncan and Richard J. Murnane. New York: Russel Sage Foundation, pp. 92–115.

Rieger, Joerg. 2013. The ethics of wealth in a world of economic inequality: A Christian perspective in a Buddhist-Christian dialogue. *Buddhist-Christian Studies* 33: 153–62. [CrossRef]

Sampson, Robert J. 2012. *The Great American City: Chicago and the Enduring Neighborhood Effect*. Chicago: University of Chicago Press.

Schlozman, Kay Lehman, Sidney Verba, and Henry E. Brady. 2012. *The Unheavenly Chorus: Unequal Political Voice and the Broken Promise of American Democracy*. Princeton: Princeton University Press.

Scherer, Michael, Pratheek Rebala, and Chris Wilson. 2014. The incredible rise in campaign spending. *Time Magazine*, October 23. Available online: http://time.com/3534117/the-incredible-rise-in-campaign-spending/ (accessed on 28 July 2016).

Silva, Diego S. 2013. Powers and Faden's concept of self-determination and what it means to 'achieve' well-being in their theory of social justice. *Public Health Ethics* 6 (1): 35–44. [CrossRef] [PubMed]

Specht, Harry, and Mark E. Courtney. 1995. *Unfaithful Angels: How Social Work Has Abandoned Its Mission*. New York: The Free Press.

Stuhldreher, Anne, and Rourke O'Brien. 2011. Family independence initiative: A new approach to help families exit poverty. *New America Foundation*. Available online: https://www.fii.org/wp-content/uploads/2017/03/newamericafiipaper_2011-1.pdf (accessed on 8 May 2017).

Thompson, Derek. 2016. Who are Donald Trump's supporters, really? *The Atlantic Politics & Policy Daily*, March 1. Available online: http://www.theatlantic.com/politics/archive/2016/03/who-are-donald-trumps-supporters-really/471714/ (accessed on 27 July 2016).

Zimmermann, Klaus, and Jo Ritzen. 2016. Fading Hope and the Rise in Inequality in the United States. Working paper no. 25, United Nations University—Maastricht Economic and Social Research Institute on Innovation and Technology (MERIT), Maastricht, The Netherlands. Available online: http://EconPapers.repec.org/RePEc:unm:unumer:2016025 (accessed on 27 July 2016).

religions

MDPI

Article

Growing Economic Inequality and Its (Partially) Political Roots

Kay Lehman Schlozman [1,*], Henry E. Brady [2] and Sidney Verba [3]

[1] Department of Political Science, Boston College, Chestnut Hill, MA 02467, USA
[2] Goldman School of Public Policy, University of California–Berkeley, Berkeley, CA 94720, USA; hbrady@berkeley.edu
[3] Department of Government, Harvard University; Cambridge, MA 02138, USA; sverba@harvard.edu
*   Correspondence: kay.schlozman@bc.edu

Academic Editors: Kate Ward and Kenneth Himes
Received: 13 February 2017; Accepted: 2 May 2017; Published: 18 May 2017

Abstract: Growing economic inequality fosters inequality in the political processes of American democracy. Since the 1970's inequalities in earnings and wealth have increased dramatically in the United States creating a higher level of inequality in disposable income than in other developed democracies. The United States also lags behind other rich nations in the way it provides for those at the bottom of the income distribution, and there is no evidence that the opportunities for success promised by the American Dream compensate for inequality in America. Technological and economic developments are significant causes of this growing economic inequality. The role of politics is more controversial, but government policy influences the distribution of income and education by the way it determines government benefits, taxes and the way markets function. For a number of reasons— including, most importantly, the relationship between education and income and the ability of the affluent to make large campaign donations—those who are economically well-off speak more loudly in politics. They are more likely to engage in most forms of individual political participation—not only ones that involve using cash but also ones that cost nothing except time. Moreover, when it comes to political voice through organizations, a professionalized domain dominated by hired experts in which the volume of political voice can be altered to reflect available economic resources, affluent interests are more likely to be organized and active. This essay considers the growing economic inequalities that form an important part of the backdrop for unequal political voice.

Keywords: economic inequality; political equality; democracy; political voice; political participation; household income and wealth; government influence on markets; labor unions

---

❖   In 2013, America's 25 highest-paid hedge fund managers made more than twice as much as all the kindergarten teachers in the country taken together (Krugman 2014).

❖   In 2013, the combined family wealth of just six members of the Walton family added up to more than the wealth of 52.5 million, or 42.9 percent, of American families[1].

❖   The minimum wage was $2.65 per hour in 1978. Had it kept up with the cost of living, it would have been $9.62—not $7.25—in 2014. If it had kept up with the increase in compensation of CEOs of large corporations, it would have been $95.97 in 2014[2].

---

[1]   Walton Family Net Worth is a Case Study Why Growing Wealth Concentration Isn't Just an Academic Worry. Economic Policy Institute Working Economics Blog, posted October 3 (Bivens 2014).

[2]   The minimum wage for 1978 is found at U.S. Department of Labor, Wage and Hour Division. 1938–2009. (Wage and Hour Division 2015); cost of living adjustment is taken from U. S. Department of Labor, Bureau of Labor Statistics (2015), CPI Inflation Calculator; the rate of growth of CEO pay (including the value of stock options exercised in a given year plus

❖ As measured by the poverty gap—that is, the percentage by which the mean income of the poor falls below the poverty line—the poor in the United States are quite poor indeed. In a group of 34 rich countries, only in Korea, Mexico, and Spain is the poverty gap higher[3].

❖ In state university systems, merit aid flows disproportionately to those who are less needy: about 1 in 5 students from households with incomes over $250,000 receive merit aid—in contrast to 1 in 10 from families making less than $30,000 (Rampell 2013).

When it comes to money, Americans are very unequal. Economic inequality has grown over the last generation, and disparities in income have consequences for which voices are heard in American politics. Those who are economically well-off speak more loudly in politics by giving more money and by engaging more frequently in almost all forms of political participation—even ones that cost nothing. The affluent are also better represented and more active when it comes to political voice through organizations where professionals can be hired as lobbyists.

Political and economic inequalities intersect in several ways. Not only is money a critical resource for both individual and organizational input into politics, but economic disparities shape the content of political conflict. Although the list of contentious political issues in contemporary America is long and varied, matters associated with differences in income and material well-being—ranging from tax policy to health care policy to Social Security—generate a great deal of political conflict[4]. Not only do economic differences produce political conflict, growing economic inequalities result from public policy as well as economic and technological change.

1. Increasing Economic Inequality

By a variety of metrics, economic inequality grew over the past generation[5]. Detailed information on household income—earnings, dividends, rents, and government transfers such as Social Security— goes back to the passage of the constitutional amendment authorizing the federal income tax in 1913. The share of pretax national income commanded by the top 10 percent and the top 1 percent of American households rose after World War I and peaked in the late 1920s. Then, during World War II, it decreased markedly, remaining relatively stable until the 1970s. During this period, increased income resulting from growth in both productivity and national income benefited the vast majority of middle-class and poor households below the top tenth while the most affluent lagged behind. Then, in the late 1970s, income inequality began to climb.

Figure 1 presents striking evidence about what happened between 1979 and 2011. As measured in constant dollars, the average after-tax household income for those at the bottom of the economic ladder—and for the middle-class households in the middle three-fifths—grew quite modestly over this period. In contrast, household incomes for those in the top fifth increased substantially: the *growth* in dollars in household income of those in the highest fifth was larger than the *average* 2011 income of those in the fourth quintile on the economic ladder. Even more notable is the extent to which this growth was concentrated in the top 1 percent of households. This upward redistribution benefited an extremely narrow slice of households: only the top 10 percent saw their share of after-tax income grow, and the gains went disproportionately to the top 1, and even the top 1, percent.

Discussions of increasing economic inequality tend to focus attention on the extent to which the rich have become richer compared to the middle class. A trend less often noticed is the fact that, by

---

salary, bonuses, restricted stock grants, and long-term incentive payouts) for chief executives of the top 350 U.S. firms is taken from Lawrence Mishel and Alyssa Davis. (Economic Policy Institute 2015).

3   Data are for the 34 members of the Organization for Economic Cooperation and Development (OECD). The poverty rate is the proportion of the population whose incomes are below half the median for the population as a whole. (OECD 2014, pp. 66–67)

4   See, for example, (Brewer 2007; Bartels 2016; Stonecash 2010, chp. 7).

5   For extensive additional bibliography and discussion of technical matters, see (Schlozman et al. 2012, chp. 3). See, also, (Piketty and Saez 2003, pp. 1–39; Burtless and Jencks 2003, chp. 3; Mishel et al. 2012; Piketty 2014, esp. Part III; Atkinson 2015, chp. 1).

some metrics, the poor have gotten poorer. After decreasing for a number of years during the 1960s, the poverty rate leveled off and has varied within a relatively narrow range since then[6]. The relative stability of the poverty rate, which separates families into groups of poor and non-poor, obscures the trend towards deeper poverty among poor households. Between 1996 and 2011, the number of people who live in extreme poverty—that is, those who live for at least one month a year on no more than $2 a day per person—has doubled[7].

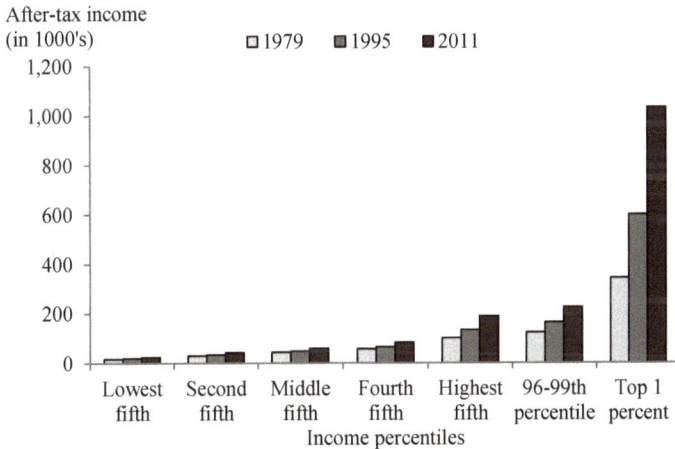

Figure 1. Growing Economic Inequality: After-Tax Household Income by Income Group, 1979–2011 (2011 Dollars). Source: (Congressional Budget Office 2014).

1.1. Earnings

The story about earnings and wealth parallels that for household income. For most households, the principal source of income is earnings, that is, wages and salaries derived from paid work. Wage and price controls during World War II resulted in substantial wage compression, especially among high-wage earners. Surprisingly, when the controls were lifted, the share of wages commanded by top earners did not immediately bounce back to prewar levels. However, in the 1970s it began to increase steadily before skyrocketing in the late 1980s and late 1990s. As shown in Figure 2, between 1979 and 2015—a period during which productivity gains were substantial—workers in the lowest decile actually lost ground in terms of real wages, and improvements in real wages for all but those in the top two deciles were modest.

Although much has been made of the increasing returns to education, what is striking is the extent to which the fruits of economic and productivity growth in recent decades accrued so disproportionately to those at the very, very top and not to the low- and middle-wage workers or even to workers who have college diplomas or advanced degrees. Between 1979 and 2010, the wage and salary income of the vast majority of Americans in the bottom 90 percent grew in real terms by 15 percent. Those at the top of the pyramid in the 90th-to-99th percentile saw their paychecks grow by 46 percent. The analogous figures for those in the stratosphere, the top 1 percent and the tippy-top 0.1 percent, are 131 percent and 278 percent, respectively (Mishel et al. 2012, p. 196).

---

[6] There is controversy among economists about the long-used official definition of poverty. An alternative measure, which takes account of in-kind government benefits, shows lower rates of poverty among children and higher rates among adults, especially the elderly. See (Bridges and Gesumaria 2015, pp. 55–81; Short 2015, pp. 60–254).

[7] (Stiglitz 2013, p. 20). On desperate poverty, see (Edin and Shaefer 2015).

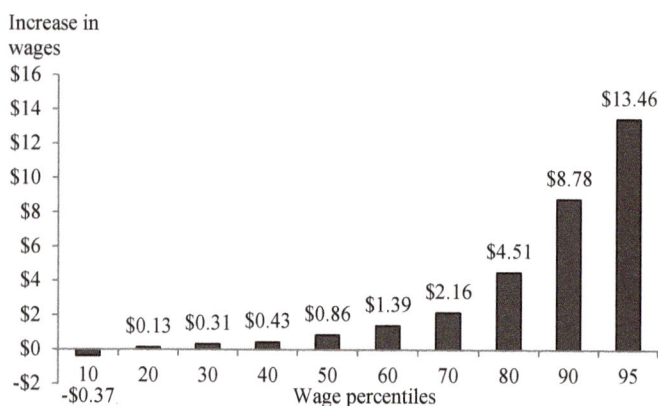

Figure 2. Growing Wage Inequality: Change in Hourly Wages by Wage Percentile, 1979–2011 (2011 Dollars). Source: Calculated from data presented in "Hourly wages of all workers, by wage percentile, 1973–2011" (Mishel et al. 2012, p. 186).

Meanwhile, the total compensation of CEOs at the nation's largest corporations shot up by almost 1000 percent between 1978 and 2014[8], a trend fueled, at least in part, by the restructuring of executive pay, in particular the inclusion of stock options in compensation packages. In 1965, CEO compensation was, on average, 20 times that of the median worker in the firm. By 2013, that ratio had jumped to 295.9 (Box 1 below provides more details). In that year, Disney's CEO earned 2238 times the median worker in his company (Morgenson 2015). What is noteworthy is that colossal CEO pay packages seem unrelated to performance[9]. One study showed the compensation of CEOs of large companies that had been through bankruptcy to be only 4 percent below the median for all CEOs of large companies[10]. A *New York Times* study of 51 Securities and Exchange Commission fraud settlements demonstrated that, even when the profits being rewarded turn out to be based on fraud, it is the corporation that is held to account, not the executives involved[11].

Box 1

❖ In the nation's largest firms, CEO compensation rose 941 percent between 1978 and 2015, a rate far higher than the increase in the stock market (543 percent) or the pay of the top 0.1 percent of earners (320 percent).
❖ Between 1973 and 2015, productivity increased 73 percent in the United States—at the same time that the average hourly earnings of nonsupervisory workers went up a mere 11 percent.

Sources: (Mishel and Schieder 2016; Economic Policy Institute 2016).

At the same time, the safety net provided by fringe benefits from private employers frayed in terms of both availability and generosity[12]. Although the Affordable Care Act increased the share of Americans with health insurance, copays and deductibles also increased. In addition, the share of workers who qualify for unemployment compensation if they lose their jobs declined and defined-contribution retirement plans replaced defined-benefit pensions so that workers cannot rely

---

8   (Economic Policy Institute 2015). The figure is for chief executives of the top 350 U.S. firms and includes the value of stock options exercised in a given year plus salary, bonuses, restricted stock grants, and long-term incentive payouts.
9   See (Bebchuk and Fried 2004)
10 Cited in (Reich 2012, p. 11)
11 Cited in (Stiglitz 2013, p. 257).
12 On the erosion of the private welfare state, see (Katz 2001, chps. 6–8; Hacker 2006).

upon a steady, predictable pension when they retire. In 1980, 84 percent of full-time workers in private establishments with at least 100 employees had defined-benefit pension plans. By 2015, that figure had fallen to 25 percent[13].

1.2. Wealth

The pattern of substantial, and increasing, inequality is even more dramatic for wealth: that is, the assets held by a household—for example, housing, consumer durables such as cars, businesses, savings, or investments—minus any outstanding mortgage, college loans, or consumer debt. Wealth—especially financial wealth like equities, bank deposits, or bonds—has always been more unevenly divided than either earnings or household income. In 2012, the top 1 percent commanded fully 42 percent of the national wealth.

Looking over time, the changes in the concentration of wealth parallel the U-shaped pattern for earnings and household income. The share of wealth owned by the top 1 percent reached a peak in the late 1920s, bottomed out in the 1970s, before turning upward again in the late 1970s. Between 1978 and 2012, the share of the nation's wealth held by the top 0.1 percent rose sharply from 7 percent to 22 percent. In fact, the share of wealth commanded by those at the very top was nearly as much as for all those in the bottom 90 percent, 23 percent, down from 35 percent in the mid-1980s (Saez and Zucman 2016, pp. 520, 523).

An important aspect of the unequal division of wealth is the divide by race or ethnicity. Black and Latino households command, on average, much less wealth than non-Hispanic white households, and these inequalities in wealth are much more pronounced than analogous inequalities in income or wages. Blacks and Latinos are less likely to be homeowners and more likely to owe more than they own[14].

2. The United States in Comparative Perspective

Most rich countries have witnessed increasing income inequality in recent decades[15], but the United States and the United Kingdom have led the way. The United States was actually less economically unequal than the powers of Europe in the early twentieth century. By the twenty-first century, the United States was the most economically unequal in a group of fourteen rich countries (Atkinson 2015, p. 26).

A key driver of increasing inequality in the United States is the explosion in compensation to those at the top. In what Thomas Piketty calls a "hypermeritocratic society," the "peak of the income hierarchy is dominated by very high incomes from labor rather than by inherited wealth" (Piketty 2014, p. 265). Whether they are quarterbacks or Oscar-winning actors or, more commonly, financiers and corporate chieftains, America's winners are very well paid indeed. In contrast, at the bottom of the hierarchy, the compensation for low-skilled work is quite stingy compared to other countries. Furthermore, government benefits are not particularly generous, and taxes are not especially redistributive in the United States. Taken together, these multiple factors interact to produce a higher level of inequality in disposable income in the United States than in other developed democracies[16].

3. Does American Affluence Compensate?

Two arguments are made to blunt concerns about the level of income inequality in the United States. The first is that the high level of affluence in America implies a higher, even though unequal,

---

[13] Figure taken from Employment Benefit Research Institute (2015, Table 5.1a), *EBRI Databook on Employee Benefits*.
[14] Discussion in this paragraph is taken from (Mishel et al. 2012, pp. 376, 385–95).
[15] This section draws on arguments and data in (Burtless and Jencks 2003; Smeeding 2005; Piketty 2014, especially chps. 8–9; Atkinson 2015, chp. 2). Making cross-national comparisons with regard to these issues poses technical dilemmas. See these sources as well the discussions and citations in (Schlozman et al. 2012, pp. 76–79).
[16] (Smeeding 2005, pp. 971–73); See, also (Krueger 2012, Figure 10); and (Gornick and Milanovic 2015).

standard of living for all. Not unexpectedly, Americans in top deciles continue to be better off than their counterparts in other affluent countries. In the middle, the United States has long outranked other affluent countries with respect to median income, but other countries are catching up fast and, in 2014, median income in Canada surpassed that in the United States (Leonhardt and Quealy 2014). Toward the bottom of the income ladder, however, the United States lags behind other rich nations. According to one comparative study, "Low paid workers in the United States—the most productive economy in the world—have markedly lower living standards than low paid workers in other advanced economies." (Freeman 1997) The combination of the relatively low wages of low-paid American workers and the lack of income support for the non-working poor implies that the incomes of households in the lowest decile in the United States are quite low when compared to their counterparts elsewhere (Mishel et al. 2009, p. 382, Figure 8E). In summary, American affluence compensates somewhat for those in the middle and not at all for those toward the bottom of the ladder.

4. What about the American Dream?

The second argument focuses on the opportunities for achieving the "American Dream." Discussions about realizing the American Dream come in two versions. One emphasizes that life gets better with absolute improvements in standard of living over the life cycle or across generations, regardless of whether the improvement also involves a relative as well as an absolute rise. The sluggish wage growth over much of the period since the mid-1970s implies that achieving this version of the American Dream has become harder for middle- and lower-income Americans. Over the life cycle, earnings tend to increase with age as workers gain experience and seniority, but they increase less sharply than they once did (Mishel et al. 2012, p. 143, Figure 3A). American standards of living have improved even though wages have stagnated but only because families are smaller than in the post–Baby Boom era; work force participation, especially by married women, has risen; and consumer indebtedness has increased.

Another definition of achieving the American Dream posits that opportunities for success, while differential, are available to the talented and industrious, irrespective of initial circumstances of disadvantage. American ideology to the contrary, rags-to-riches—and riches-to-rags—stories, however newsworthy, are exceptional. We are not all equal at the starting point, and recent research shows considerable correspondence in the economic deserts of successive generations[17]. Children who have the good fortune to be born to affluent well-educated parents are better off in a myriad of ways. Among others, they are more likely to

- Grow up with two biological parents;
- Live in a home environment that cultivates attitudes, interests, habits, and personality traits that are helpful in school and the marketplace;
- Benefit from parental investments in their development ranging from stimulating conversations to music lessons to summer camp;
- Attend schools with experienced teachers, educationally engaged fellow students, AP courses, and organized sports;
- Achieve academically in school;
- Be able to afford rising college tuitions and to have advisors at home and school able to guide them through the process of applying to college and finding financial aid, if needed;
- Matriculate in college and, ultimately, graduate;

---

[17] In a vast literature, see, for example, (Blau and Duncan 1967; Hauser and Featherman 1977; Hout 1988, pp. 1358–400; Ganzeboom et al. 1991, p. 284; Burtless and Jencks 2003); the essays in (Bowles et al. 2005); and the essays in (Isaacs et al. 2008).

Be located in social networks that provide mentors and contacts along the way[18].

The investments made by parents in their children's development and well-being are not necessarily financial. Although many of the enrichment opportunities provided by affluent parents are expensive, many aspects of a stimulating and nurturing home environment have no price tag. In fact, on average, it is probably more advantageous to have well-educated parents than rich ones. Still, it is hardly surprising that those who are savvy enough to have chosen affluent, well-educated parents are much more likely to end up affluent and well educated themselves (see Box 2 below for more details).

Box 2

> The class-based gap in parental expenditures on their children's development—in such things as books, high-quality child care, summer camp, and private school—has grown. In the 1972–1973 period, families in the highest income group spent $2701 more per year on child enrichment than did families in the lowest income group. By the 2005–2006 period, the disparity had grown to $7,557.
>
> Source: (Duncan and Murnane 2011b, p. 11). Data for lowest and highest income quintiles in 2008 dollars.

These class-based gaps in the experiences and well-being of children have, unfortunately, grown markedly in recent decades—a cause for concern about both the current circumstances and future mobility prospects of children whose parents are less affluent and well-educated[19].

The United States is anything but the leader when it comes to providing opportunities for success regardless of the previous condition of disadvantage. In a group of thirteen affluent democracies, the Nordic countries exhibit the most social mobility from generation to generation as measured by the correspondence between fathers' and son's earnings. Along with the U.K. and Italy, the United States has the least. What is more, among rich countries, those with higher levels of income inequality tend also to be those where the advantage passes from one generation to the next[20]. In summary, there is no evidence at all that the opportunities for success to the talented and industrious promised by the American Dream compensate for inequality in America.

5. How Do We Explain Increasing Economic Inequality?

There is widespread agreement that multiple factors contribute to increasing income inequality and that those factors are difficult to disentangle. There is also consensus that structural and economic trends exacerbate economic inequality. Among them is skill-based technological change in which machine tools, computers, and robots operated by high-skilled workers replace low-skilled workers; international trade and domestic outsourcing in which lower-paid workers are substituted for better-paid ones; and winner-take-all markets in which the most successful, not only in athletics and entertainment but also in the corporate and financial sectors, are able to command stratospheric compensation[21].

At this point, the agreement breaks down. Some maintain that the growth of economic inequality can be explained primarily by the operations of increasingly efficient markets. Others point out that markets reflect more than simply an equilibrium achieved by impersonal forces of supply and demand and that market outcomes are "the result of the bargaining power of different participants,"

---

[18] On the class gaps in child well-being, see (Putnam 2015). With respect to the educational system, see the essays and references in (Duncan and Murnane 2011a), in particular, (Duncan and Murnane, "Introduction," chp. 1; Reardon, Sean F. "The Widening Academic Achievement Gap between the Rich and the Poor: New Evidence and Possible Explanations," chap. 5; and Bailey, Martha J., and Susan M. Dynarski, "Inequality in Postsecondary Education," chap. 6.)

[19] An exception to the pattern of growing gaps between rich and poor children is diminution in the disparity in health between rich and poor for children and young adults. See (Sanger-Katz 2016)

[20] (Corak 2013, Figure 1). See also, (Krueger 2012).

[21] Discussion of such factors is contained in (Dadush et al. 2012, chp. 4). See also, (Atkinson 2015, chp. 3).

(Atkinson 2015, p. 147) an insight that provides the conceptual framework for the Progressive-era observation that "an empty stomach can make no contracts."[22]

A special point of contention is the role of politics. Economists differ with regard to the weight they place on government policy in explaining increasing economic inequality. Clearly, technological and economic developments are significant causes of growing economic inequality. Still, the economic argument about increasing return to education does not explain the explosion of compensation at the very top. Furthermore, these economic and technological changes, which are present across developed economies, cannot explain why the growth of inequality has differed so substantially across nations and why it has been especially pronounced in the United States. Christopher Jencks has a blunt rejoinder, "The answer turns out to be pretty simple: 'It's politics, stupid.'" (Jencks 2005, p. 134). If it is politics, then to what extent have policies exacerbated inequality or failed to deter its growth?

5.1. Benefits and Taxes

Discussions of how policy affects income inequality usually begin with the government benefits and taxes that modify market outcomes. In all rich democracies, the sum total of what governments distribute, often on a means-tested basis, in benefits and extract in taxes ameliorates income inequality. The reduction in inequality from these tools is not especially pronounced in the United States. Clearly, since the late 1970s, the redistributive effects of benefits and taxes have not kept pace with growing inequality in market outcomes before benefits and taxes.

In 1988, Ronald Reagan famously observed, "We fought a war against poverty, and poverty won." While Reagan may have the better quotation, in fact, government benefits do reduce poverty,[23] and decreases in benefits increase poverty. The 1996 welfare reform replaced the major income support, Aid to Families with Dependent Children (AFDC), with Temporary Assistance to Needy Families (TANF), which is time-limited and, on average, provides a less generous level of support. While the welfare rolls were already declining at the time that welfare reform was passed, the drop in coverage has been marked: in 2014, the TANF caseload was only 27 percent of what it was at the height of the old welfare program in 1994 (Edin and Shaefer 2015, p. 7). That a much smaller share of poor families receive TANF benefits and that inflation-adjusted TANF benefits are, on average, lower than at the time of welfare reform is at least part of the story of the increase of the proportion of families with children that are deeply poor. The decline of TANF has reduced government benefits that redistribute income, but that is not the end of the story.

The main income support for the poor is now the Earned Income Tax Credit (EITC), a tax benefit that is tied to work. The EITC ameliorates income inequality, but the link to employment means that it only helps those who are able to find jobs. As a result, it has limited countercyclical impact in economic downturns (Bitler and Hoynes 2016). Two other programs partly fill the gap. During the Great Recession, SNAP—the Supplemental Nutrition Assistance Program, the heir to what was known as "food stamps"—and Unemployment Insurance provided compensatory assistance with the result that, according to a Congressional Budget Office Report, the reduction in income inequality from government benefits was somewhat higher in 2011 than it had been in 1979[24]. With economic recovery and the expiration of the temporary boost to SNAP benefits, SNAP spending has declined and with it the temporary boost in the redistributive impact of government benefits (Rosenbaum and Keith-Jennings 2016).

---

[22] Testimony before the Massachusetts legislature, cited without additional bibliographic information in (Kens 1998, p. 19). On the extent to which executive pay reflects forces other than the operations of markets, see (Bebchuk and Fried 2004, Parts I and II).

[23] For evidence and citations supporting the contention that government benefits reduce poverty, see (Ziliak 2015, pp. 34–36).

[24] (Congressional Budget Office 2014, pp. 25–27). A parallel CBO analysis undertaken three years earlier found the opposite, a decrease in the redistributive impact of government benefits, for the period between 1979 and 2007. See (Congressional Budget Office 2011, Xii).

The American tax system is complicated. While it is broadly progressive, in certain respects, it is friendlier to those with higher incomes. Most people's federal taxes are fairly straightforward and are withheld from their paychecks[25]. In contrast, for those with complex investments and financial dealings, the federal tax code is riddled with tax-reducing deductions and loopholes inserted by lobbyists and exploited by lawyers and accountants. Because such provisions are so byzantine, they are open to legitimate differences of interpretation as well as flagrant dishonesty. Significantly, in the late 1990s, Congress passed legislation crippling the tax enforcement capacity of the IRS and has subsequently eroded its funding. Nevertheless, after federal taxes, income inequality is somewhat less pronounced than before the federal government takes its bite.

Unlike federal taxes, state and local taxes, which vary substantially from state to state, are not progressive overall. With each rung up the economic ladder, the proportion of income paid in state and local taxes diminishes. In 2015, the share of income paid by the lowest 20 percent of households, those with incomes below $19,000, was 10.9 percent; by the middle 20 percent, those with incomes between $35,000 and $56,000, 9.4 percent; and by the top 1 percent, who had incomes over $471,000, only 5.4 percent (Institute on Taxation and Economic Policy 2015).

After decades of tinkering with the federal tax code, federal taxes now do less to ameliorate income inequality than they did in 1979[26]. A number of the alterations to federal taxes have had a regressive impact[27]. Compared to those further down, the affluent realize a higher share of their incomes from unearned income—that is, income like rents and dividends not derived from wages and salary. Therefore, the successive reductions of the capital gains tax to 15 percent have, on average, reduced the tax bills of those at the top of the income ladder. Similarly, changes to the federal estate tax have reduced estate taxes for the very wealthy[28].

Perhaps most notably, income taxes on high salaries have been reduced substantially. Beginning in the 1980s, most affluent countries lowered marginal income tax rates, but the U.S and the U.K., which had relatively higher rates during the 1960s, went further than most[29]. During the Reagan administration, the marginal federal income tax rate fell from 70 percent to 28 percent. Under Clinton, it rose to 39.6 percent before being lowered to 35 percent under George W. Bush. In fact, the most important effect of reductions in the marginal rate on earned incomes may be less on who pays what in taxes than on the pay itself. The era of lower marginal income tax rates has also been the era of soaring compensation. When federal taxes gobbled so much of the high pay, there was less incentive to try to extract the last dollar. With lower marginal rates, the payoff for demanding a big raise has skyrocketed[30].

5.2. Government Policy and the Shaping of Market Outcomes

Less widely discussed than the way that government benefits and tax policies modify market incomes is how profoundly government policies shape the operations of markets. Beginning with the capacity of governments to enforce the contracts upon which market exchanges rely, capitalist systems are embedded in a myriad of policies that shape their functioning. Two issues at stake in the 2016 presidential election—immigration and trade agreements, both of which have implications for economic distribution—are shaped fundamentally by policy decisions. They are but two of the many matters germane to economic inequality in which both market operations and government policies have consequences. That is why, according to Joseph Stiglitz, we must understand "the array of laws

---

25 Material in the paragraph is taken from (Johnston 2007, pp. 168–73).
26 (Congressional Budget Office 2014, Figure 15). See also, (Fieldhouse 2013).
27 Information in this paragraph is taken from (Stiglitz 2013, pp. 89–92); and (Formisano 2015, pp. 77–80).
28 For information about the estate tax, see (Jacobson et al. 2007, volume 2, chp. 1); (Jacobson et al. 2007) and (Huang and DeBot 2015).
29 (Atkinson 2015, pp. 181–82). See also, (Piketty 2014, pp. 499, 508).
30 Among others, this argument is made by (Piketty 2014, pp. 508–12)), who finds no evidence that the explosion in compensation has been accompanied by enhanced productivity by high earners.

and policies that lie beneath the surface—the rules that determine the balance of power between public and private, employers and workers, innovation and shared growth and all the other interests that make up the modern economy." (Stiglitz 2015)

As with immigration and trade, policies with the potential to enhance workers' paychecks often have politically powerful opponents and inevitably involve tradeoffs among valued outcomes. Furthermore, agreement on a desired result may not be matched by consensus among economists on how to achieve it.

One policy, not always cited in discussions of growing economic inequality, is the use of fiscal and monetary tools to maintain full employment and, thus, promote higher wages. Slack labor markets tend to place workers, especially low-wage workers, at a disadvantage. Since the Reagan years, economic policy has not always made full employment a priority (Baker and Bernstein 2013; Mishel et al. 2014, pp. 26–31). Another rarely cited partial explanation for growing economic inequality is reduced competition among firms in various economic sectors. When fewer employers are competing for workers, employers gain leverage in setting wages. Concerns about the impact of mergers on competition for employees, and therefore on wages, are notably absent from merger complaints (Council of Economic Advisers Brief 2016). Besides, antitrust enforcement has not been especially vigorous in recent decades.

A policy that is mentioned more frequently is the minimum wage which, by placing a floor under wages, has a mildly equalizing effect on earnings. Unlike many policies ranging from Social Security benefits to the cap on payroll taxes, the minimum wage, established in the Fair Labor Standards Act of 1938, is not indexed to inflation or to the median wage. The value of the minimum wage peaked in real terms in 1968 and has declined 24 percent since then, even though the half century since then has witnessed substantial economic growth (Elwell 2014, Table 1). It is also not especially generous in comparison with other affluent democracies. In a group of 13 affluent countries, only in Spain and Japan is the minimum wage a smaller percentage of median earnings than in the United States (Atkinson 2015, p. 149). Therefore, what the government has not done—or, at least, what it has not done very often since the Reagan Administration—raise the minimum wage, has contributed to income inequality.

Overtime pay presents a parallel case. Like the minimum wage, guaranteed overtime pay, mandated in the Fair Labor Standards Act, is not indexed. Because the threshold for overtime eligibility is not automatically adjusted with inflation, the share of salaried workers who qualify for overtime pay had sunk to 11 percent in 2014—from 65 percent in 1975[31].

In an era when workers have, on average, reduced leverage in bargaining with employers, employers have adopted a number of practices to keep labor costs down. Among them are hiring outside contractors to do work once undertaken by regular employees who qualified for such fringe benefits as health insurance; requiring employees with complaints about pay or employment practices to submit to binding arbitration rather than to sue in court; enjoining employees from discussing matters of pay with one another; failing to pay mandated minimum wage or overtime; and requiring new employees—not just engineers in Silicon Valley who might have access to trade secrets but such low-wage employees as fast-food workers or camp counselors—to sign non-compete agreements limiting their freedom to seek better-paid jobs[32].

All of these practices could be modified by government policy. In some cases, policy makers have chosen to eschew any policy remedy or have been met with successful opposition by affected business interests. In others, the policy tools are in place but inadequately enforced. For example,

---

[31] (Mishel and Eisenbrey 2015, p. 10). In the final year of the Obama administration, the Department of Labor put out a rule making many additional workers eligible for overtime pay. Immediately after Trump took office, this rule was suspended. See (Opfer 2017).

[32] These and other practices are discussed in (Stiglitz 2015) and (Council of Economic Advisers Brief 2016). The specific examples of lower-wage workers who are required to sign non-competes are in (Council of Economic Advisers Brief 2016, p. 8).

when it comes to paying below minimum wage or depriving employees of overtime, the number of federal inspectors was cut by nearly a third between 1980 and 2007. Even with the reduced capacity to enforce wage and overtime guarantees, more than $1 billion of stolen wages were recovered in 2012, a figure that is thought to be a small fraction of the national total (Stiglitz 2015, p. 47).

The growth of the financial sector and the explosion of its profitability and the compensation of its higher-ups along with consumer losses during the Great Recession clearly exacerbated income inequality. Nevertheless, it is difficult to assess the contribution to that outcome of government action and inaction with respect to investments, borrowing, and other financial transactions[33]. Political conflict about government regulation of finance tends to involve lobbying by organized interests—for example, credit card companies, banks, and other financial institutions. As is so often the case, policy impact is buried in the details, details that have been scrutinized and shaped by interests with insider status, policy expertise, and deep pockets.

A number of government actions in the post-2000 era seem to have been particularly friendly to business. For example, the 2005 bankruptcy reform that made it harder for consumers—and nearly impossible for indebted students[34]—to discharge debts by declaring bankruptcy is surely more advantageous to credit card companies, mortgage lenders, car lenders, and for-profit universities than to indebted consumers. Similar arguments are made about policy developments with regard to the increased protection of intellectual property and the relaxation of antitrust enforcement (Reich 2015).

Much of the story of the financial sector in recent decades, however, involves the absence of regulation. The 1999 repeal of the 1933 Glass-Steagall Act, which had separated investment banking from commercial banking, involved explicit deregulation. However, the absence of regulation can also reflect successful industry opposition, as in the case of the complex financial instruments known as derivatives, as well as the failure of enforcing agencies to regulate vigorously—whether out of ideological conviction, coziness with the industry, or insufficient budgets.

Combined with technological developments that transformed how financial transactions take place, this unregulated environment incubated new ways of doing financial business. Speculation in arcane and complex financial instruments and other forms of financial risk-taking, predatory lending and, sometimes, actual fraud ended up jeopardizing the solvency of financial institutions and leaving many consumers indebted or foreclosed. When the collapse of major financial institutions was imminent, the government came through with a bailout that, while eventually repaid in full, cost more than the government spent on the unemployed who lost jobs during the ensuing recession and helped bankers retain their bonuses while leaving behind those who had lost homes to foreclosure. In the aftermath, Congress legislated new financial regulations in the 2010 Dodd-Frank Wall Street Reform and Consumer Protection Act. Although passed with a party-line vote, the bill involved substantial compromise. Both the bill itself and its implementation, which has not been especially forceful, have been controversial. With the recent transition to the Trump administration, the fate of Dodd-Frank remains in doubt.

5.3. Declining Unions and Growing Economic Inequality

Any account of the growth of economic inequality must include a discussion of the decline of labor union membership and power, a development with consequences for both economic and political inequality. Unions operate in several ways to boost workers' power and enhance their earnings. Union members are more likely to be politically active even beyond what we would expect on the basis of their education and incomes. Furthermore, labor unions represent their members' economic interests—and

---

[33] For conflicting views on the causes of the 2008 financial crisis, see (Financial Crisis Inquiry Commission 2011), including the two dissenting reports. Material in the remainder of this section is taken from (Warren and Tyagi 2003, pp. 126–29, 152–56; Stiglitz 2013, pp. 46, 93, 112–15, 239–45, 252, 310; Reich 2012, pp. 57–58).

[34] One provision in the 2005 bankruptcy act made it extremely difficult to discharge private student loans—in contrast to, for example, consumer debt—through bankruptcy. See (Lieber 2010).

the economic interests of ordinary citizens more generally—in politics. Unions also provide workers a collective voice in the workplace.

The share of the workforce that is unionized actually peaked in the 1950s, but the past three decades have witnessed striking attrition in the proportion of workers who are union members and the slightly higher proportion who are covered by union contracts. It is notable that, even as the size of the workforce expanded substantially, the absolute number of union members declined by nearly five million over this period. In 1977, 26.5 percent of all wage and salary workers were members of unions; by 2014, the figure had dropped to 11.1 percent[35]. America's circumstances are not unique and over the last generation, the erosion in the proportion of the workforce that is unionized has been common across industrial democracies. In a group of twenty advanced democracies, the proportion of unionized workers diminished between 1979 and the late 1990s in fourteen of them[36]. Still, even if the United States is hardly alone in the drop in union density, the United States has, in comparative terms, very low levels of union membership.

The decrease in union ranks has occurred entirely in the private sector. The proportion of private-sector workers who were union members decreased steadily, from 21.7 percent in 1977 to 6.6 percent in 2014. In contrast, the share of public-sector workers who are union members fluctuated within a very narrow range and ended the period at a slightly higher level, 35.7 percent, than at the beginning. While the share of the workforce employed in the public sector fell from 18.7 percent to 15.2 percent over this period, the share of union members who are public-sector employees rose sharply, from 31.4 percent to 54.4 percent.

There is no question that the decline of union membership has had an impact on the growth of income inequality, although there is disagreement about how much. The union wage premium—that is, the increment to wages and benefits accruing solely from union membership with other relevant factors taken into account—has diminished since the 1980s. Still, union membership clearly boosts compensation—especially for private-sector employees, for men, for blue-collar workers, and for workers with no post-secondary education[37]. In fact, one study estimates that union decline explains between a fifth and a third of the growth in wage inequality among men (Western and Rosenfeld 2011).

At the same time that the weakening of union economic power has had consequences for the size of workers' paychecks and the conditions under which they work, union decline has diminished their political capacity to support policies that protect the economic interests of ordinary workers and to oppose policies that benefit the privileged. An indicator of the political weakness of organized labor is the finding in a recent study that when asked to name their principal antagonists on the issues on which they were currently working, not one of the corporate lobbyists mentioned a union (Drutman 2015, pp. 78–79). Thus, union decline has operated through both the workplace and politics to enhance income inequality.

What explains the steep decline in the share of American workers who are union members? A number of factors account for this trend[38]. One is structural changes in the American economy, in particular the decrease in manufacturing employment. Another is diminished support for unionization among workers. Unions themselves made miscalculations. There is evidence that the leadership of the American Federation of Labor and Congress of Industrial Organizations (AFL-CIO), especially George Meany, did not devote sufficient attention or resources to organizing. Furthermore, employers have

---

[35] Data taken from the Union Membership and Coverage Database constructed by Barry Hirsch and David Macpherson. (Hirsch and Macpherson 2015)

[36] (Flanagan 2005, p. 35. Table 1). See (Mishel et al. 2009, p. 375). Of the thirteen countries about which they present data, union coverage is lowest in the United States.

[37] See (Mishel 2012; Rosenfeld 2014, chps. 2–3).

[38] For a more extensive discussion and additional bibliographical sources, see (Schlozman et al. 2012, pp. 87–94); as well as (Freeman 2007, chp. 5). See also (Goldfield 1987; Freeman and Katz 1994; Hacker and Pierson 2010, pp. 56–61; Rosenfeld 2014, chp. 1).

been increasingly aggressive. Aided by consultants who specialize in "union prevention," businesses have become substantially more hostile to union-organizing drives in both tone and tactics.

Finally, the weakening of labor has undoubtedly had a political component[39]. A significant blow to organized labor unions was the passage in 1947 of the employer-friendly Taft-Hartley Act, which proscribed a number of labor practices and permitted states to pass "right-to-work" laws outlawing the union shop. Although attempts have been made to alter or repeal it, Taft-Hartley remains in place today. In fact, organized labor has not succeeded in realizing any of its major legislative goals in decades. During both the Carter and Obama administrations, Congresses controlled by Democrats handed legislative defeats to organized labor[40].

Political developments in the early years of the Reagan administration are critical. In a turning point in labor history, during the summer of 1981, Reagan dismissed striking air traffic controllers and replaced them with nonunion employees, after which employers have felt free to replace striking workers. In addition, Reagan was able to name appointees to the National Labor Relations Board (NLRB) who were unfriendly to labor. The result was policy changes that have facilitated management's capacity to act aggressively against unions[41]. The NLRB was able to weaken worker protections under the National Labor Relations Act by overturning worker-friendly precedents, many of them long standing, through a series of decisions in carefully selected cases. At the same time, whether by accident or design, the number of decisions in cases of unfair labor practices dwindled, and the backlog of unresolved cases expanded to the largest number in history (Gross 1995, p. 253). More recently, at the state level, bolstered by friendly state legislatures, Republican governors in a number of states have dealt with revenue shortfalls by cutting the medical benefits and pensions of unionized public employees and, more fundamentally, targeting their collective bargaining rights.

6. Conclusions

Economic deserts are not only unequally distributed but are more unequally distributed now than at any time in several generations and are more unequal in the United States than in most developed democracies. Those at the top have garnered most of the income gains while incomes in the middle and lower ranges have stagnated, and the number of desperately poor has risen.

What we have seen undermines several clichés about economic life in America. For one, it is often argued that a rising economic tide lifts all boats. However, growing prosperity and productivity in recent decades have lifted the yachts but left the dinghies still grounded. Moreover, with the stagnation in middle- and lower-class income and earnings, no longer does American affluence imply that low-income workers are better off in absolute terms than they are elsewhere. Finally, in spite of rhetoric about America as the land of opportunity, well-educated, affluent parents are ordinarily able to pass their high status along to their children, and the rates of upward mobility in the United States are actually lower than in most affluent democracies. Besides, the possibilities for those of modest origins to become successful have surely not increased in this era of increasing economic inequality. Indeed, they may have diminished.

It is difficult to sort out the causes of economic inequality, but there is agreement that technological change, international trade, and domestic outsourcing are significant factors. Although the role of politics is more controversial, an environment of government policy shapes the way the markets function, and government policies influence the distribution of income. In addition, government inaction has exacerbated income inequality. Public officials have had policy instruments at their disposal—for example, raising the minimum wage regularly or establishing prudent standards for mortgage loans—that might have decelerated the rate of growth of economic inequality. Thus, the sum

---

[39] On these factors, see (Lichtenstein 2002, chps. 3–4).
[40] See (Hacker and Pierson 2010, pp. 127–32, 278–79).
[41] On the NLRB under Reagan, see (Levy 1985, pp. 269–390; Moe 1987, pp. 266–71; Gross 1995, chp. 13).

total of government action and inaction has been insufficient to keep up with growing income inequality in the United States and has had less impact on the increase than in other affluent democracies.

Another factor that has added to economic inequality is the decline of unions and the resulting reduction in the economic and political power of workers. Even though private-sector union membership is a fraction of what it once was, unionized workers still command better wages and benefits than otherwise similar non-union workers. The weakness of unions also has implications for the inequalities of political voice. Among organized interests, unions are the most important advocates for the economic needs and concerns of ordinary workers. Labor union membership has a mobilizing effect for individuals: compared to their non-union counterparts, union members are more likely to vote or to engage in other political activity.

We are concluding this essay in the same week as the announcement of the broad outlines of a tax plan that, in one assessment, "shifts trillions to the wealthiest." (Davis and Cohen 2017). Should this tax plan be enacted in roughly its proposed form, it would hardly ameliorate the current levels of economic inequality and would serve as additional evidence that politics matters for economic outcomes.

Author Contributions: Kay Lehman Schlozman took the lead in drafting this chapter but all authors contributed to it.

Conflicts of Interest: The authors declare no conflict of interest.

References

Atkinson, Anthony. 2015. *Inequality: What Can Be Done?* Cambridge: Harvard University Press.

Baker, Dean, and Jared Bernstein. 2013. *Getting Back to Full Employment*. Washington: Center for Economic and Policy Research.

Bartels, Larry M. 2016. *Unequal Democracy*, 2nd ed. Princeton: Princeton University Press.

Bebchuk, Lucian, and Jesse Fried. 2004. *Pay without Performance: The Unfulfilled Promise of Executive Compensation*. Cambridge: Harvard University Press.

Bitler, Marianne, and Hilary Hoynes. 2016. The More Things Change, the More They Stay the Same? The Safety Net and Poverty in the Great Recession. *Journal of Labor Economics* 34: S403–44. [CrossRef]

Bivens, Josh. 2014. Walton Family Net Worth is a Case Study Why Growing Wealth Concentration Isn't Just an Academic Worry. *Economic Policy Institute Working Economics Blog*, October 3. Available online: http://www.epi.org/blog/walton-family-net-worth-case-study-growing/ (accessed on 18 December 2015).

Blau, Peter M., and Otis Dudley Duncan. 1967. *The American Occupational Structure*. New York: Wiley.

Samuel Bowles, Herbert Gintis, and Melissa Osborne Groves, eds. 2005. *Unequal Chances: Family Background and Economic Success*. Princeton: Princeton University Press.

Brewer, Mark D. 2007. *Split: Class and Cultural Divides in American Politics*. Washington: CQ Press, 2007.

Bridges, Benjamin, and Robert V. Gesumaria. 2015. The Supplemental Poverty Measure (SPM) and Children: How and Why the SPM and Official Poverty Estimates Differ. *Social Security Bulletin* 75: 55–81.

Bureau of Labor Statistics. 2015. CPI Inflation Calculator. Available online: http://www.bls.gov/data/inflation_calculator.htm (accessed on 26 December 2015).

Burtless, Gary, and Christopher Jencks. 2003. American Inequality and Its Consequences. In *Agenda for the Nation*. Edited by Henry J. Aaron, James M Lindsay and Pietro S. Nivola. Washington: Brookings Institution.

Congressional Budget Office. 2011. Trends in the Distribution of Household Income between 1979 and 2007. October 25, Xii. Available online: https://www.cbo.gov/publication/42729 (accessed on 2 January 2016).

Congressional Budget Office. 2014. The Distribution of Household Income and Federal Taxes, 2011. November 12. Available online: https://www.cbo.gov/publication/49440 (accessed on 2 January 2016).

Corak, Miles. 2013. Income Equality, Equality of Opportunity, and Intergenerational Mobility. *Journal of Economic Perspectives* 27: 79–102. [CrossRef]

Council of Economic Advisers Brief. 2016. Labor Market Monopsony: Trends, Consequences, and Policy Responses. October. Available online: https://www.whitehouse.gov/sites/default/files/page/files/20161025_monopsony_labor_mrkt_cea.pdf (accessed on 15 January 2017).

Dadush, Uri, Kemal Dervis, Sarah Puritz Milsom, and Bennett Stancil. 2012. *Inequality in America: Facts, Trends, and International Perspectives*. Washington: Brookings.

Davis, Julie Hirschfield, and Patricia Cohen. 2017. Trumps Plan Shifts Trillions to Wealthiest. *New York Times*, April 28.

Drutman, Lee. 2015. *The Business of America Is Lobbying*. Oxford and New York: Oxford University Press.

Greg J. Duncan, and Richard J. Murnane, eds. 2011a. *Whither Opportunity? Rising Inequality, Schools, and Children's Life Chances*. New York: Russell Sage.

Duncan, Greg J., and Richard J. Murnane. 2011b. Introduction: The American Dream, Then and Now. In *Whither Opportunity? Rising Inequality, Schools, and Children's Life Chances*. Edited by Greg J. Duncan and Richard J. Murnane. New York: Russell Sage.

Economic Policy Institute. 2015. CEO Pay Has Grown 90 Times Faster than Typical Worker Pay Since 1978. July 1. Available online: http://www.epi.org/publication/ceo-pay-has-grown-90-times-faster-than-typical-worker-pay-since-1978/ (accessed on 26 December 2015).

Economic Policy Institute. 2016. The Productivity–Pay Gap. August. Available online: http://www.epi.org/productivity-pay-gap/ (accessed on 14 January 2017).

Edin, Kathryn J., and H. Luke Shaefer. 2015. *$2.00 a Day: Living on Almost Nothing in America*. Boston: Houghton Mifflin Harcourt.

Elwell, Craig K. 2014. Inflation and the Real Minimum Wage: A Fact Sheet. *Congressional Research Service*. Available online: https://www.fas.org/sgp/crs/misc/R42973.pdf (accessed on 8 March 2016).

Employment Benefit Research Institute. 2015. EBRI Databook on Employee Benefits. Available online: https://www.ebri.org/pdf/publications/books/databook/DB.Chapter%2005.pdf (accessed on 8 March 2016).

Fieldhouse, Andrew. 2013. Rising Income Inequality and the Role of Shifting Market-Income Distribution, Tax Burdens, and Tax Rates. Economic Policy Institute. June 14. Available online: http://www.epi.org/publication/rising-income-inequality-role-shifting-market/ (accessed on 2 January 2016).

Financial Crisis Inquiry Commission. 2011. The Financial Crisis Inquiry Report. *U.S. Government Printing Office*. Available online: https://www.gpo.gov/fdsys/pkg/GPO-FCIC/pdf/GPO-FCIC.pdf (accessed on 14 January 2016).

Flanagan, Robert J. 2005. Has Management Strangled U.S. Unions? *Journal of Labor Research* 26: 35. [CrossRef]

Formisano, Ronald P. 2015. *Plutocracy in America*. Baltimore: Johns Hopkins University Press, pp. 77–80.

Freeman, Richard B. 1997. *When Earnings Diverge: Causes, Consequences, and Cures for the New Inequality in the United States*. Washington: National Policy Association, p. 19.

Freeman, Richard B. 2007. *America Works: The Exceptional U.S. Market*. New York: Russell Sage Foundation.

Freeman, Richard B., and Lawrence Katz. 1994. Rising Wage Inequality: The United States vs. Other Advanced Countries. In *Working under Different Rules*. Edited by Richard B. Freeman. New York: Russell Sage Foundation.

Ganzeboom, Harry B. G., Donald J. Treiman, and Wout C. Ultee. 1991. Comparative Intergenerational Stratification Research: Three Generations and Beyond. *Annual Review of Sociology* 17: 277–302. [CrossRef]

Goldfield, Michael. 1987. *The Decline of Organized Labor in the United States*. Chicago: University of Chicago Press.

Gornick, Janet C., and Branko Milanovic. 2015. Income Inequality in the United States in Cross-National Perspective: Redistribution Revisited. LIS Center Research Brief. May 4. Available online: https://www.gc.cuny.edu/CUNY_GC/media/CUNY-Graduate-Center/PDF/Centers/LIS/LIS-Center-Research-Brief-1-2015.pdf (accessed on 14 January 2017).

Gross, James A. 1995. *Broken Promise: The Subversion of U.S. Labor Relations Policy, 1947–1994*. Philadelphia: Temple University Press.

Hacker, Jacob S. 2006. *The Great Risk Shift: The Assault on American Jobs, Families, Health Care, and Retirement and How You Can Fight Back*. Oxford: Oxford University Press.

Hacker, Jacob S., and Paul Pierson. 2010. *Winner-Take-All Politics*. New York: Simon and Schuster.

Hauser, Robert M., and David L. Featherman. 1977. *The Process of Stratification*. New York: Academic Press.

Hirsch, Barry, and David Macpherson. 2015. Union Membership and Coverage Database from the CPS. Available online: http://www.unionstats.com/ (accessed on 31 December 2015).

Hout, Michael. 1988. More Universalism, Less Structural Mobility. *American Journal of Sociology* 93: 1358–400. [CrossRef]

Huang, Chye-Ching, and Brandon DeBot. 2015. Ten Facts You Should Know About the Federal Estate Tax. Center on Budget and Policy Priorities, March 23. Available online: http://www.cbpp.org/sites/default/files/atoms/files/1-8-15tax.pdf (accessed on 2 January 2016).

Institute on Taxation and Economic Policy. 2015. Who Pays?: A Distributional Analysis of the Tax Systems in All Fifty States, 5th ed. January. Available online: http://www.itep.org/whopays/full_report.php (accessed on 2 January 2016).

Julia B. Isaacs, Isabel V. Sawhill, and Ron Haskins, eds. 2008. *Getting Ahead or Losing Ground: Economic Mobility in America*. Washington: Brookings Institution and Economic Mobility Project.

Jacobson, Darien B., Brian G. Raub, and Barry W. Johnson. 2007. The Estate Tax: Ninety Years and Counting. Internal Revenue Service. In *Compendium of Federal Transfer Tax and Personal Wealth Studies*. Available online: https://www.irs.gov/pub/irs-soi/11pwcompench1aestate.pdf (accessed on 15 May 2017).

Jencks, Christopher. 2005. Why Do So Many Jobs Pay So Badly? In *Inequality Matters*. Edited by James Lardner and David A. Smith. New York: New Press.

Johnston, David Cay. 2007. The Great Tax Shift. In *Inequality Matters*. Edited by Lardner and Smith. New York: The New Press, pp. 168–73.

Katz, Michael B. 2001. *The Price of Citizenship: Redefining the American Welfare State*. New York: Henry Holt.

Kens, Paul. 1998. *Lochner v. New York: Economic Regulation on Trial*. Lawrence: University Press of Kansas.

Krueger, Alan. 2012. The Rise and Consequences of Inequality. Presentation Made to the Center for American Progress. January 12. Available online: https://www.americanprogress.org/events/2012/01/12/17181/the-rise-and-consequences-of-inequality/ (accessed on 30 December 2015).

Krugman, Paul. 2014. Now That's Rich. *New York Times*, May 9.

Leonhardt, David, and Kevin Quealy. 2014. U.S. Middle Class Is No Longer the World's Richest. *New York Times*, April 23.

Levy, Paul Alan. 1985. The Unidimensional Perspective of the Reagan Labor Board. *Rutgers Law Journal* 16: 269–390.

Lichtenstein, Nelson. 2002. *State of the Union*. Princeton: Princeton University Press.

Lieber, Ron. 2010. Student Debt and a Push for Fairness. *New York Times*, June 5.

Mishel, Lawrence. 2012. Unions, Inequality, and Faltering Middle-Class Wages. *Economic Policy Institute*, August 29. Available online: http://www.epi.org/publication/ib342-unions-inequality-faltering-middle-class/ (accessed on 4 January 2016).

Mishel, Lawrence, and Jessica Schieder. 2016. Economic Policy Institute. CEO Compensation Grew Faster Than The Wages of the Top 0.1 Percent and the Stock Market. July 13. Available online: http://www.epi.org/publication/ceo-compensation-grew-faster-than-the-wages-of-the-top-0-1-percent-and-the-stock-market/ (accessed on 16 May 2017).

Mishel, Lawrence, and Ross Eisenbrey. 2015. How to Raise Wages: Policies That Work and Policies That Don't. Briefing Paper #391. Washington: Economic Policy Institute, March 16.

Mishel, Lawrence, Jared Bernstein, and Heidi Shierholz. 2009. *The State of Working America, 2008/2009*. Ithaca: Cornell University Press, ILR Press.

Mishel, Lawrence, Josh Bivens, Elise Gould, and Heidi Shierholz. 2012. *The State of Working America*, 12th ed. Ithaca: Cornell University Press.

Mishel, Lawrence, John Schmitt, and Heidi Shierholz. 2014. Wage Inequality: A Story of Policy Choices. *New Labor Forum* 23: 26–31. [CrossRef]

Moe, Terry. 1987. Interests, Institutions, and Positive Theory: The Politics of the NLRB. *Studies in American Political Development* 2: 266–71. [CrossRef]

Morgenson, Gretchen. 2015. Comparing Paychecks with CEOs. *New York Times*, April 12.

OECD. 2014. *OECD Factbook 2014: Economic, Environmental and Social Statistics*. Paris: OECD Publishing, pp. 66–67. Available online: http://dx.doi.org/10.1787/factbook-2014-en (accessed on 18 December 2015).

Opfer, Chris. 2017. Trump Freezes Overtime, Pay Regulations. *Bloomberg BNA*, January 24. Available online: https://www.bna.com/trump-freezes-overtime-n73014450151/ (accessed on 26 April 2017).

Piketty, Thomas. 2014. *Capital in the Twenty-First Century*. Cambridge: Harvard University Press.

Piketty, Thomas, and Emmanuel Saez. 2003. Income Inequality in the United States, 1913–1998. *Quarterly Journal of Economics* 118: 1–39. [CrossRef]

Putnam, Robert D. 2015. *Our Kids: The American Dream in Crisis*. New York: Simon and Schuster.

Rampell, Catherine. 2013. Freebies for the Rich. *New York Times Magazine*, September 29, p. 14.

Reich, Robert B. 2012. *Beyond Outrage*. New York: Random House, Vintage Books.

Reich, Robert B. 2015. The Political Roots of Widening Inequality. *The American Prospect*, April 28, pp. 28–29.

Rosenbaum, Dottie, and Brynne Keith-Jennings. 2016. SNAP Costs and Caseloads Declining. Center on Budget and Policy Priorities. March 8. Available online: http://www.cbpp.org/research/food-assistance/snap-costs-and-caseloads-declining (accessed on 16 August 2016).

Rosenfeld, Jake. 2014. *What Unions No Longer Do*. Cambridge: Harvard University Press.

Saez, Emmanuel, and Gabriel Zucman. 2016. Wealth Inequality in the United States since 1913: Evidence from Capitalized Income Data. *Quarterly Journal of Economics* 131: 519–78. [CrossRef]

Sanger-Katz, Margot. 2016. Bucking a Health Trend, Fewer Kids Are Dying. *New York Times*, June 19.

Schlozman, Kay Lehman, Sidney Verba, and Henry E. Brady. 2012. *The Unheavenly Chorus: Unequal Political Voice and the Broken Promise of American Democracy*. Princeton: Princeton University Press.

Short, Kathleen. 2015. The Supplemental Poverty Measure: 2014. *Current Population Reports*. September. Available online: https://www.census.gov/content/dam/Census/library/publications/2015/demo/p60-254.pdf (accessed on 16 May 2017).

Smeeding, Timothy M. 2005. Public Policy, Economic Inequality, and Poverty: The United States in Comparative Perspective. *Social Science Quarterly* 86: 955–83. [CrossRef]

Stiglitz, Joseph E. 2013. *The Price of Inequality*. New York: W.W. Norton.

Stiglitz, Joseph E. 2015. Rewriting the Rules of the American Economy. *The Roosevelt Institute*. Available online: http://rooseveltinstitute.org/rewriting-rules-report/ (accessed on 14 January 2017).

Stonecash, Jeffrey M. 2010. Class in American Politics. In *New Directions in American Politics*. Edited by Jeffrey M. Stonecash. New York: Routledge.

Wage and Hour Division. 2015. History of Federal Minimum Wage Rates under the Fair Labor Standards Act. Available online: https://www.dol.gov/whd/minwage/chart.htm (accessed on 16 May 2017).

Warren, Elizabeth, and Amelia Warren Tyagi. 2003. *The Two-Income Trap*. New York: Basic Books.

Western, Bruce, and Jake Rosenfeld. 2011. Unions, Norms, and the Rise in U.S. Wage Inequality. *American Sociological Review* 76: 532. [CrossRef]

Ziliak, James P. 2015. Income, Program Participation, and Financial Vulnerability: Research and Data Needs. *Journal of Economic and Social Measurement* 40: 34–36. [CrossRef]

religions

MDPI

Article

The Impact of Economic Inequality on Children's Development and Achievement

Mary E. Walsh * and Maria D. Theodorakakis

Department of Counseling, Developmental, and Educational Psychology, Boston College, Campion Hall 305C, 140 Commonwealth Avenue, Chestnut Hill, MA 02467-0123, USA; theodomc@bc.edu
* Correspondence: walshhur@bc.edu; Tel.: +1-617-552-8973

Academic Editors: Kenneth Himes and Kate Ward
Received: 13 February 2017; Accepted: 7 April 2017; Published: 14 April 2017

Abstract: Child poverty leads to many challenges at both societal and individual levels, and the two levels are interrelated. It is critical to recognize the complex implications of poverty, including short-term and long-term effects for children and families. After reviewing both the societal (e.g., economic costs, segregation, and unequal opportunity) and individual (e.g., effects on children's health, development, learning, and academic achievement) implications of poverty, this paper will describe a framework for action that incorporates multiple existing approaches, and offer an example of one intervention that aims to address the challenges associated with economic inequality for children in the United States in a comprehensive, multifaceted manner.

Keywords: child poverty; academic achievement gap; educational disparity; City Connects; school-based intervention

1. Introduction

Child poverty is a significant problem in the United States. Children who experience poverty are at risk for a multitude of adverse developmental outcomes throughout the lifespan. Rates of child poverty are higher in the United States than in other countries with equivalent resources (American Academy of Pediatrics 2016), and the numbers have risen steadily since the 1980s (Reardon 2011). Currently, more than 16 million children in the United States are impacted by poverty, with approximately twenty-one percent of the nation's children living in a family that is defined as "poor," based on a family income that is below 100% of the federal poverty threshold (National Center for Children in Poverty 2016). In fact, recent statistics suggest that economic disadvantage now affects the *majority* of the nation's children, with 52% of all public school students qualifying for free or reduced-priced school lunch (Southern Education Foundation 2015; U.S. Department of Education 2016). Economic disparity, which has historically been deeply tied to race in the United States, is even greater for African American, Hispanic, and Native American children, who are three times more likely to experience poverty than their White and Asian counterparts (American Academy of Pediatrics 2016). In light of these staggering statistics, the challenge of educating and caring for low-income children can no longer be considered a "side issue" in our nation, and should instead be conceptualized as "the central mission of American public schools and, by extension, a central responsibility of the American public" (Tough 2016, p. 6).

2. Societal Implications of Poverty

According to the United Nations Educational, Scientific and Cultural Organization, poverty can be defined in either absolute or relative terms. "Absolute" poverty measures poverty in relation to the amount of money necessary to meet basic needs (e.g., food, clothing, shelter) and is not directly concerned with broader "quality of life issues" or overall level of inequality and human suffering; in contrast, the concept of "relative" poverty defines poverty in relation to the economic status of other members in the society in which they live—including how individuals' life chances are impacted (United Nations Educational, Scientific and Cultural Organization 2017). For purposes of this paper, both conceptualizations of poverty will be considered.

The societal implications of poverty lead to heavy economic and social costs. The economic cost of poverty is high, as children who grow up in poverty and do not complete high school are more likely to become teenage parents, to be unemployed, or to be incarcerated, which eventually leads to lost productivity and increased social expenditure (American Academy of Pediatrics 2016). In addition to reduced productivity and monetary output, the economic costs of poverty can include increased propensity to commit crimes and lower quality of health later in life (Holzer et al. 2008, p. 41). When the costs of the conditions associated with poverty are aggregated, including all forms of societal intervention initiatives, it is estimated that they total about five hundred billion dollars per year; this is "the equivalent of nearly 4% of gross domestic product" (Holzer et al. 2008, p. 41).

Poverty also results in significant social costs. It has undoubtedly led to disparity and segregation in our society. Though race-based neighborhood segregation has been slowly declining overall, socioeconomic segregation has steadily increased (Kirsch et al. 2016, p. 37), and serves as one important example of the societal implications of poverty (see the essay by Himes in this volume and his comment on Secession of the Successful). Arguably, the biggest threat to national cohesion is not income inequality itself but the social segregation that inequality helped to create because this segregation dictates where individuals live, the quality of education to which they have access, and the support services and enrichment opportunities that are readily available (Putnam 2015).

Low-income families are most vulnerable to the deleterious effects of segregation, as articulated by a recent article in the Boston Globe daily newspaper: "One thing is being layered over another. It's not just that you're growing up in a poor neighborhood; you're growing up in a neighborhood with unhealthy conditions and high exposure to violence" (Scharfenberg 2016). Kirsch and colleagues (2016) echo this sentiment, explaining that neighborhoods "either nurture or crush opportunity" and that "education, employment, housing, and a host of other variables—including police protection, health care, and libraries, to name a few—are largely determined in the United States by where one resides" (Kirsch et al. 2016, p. 37).

It is imperative to remember that the economic disparity in America today is "not simply the result of forces beyond our control" (Kirsch et al. 2016, p. 39). While economic disparity is in part due to the nature of capitalism and innovation (e.g., globalization and rapid technological advancements), the "stratified nature of opportunity, with access that varies based on economic status, geographic location, and race and ethnicity, has been strongly impacted by a range of choices made over time by policy makers at all levels of government, as well as by corporations and individuals" (see the essay by Schlozman on the impact of political choices in this volume) (Kirsch et al. 2016, p. 39). For example, Kirsch and colleagues believe that residential segregation by race and class has been driven by "weak enforcement of antidiscrimination policies" and "exclusionary zoning practices that allow affluent areas to prevent any incursion of affordable-housing units into their neighborhoods" (Kirsch et al. 2016, p. 39).

3. Implications of Poverty for Individual Children

Poverty leads to significant individual suffering and has been identified as the single greatest threat to children's health and wellbeing; it negatively impacts multiple dimensions of child development simultaneously, including physical health, mental health, executive functioning, and learning (American Academy of Pediatrics 2016). We will highlight two aspects of the multiple and cumulative effects of poverty on individual children: its impact on health and development and its subsequent effect on learning and academic achievement.

3.1. Impact on Health and Development

Poverty directly impacts children's health and development by increasing the likelihood of language delays, poor nutrition, chronic illness, and, most critically, by leading to toxic stress and compromising brain development (American Academy of Pediatrics 2016; National Center for Children in Poverty 2016; Noble et al. 2015). In the context of child poverty, adversity and stress shape neural development and dictate adaptations in behavioral patterns and mental states (Blaire and Raver 2012, p. 312). Toxic stress is defined by Garner and colleagues (2012) as: "excessive or prolonged activation of the physiologic stress response systems in the absence of the buffering protection afforded by stable, responsive relationships" (Garner et al. 2012, p. 225). Toxic stress is associated with lifelong hardship, and can result in difficulties with self-regulation (e.g., inattention, impulsivity, and defiance), executive function, learning, and memory (American Academy of Pediatrics 2016; Anda et al. 2006). It can also increase susceptibility to "physical illness (such as cardiovascular disease, hypertension, obesity, diabetes, and stroke)" and "mental health problems (such as depression, anxiety disorders, and substance abuse)" (National Scientific Council on the Developing Child and National Forum on Early Childhood Policy and Programs 2011, p. 9).

The primary mechanism through which children's environments affect their development is stress (National Scientific Council on the Developing Child 2014). Adverse experiences in childhood (such as those related to poverty) can undermine the development of adaptive processes and coping skills and negatively impact the development of the stress response system, which aims to predict life patterns and detect threats via environmental cues (Garner et al. 2012; Tough 2016). When children learn to expect that life will be difficult or chaotic, the stress-response system is constantly on high-alert, which manifests in the form of elevated cortisol levels and other stress-related reactions (Blaire and Raver 2012). While this can serve as a protective factor in the short term, it also results in long-term psychological and physical "costs" to the organism related to alterations to stress and immune system functioning (Blaire and Raver 2012, p. 312).

The emotional repercussions of toxic stress include difficulty with navigating disappointments and provocations, and the cognitive repercussions can include disruption in the development of executive functioning skills (National Scientific Council on the Developing Child and National Forum on Early Childhood Policy and Programs 2011; Tough 2016). Executive functions serve as building blocks for the successful development of important cognitive and social capacities, and underlie a broad range of life skills, competencies, and behaviors such as working memory, inhibitory control, and cognitive flexibility (National Scientific Council on the Developing Child and National Forum on Early Childhood Policy and Programs 2011, p. 3). Toxic stress, adversity, and trauma ultimately compromise children's development and ability to learn and grow in a healthy manner. There is, therefore, a high emotional cost associated with poverty, as well as a significant overall cost to an individual's wellbeing and human experience. In order to counteract and mitigate the effects of toxic stress, it is critical to foster children's strengths and promote resilience; this can be done through targeted prevention and intervention programming across the course of a child's development.

3.2. Poverty Limits Learning and Academic Achievement

It has been established that up to two-thirds of the academic achievement gap is attributable to societal inequality (e.g., poverty) and contexts beyond school (Noguera and Morell 2011; Rothstein 2010). The academic achievement gap between high-and low-income children in the United States has grown by forty percent in a generation (Reardon 2011). For example, the gap in SAT scores between wealthy and poor high school seniors has increased by 35 points on an 800-point scale over the last thirty years (Reardon 2011). This leads to disparity in the college graduation rate between wealthy and poor students, which has also risen steadily in recent decades; without a college degree, economic mobility becomes next to impossible for children from families in the lowest socioeconomic brackets (Reardon 2011).

The academic achievement gap between students from affluent and low-income families is large when children enter kindergarten and does not appear to grow or narrow significantly as children progress through school (Reardon 2011). Thus, the timing of opportunities and supports is critical with respect to gaps in achievement because "the earlier we intervene to reduce them, the more effective we will be at eliminating them in the long run" (Reardon 2013, p. 15). In other words, without deliberate intervention, income-related achievement gaps will likely persist for the entirety of children's school careers.

One major factor impacting poor children's ability to learn and achieve academically is the disparity in quality and quantity of learning supports available (Reardon 2011). While wealthier families are able to purchase materials, experiences, and services to invest in their children (e.g., books, computers, educational outings to museums, or tutoring) (Garrett et al. 1994), children from families with limited resources may not have access to these investments. Furthermore, these families' housing conditions may not be conducive to learning (e.g., poor lighting, limited space, or high noise levels) (Dearing and Taylor 2007; Evans 2004).

It is clear that children living in impoverished neighborhoods have inadequate access to support services and enrichment opportunities, as well as heightened stress response systems that interfere with the learning process. Because children who grow up in high-stress, high-poverty environments are "constantly on the lookout for threats," they can enter behavioral patterns in school that are "self-defeating" and directly hinder their ability to learn (e.g., fighting, talking back, acting out in class, etc.); they may also have increased difficulty following complicated directions or be easily distracted, leading to frustration and learned helplessness in the classroom (Tough 2016, p. 21).

As a result of limited resources and opportunities, as well as the detrimental impact of stress on brain development and neurological functioning, it can be concluded that poverty limits learning. Poverty has therefore become one of the most salient factors impacting students' academic achievement, and has infiltrated the national discussion on education reform. In fact, Berliner (2013) has identified poverty as the single most critical factor to address in educational reform (Berliner 2013).

Beginning in the 1960s with the Coleman Report, there has been increasing recognition that life outside of school has considerable consequences for achievement in school, and this is especially true for students from low-income families (Coleman et al. 1966; Dearing 2008). In 1983, "A Nation at Risk" was published, clearly articulating these concerns and describing the American education system as a "rising tide of mediocrity." In response to the concerns that have been repeatedly raised about income-based inequality in American education throughout the last several decades, the No Child Left Behind legislation was passed in 2002. Considered the most comprehensive educational reform legislation ever implemented in the United States, No Child Left Behind targeted underperforming schools and measured school improvement via high-stakes standardized assessments. The vast majority of these underperforming schools were located in high-poverty urban centers or remote rural areas. More recently, President Obama's Race to the Top program continued to place an emphasis on closing the achievement gap and providing higher-quality education to the nation's children. In spite of ample attention and significant improvements in curriculum and instruction introduced by the No Child Left Behind legislation and Race to the Top program, the academic achievement gap in the United States has remained steadfastly stubborn.

The academic achievement gap was originally conceptualized as a discrepancy in standardized assessment scores between students of different racial groups, but recent data highlights a more nuanced understanding that includes the connection between poverty and racially minoritized groups. While the academic achievement gaps between racial groups continue to warrant attention, standardized assessment results demonstrate that they have narrowed since the 1970s; in contrast, income-related academic achievement gaps have grown substantially (Kirsch et al. 2016). In fact, the gap between children from high-and low-income families is now more than twice as large as the Black-White achievement gap (Kirsch et al. 2016). This highlights the inextricable link between poverty and race in our nation, and identifies economic segregation, inadequate resources, and lack of opportunities as major contributors to the persistent academic achievement gap. As a result, it is critical to acknowledge the complex role of identity-based intersectionality (e.g., students of Color who are also from low-income families) on the nation's achievement gap.

In an attempt to highlight the impact of systemic barriers and inequality many schoolchildren face, the persistent gap in students' academic achievement has also been referred to as an "opportunity gap" (Darling-Hammond 2010; Darling-Hammond 2014; Milner 2013). The rationale behind this term is a clear understanding of how important it is to create opportunities that compound economic and social advantages for children from marginalized groups.

It thus becomes imperative to provide children with opportunities and recognize the importance of "human and social capital," which "impacts the transmission of opportunity from one generation to the next" (Kirsch et al. 2016, p. 26). Reardon (2011) asserts: "We tend to think of the relationship between socioeconomic status and children's academic achievement as a sociological necessity, rather than as the product of a set of social conditions, policy choices, and educational practices" (Reardon 2011, p. 92). If we operate from this perspective, it becomes even more logical to conceptualize disparities in academic achievement as an "opportunity gap" that we can actively work toward closing.

4. Framework for Action

There is a paradox inherent in the cutting-edge research on poverty and children's learning and achievement: "while the problems that accompany poverty may be best understood on the molecular level, the solutions are not" (Tough 2016, p. 22). In other words, even though it is important to cultivate a deeper understanding of the intricate scientific impact of poverty on brain development, this does not provide sufficient information about how to help children or bring about change.

The majority of what we know about how socioeconomic inequality leads to educational inequality is rooted in the child development literature, which has identified ways in which children's risk and protective factors interact with one another and impact a child's developmental trajectory. For children living in poverty, risk factors are present across developmental domains (e.g., cognitive, social, emotional, and behavioral) as well as across contexts (e.g., home, neighborhood, and school). Despite the innumerable risk factors children living in poverty face, it is imperative to recognize that risk factors are often counterbalanced by protective factors, as well as by children's resilience. Thus, by ameliorating the effects of poverty via coordinated intervention efforts, children's developmental trajectories can be altered (Cicchetti and Sroufe 2000; Sameroff 2009).

Due to the reality that the problem of poverty and its subsequent impact on child development and education defies simple solutions (Kirsch et al. 2016), approaches operating at both the societal level—addressed by economists and policymakers—and at the individual level—addressed by human services providers such as social workers or psychologists—are needed. The conversation, according to Tough (2016), cannot be confined to "policy makers and philanthropists"; it should also include those who are most familiar with the struggles of children experiencing adversity related to poverty—including educators, pediatricians, parents, social workers, etc. (Tough 2016, p. 8).

Examples of solutions at the societal level involve tax policies and direct financial aid such as earned income tax credit (see the essay by Quinn and Cahill in this volume), access to comprehensive healthcare provided by Medicaid and the Affordable Care Act, participation in early childhood education initiatives such as Head Start, and access to adequate nutrition support such as the Supplemental Nutrition Assistance Program (SNAP) or Women, Infants, and Children (WIC) program benefits (American Academy of Pediatrics 2016). These services and interventions are designed to be widely available to families in our nation in order to ensure that children's basic needs are met; however, universal services are often insufficient without individually tailored support and attention for every child and family.

Individual-level solutions can take on a variety of forms (e.g., in-home family therapy, tutoring, after-school enrichment programs, etc.), and can drastically range in terms of depth and breadth (i.e., targeted vs. comprehensive). With this in mind, Kirsch and colleagues (2016) offer five principles upon which individual-level solutions can be built: (1) interventions must be implemented systematically across the lifespan, (2) interventions must be systemic, drawing on all relevant stakeholders and institutions, (3) efforts must be sustainable, (4) a strategy of continuous improvement must guide initiatives, and (5) efforts must be adaptable to local contexts. A framework for action regarding individual-level solutions should also include a long-term commitment to evidence-based interventions and policies, a focus on building coalitions among multiple institutions, and an openness to interweaving already-successful approaches with new interventions (Kirsch et al. 2016, p. 6).

It is also possible for an intervention to exist at the nexus between these two different approaches, and incorporate key elements of both individual-level and societal-level solutions. The value of such an intervention is the concurrent consideration of individual children's needs and the context or environment in which they are learning and growing. In addition to providing tailored supports to each child, these interventions can operate in a systemic manner and be connected to policy updates or other large-scale changes. One example of such an intervention that exists at the nexus between individual and societal levels is City Connects, a national organization that aims to create tailored networks of supports and opportunities for children in the United States. The City Connects intervention's practice and outcomes will be discussed in the following section of this paper.

5. The City Connects Intervention

5.1. Introduction and Rationale

The City Connects intervention began in Boston, Massachusetts in 2001 and is now implemented in 84 urban schools across the United States (in Massachusetts, New York, Ohio, Minnesota, and Connecticut). City Connects currently serves over 27,000 children, the vast majority of which come from low-income families. The mission of City Connects is to have children engage and learn in school by connecting each student with the tailored set of prevention, intervention, and enrichment services he or she needs to thrive. The authors of this paper are directly affiliated with City Connects; the first author directs the City Connects research and intervention program and the second author is an advanced graduate assistant. City Connects is housed within the Lynch School of Education at Boston College and funded via contributions from philanthropic partners as well as by individual school districts that choose to implement the intervention.

The City Connects intervention is grounded in a deep understanding of the deleterious impact of poverty on learning and academic achievement. This includes recognizing that, for all children, life outside of school affects what happens in school, and that for children living in poverty, life outside of school may include tremendous stressors such as hunger, a stay in a homeless shelter, or medical needs that are difficult to meet. Low-income families may also have less time and fewer resources to invest in supporting their children's education, and the chronic financial stress experienced by parents may negatively impact the ability to positively interact with children and with school staff.

Research shows that poverty profoundly impacts all domains of child development (e.g., academic achievement, health, family, or social-emotional), that these domains interact, and that the consequences for one domain multiply across the others (Cicchetti and Sroufe 2000; Sameroff 2009). In response, effective student support interventions should address each of these domains while strongly considering a child's context (e.g., school and neighborhood environments) and tailoring services to the particular risks and strengths of individual children (Rutter 2007; and see Dearing's essay in this volume). In order to provide this comprehensive care, effective student support interventions should concurrently operate at individual and societal levels.

It is clear that schools provide an obvious and appropriate setting for the core functions of effective student support interventions due to the amount of time children spend in schools and their role in student's socialization (O'Connor et al. 2011). Recognizing the complexity of the challenges at hand, Reardon (2013) asserts: "U.S. schools have historically been thought of as the great equalizer—the social institution best suited to ensure that all children have equal opportunity to learn, develop, and thrive. It is unrealistic, however, to think that school-based strategies alone will eliminate stark disparities in academic success" (Reardon 2013, p. 14). Thus, in addition to acknowledging that schools serve as a hub in which teachers, school staff, families, community partners, and policymakers can come together to support students' learning and achievement, the City Connects intervention recognizes the value of collaborating with community partners, policymakers, and other stakeholders in order to address students' needs in a comprehensive manner.

With respect to theoretical foundation, the City Connects intervention is rooted in the child development literature. This body of literature suggests that, while early childhood experiences impact long-term trajectories, they do not dictate absolute outcomes; this implies that developmental trajectories can be altered and highlights the innate malleability of child development as a function of children's brain plasticity (Cicchetti 2015; Ford and Lerner 1992; Lerner 1995; Rutter 2007; Sameroff 2009; Shonkoff 2010). Therefore, change—via evidence-based intervention—is possible, as the intervention serves as the mechanism to elicit and guide a change in developmental trajectories.

5.2. Codified Practice

City Connects is a school-based intervention that provides an infrastructure for student support efforts in schools and includes a systemic and codified practice. At the heart of the City Connects intervention is a City Connects Coordinator in each school. Coordinators hold Master's degrees in fields such as school counseling or school social work, and also receive training, professional development, coaching, and supervision from City Connects. City Connects has developed materials and guidance for the staff members who coach and supervise practitioners, referred to as Program Managers. Program Managers are also trained by City Connects, and are each responsible for supervising Coordinators in up to ten schools.

Every year, the City Connects Coordinator in each school collaborates with teachers to identify each child's unique strengths and needs across major developmental domains. Based on this assessment, the Coordinator develops a plan for every student in order to connect him or her to a tailored set of support services and enrichment opportunities, both in the school and throughout the community. City Connects Coordinators then collaborate with the students' family to finalize and implement the plans, providing support as needed with respect to logistics (e.g., registration forms, fees, transportation, etc.). Students identified as having intensive needs at any point during the school year receive an individual review during which a wider team of education, human services, and health professionals discuss and develop specific measureable goals and strategies for the student (City Connects 2014a). City Connects pays particular attention to children's health and links children to health services from pediatricians and other healthcare providers.

City Connects Coordinators document, track, and follow up on the delivery of the tailored set of services for each student via a proprietary online database, which allows for secure collection of data on student reviews, individual student plans, service referrals, and providers who deliver services; it also allows Coordinators to run reports that are used to guide practice and to develop priorities.

Coordinators themselves directly provide a range of support services within the school and classrooms, consistent with the principal's objectives and school wide curricula (e.g., social-emotional learning or healthy life skills groups with topics such as friendships, family relationships, bullying, or nutrition). Another critical aspect of the role of the City Connects Coordinator is cultivating relationships with children and families throughout the course of the school year, as well as developing partnerships with local community agencies and institutions. These partnerships collectively provide a range of prevention, early intervention, and enrichment services. Recognition of the critical role of systematic partnerships with community and school supports is a unique aspect of the City Connects intervention, which greatly impacts efficiency of matching students to resources.

With these codified practices and procedures in place, City Connects is able to implement personally tailored supports in a systemic manner—existing at the intersection between individual and societal approaches to supporting students. City Connects stands apart from similar initiatives, which are sometimes termed "wraparound" programming, because it is both theory-based and research driven. The City Connects intervention is designed as a systemic practice, which is well-documented and learned through specific trainings and professional development initiatives. This practice is rigid and flexible at the same time; it is carried out in a similar way from school to school, with the ability to measure fidelity of implementation, but also flexible enough to adapt to each context in which it is implemented.

City Connects is grounded in theoretical principles of effective practice that emerge from the research on child development; these principles specify that a "wraparound" intervention should be: (1) *customized* to meet the needs of every single individual child within the school, (2) *comprehensive* in order to assess the needs of the "whole child" across all developmental domains (academic, social-emotional, health, and family) and provide multi-tiered supports ranging from prevention to intensive intervention, (3) *coordinated* through an intentional practice that involves organized collaboration among school staff and family members and provides a system for collecting and utilizing student-level data, and (4) *continuous* in how it is systemically integrated into the functioning of the school, allowing for regular follow-up over time, evaluation of fidelity of implementation, and measurement the intervention's outcomes/impact (Walsh et al. 2016)

5.3. Outcomes

Over a decade of research has demonstrated that City Connects serves as an effective mechanism for changing children's academic and non-academic outcomes, thereby increasing the life chances of children in poverty. Data show that City Connects significantly improves academic performance and thriving, and narrows the achievement gap for low-income students in participating schools (City Connects 2014a; City Connects 2014b; Walsh et al. 2014). Students enrolled in City Connects elementary schools outperform their peers who were never enrolled in a City Connects school on measures of academic achievement (i.e., standardized assessments and classroom report cards) and demonstrate improved thriving in areas such as behavior, work habits, and effort (City Connects 2014a; City Connects 2014b; Walsh et al. 2014).

After students leave City Connects schools in the fifth grade, they continue to thrive and outperform their counterparts. For example, relative to the Massachusetts state average, the achievement gap for students in City Connects schools is closed by half in English Language Arts and by two-thirds in Mathematics. Students who participated in the City Connects intervention in elementary school also earn higher grades on middle school report cards, have lower rates of being held back, are less likely to be chronically absent, and drop out of high school at only half the rate of their peers who were never enrolled in a City Connects school (City Connects 2014a; City Connects 2014b). This is important because in the United States, children's opportunities and life chances are notably enhanced by receiving a high school diploma. City Connects student outcomes are also consistent across important subgroups of students. For example, the City Connects intervention considerably narrowed academic achievement gaps between English language learners and immigrant children who were proficient in English (Dearing et al. 2016).

In addition to leading to positive outcomes for individual students, the City Connects intervention is cost-effective. Economists at the Center for Benefit-Cost Studies of Education at Columbia University concluded that City Connects provides a societal return on investment of 11:1 and a return on investment of 3:1 including the costs of the intervention and all services to which children and families may be connected (Bowden et al. 2015). This means that society will save three dollars for every dollar invested in the City Connects model and the associated support services and enrichment opportunities, saving a minimum of a third of societal costs (Bowden et al. 2015). In other words, the short-and long-term outcomes of City Connects demonstrate that the economic costs of poverty are ameliorated by the intervention. To the extent that the intervention is cost-effective, it is rendered more valuable to a larger number of children in poverty and more able to relieve human suffering.

The impact of City Connects has been recognized by Child Trends, a non-profit, non-partisan research center. Following a national review of prominent systemic student support interventions, City Connects was designated as one of three interventions that meets the Child Trends standards for rigorous research; these interventions are described by Child Trends as "a promising approach for helping more disadvantaged children and youth improve in school and have a brighter path to life," and it is asserted that their salutary effects may be cumulative (Moore and Emig 2014, p. 8).

6. Conclusions

It is widely asserted that the system that currently exists in this country to support children living in poverty is "profoundly broken," and the problems most of these children face are "relentless and pervasive" (Tough 2016, p. 127). Statistically, children who grow up in low-income families are "likely to live in chaotic disrupted families, in neighborhoods or regions of concentrated poverty where there are few resources to nurture children and countless perils to wound them, physically or psychologically or both"—furthermore, "the schools they attend are likely to be segregated by race and class and to have less money to spend on instruction than the schools well-off students attend, and their teachers are likely to be less experienced and less well-trained than teachers at other schools" (Tough 2016, p. 128).

In spite of the daunting challenges associated with child poverty in the United States, it is critical to acknowledge that the course of a child's development can be altered via intervention and that—with sufficient supports, opportunities, and resources—every child can thrive. In other words, the deleterious effects of poverty and inequality can be mitigated. This can be done by assessing students' individual strengths and needs and subsequently ensuring children are connected to the supports they need to be successful both at school and at home.

City Connects is one example of an evidence-based, theoretically-grounded intervention that can provide these necessary supports, opportunities, and resources in a sustainable, cost-effective manner. Due to its underlying mission and philosophy, the City Connects intervention also serves as an example of an approach that exists at the nexus between individual and societal solutions. By improving academic outcomes and student thriving, decreasing rates of chronic absenteeism and high school dropout, and connecting students to critical social-emotional, behavioral, health, and family-related supports, we assert that City Connects improves children's life chances and alleviates some of the burdens associated with poverty for children and families. As Kirsch and colleagues (2016) suggest: "America's future will depend not only on the choices we make, but also the urgency and persistence with which we work together to take the actions consistent with those choices" (Kirsch et al. 2016, p. 45).

In order to implement effective interventions that can bring about the change needed to combat the effects of poverty on children's achievement, it is clear that we must reach beyond simply weaving programs together, and engage in comprehensive cross-sector collaboration (including health, mental health, education, family systems, etc.). Furthermore, if change is to occur at both individual and societal levels, we must expand our definition of "community" and increase our sense of reciprocity and obligation to one another. This includes both our immediate community (e.g., neighborhood, local schools, etc.) and a broader definition of community at a societal level (e.g., country and world) (on this last point, see the essay by Garcia in this volume). Only when communities unite can the problems associated with child poverty and education be addressed. Continuing to build the human community is both the challenge and the solution.

Acknowledgments: We would like to thank the funders of this research, including the Barr Foundation, the Better Way Foundation, the Charles Hayden Foundation, and the Mathile Family Foundation. We also would like to thank the staff of the Center for Optimized Student Support at Boston College and at all schools in which the City Connects intervention is implemented.

Author Contributions: Mary Walsh and Maria Theodorakakis contributed equally to this paper. Mary Walsh led the design and development of the City Connects intervention. Maria Theodorakakis has participated in multiple phases of the evaluation of the intervention.

Conflicts of Interest: The authors declare no conflict of interest.

References

American Academy of Pediatrics. 2016. Poverty and child health in the United States. *Pediatrics* 137: 1–16.

Anda, Rorbert, Vincent Felitti, J. Douglas Bremner, John Walker, Charles Whitfield, Bruce Perry, Shanta R. Dube, and Wayne H. Giles. 2006. The enduring effects of abuse and related adverse experiences in childhood. *European Archives of Psychiatry and Clinical Neuroscience* 256: 174–86. [CrossRef] [PubMed]

Berliner, David. 2013. Effects of inequality and poverty vs. teachers and schooling on America's youth. *Teacher's College Record* 115: 1–26.

Blaire, Clancy, and Cybele Raver. 2012. Child development and the context of adversity: Experimental canalization of brain and behavior. *American Psychologist* 67: 309–18. [CrossRef] [PubMed]

Bowden, A. Brooks, Clive R. Belfield, Henry M. Levin, Robert Shand, Anyi Wang, and Melisa Morales. 2015. A benefit-cost analysis of City Connects. Available online: http://cbcse.org/wordpress/wp-content/uploads/2015/08/CityConnects.pdf (accessed on 10 April 2017).

Cicchetti, Dante. 2015. Neural plasticity, sensitive periods, and psychopathology. *Development and Psychopathology* 27: 319–20. [CrossRef] [PubMed]

Cicchetti, Dante, and L. Alan Sroufe. 2000. The past as prologue to the future: The times, they've been a-changin'. *Reflecting on the Past and Planning for the Future of Developmental Psychopathology* 12: 255–64. [CrossRef]

City Connects. 2014. *The Impact of City Connects: Progress Report 2014*. Available online: http://www.bc.edu/content/dam/files/schools/lsoe/cityconnects/pdf/CityConnects_ProgressReport_2014.pdf (accessed on 10 April 2017).

City Connects. 2014. City Connects: The lasting impact of optimized student support. Available online: http://www.bc.edu/content/dam/files/schools/lsoe/cityconnects/pdf/City%20Connects%20Impact%20Winter%202014.pdf (accessed on 10 April 2017).

Coleman, James S., Ernest Q. Campbell, Carol. J. Hobson, James McPartland, Alexander M. Mood, Frederic D. Weinfeld, and Robert L. York. 1966. *Equality of Educational Opportunity*. Washington: Office of Education, U.S. Department of Health, Education, and Welfare.

Darling-Hammond, Linda. 2010. *The Flat World and Education: How America's Commitment to Equity will Determine our Future*. New York: Teachers College Press.

Darling-Hammond, Linda. 2014. Closing the achievement gap: A systemic view. In *Closing the Achievement Gap from an International Perspective*. Dordrecht: Springer, pp. 7–20.

Dearing, Eric. 2008. The psychological costs of growing up poor. *Annals of the New York Science Academy of Sciences* 1136: 324–32. [CrossRef] [PubMed]

Dearing, Eric, and Beck A. Taylor. 2007. Home improvements: Within-family associations between income and the quality of children's home environments. *Journal of Applied Developmental Psychology* 28: 427–44. [CrossRef]

Dearing, Eric, Mary E. Walsh, Erin Sibley, Terrence Lee-St John, Claire Foley, and Anastasia Raczek. 2016. Can Community and School-Based Supports Improve the Achievement of First-Generation Immigrant Children Attending High-Poverty Schools? *Child Development* 87: 883–97. [CrossRef] [PubMed]

Evans, Gary W. 2004. The environment of childhood poverty. *American Psychologist* 59: 77–92. [CrossRef] [PubMed]

Ford, Donald H., and Richard M. Lerner. 1992. *Developmental Systems Theory: An Integrative Approach*. Newbury Park: Sage.

Garrett, Patricia, Nicholas Ng'andu, and John Ferron. 1994. Poverty experience of young children and the quality of their home environments. *Child Development* 65: 331–45. [CrossRef]

Garner, Andrew S., Jack P. Shonkoff, Benjamin S. Siegel, Mary I. Dobbins, Marion F. Earls, Laura McGuinn, John Pascoe, and David L. Wood. 2012. Early childhood adversity, toxic stress, and the role of the pediatrician: Translating developmental science into lifelong health. *Pediatrics* 129: 224–31.

Holzer, Harry J., Diane W. Schanzenbach, Greg J. Duncan, and Jens Ludwig. 2008. The economic costs of childhood poverty in the United States. *Journal of Children and Poverty* 14: 41–61. [CrossRef]

Kirsch, I., H. Braun, M. L. Lennon, and A. Sands. 2016. *Choosing Our Future: A Story of Opportunity in America*. Princeton: Educational Testing Service Project.

Lerner, Richard M. 1995. Developing individuals within changing contexts: Implications of developmental contextualism for human development research, policy, and programs. In *Development of Person-Context Relations*. Edited by Thomas A. Kindermann and Jaan Valsiner. Hillsdale: Lawrence Erlbaum.

Milner, H. Richard. 2013. Rethinking achievement gap talk in urban education. *Urban Education* 48: 3–8.

Moore, Kristin A., and Carol Emig. 2014. Integrated student supports: A summary of the evidence base for policymakers. Available online: http://www.childtrends.org/wp-content/uploads/2014/02/2014-05ISSWhitePaper1.pdf (accessed on 10 April 2017).

National Center for Children in Poverty. 2016. Child Poverty. Available online: http://www.nccp.org/topics/childpoverty.html (accessed on 10 April 2017).

National Scientific Council on the Developing Child. 2014. Excessive Stress Disrupts the Architecture of the Developing Brain. Working Paper 3. Cambridge, MA, USA: Harvard University.

National Scientific Council on the Developing Child and National Forum on Early Childhood Policy and Programs. 2011. Building the Brain's "Air Traffic Control" System: How Early Experiences Shape the Development of Executive Function. Working Paper No. 11. Cambridge, MA, USA: Center on the Developing Child, Harvard University.

Noble, Kimberly G., Susan M. Houston, Natalie H. Brito, Hauke Bartsch, Eric Kan, Joshua M. Kuperman, Natacha Akshoomoff, David G. Amaral, Cinnamon S. Bloss, Ondrej Libiger, and et al. 2015. Family income, parental education and brain structure in children and adolescents. *Natural Neuroscience* 18: 773–78. [CrossRef] [PubMed]

Noguera, Peter, and Ernest Morrell. 2011. A Framework for Change: A Broader and Bolder Approach to School Reform. *Teachers College Record*, August 4. Available online: http://www.tcrecord.org (accessed on 10 April 2017).

O'Connor, Erin E., Eric Dearing, and Brian A. Collins. 2011. Teacher-child relationship and behavior problem trajectories in elementary school. *American Educational Research Journal* 48: 120–62. [CrossRef]

Putnam, Robert. 2015. *Our Kids: The American Dream in Crisis*. New York: Simon and Schuster.

Reardon, Sean. 2011. The widening academic achievement gap between the rich and the poor: New evidence and possible explanations. In *Whither Opportunity?: Rising Inequality, Schools, and Children's Life Chances*. Edited by Greg J. Duncan and Richard J. Murnane. New York: Russell Sage Foundation.

Reardon, Sean. 2013. The widening income achievement gap. *Educational Leadership* 70: 10–16.

Rothstein, Richard. 2010. How to fix our schools. Washington: Economic Policy Institute, October 14. Available online: www.epi.org (accessed on 10 April 2017).

Rutter, Michael. 2007. Gene-environment interdependence. *Developmental Science* 10: 12–18. [CrossRef] [PubMed]

Sameroff, Arnold. 2009. *The Transactional Model*. Washington: American Psychological Association.

Scharfenberg, David. 2016. Boston's struggle with income segregation. *The Boston Globe*, March 6. Available online: https://www.bostonglobe.com/metro/2016/03/05/segregation/NiQBy000TZsGgLnAT0tHsL/story.html (accessed on 6 March 2017).

Shonkoff, Jack P. 2010. Building a new biodevelopmental framework to guide the future of early childhood policy. *Child Development* 81: 357–67. [CrossRef] [PubMed]

Southern Education Foundation. 2015. A new majority: Low income students now a majority in the nation's public schools (Research Bulletin). Available online: http://www.southerneducation.org/getattachment/4ac62e27-5260-47a5-9d02-14896ec3a531/A-New-Majority-2015-Update-Low-Income-Students-Now.aspx (accessed on 10 April 2017).

Tough, Paul. 2016. Helping children succeed: What works and why. Available online: paultough.com/helping (accessed on 10 April 2017).

U.S. Department of Education. 2016. *Public Elementary/Secondary School Universe Survey 2013–14*. Washington: National Center for Education Statistics, Common Core of Data (CCD). Available online: https://nces.ed.gov/programs/digest/d15/tables/dt15_204.10.asp?current=yes (accessed on 10 April 2017).

United Nations Educational, Scientific and Cultural Organization. 2017. Poverty. Available online: http://www.unesco.org/new/en/social-and-human-sciences/themes/international-migration/glossary/poverty (accessed on 30 March 2017).

Walsh, Mary E., George F. Madaus, Anastasia E. Raczek, Eric Dearing, Claire Foley, Chen An, and Albert Beaton. 2014. A New Model for Student Support in High-Poverty Urban Elementary Schools Effects on Elementary and Middle School Academic Outcomes. *American Educational Research Journal* 51: 704–37. [CrossRef]

Walsh, Mary E., Joan Wasser Gish, Claire Foley, Maria Theodorakakis, and Kirsten Rene. 2016. Policy Brief: Principles of Effective Practice for Integrated Student Support. Available online: http://wwwbc.edu/content/dam/files/schools/lsoe/cityconnects/pdf/Policy%20Brief%20%20Building%20Sustainable%20Interventions%20web.pdf (accessed on 10 April 2017).

religions

MDPI

Article

The Relative Effectiveness of the Minimum Wage and the Earned Income Tax Credit as Anti-Poverty Tools

Joseph F. Quinn [1] and Kevin E. Cahill [2,*]

[1]   Department of Economics, Boston College, Chestnut Hill, MA 02467-3859, USA; joseph.quinn@bc.edu
[2]   Center on Aging & Work, Boston College, Chestnut Hill, MA 02467-3859, USA
*   Correspondence: kevin.e.cahill@bc.edu; Tel.: +1-857-222-4101

Academic Editors: Kenneth Himes and Kate Ward
Received: 13 February 2017; Accepted: 6 April 2017; Published: 17 April 2017

Abstract: In the search for effective measures to combat poverty, two government policies have been given much attention. One is the establishment of a federal minimum wage to help workers secure a decent standard of living. The second measure is the Earned Income Tax Credit, which gives tax refunds to workers in households that fall below a set standard of income. Both policies have supporters and critics regarding the effectiveness of the policies. This essay provides an economic analysis of the two measures. Among the issues discussed are how the policies affect employment and poverty, and how well targeted they are at the population at risk.

Keywords: minimum wage; earned Income Tax Credit; employment; poverty line; cash transfers; in-kind transfers; anti-poverty measures

---

Capitalist and other societies generate income distributions that many view as unacceptably unequal, so governments intervene to alter these market outcomes. Modern developed countries typically have progressive personal income tax structures, in which citizens pay no federal income tax on some amount of income (that amount usually based on family size), and then pay marginal tax rates that increase with taxable income. The goal of such systems is to generate average tax rates that increase with the level of income, making after-tax distributions less unequal than pre-tax ones[1,2] In addition, governments make transfer payments to households, many of which also make the income distribution less unequal. In the United States, we have important cash and in-kind transfer programs. Cash programs include Social Security, unemployment compensation, workers compensation (for injuries on the job), Supplementary Security Income, and Temporary Assistance for Needy Families (formerly Aid to Families with Dependent Children.) Even more resources are transferred through in-kind (non-cash) programs such as Medicare and Medicaid, food stamps (now SNAP, the Supplemental Nutrition Food Program), housing assistance and Pell grants, in which

---

[1]   In addition to making after-tax incomes less unequal, economists have noted three additional objectives of tax systems: economic stabilization (i.e., to move towards full employment), intergenerational equity (i.e., to maintain fairness between generations), and market efficiency (e.g., to minimize distortions to decision making) (Mankiw 2008). Regarding the first objective, economists at the Federal Reserve Bank of Boston find that, while federal taxes do indeed mitigate wage inequality, the impact varies by state due to differences in state tax policies. Further, the authors find that the impact of taxation on inequality has been relatively constant over time, so that increases in before-tax wage inequality since the mid-1980s have led to increases in after-tax wage inequality (Cooper et al. 2011).

[2]   In addition to making after-tax incomes less unequal, economists have noted three additional objectives of tax systems: economic stabilization (i.e., to move towards full employment), intergenerational equity (i.e., to maintain fairness between generations), and market efficiency (e.g., to minimize distortions to decision making) (Mankiw 2008). Regarding the first objective, economists at the Federal Reserve Bank of Boston find that, while federal taxes do indeed mitigate wage inequality, the impact varies by state due to differences in state tax policies. Further, the authors find that the impact of taxation on inequality has been relatively constant over time, so that increases in before-tax wage inequality since the mid-1980s have led to increases in after-tax wage inequality (Cooper et al. 2011).

the aid is a particular form of assistance, not the cash with which to purchase it[3]. Some programs are need-based, like Medicaid and housing assistance, with income and often asset requirements; others, like Social Security, Medicare, and unemployment and workers' compensation, are not.[4]

These very important alterations to the income distribution occur *after* market incomes like earnings and returns on assets have been generated. But countries intervene to affect market income as well. Two very important programs are designed to increase the market earnings of some workers: minimum wage policies set by various levels of government (the federal government as well as some states and a few cities), which are now very much in the news, and the federal Earned Income Tax Credit (EITC), a much less well understood but also very important program. Both aim to alter the final distribution of income and, at the lower end, to reduce the extent and impact of poverty. In this paper, we will discuss the pros and cons of both, particularly their effectiveness as anti-poverty tools.

1. The Minimum Wage in the United States

The 1938 Fair Labor Standards Act, which legislated the first federal minimum wage of $0.25/hour, emerged from the ravages of the Great Depression.[5] It was controversial then and has remained so to this day. Prior federal and state minimum wages laws had been struck down as unconstitutional by a 5-4 United States Supreme Court decision, which deemed them a violation of freedom of contract. This unpopular judicial decision earned the ire of President Franklin Roosevelt, who criticized "nine old men," and it prompted his threat to increase the size of the Court by adding six sympathetic justices. One sitting justice quickly saw the light and reversed his vote on a similar case in 1937, deeming the minimum wage constitutional after all, paving the way for the historic 1938 legislation and generating the quip, "a switch in time saved nine" (Grossman 1978).

Congress has increased the federal minimum wage 22 times, most recently in 2007, 2008 and 2009, when it was raised to $5.85, $6.55 and then $7.25 per hour, where it remains today.[6]

As seen in Figure 1, the minimum wage peaked in 1968 at $1.60/hour, which is $10.86/hour in current (2015) dollars. Since the peak, the real value (all in 2015 dollars) fell by 46 percent to $6.04 in in 2006, rose back to $7.98 in 2009 following the three increases in three years, and has since declined to $7.25/hour in 2015—one-third below its peak. Without a legislative increase, the real value of the minimum wages declines each year with inflation.

State minimum wages are higher than the federal standard in 29 states and the District of Columbia, led in 2016 by DC ($11.50), California ($10.00) and Massachusetts ($10.00). The federal minimum wage applies in 16 states that have minimum wages the same as or lower than the federal level, and the remaining five, all in the south, that have no state minimum wage.[7] Unlike the federal government, 11 states currently index their minimum wage to the cost of living, and another four will soon do so (National Employment Law Project 2016). New York State and California have passed $15/hour

---

[3] In-kind benefits provide considerably more assistance than cash benefits do and the ratio of in-kind to cash has been growing over time (Glaeser 2012).

[4] In subtle ways, Social Security and Medicare do have need-based components. For example, although the Social Security benefit one receives after reaching one's full retirement age does not decline as current earnings or income rise, a proportion of the benefit becomes taxable if one's income is high enough (Purcell 2015). Similarly, although Medicare eligibility does not depend on income, as Medicaid eligibility does, the premiums paid for Medicare Parts B and C do rise with income (Kaiser Family Foundation 2015).

[5] The first minimum wage was passed in New Zealand in 1894. Massachusetts passed the first state minimum wage in the U.S. in 1912, and 16 other states and the District of Columbia followed suit by 1930 (BeBusinessed.com 2016).

[6] The Fair Labor Standards Act (FLSA) establishes the federal minimum wage and covers about 84% of workers in the labor force (Bradley 2015). Excluded are some seasonal workers (e.g., in summer camps or amusement parks), some agricultural workers (e.g., family members), casual babysitters and newspaper deliverers. In addition, some workers are temporarily exempt from coverage. There is a lower teenage minimum of $4.25/hour for first 90 days of employment, and full time students in retail, service, agriculture, or at an institution of higher learning can be paid 85% of the federal minimum wage. Finally, there is a lower minimum wage ($2.13/hour) for those who depend heavily on tips, but the regular minimum wage applies to the sum of salary and tips.

[7] The Congressional Budget Office (CBO 2014, p. 4) estimates that "about half of workers in the United States live in states where the applicable minimum wage is more than $7.25/hour."

minimum wages, to be phased in over time, by 2021 for New York City and its suburbs and by 2022 statewide in the case of California (Lazo and Orden 2016). More than two dozen localities, including Seattle, San Francisco, Los Angeles and Chicago, have adopted minimum wages in excess of their state minimum (Economic Policy Institute 2016). There is discussion by some of raising the national minimum to $9.00, $10.10 or $15.00/hour over the near future (Cooper and Hall 2013; Nicholas 2016). The 2016 Democratic Party Platform (Democrats.org 2016, p. 3) labels the current minimum wage "a starvation wage" and proposes increasing it to $15/hour and indexing it to the cost of living. Many interested parties, especially business owners (and most importantly, restaurants and other food providers) oppose these proposed minimum wage increases in part because they increase the cost of production.

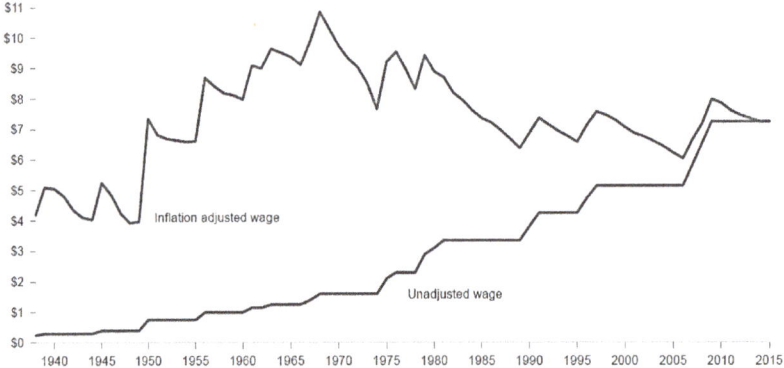

Figure 1. Minimum wage rate in nominal and 2015 dollars (Kurtz and Yellin 2016).

Is a minimum wage, or an increase in the minimum wage, a good public policy?[8] Whom does it help and whom does it hurt, with particular interest on those earning at the low end of the earnings distribution. The good news and the bad news can be illustrated in a very simple graph showing the supply and demand curved in a competitive low-skilled labor market (Figure 2).

Without a minimum wage, the market-clearing (supply = demand) wage is W_{before} and the number of workers employed is E_{before}. If the market wage is higher or lower than this, there will be pressures driving the wage toward equilibrium, either an excess supply of unemployed workers driving the wage down or an excess demand by employers driving the wage up.

If we now introduce a minimum wage of W_{after}, above the prior equilibrium wage, we see that employment declines (fewer workers are hired at the higher wage) but the wages of those still employed (E_{after}) have increased. Employment declines for two reasons. Even if the level of production in a firm now paying a higher wage stays the same, employers might shift (and more so in the long run than immediately, as adjustments take time) from the now relatively more expensive input (labor) to alternative inputs (like capital or technology)—this is the substitution effect. In addition, however, if the prices of the products produced increase because of the higher input costs, total sales may decline, further decreasing the demand for labor across the wage distribution (the output or scale effect). In addition, a higher minimum wage might discourage firm openings and/or increase the rate of firm closings. In the end, some workers will be better off (those still employed but at a higher wage), but others, and some among those that minimum-wage legislation is designed to help, will be worse off. They were employed at the lower minimum-wage but are now unemployed at the higher

---

[8] There are extensive literatures on various impacts of the minimum wage. Appendix B in (CBO 2014) lists five pages of references, including 14 reviews of the literature.

minimum-wage. Given turnover in the low-wage sector, some individual workers may be both worse off (e.g., laid off from one job after an increase in the minimum wage) and then better off (hired at a new position at the higher wage) or the reverse.

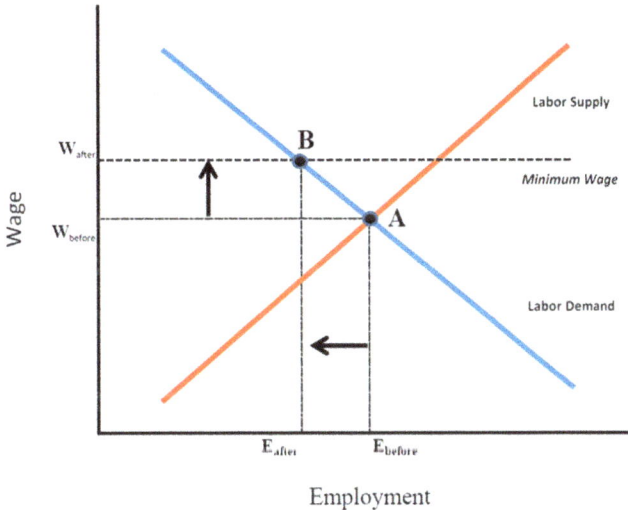

Figure 2. How a minimum wage impacts employment (Authors' illustration).

Others in society can be affected as well. Workers already earning above but near a new higher minimum wage might enjoy pay increases as well (good news for those workers), as employers try to maintain traditional wage differentials among various categories of employees—but some of these better paid workers might be laid off as well (bad news for them). Workers with collectively bargained wages tied to the minimum wage would also gain. If prices of products in this industry rise, as noted above, consumers of these products will pay more, consume less and be made worse off. Demand for components of these products might decrease, with ripple effects in other industries. And of course those paying the higher minimum wages (the employers directly affected) may be worse off as well, earning lower profits as production costs rise and sales volumes decline.

Some of these effects may be partially offset. Those now earning more might purchase more of these now higher priced products. At higher wages, these jobs are now more attractive to workers, which might instill a higher work ethic leading to lower turnover, which saves employers hiring and training costs, and to higher productivity.

There are societal implications as well. Higher paid workers will pay more in income taxes and may rely less on federal, state and local transfer payments. But those laid off will do just the opposite. Overall, earnings inequality and therefore income inequality may decline, which is one of the goals of minimum wage advocates.

Many economists, even those on opposite sides of the minimum wage debate, would agree on the *direction* of these effects. An increase in the minimum wage is likely to increase the income of those affected workers who are still employed and may reduce inequality, turnover, and welfare expenditures. The higher minimum wage may also reduce employment in the low-wage market, increase product prices and lower profits. But these same economists may disagree dramatically on the *magnitude* of these effects, and on the characteristics of the individuals on whom they fall. How many low-wage workers will remain employed at the higher wage? How many will be laid off? Who are those who are laid off? Are they family breadwinners on whose earnings other rely or are they supplementary workers or teenagers looking for summer jobs? If the latter, which teenagers are they—those in middle-income or wealthy families, looking for some spending money or inner city youth looking for desperately needed income and vital job experiences? Although those affected are clearly low-wage *earners*, if they are earning near the minimum wage, are they members of low-income *households*? How should policymakers and society compare the gains of the winners and the losses of the losers? Does the good news justify the bad?

It is interesting to note the diversity of opinion among economists on the magnitude of the dis-employment effects of an increase in the minimum wage. The Initiative on Global Markets (The Initiative on Global Markets 2015) at the University of Chicago Booth School of Business periodically surveys a panel of about 50 prominent economists about a series of economic statements, including, in 2015, "If the federal minimum wage is raised gradually to $15-per-hour by 2020, the employment rate for low-wage US workers will be substantially lower than it would be under the status quo."[9] The results are symmetrical. About one-quarter of these economists agree, another quarter disagree and most of the remainder are uncertain.

Researchers in this field also disagree on these issues, but the current dominant view is that the magnitude of the job loss would be modest for moderate increases in the minimum wage.[10] In a recent book that surveys this extensive literature, (Belman and Wolfson 2014) conclude that,

> "Bearing in mind that the estimates for the United States reflect a historic experience of moderate increases in the minimum wage, it appears that if negative effects on employment are present, they are too small to be statistically detectable."[11] (Belman and Wolfson 2014, p. 178)

and that, of the research that has avoided some statistical problems they describe,

> "little has been able to detect a substantially significant response of employment, measured as the number of jobs, the number of people working, or the number of hours. Although this does not close the issue, the preponderance of the evidence currently leans that way...The corresponding elasticities for eating and drinking establishments in the United States appear to be somewhat larger, with precision weighted means near −0.05." (Belman and Wolfson 2014, p. 402)

The latter estimate suggests that for each 1% increase in the minimum wage, employment in these establishments would decline by 0.05%. If correct, a 50% increase (e.g., from the current $7.25 to $10.87/hour) could decrease employment by 2.5%, and doubling the minimum wage to $14.50 would create a 5.0% decline in employment. It should be noted that the research on which these estimates are based typically studied prior changes in minimum wages or differentials in the minimum wage in different geographic regions, and extrapolations from these historical experiences to very different hypothetic minimum wages (e.g., to $15/hour) are accompanied by increasing uncertainty in the estimated impacts.

A recent study by the nonpartisan Congressional Budget Office (CBO) (CBO 2014) tried to estimate the effects of a change in the federal minimum wage from 7.25 to $10.10/hour—a nearly 40 percent increase—over three years. They note that the employment effects can differ dramatically by firm,

---

[9] For a list of the economists surveyed and the results see (The Initiative on Global Markets 2015).

[10] This is not the universal view. For example, in a Wall Street Journal op-ed, David Neumark (Neumark 2015) argues that "the evidence is piling up that minimum wages kill jobs," and notes that the elasticities on job displacement differ by demographic group, and are higher for teenagers and for those with very low skills. See also (Neumark and Wascher 2008, p. 286) for an extensive review of the literature at that time. In their conclusions, they emphasize the "reduction in employment opportunities for low-skilled and directly affected workers" and find "virtually no evidence that minimum wages reduce the proportion of families near or below the poverty line … "

[11] Burkhauser (Burkhauser 2015, p. 5) notes that European minimum wages are typically higher relative to the average wage than they are in the U.S., and that "there has been almost no evidence for adverse employment effects." The fact that recent changes in the U.S. (real) minimum wage have been modest, and that those historical experiences provide the data on which projections of the impacts of future change will be based, should give one pause when dramatic increases in the minimum wage (e.g., to $10.10, $12 or $15/hour) are being considered. Unless the impacts are linear, and there is no reason to believe they are, past experiences may be a poor guide for future impacts.

depending, among other things, on the importance of wage costs in the total costs of production, on the firm's ability to substitute other factors of production for labor, and on the price sensitivity of their customers.[12] The impacts will also increase over time, as firms find additional ways to reduce the use of more expensive inputs. On the other hand, some firms might be able to minimize the employment impacts, if they can reduce other components of compensation (like training or fringe benefits, admittedly less likely in these low-wage settings) in response to the increased wage.

The CBO notes that, as mentioned above, workers making slightly above the new minimum wage (in this case, already making more than $10.10/hour) might also enjoy wage gains, as workers below them receive raises and employers try to maintain prior wage differentials. The authors assumed that these positive "ripple effects" might occur up to a wage 50 percent higher than the increase in the actual minimum wage; in this case, up to $11.50/hour.[13]

The CBO's best estimate is that at the end of the three-year transition period to a $10.10/hour minimum wage, employment would be reduced by about 500,000 workers, a decline of about 3% of the workers affected.[14] This is the bad news. The good news is that the rest of the covered low-wage workers—those still employed, about 16.5 million of them—would have higher earnings because of the change. The winners at this stage outnumber the losers by over 30:1. But these changes in earnings (to losers and winners) are only the first stage effects. The CBO also estimates the negative impacts of product price increases, the positive impacts of increases in demand for goods and services by those now earning more, and the losses in income of those business owners now paying the higher wages.

Figure 3 illustrates the estimated increases in net earnings for low-wage earners and the aggregate effect on families' real income, disaggregated by the ratio of family income to the appropriate poverty threshold (anticipating our next topic—the anti-poverty efficacy of minimum wage legislation). The dark blue bars show just the changes in earnings (both increases to those still employed at $10.10/hour and losses to those who lose their jobs). The light blue bars include the other impacts on real incomes as well, several of which are negative, like price increases and reduced profits. The sum of the light blue bars for the families *up to 6 times* their poverty threshold is +$19 billion (in 2013 dollars), with $5 billion going to families below the poverty line, $12 billion to families between 1 and 3 times the line and $2 billion to those between 3 and 6 times the line. The big losers are those families *above 6 times* the poverty line, who reap very little of the good news (higher wages for low wage workers) and much of the bad news (like higher prices and lower profits), with a net loss summing to −$17 billion (see (CBO 2014), Figure 3).[15] The net result for all those affected (+19b − $17b = +$2b) is nearly a wash, but the redistribution is progressive, with families at the lower end and in the middle of the income distribution in aggregate better off and those at the very upper end worse off. The vast majority of the net gain goes to workers in families above the poverty line, although some of the net gain goes to those close to it (within 2 times their poverty threshold). Below we will compare these anti-poverty results with those of an important alternative, the Earned Income Tax Credit.

---

12   The importance of the cost of other factors of production suggests that the impact of a minimum wage increase will differ geographically. A given increase in a firm's labor costs in a rural area, where rents and other costs are low, will have a much larger percentage impact on total costs than the same increase in the wage bill would have in Manhattan, where rents and other costs are much higher. The more important wages are in total costs, the larger the likely impact of change in the minimum wage.

13   The increase analyzed, from $7.25 to $10.10, is an increase of $2.85/hour. An increase 50% larger than that would be an increase of $4.27/hour. Adding that to the original $7.25 yields $11.52, rounded to the $11.50/hour used in the CBO study.

14   This 500,000 decline includes only workers who would have made less than $10.10/hour before the increase in the minimum wage. The authors assume some of those already earning slightly above $10.10/hour (up to $11.50/hour—see footnote 11) would enjoy some wage increase (the "ripple effect"), but none would suffer job losses. This −500,000 is the researchers' best estimate. Their 67% confidence interval for the loss in jobs ranges from approximately 0 to a loss of 1 million, implying a 33% chance that the change could be outside that range, from a gain in employment to a loss of over 1 million jobs.

15   In 2016, 6 times the poverty line is roughly $120,000 for a family of three and $150,000 for a family of 6. See (CBO 2014, p. 11).

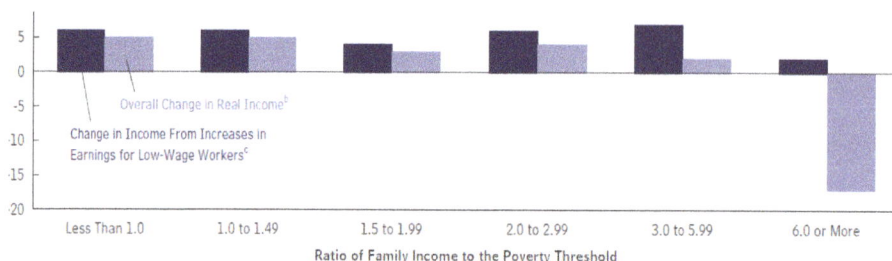

Figure 3. Estimated effects on real family income of an increase in the federal minimum wage, second half of 2016, $10.10 option[a] (billions of 2013 dollars, annualized). See (CBO 2014). Notes: Calculated using before-tax family cash income. Poverty thresholds vary with family size and composition. The definitions of income and of poverty thresholds are those used to determine the official poverty rate and are as defined by the Census Bureau. CBO projects that in 2016 the poverty threshold (in 2013 dollars) will be about $18,700 for a family of three and $24,100 for a family of four. a. The minimum wage would rise (in three steps, starting in 2014) to $10.10 by 1 July 2016, and then be indexed to inflation. b. Changes in real (inflation-adjusted) income include increases in earnings for workers who would receive a higher wage, decreases in earnings for workers who would be jobless because of the minimum-wage increase, losses in income for business owners, decreases in income because of increases in prices, and increases in income generated by higher demand for goods and services. c. Increases in earnings for workers who are projected, under current law, to be paid less than $11.50 per hour.

Douglas Holtz-Eakin and Ben Gitis (Holtz-Eakin and Gitis 2015) duplicated the CBO analysis for larger minimum wages increase, to $12/hour and $15/hour by the year 2020, both of which have been proposed.[16] They used the CBO methodology, as well as some higher dis-employment effects proposed by other researchers: Jonathan Meer and Jeremy West (Meer and West 2016), who estimated intermediate-sized job loss effects, but much larger than the CBO estimates, and Jeffrey Clemens and Michael Wither (Clemens and Wither 2014), who estimated extremely large dis-employment effects.

The Holtz-Eakin and Gitis results using the CBO methodology are qualitatively similar to the $10.10/hour minimum wage estimates discussed above.[17] For example, following an increase to $12/hour, about 1.3 million jobs would be lost, but 37 million affected workers (earning up to $14.40/hour) would still be employed—a good news : bad news ratio of about 28:1.[18] For the larger increase to $15/hour, 3.3 million workers would lose their jobs but 52 million would be employed at a higher wage, a ratio of almost 16:1. In terms of individuals, the number enjoying the good news significantly outweighs the number suffering the bad, although the loss in economic well-being and morale for an individual now without a job most likely outweighs the increase in well-being for someone who remain employed at a higher wage (Sabia 2014b, p. 1045). How one weighs the numbers who are better and worse off versus the differential impact of the change per person still employed

---

[16] See (Holtz-Eakin and Gitis 2015, p. 4, footnotes 8–9).

[17] For example, Holtz-Eakin and Gitis (Holtz-Eakin and Gitis 2015, Figures 1–4) used the same definition of workers already earning above the minimum wage who might nonetheless enjoy a wage increase—up to wage rates 50% higher than the difference between the old and new minimum wage (see footnote 11). In their $12/hour example, the ripple effects (higher wages after an increase in the minimum wage) occur up to $14.40/hour and in the $15/hour case, up to $18.90/hour.

[18] Holtz-Eakin and Gitis (Holtz-Eakin and Gitis 2015, p. 6) estimate that 25.8 million workers would have earned between $7.25 and $12/hour and another 12.5 million between $12 and $14.40/hour in the absence of an increase in the federal minimum wage, for a total of 38.3 million affected by the increase. Of those, following the increase, 1.3 million would lose their jobs and be worse off, and the remainder (37.0 million) would keep their jobs at the higher wage and be better off. In the $15/hour case, 55.1 million (those earning between $7.25 and $18.90/hour) would be affected, 3.3 million would lose their jobs and the remaining 51.8 million would remain employed.

versus now unemployed is one reason why analysts can differ in their views on increases in the minimum wage.[19]

2. The Earned Income Tax Credit

The federal Earned Income Tax Credit (EITC) is a wage supplement, via a refundable tax credit, to wage earners in low- and modest-income families. It increases hourly earnings, just like a raise, if the family's income is low enough, and it is designed to encourage work.

The EITC does not change one's gross paycheck. Rather, with each hour worked by anyone in the family, the credit first negates any income or Social Security taxes the family owes for the year, and then any additional unused credit is refunded to the family after the annual tax forms are filed. The fact that the credit is *refundable*, and does not only cancel taxes owed, is very important because, although nearly all workers pay Social Security taxes, from the first dollar earned, almost half (about 45% in 2015) of the households in the United States do not have enough income to owe federal income taxes (Tax Policy Center 2015).

Figure 4 illustrates how the EITC works, in this case, for a married couple with two children in 2015 (CBPP 2016c). Family earnings are supplemented by about 40 percent up to a maximum of $5,548 per year, which occurs when earnings reach about $14,000.[20] The annual EITC remains at this level as family earnings increase to about $23,400, during which workers earn just their wage from their employer. After this flat range on the graph, the supplement declines by about $0.20 for each additional $1 earned, until it disappears at earnings of just over $50,000. During this downward section, the worker actually nets less than the wage from the employer, because the EITC declines with each hour worked, providing a work disincentive along this range of the graph. For a single head of household with two children, the first part of the graph is the same but the decline starts earlier, at earnings of about $18,000. For a couple with three children, the maximum EITC and the earnings at which it declines to $0 are both higher ($6,242 and about $53,500); with one child, both are lower ($3,359 and about $44,800). The EITC once applied only to families with children. Low earners without children are now eligible, but for a maximum of only about $500 per year, or less than $10 per week.[21] Although the amount of the EITC depends on the head of household (single or couple) and the number of children (up to a maximum of 3), the structure of the benefit always looks like Figure 4, with a wage supplement up to a maximum amount, which then stays constant for a while and then declines at a rate lower than the increase. The EITC acts as a supplement (of about 40%) to the wage rate on the way up, and then acts as a tax (of about 20%) on the way down, since the credit declines as anyone in the family earns more.

In 2013, the average EITC recipient with children received about $3100 (CBPP 2016c). The grant differs significantly by number of children as seen in Figure 5. Families of three or more children averaged over $4000 (in 2013), those with three children about $3700, those with one child about $2300 and those with no children less than $300 (CBPP 2016b). The District of Columbia and 26 states supplement the federal EITC, usually adding a percentage to the federal grant (Marr et al. 2015).[22]

---

[19] The number of individuals who are better off and worse off could also be influenced by migration if higher minimum wages attract low-skilled immigrants or induce relocations among recent migrants. A recent review of the literature on migration flows in response to minimum wage laws concludes that the evidence is mixed regarding these potential migration effects (Giulietti 2015).

[20] Unlike the federal minimum wage, which changes only with legislation, the EITC amounts change each year. For example, the 2015 maximum EITC for a household with two qualifying children, $5,548, increased marginally to $5,572 in 2016. Eligibility also requires that the family have less than $3,400 in investment income for the year. See (IRS 2016a).

[21] How the EITC amount changes with head of household (single or couple), number of children (0 to 3) and family earnings can be seen in a neat interactive graph available at the Center for Budget and Policy Priorities (CBPP 2016b).

[22] Of the states (and DC) that supplement the federal EITC, 24 have refundable grants, like the federal program; four have non-refundable grants, meaning that they can decrease or eliminate tax obligations but any remainder does not go to the family (CBPP 2016d).

Figure 4. Value of federal Earned Income Tax Credit, 2015 (filing status: married, two children, $14,162 in household wage income). See (CBPP 2016c).

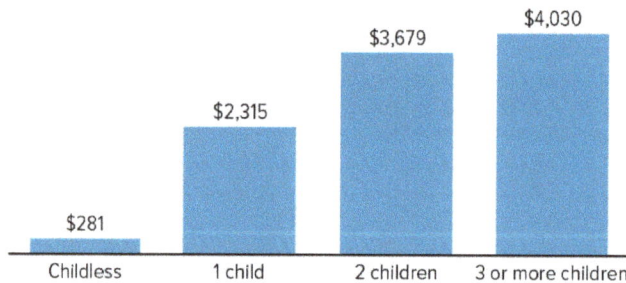

Figure 5. Average Earned Income Tax Credit benefit. See (Center for Budget and Policy Priorities (CBPP 2016b).

Figure 6 illustrates the impact of the EITC on a low-wage labor market for someone on the upward section of Figure 4. Point A is the market equilibrium with no minimum wage and no EITC, with E_{before} workers employed at wage W_{before}. The EITC then creates a positive wedge between what the employer pays per hour (W_{after}-employer, assumed to be above the minimum wage) and what the worker receives (W_{after}-employee)—with the EITC subsidy (per hour) creating the difference. At the new equilibrium, point B, labor supply (which depends on W_{after}-employee—the wage rate received by the employee, *including* the EITC) equals labor demand (which depends on W_{after}-employer—the lower amount paid by the employer).

Note that compared to the single wage before the EITC, W_{before}, the worker earns more and the employer pays less. The government subsidy is shared, and who gets what proportion of the subsidy depends on the shapes (the elasticities) of the supply and demand curves.[23]

The most important feature of this graph, and a crucial difference from the minimum wage example in Figure 2, is that employment *increases*. Employees want to work more because they are

---

[23] In Figure 5, the subsidy appears to be shared about equally, but that is just because of how these supply and demand curves are drawn; there is no reason to expect equal sharing in a real case. Bernstein and Shierholz (Bernstein and Shierholz 2014, p. 1038) cite (Rothstein 2010) who estimates that employers capture about one-quarter of the subsidy via lower pre-tax wages. Rothstein (Rothstein 2010, pp. 6, 205) concludes that "under reasonable demand elasticities substantial portions of the funds expended on the EITC are shifted to employers ... Although the exact magnitudes of these effects are sensitive to the details of the simulation, their qualitative importance is quite robust."

earning more; employers want to hire more because they are paying less. Both sides gain, with that gain funded by taxpayers, who may very well include these employers and employees.

The EITC appeals to many. Many conservatives like it because it encourages work, it helps only those who do work, and it increases total employment. Many liberals like it because it helps workers who live in poor or modest-income households. Many employers like it because it is funded by taxpayers, not just by employers, and because the wages they pay might decline, as seen in Figure 6. Many economists like that it encourages work and because it is well targeted, not on those earning low wages, who may live in wealthy households, but rather on those living in low-income households, a topic to be discussed further below.

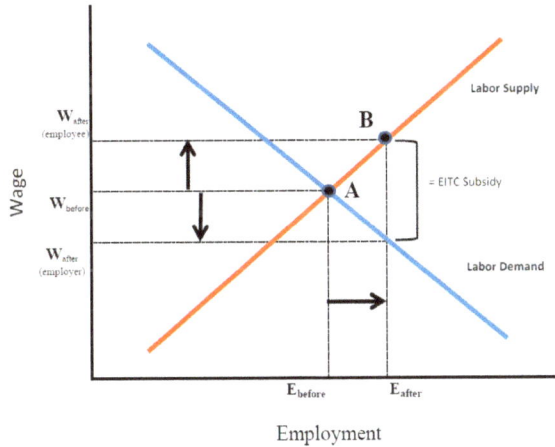

Figure 6. How the Earned Income Tax Credit impacts employment (Authors' illustration).

The EITC is a large and very important federal program. In 2014, over 27 million Americans received nearly $67 billion in refundable credits (IRS 2016b). It is about the same size as the Supplemental Nutrition Assistance (food stamps) Program ($75 billion in 2015), is larger than federal housing assistance to low-income households ($50 billion in 2014), and is much larger than traditional welfare, Temporary Assistance for Needy Families, formerly AFDC (less than $20 billion in 2014). The IRS (IRS 2016b) estimates that about 80 percent of those who are eligible for the benefit file tax forms, and apply for and receive the EITC. Among those eligible who do not apply are disproportionately the self-employed, rural residents and those not proficient in English, and some of those who do not claim the EITC might be eligible for only small amounts, and deem it not worth the effort. Outreach programs exist to reach and inform those who are missing out on these benefits (IRS 2016b).

Although both the minimum wage and the EITC can raise a worker's wage, they differ in important ways. First, unlike the minimum wage, the benefit of which appears in each paycheck, the EITC is refunded just once per year, via the income tax system. This may be a disadvantage to those who would like to increase weekly expenditures, or an advantage to others who then purchase or repair durable goods with the lump sum payment. Second, the EITC is funded by the government (by taxpayers), through foregone tax receipts and checks for the remainder, not by employers, who pay the minimum wage and who pay more when it is increased. In fact, as we will see below, employers might actually be beneficiaries of the EITC, capturing some of the benefit by paying lower wages.

3. The Anti-Poverty Effectiveness of the Minimum Wage and the EITC

Among the goals of both the minimum wage and the EITC is improving the financial status of those at the lower end of the income distribution, which includes those below and those above but near the poverty line. As noted above, the (CBO 2014) estimates that about 16.5 million low-wage (earning less than $10.10/hour) workers would receive higher wages with a $10.10/hour federal minimum wage, as would some additional workers earning up to $11.50/hour.[24] The light blue bars in Figure 3 show the changes in earnings disaggregated by family income, measured here as multiples of the each family's poverty threshold, which depends on family size. In total, the increase in the minimum wage to $10.10/hour raises aggregate earnings by $31 billion per year (CBO 2014, p. 2). Of that $31 billion, less than one-fifth (19%) goes to poor families, about one-third (32%) goes to families between 1 and 2 times the poverty line, another fifth (19%) to those between 2 and 3 times the line, nearly a quarter (23%) to families between 3 and 6 times the poverty threshold, and the remaining 6 percent to those over 6 times the poverty line (derived from (CBO 2014, figure 3)). If we define those below 1.5 times the poverty line (in 2016, 1.5 x the poverty line = $36,375 for a family of 4) as poor and near-poor, they reap less than 40 percent of the total increase in earnings. If we include all below 2 times the line ($48,500 for a family of 4), they get about half of the gain, with the other half going to families above 2 times and almost 30 percent going to those in families over 3 times the poverty threshold ($72,750).

Holtz-Eakin and Gitis perform a similar exercise, focusing on the net pay change following minimum wage increases to $12 and $15/hour. As seen in Table 1, very little of the gain goes to those below the poverty line (8% in the $12/hour case and 7% in the $15/hour case)—even less than in the $10.10 example because the impacts reach higher up into the wage distribution. The majority of the gain goes to those between 1 and 3 times the poverty threshold (45%–47%) and almost half (45%–48%) goes to families far from poverty.

Table 1. Percentage distribution of new pay change, by income level, from a minimum wage level of $12/hour and $15/hour. See (Holtz-Eakin and Gitis 2015, Tables 8 and 10).

Poverty Level	Percentage Distribution of New Pay Change (%)	
	$12/hour	$15/hour
less than 1x	8.1	7.0
1x–3x	46.9	45.1
3x–6x	33.3	35.0
6x plus	11.7	13.0

Why is the minimum wage poorly targeted? The minimum wage focuses on the *hourly earnings of individuals*, while the EITC focuses on the *total income of families*—a much better indicator of financial well-being. The CBO (CBO 2014, table 3) estimates that only about half of low-wage workers (making less than $11.50/hour) are in families with income below 2 times their poverty threshold, and only 20 of that 50 percent are in families below the poverty line; that is, officially poor. Of the other half of low-wage earners, nearly 20 percent are in families between 2 and 3 times the line, almost a quarter are in families between 3 and 6 times the line, and 9 percent of low-wage workers reside in families with income more than 6 times their poverty threshold. Hourly wage is not a very precise predictor of family income status.

Joseph Sabia (Sabia 2014a, table 2) makes the same point and shows how dramatically the poverty status of low-wage workers has changed over time.[25] In 1959, 42 percent of low-wage workers were in

---

[24] The CBO estimates that, in addition to the 16.5 million workers whose wages are below the new minimum, another 8 million workers would be in this "ripple" range, between $10.10 and $11.50/hour, but the CBO "did not have a basis for estimating the total number of (these "ripple") workers whose earnings would rise." (CBO 2014, p. 21) To the extent that any of workers received a raise, the ratio of workers better off: workers worse off would rise above the over 30:1 estimated above.

[25] In this article, Sabia (Sabia 2014a, p. 1031) defines low-wage workers as those "earning less than half of the average private sector wage ($9.87 in 2012) and working at least 15 hours per week and at least 14 weeks in the last year..." With a different definition of 'low wage', Sabia's quantitative results differ from those of the Congressional Budget Office (CBO 2014), but the qualitative results are the same. Sabia extends the work of Burkhauser and Finegan (Burkhauser and Finegan 1989), who were among the first to point out the declining proportion of low-wage workers who were in poor families. Studying the

poor families, and 74 percent were in families below 2 times the poverty line. Thirty years later, these numbers had declined to 22 and 51, and by 2012, only 13 percent of low-wage workers were in poor families, and only 40 percent in families below twice the poverty line. A policy tool that was once well targeted, when many families had one primary earner, has become considerably less so over time.

Overall, counting just those moving out of poverty (or moving into poverty, because of job losses caused by the higher minimum wage), the CBO estimates that about 900,000 fewer people would be in poor families following an increase in the minimum wage to $10.10 per hour, a reduction of about 2 percent of a pool of about 45 million poor (CBO 2014, p. 11)[26]. This number is modest because many low-wage earners are not in poor households, as noted above, and because some of those who are may remain poor even after the wage increase. On the other hand, counting as a success only those who cross a poverty line is a very narrow and restrictive criterion. Those who earn more under a higher minimum wage but whose families remain poor are still better off than they were before, as are those already above but near the poverty line who move further away from it. Certainly those within two times the poverty threshold are not well off and gains to them will reduce income inequality.

In contrast, the EITC is very well-targeted toward the low end of the income distribution since eligibility depends on family income, not individual earnings. A low-wage worker in a wealthy family would not be eligible for this credit. The EITC also *increases* employment rather than decreasing it, as the minimum wage does, even if only to a modest degree. The Center on Budget and Policy Priorities (CBPP 2016c) estimates that the EITC, in conjunction with the smaller related Child Tax Credit, lifted over 9 million persons out of poverty in 2013 (about 10 times the estimate for the $10.10 per hour minimum wage) and made another 22 million persons less poor (Figure 7).[27]

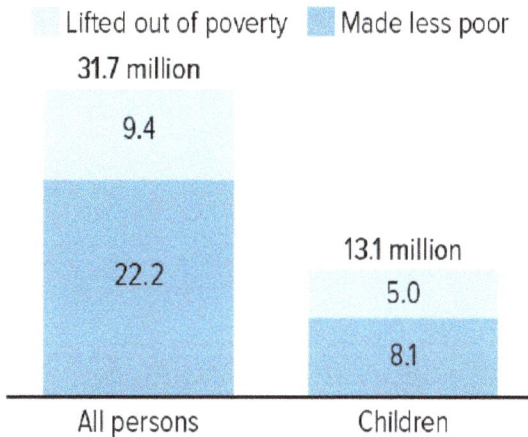

Figure 7. Millions of persons lifted out of poverty or made less poor (using supplemental poverty measure), by Earned Income Tax Credit and Child Tax Credit, 2013. See (CBPP 2016c).

relationship through 1985, Burkhauser and Finegan (Burkhauser and Finegan 1989, p. 65) conclude that "Economists...have mostly ignored the dramatic decline in the target efficiency of minimum-wage legislation...The overwhelming majority of low-wage workers are not poor; over half of the full-time working poor are not helped by the minimum wage; and most of the nonworking poor are hurt by its inflationary side effects."

26 These official poverty rates count only gross cash income, and exclude taxes (an important deficiency at the upper end of the income distribution) and tax credits (like the EITC, much more important at the lower end) as well as non-cash government benefits like Medicaid, housing assistance and the Supplemental Nutrition Assistance Program.

27 The Child Tax Credit provides an additional 15% earning supplement, but only after the first $3000 in earnings, to a maximum of $1,000 per eligible child under age 17 (CBPP 2016a). For more detail on the Child Tax Credit and the Earned Income Tax Credit, see (CBO 2013).

Over 30 million people had their finances improved, although these head counts do not reveal by how much. A low-income couple without children could be included in these statistics, even though the average EITC amount for those without children is about $6 per week, which could hardly make a big difference. Nonetheless, the EITC does a better job than the minimum wage at reducing economic distress at the lower end of the income distribution. And, as Richard Burkhauser (Burkhauser 2015, p. 6) points out, for a given change in the well-being of poor families, "(T)he cost of a higher minimum wage to employers (and to consumers who purchase their products) was much larger than the cost to the government (and the taxpayers who provide these revenues) of an enhancement of the earned income tax credit."

4. Some Other Aspects of the Minimum Wage and the EITC

Research suggests that the EITC not only encourages work and raises the income of poor and near-poor families, but also has other positive effects throughout the life cycle. There is evidence that the financial subsidy to workers improves maternal and infant health, reduces the number of low birth-weight infants, and leads to improved educational performance among youth in low-income households, including higher academic test scores, higher high school graduation rates and higher college attendance rates (Marr et al. 2015; Hoynes 2014). Higher earnings will lead to higher Social Security benefits later. (Since these positive results stem from the additional income, not the EITC per se, a higher minimum wage would likely have similar effects among those still employed.) The EITC also acts as a temporary safety net during times of financial stress; e.g., following the loss of a spouse's job or the birth of a child. In fact, as seen in Figure 8, a majority of families utilize the EITC for only one (42%) or two years (19%) at a time; only 20 percent remain on the program for five or more consecutive years (Marr et al. 2015). Hilary Hoynes (Hoynes 2014) suggests that the EITC "may ultimately be judged one of the most successful labor market innovations in U.S. history."

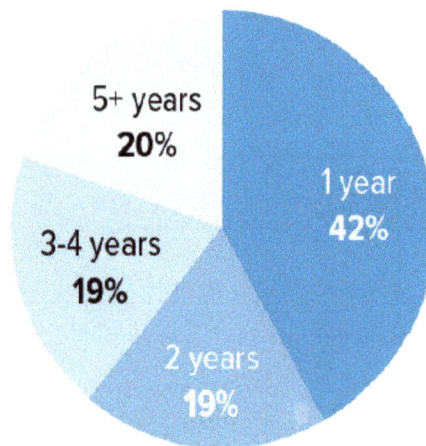

Figure 8. Share of Earned Income Tax Credit families by consecutive years with EITC. See (Marr et al. 2015).

The minimum wage likewise has impacts beyond its direct effects on the incomes of households with low-wage workers. Jared Bernstein and Heidi Shierholz (Bernstein and Shierholz 2014) argue that minimum wage legislation creates an important labor standard, reflecting a societal determination of "what's right," just like "laws against child labor, unpaid overtime for covered workers, (and) discrimination..." all of which intervene in and override the natural equilibrium conditions of competitive labor markets and raise the costs of employers.[28]

Bernstein and Shierholz (Bernstein and Shierholz 2014, p. 1039) are also supporters of the EITC, but point out that with a $7.25/hour minimum wage, the EITC alone would leave the cash income of a solo worker with a family of four well (-17%) below the poverty line, whereas the same EITC rules would put them slightly (5%) above the poverty threshold with a minimum wage of $10.10/hour. They also note that the EITC is a once-per-year tax refund, far from ideal for a family living near the edge, compared to the benefits of an increased minimum wage which appear in each paycheck. Also, since the minimum wage is not means-tested, recipients do not have to submit documentation to meet income or asset standards in order to qualify.

Finally, as a participant in a recent conference on issues of inequality hypothesized, the same financial outcome may provide different levels of satisfaction depending on the source of the income. Many individuals prefer to work than to be on the dole, given the many positive non-pecuniary social aspects of employment, and similarly, a wage paid by an employer, reflecting what that employer deems that employee to be worth, may feel better to the worker than a lower wage, supplemented by a government income redistribution policy like the EITC, even if the net wages are the same. These subtleties go beyond the simplest of economics models, in which leisure is a good and work, therefore, a bad. The conference participant noted that there have been many public rallies in favor of increasing the minimum wage, but few if any advocating for a higher EITC, even if the latter is the more effective social policy.

5. Conclusions

The minimum wage and the Earned Income Tax Credit both have advantages and disadvantages. The minimum wage shows up in every weekly, bi-weekly and monthly paycheck of the workers affected. It is funded by employers, and results in job losses to workers who would have been hired at a lower wage but are not hired at the higher minimum wage. The good news is that in recent examples of minimum wage increases many more workers remained employed at the higher wage than were laid off, but the impact of a job loss to an individual is probably much larger than the benefit to another who remained employed. And it is not clear how well past experiences with modest changes in the minimum wage will predict the impacts of the much larger increases being contemplated and legislated today. A drawback of minimum wage policy is that many of those better off after a minimum wage increase are not in poor or even near-poor families, but rather in families with earnings and other income sources that place them far above the poverty threshold. These are not workers for whom the minimum wage was designed. This phenomenon has grown over time, as the average number of workers per family has grown, and as the instances in which a minimum wage worker is a family's only or even primary worker has decreased (Burkhauser 2015, p. 9).

The Earned Income Tax Credit is a once-per-year refund (not ideal timing for a poor family) and requires recipients to file income tax forms, which the vast majority of those eligible for the EITC do. It is very well targeted towards the poor and near-poor because eligibility depends on family income, not individual wage rates, and it is financed by taxpayers, not by employers.[29] In fact, employers may find that the wages rates they pay decline and that they are able to capture some of the government transfers designed to assist workers. As the wage that employers pay declines and the wage received

---

[28] Frances Perkins, the Secretary of Labor when the original minimum wage was legislated, described the goal of the Fair Labor Standards Act as the "elimination of labor conditions detrimental to the maintenance of the minimum standards of living necessary for health, efficiency and well-being of workers" (Bernstein and Shierholz 2014, p. 1038). A minimum wage was only one such mechanism.

[29] See footnote 21. Although the EITC is an expensive program, costing the federal government nearly $70 billion in 2014, some of the cost if recouped by the governments (federal and the states that supplement it) by additional tax revenues from the economic activity associated with the additional employment.

by workers rises, employment will increase rather than decline, which is a major advantage of the EITC.[30]

Fortunately, these policies are not mutually exclusive, and in the United States, policy-makers have chosen to utilize both—the EITC because it encourages work, raises both wage rates and employment, is well targeted toward workers in low-income families, and because its costs are shared widely; and the minimum wage because it shows up in each paycheck, helps many more than it hurts and does not significantly affect the federal budget.[31] Both policies should result in reduced reliance on government welfare policies. Both may also reduce employee turnover, reducing hiring and training costs for employers, and both policies should reduce income inequality, an important goal for many.

The EITC and the minimum wage interact in interesting ways. An increase in the minimum wage directly increases the earnings in families in which workers are not laid off, which in turn increases the EITC for those on the (rising) subsidy side of the graph in Figure 4. They gain twice. For those who are on and remain on the flat part, their EITC amount is unaffected. But for those on the downward sloping phase-out side, the minimum wage gains would be partially offset by the reduction in EITC benefits, discouraging work at the margin (CBO 2014, p. 15)

The best policy is not one or the other but both. They are complements not substitutes, as Bernstein and Shierholz (Bernstein and Shierholz 2014, p. 1038) argue, noting that relying on just the EITC to get the outcome generated by both would impose a much higher and perhaps unacceptable financial burden on taxpayers. If only one were allowed, and the primary goal were to improve the financial well-being of workers near the bottom on the income distribution, the EITC would dominate, although neither it nor the minimum wage helps those who do not or cannot work. But each has its advantages, some economic and some symbolic, and we expect policymakers in the United States to continue to use both in the future.

Author Contributions: Joseph F. Quinn and Kevin E. Cahill conceived the idea for this paper, researched the literature and wrote the paper.

Conflicts of Interest: The authors declare no conflict of interest.

References

History of minimum wage. *BeBusinessed.com*. Available online: http://bebusinessed.com/history/history-of-minimum-wage (accessed on 13 April 2017).

Belman, Dale, and Paul Wolfson. 2014. *What Does the Minimum Wage Do?* Kalamazoo: Upjohn Institute Press.

Bernstein, Jared, and Heidi Shierholz. 2014. The minimum wage: A crucial labor standard that is well targeted to low and moderate-income households. *Journal of Policy Analysis and Management* 33: 1036–43. [CrossRef]

Bradley, David. 2015. *The Federal Minimum Wage: in Brief*. Washington: Congressional Research Service.

Burkhauser, Richard. 2015. *The Minimum Wage versus the Earned Income Tax Credit for Reducing Poverty*. Bonn: IZA World of Labor.

Burkhauser, Richard, and T. Aldrich Finegan. 1989. The minimum wage and the poor: The end of a relationship. *Journal of Policy Analysis and Management* 8: 53–71. [CrossRef]

---

[30] It is interesting to note that, despite this major advantage of the EITC, only the U.S., the U.K. (in 1999) and Canada (a small program in 2007) have adopted some version of the EITC, whereas many countries, including almost all European countries, have minimum wage legislation (Burkhauser 2015, pp. 2, 5, 7).

[31] An increase in the minimum wage would have several offsetting effects on the federal deficit. The deficit will tend to rise as the federal government pays higher wages to a small number of low-paid hourly employees, pays more for some goods and services whose prices rise, receives less tax revenue from businesses whose profits decline, and makes additional transfer payments to workers laid off. But at the same time, the deficit will decline as the government receives more tax revenues from minimum and near-minimum wage workers who now earn more, and as the government pays less in transfer payments to those same workers still employed and enjoying higher incomes. The CBO (CBO 2014, p 14) concludes that "it is unclear whether the effect for the coming decade as a whole would be a small increase of a small decrease in budget deficits."

CBPP (Center on Budget, Policy Priorities). 2016a. Policy basics: the Child Tax Credit. Available online: http://www.cbpp.org/research/policy-basics-the-child-tax-credit (accessed on 13 April 2017).

CBPP (Center on Budget, Policy Priorities). 2016b. Chart Book: the Earned Income Tax Credit and Child Tax Credit. Available online: http://www.cbpp.org/sites/default/files/atoms/files/1-7-15tax-chartbook.pdf (accessed on 13 April 2017).

CBPP (Center on Budget, Policy Priorities). 2016c. Policy basics: the Earned Income Tax Credit. Available online: http://www.cbpp.org/research/federal-tax/policy-basics-the-earned-income-tax-credit (accessed on 13 April 2017).

CBPP (Center on Budget, Policy Priorities). 2016d. Policy basics: State Earned Income Tax Credits. Available online: http://www.cbpp.org/research/state-budget-and-tax/policy-basics-state-earned-income-tax-credits (accessed on 13 April 2017).

CBO (Congressional Budget Office). 2013. *Refundable Tax Credits*. Washington: U. S. Government Printing Office.

CBO (Congressional Budget Office). 2014. *The Effects of a Minimum-wage Increase on Employment and Family Income*. Washington: U. S. Government Printing Office.

Clemens, Jeffrey, and Michael Wither. 2014. The Minimum Wage and the Great Recession: Evidence on the Effects on the Employment and Income Trajectory of Low-skilled Workers. Working Paper 20724, National Bureau of Economic Research, Cambridge, MA, USA. Available online: http://www.nber.org/papers/w20724 (accessed on 13 April 2017).

Cooper, Daniel H., Byron F. Lutz, and Michael G. Palumbo. 2011. *Quantifying the Role of Federal and State Taxes in Mitigating Income Inequality*. Public Policy Discussion Papers No. 11-7, Federal Reserve Bank of Boston, Boston, MA, USA.

Cooper, David, and Douglas Hall. 2013. *Raising the Federal Minimum Wage to $10.10 Would Give Working Families, and the overall Economy, a Much-Needed Boost*. Briefing Paper #357, Economic Policy Institute, Washington, DC, USA.

The 2016 Democratic Platform. 2016. Available online: https://www.democrats.org/party-platform (accessed on 13 April 2017).

Economic Policy Institute. 2016. Minimum Wage Tracker. Available online: http://www.epi.org/minimum-wage-tracker/ (accessed on 13 April 2017).

Glaeser, Edward. 2012. Cash Better Than Food Stamps in Helping Poor: Glaeser. *Bloomberg View*, February 27. Available online: https://www.bloomberg.com/view/articles/2012-02-28/cash-better-than-food-stamps-in-helping-poor-commentary-by-edward-glaeser (accessed on 13 April 2017).

Grossman, Jonathan. 1978. Fair Labor Standards Act of 1938: Maximum struggle for minimum wage. *Monthly Labor Review* 101: 22–30. [PubMed]

Giulietti, Corrado. 2015. Do minimum wages induce immigration? *IZA World of Labor*. Available online: http://wol.iza.org/articles/do-minimum-wages-induce-immigration (accessed on 13 April 2017).

Holtz-Eakin, Douglas, and Ben Gitis. 2015. *Counterproductive: The Employment and Income Effects of Raising America's Minimum Wage to $12 and to $15 per Hour*. Issue Brief No. 36, Manhattan Institute for Policy Research, American Action Forum, New York, NY, USA. Available online: http://americanactionforum.aaf.rededge.com/uploads/files/research/Counterproductive.pdf (accessed on 13 April 2017).

Hoynes, Hilary W. 2014. A revolution on poverty policy: The Earned Income Tax Credit and the well-being of American families. Available online: https://web.stanford.edu/group/scspi/_media/pdf/pathways/summer_2014/Pathways_Summer_2014_Hoynes.pdf (accessed on 13 April 2017).

IRS (Internal Revenue Service). 2016a. 2015 EITC income limits, maximum credit amounts and tax law updates. Available online: https://www.irs.gov/credits-deductions/individuals/earned-income-tax-credit/eitc-income-limits-maximum-credit-amounts (accessed on 13 April 2017).

IRS (Internal Revenue Service). 2016b. About EITC. Available online: https://www.eitc.irs.gov/EITC-Central/abouteitc (accessed on 13 April 2017).

Kaiser Family Foundation. 2015. The facts on Medicare spending and financing. (Fact Sheet). Available online: http://kff.org/medicare/fact-sheet/medicare-spending-and-financing-fact-sheet/ (accessed on 13 April 2017).

Kurtz, Annalyn, and Tal Yellin. 2016. Minimum wage since 1938. *CNN Money*. Available online: http://money.cnn.com/interactive/economy/minimum-wage-since-1938/ (accessed on 13 April 2017).

Lazo, Alejandro, and Erica Orden. 2016. California, New York governors sign minimum wage increase into law. *The Wall Street Journal*, April 4. Available online: https://www.wsj.com/articles/california-new-york-governors-sign-minimum-wage-increase-into-law-1459794036 (accessed on 13 April 2017).

Mankiw, Greg. 2008. Four goals of tax policy. *Greg Mankiw's Blog*, January 31. Available online: http://gregmankiw.blogspot.com/2008/01/four-goals-of-tax-policy.html (accessed on 13 April 2017).

Marr, Chuck, Chye-Ching Huang, Arloc Sherman, and Brandon Debot. 2015. EITC and Child Tax Credit promote work, reduce poverty, and support children's development, research finds. *Center on Budget and Policy Priorities*, October 1. Available online: http://www.cbpp.org/research/federal-tax/eitc-and-child-tax-credit-promote-work-reduce-poverty-and-support-childrens (accessed on 13 April 2017).

Meer, Jonathan, and Jeremy West. 2016. Effects of the minimum wage on employment dynamics. *Journal of Human Resources* 51: 500–22. [CrossRef]

National Employment Law Project. 2016. What's the minimum wage in your state? Available online: http://www.raisetheminimumwage.com/pages/minimum-wage-state (accessed on 13 April 2017).

Neumark, David. 2015. The evidence is piling up that higher minimum wages kill jobs. *The Wall Street Journal*, December 15. Available online: https://www.wsj.com/articles/the-evidence-is-piling-up-that-higher-minimum-wages-kill-jobs-1450220824 (accessed on 13 April 2017).

Neumark, David, and William Wascher. 2008. *Minimum Wages*. Cambridge: MIT University Press.

Nicholas, Peter. 2016. Democrats add Bernie Sanders's $15 minimum wage call to party platform. *The Wall Street Journal*, July 9. Available online: https://blogs.wsj.com/washwire/2016/07/09/democrats-add-bernie-sanderss-15-minimum-wage-call-to-party-platform/ (accessed on 13 April 2017).

Purcell, Patrick J. 2015. *Income Taxes on Social Security Benefits*; Issue Paper No. 2015-02, US Social Security Administration, Washington, DC, USA. Available online: https://www.ssa.gov/policy/docs/issuepapers/ip2015-02.pdf (accessed on 13 April 2017).

Rothstein, Jesse. 2010. Is the EITC as good as an NIT? Conditional cash transfers and tax incidence. *American Economic Journal: Economic Policy* 2: 177–208. [CrossRef]

Sabia, Joseph J. 2014a. Minimum wages: An antiquated and ineffective policy tool. *Journal of Policy Analysis and Management* 33: 1028–36. [CrossRef]

Sabia, Joseph J. 2014b. The minimum wage: No feature, all bugs. *Journal of Policy Analysis and Management* 33: 1043–46. [CrossRef]

Tax Policy Center. 2015. Model estimates: T15-0138—Tax units with zero or negative income tax. Available online: http://www.taxpolicycenter.org/model-estimates/tax-units-zero-or-negative-income-tax/tax-units-zero-or-negative-income-tax (accessed on 13 April 2017).

The Initiative on Global Markets. 2015. *IGM Forum: $15 Minimum Wage*. Chicago: The University of Chicago Booth School of Business. Available online: http://www.igmchicago.org/surveys/15-minimum-wage (accessed on 13 April 2017).

religions

MDPI

Article

Globalization, Inequality & International Economic Law

Frank J. Garcia

Boston College Law school, Boston College, 885 Centre Street, Newton Centre, MA 02459, USA;
frank.garcia@bc.edu

Academic Editors: Kate Ward and Kenneth Himes
Received: 7 February 2017; Accepted: 4 April 2017; Published: 26 April 2017

Abstract: International law in general, and international economic law in particular, to the extent that either has focused on the issue of inequality, has done so in terms of inequality between states. Largely overlooked has been the topic of inequality within states and how international law has influenced that reality. From the perspective of international economic law, the inequality issue is closely entwined with the topics of colonialism and post-colonialism, the proper meaning of development, and globalization. While international economic law has undoubtedly contributed to the rise of inequality, it is now vital that the subject of international economic law be examined for how it may contribute to the lessening of inequality. To do so will require a shift in the way that we think, in order to address inequality as a problem of an emerging global market society, and how best to regulate that society and its institutions.

Keywords: international economic law; globalization; international trade; global market society; John Rawls; global inequality

1. Introduction

International Economic Law (IEL) is the branch of international law that includes trade law, investment law, global banking and finance law, development lending and crisis lending and international commercial law. Given its subject matter, it is not surprising that the problem of inequality is central to IEL, and vice versa. While the field has, to some extent, addressed inequality between states, inequality within states has largely been ignored; only recently has the field struggled to take into account the extent to which inequalities within states are influenced by laws and policies set at the inter-state level[1]. This essay, part of a larger interdisciplinary working group on inequality, seeks to introduce the reader to the way inequality questions present themselves in international economic law, to some of the current thinking within the field on how to address inequality, and what international economic law can contribute to the larger inquiry into inequality and its drivers, and to broader societal efforts at remediation.

In the field of IEL, the question of inequality is shadowed by three inter-related concerns: the history and legacies of colonialism and post-colonialism (Chimni 2007); the related notion of "development," itself a fraught term (Boas and Bull 2010; Garcia 2016b)[2]; and now by the transformative effects of globalization (Carmody et al. 2012). How much should our efforts to address pernicious

---

[1] See, e.g., (Garcia 2006), "Trade, Justice and Security" explores impact of trade law on domestic inequality, and impact of trade-related inequalities on security and other policy concerns.

[2] See (Boas and Bull 2010), "The main lesson from the first 60 or so years of development theory as a field of study is that any sweeping, general argument about processes as complex and involving as many facets of human life as development will be refuted at one point or the other."

inequalities focus on rectifying past injustice (i.e. reparations, corrective justice etc.), and how much on re-setting the current terms of engagement (institutional reform, distributive justice etc.)? (UN General Assembly 1974) How should development be defined, measured, and most importantly, supported by the IEL system? (Rolland 2012) And how do we best let such questions reframe themselves in view of the fundamental transformations globalization is bringing about in terms of the economy, governance, and society? (Garcia 2013a)

For IEL as for many disciplines, a crucial question is whether engagement with the global economy as currently regulated increases or reduces national, international and global inequalities. If it is increasing inequality in any dimension, where does the fault lie: in the laws and policies of global economic regulation, in domestic economic laws and policies, in the quality of domestic political institutions generally, or all three? These are complex, fundamental questions.

Whether the domain is a domestic, international or "global" space, IEL must also try to understand which inequalities matter and why. This is of course part of a larger set of questions not unique to IEL, but it has unique wrinkles here. For example, comparative advantage in trade depends upon there being "inequalities" in the distribution of factor endowments between economies ("good" or "natural" inequalities?), yet the global justice debate is fueled by concerns over inequalities in the distribution of social resources such as market access, investment capital, intellectual property etc. ("bad" or "social" inequalities?). How can we be sure we are facilitating or remediating the appropriate inequalities?

Much of this boils down to ensuring the right balance of equal and unequal treatment under the law. When should states be treated equally, and when unequally? For example, if we are concerned about "development", in which cases should developing countries be treated equally under the law, and in which cases unequally? For example, with respect to treaty obligations, should developing countries shoulder reciprocal treaty obligations (i.e. equal treatment), or should they be allowed non-reciprocal concessions, the cornerstone of what we call Special & Differential Treatment, the key trade policy for developing countries? (Garcia 2003) To take another example, the Doha Development Round of World Trade Organization (WTO) trade negotiations was founded to address inequality (i.e. WTO rules are not "fair" to developing countries, i.e. the trading rules are not equal and unequal in the right ways), but has foundered on the problem of inequality as well: are states like India or China as "unequal" as they claim to be when it comes to the treatment they claim they need/deserve, and who decides? To frame it a different way, what happens when special treatment claimed by one state on behalf of its least advantaged citizens, negatively impacts the least advantaged (or politically sensitive) citizens in another state?[3]

IEL is thus at the center of our efforts to address inequality, even as many argue it has contributed to the problem through its policies and institutions. In the same way, globalization both intensifies inequality, and suggests new avenues for response. This means that any inquiry into the relationship between IEL and inequality raises more issues and questions than can be answered by any one author in any one submission, and this essay does not try. Instead, this essay will focus on the intersection of IEL and globalization, and argue, first, that questions of inequality must be addressed within the context of a shared global space. Within that frame, the essay will outline a normative view of the problem of global inequality and its relationship to globalization and international economic law. In the author's view, the most fundamental response needed within IEL to the problem of inequality is not so much specific legal and policy reforms—although those matter a great deal—but a fundamental paradigm shift concerning how we understand the regulatory space within which IEL and domestic inequality policies operate: a global space which requires an integrated global approach at both global and national institutional levels.

---

[3] See, e.g., (Jones 2010) "While the United States and EU blamed primarily each other for the collapse, it was clear that India, in particular, was also unwilling to negotiate further without major cuts in U.S. farm subsidies."

2. The Global Context for Addressing Inequality

Because of globalization, inequality is a problem happening within a shared space. Globalization is transforming human relationships in ways that affect our interconnectedness, the basis for solidarity, and the effective reach of our awareness, understanding and actions with respect to others. In essence, globalization is contributing to the emergence of global social bonds—perhaps even a global community or elements of one, but certainly a global market society—built around a range of institutional practices and common challenges (Garcia 2013a; Garcia 2013b; Garcia 2016a).

First, globalization is building communities of risk—David Held calls them communities of fate—around the shared challenges characteristic of global life today: the natural environment, poverty and inequality, security etc. The intensification of global social and economic interaction—in areas as diverse as global finance, refugee crises, terrorism, climate change—create common interests and can contribute to the subjective awareness of a shared fate. This builds on what can be called a community of knowledge, created by the global social media and information revolutions so characteristic of our everyday experience of globalization. Thanks to these infrastructures, we know so much—more than ever before—about how we collectively experience these and other risks, 24/7, around the globe, instantaneously. Finally, and perhaps most importantly, globalization is building a set of shared understandings and practices around how we respond to such risks, and to globalization's opportunities as well (Garcia 2013a). We see this in areas such as the use of markets and the regulation of markets through law and institutions (about which I will have more to say below), as well as in new and emerging regimes around challenges as diverse as climate change and global tax avoidance. (OECD 2013a; Harvey 2015)

Together this represents a fundamental shift in social organization on the planet.[4] One of the surprising features of this new global social space is how it resembles what we used to call "domestic" space, which also consists of regions of wealth, urbanization and industrialization, and regions of agrarianism, poverty and underdevelopment, all linked by an overarching framework of economic, legal, political and social networks of causality, influence and responsibility. We are in the habit of associating this "domestic" space with an identifiable community structured by a set of shared social norms and governance institutions. Because of globalization, we can no longer easily oppose this "domestic" space to the "international" space "between" communities, and insist the latter lacks shared understandings and institutions. What we see emerging through globalization may in fact be a global community, or elements of it, within which global norms and global institutions permeate and interweave with persistent (and valued) local spaces, communities and norms. It is all simultaneously local and global (Sassen 2008).

This trend is nowhere clearer than in the economy, which is of course central to both IEL and the global inequality problem. Contemporary data suggests the emergence of a global economy characterized by diminishing geographic segregation, decreasing discrimination according to source and increasingly integrated global production processes (Lloyd 2010). The magnitude of global economic integration can be gauged by both institutions and outcomes (Prakash and Hart 2000). Removal of institutional impediments is a necessary condition for cross-border integration and, in this respect, institutions (and through them, states) have largely demonstrated a commitment to global economic integration (Prakash and Hart 2000, p. 95). Since at least 1991, states have liberalized the market for capital, with 85% of new investment policy measures in 2015 being favorable to investors ((United Nations Conference on Trade and Development(UNCTAD) 2016)). The market for goods has long been the focus of global economic integration through the GATT/WTO system, which has dramatically reduced tariffs and border measures and effectively addressed beyond-the-border

---

4   See, e.g., (Buber 2004). Perhaps, if not a world of "us," at least a world of "I and Thou"? See, e.g., (Messner 2001).

discrimination of goods through the principle of national treatment (Lloyd 2010, pp. 78, 80)[5]. While the market for labor has remained stubbornly restrictive (Lloyd 2010, p. 81; Prakash and Hart 2000, p. 104), taken as a whole states and institutions have actively worked to facilitate an integrated global economy.

While institutions facilitate and encourage integration through policy-based efforts, ultimately key state and private actors must assess and respond to them, and for this reason it is significant that outcomes also demonstrate a deepening global economy (Prakash and Hart 2000, p. 97). Trade as a percentage of global gross domestic product rose from 27% in 1970 to 43% by 1995, and then to 59% by 2014 (The World Bank 2017c). Foreign direct investment (FDI) has risen from approximately $10 billion in 1970 to $320 billion by 1995, and then to $1.56 trillion by 2014 (The World Bank 2017b).[6] This surge in FDI has in turn facilitated the development of global value chains, within which nearly half of world trade in goods and services takes place (World Trade Organization 2015).[7] Therefore both in absolute and relative terms, and over time and to the present day, outcome-based indicators also illustrate the deep connections characteristic of a global economy.

One way to characterize the social relationships emerging from all of this is as a global market society. Markets and how we regulate them are central to our 21st-century social reality: at this point in world history, it is possible to say that virtually all people live in some form of organized market economy.[8] Globalization has been both a facilitator and accelerator of this trend, and not without significant controversy, due both to the nature of market society versus traditional societies,[9] and to the dominant market ideology in globalization today.[10]

While globalization is extending and deepening the worldwide reliance on markets as a tool for organizing economic life, this in itself is no guarantee of a shared economic culture (Slater and Tonkiss 2013).[11] This brings me to my second point, namely, the regulation of the market through institutions as a shared practice. Market society—or the set of social practices within which markets are embedded—has certain attributes—the need for bureaucratic regulation, recognition of private property, and functioning civil courts, to name a few—which by virtue of their significant spill-over effects, both challenge traditional social bonds and contribute to the formation of important new shared interests among participants.[12] Societies relying on markets also develop, even minimally, some set of social practices or domestic institutions capable of supplementing and mitigating the rigors of capitalism, for example by compensating the "losers" through some form of wealth transfer. We can

---

5 The principle of national treatment prohibits discrimination in taxation or regulation between domestically produced and imported goods. There are several factors that undermine the unconditional commitment by WTO members to the principle of national treatment for goods, including regional trade agreements, and exceptions for subsidies and government purchases (Lloyd 2010, pp. 80–81). Further, the market for services, which is within the WTO's purview, is not as completely integrated as the market for goods (Lloyd 2010, pp. 78–79). However, the WTO's virtually universal membership is itself a testament to states' commitment to global economic integration. See generally (Allee and Scalera 2012).

6 Between 1970 and 2014, FDI as a percentage of global GDP has risen continuously, from 0.5% in 1970 to 2% in 2014 (The World Bank 2017a).

7 Global value chains allow firms to "do" the part of the process they are best at, using intermediate goods and services from elsewhere without having to develop a whole industry (OECD 2013b).

8 This point is acknowledged across a range of perspectives towards markets. See, e.g., (Simmons et al. 2008; Herman 1999).

9 One way to view globalization is as the world-wide extension of the transition to market society that European culture went through in the 17th to 19th centuries. See (Giddens 2000) (citing globalization as the global spread of modernity, with all of its characteristic features and complications).

10 Global market society could be seen as a regressive development if confused with current neoliberal market ideology, but I think this is a mistake. This complaint is more a normative judgment about the global spread of under-regulated capitalism than a judgment on the global economy per se. (Hopkins 2003) (dangers posed by weakened regulatory power over capitalist system). For our purposes here, it is the ubiquity of the market itself that is significant from the perspective of shared understandings and practices, not its shifting regulatory ideologies.

11 Warning that transnational economic activity can also thin out economic ties and the cultural embeddedness of economic activity.

12 See, e.g., (Slater and Tonkiss 2013, pp. 92–116) (surveying the range of institutions which markets require and/or are embedded in).

see this at the global level—what is truly distinctive about the emerging global economy is the shared recognition of the need for institutions regulating the market at a trans-national level.[13]

The emergence of a global market society thus has profound consequences for how we approach transnational problems of politics, economics and law such as inequality.[14] In particularly, these trends suggest that our response to the problem of inequality must be global in nature, and operate within a shared global market society. *Put simply, we need to address inequality as a problem of global market society.* But what is inequality like at the global level? In particular—and this is one of the most urgent challenges of globalization today—what *kind* of global economy are we creating? There are reasons for concern.

3. The Global Inequality Problem

The problem of inequality is not new, yet globalization has intensified the nature of inequality today to worrisome proportions. The forces of inequality are global in nature and intensity. We should be concerned about global inequality for the same reasons we are concerned about national inequality, as well as some new ones.

On the face of it, the outlook for equality is not encouraging (Keeley 2015). To attempt to summarize some very contentious statistics, overall we see a disturbing reversal of the 20th-century trend towards growth with lower inequality (Piketty 2014; Garcia 2015). The OECD has forecasted that by 2060, and without a change in policy approaches, inequality in the average OECD country will match that found today in the most unequal countries (Piketty 2014). Most importantly, global inequality (inequality between people, across countries) greatly exceeds national inequality (inequality within countries).[15] While it may be that inequality *between* countries (international inequality) is decreasing (thanks largely to the gains by China and India), inequality *within* countries is increasing, at least partially offsetting any reductions in global inequality.[16] Moreover, digging behind national aggregates reveals huge differences in income and wealth at the individual and household levels (Oxfam International 2016). The most disturbing conclusion of them all is that, depending how one reads the data, it could be that domestic inequality entirely offsets reductions in international inequality—it could even be that overall global inequality has increased despite the gains between states and the gains in poverty reduction.[17]

Everything about globalization is having an impact on inequality and our responses to it. At a macro/systemic level, for example, globalization's territorial effects raise very basic questions central to inequality policy: who is "inside" or "outside" a bounded space? Whose inequality counts and for what? These are related to globalization's governance effects: where are rules made and by whom and for whose benefit? Globalization's social and subjective effects also complicate our responses to inequality: how do we construct identity (and stigma) in a global space? Who do we consider our "neighbor"? How do we feel about what we have versus what others have? Where does our

---

[13] This does not mean, of course, that there is agreement on the nature of such institutions or on what ideology should guide their market regulation. See, e.g., (James 2012).

[14] For one thing, it shifts the frame through which we try to understand relations between advanced market societies and societies still transitioning from traditional to market principles, such as most Middle Eastern societies.

[15] Global inequality stands at 70 Gini versus 40s for US, 20s and 30s for Europe (Bourguignon 2016).

[16] The top 1% of global wealth holders started the millennium owning 48.9% of all household wealth but have ended up owning half of all household assets in the world as of 2015 (Credit Suisse 2015). Data on global income shares show that interpersonal income inequality is extremely high and that between 1988 and 2011, 46% of overall income growth accrued to the top 10 percent of the world population (Oxfam International 2016).

[17] (Lakner and Milanovich 2013), correcting for underreporting of high income levels across national data sets leads to significantly higher levels of global inequality (76 as measured by national Gini coefficients); see also (Bourguignon 2016), noting this possibility.

responsibility end? How much inequality are we prepared to accept? Are we motivated or paralyzed by seeing so much about how other people live and suffer around the world?[18]

More specific to the subject of this essay, we can see that key elements of the international economic law system favor the intensification of inequality at national and global levels. First, at the level of trade and investment flows, while trade has grown within this framework, and *may* decrease inequality in developing countries, such decreases come in part by *flattening* wages in the middle class; moreover, trade may be *increasing* inequality in developed countries by decreasing wages and shifting jobs at the bottom (Dabla-Norris et al. 2015; Keeley 2015, pp. 33–50). Similarly, foreign investment increases inequality in home and host countries, outbound by facilitating transfer of low-skill jobs from developed countries, increasing returns to capital; and inbound in developing countries by increasing the skill premium (a good thing in certain respects, but also un-equalizing, promoting new elites) (Dabla-Norris et al. 2015; The World Bank 2016; Keeley 2015, p. 42). Thus, while trade openness is generally associated with lower inequality (though at some cost to absolute income levels), greater financial openness is associated with rising income inequality (Dabla-Norris et al. 2015, p. 23).

Technological change also has a well-understood effect on inequality, which is magnified through trade and investment channels. New technologies intensify inequality within countries by increasing skill premiums, substituting automation for human labor, and promoting non-traditional work. The effect of new technologies is particularly acute in developed economies, themselves ironically also the lead innovators, where new technologies have contributed to the destruction or offshoring of old jobs in traditional areas of employment.[19] As older, less-skilled work is destroyed or moved offshore, a premium is attached to higher-skilled labor. Technology thus helps deliver a larger share of income gains to the owners of capital, and a smaller share to the people who work for them through a reduction in human labor.[20]

Third, social regulation is often both more complex and less effective on a global level, and national regulation is under great pressure. To take just one example, the global structure for income taxation facilitates tax avoidance, which in turn depresses national budgets when states can least afford lost revenues in confronting inequality problems, among others (OECD 2015; Ault et al. 2014). At the ideological level, the dominant global regulatory ideology, neoliberalism, depresses national social welfare systems in both dominant and client states by labeling them either protectionist or unsustainable and then dismantling them, thereby exacerbating inequality and limiting the range of domestic policy tools through which to ameliorate it.[21]

Finally, global inequality is having domestic political effects, intensifying the reactivity of domestic politics and further complicating our policies towards inequality and political reform.[22] One can see this in everything from the Euro crisis to Brexit to the reactionary nationalism of U.S., French, Hungarian, Polish and Austrian politics, to list only a few examples.[23] Global inequality thus creates unique political problems for domestic societies, when socio-economic resentments and migration pressures stoke nativism, xenophobia and reactive domestic politics.

---

[18] These questions have prompted theological as well as legal and philosophical reflection, and are if anything even more complicated when one includes the varying theological interpretations of the meaning and causes of inequality. See e.g., (Rieger 2013).

[19] See (Keeley 2015, pp. 42, 50). The growing importance of skill-biased technological progress for growth and rising demand for higher skills will lead to continued polarization of the wage distribution.

[20] See (Keeley 2015). The labor share has declined in nearly all OECD countries over the past 30 years and in two-thirds of low-and middle-income countries between 1995 and 2007. (Oxfam International 2016, p. 12) A declining labor share reflects the fact that improvements in productivity and growth in output do not translate into a proportional rise in earnings for workers, thereby severing the link between productivity and prosperity.

[21] See (Kotz and McDonough 2010), documenting the hollowing out of the modern welfare state under neoliberalism.

[22] See generally (Schlozman et al. 2016), on file with author.

[23] (Aisch et al. 2016), graphically demonstrating the rise of nationalistic politics across Europe.

Even if such inequality trends were not themselves a problem (and there are many good reasons to consider them a problem, and a serious one),[24] the pattern of allocations generated by the international institutions regulating the global economy raise serious distributive concerns, in areas as diverse as taxation, access to capital, control over natural resources and the social costs of investment, to name a few (Pogge 2010). Wealthy states bear some corrective and distributive responsibilities due to the legacy of colonialism, their dominant influence in shaping the institutions that manage globalization today, and the flawed structural incentives (resource and borrowing privileges) inherent in the international legal system (Pogge 2008; Chimni 2007).

Together, these trends raise a host of compelling social, political, legal and normative issues for international economic law—as the regulatory framework of the global economy, all of these issues land in its lap, so to speak. There is much work to be done to ensure that the global economy works fairly for everyone.

4. A Paradigm Shift for Addressing Inequality

Globalization is not simply intensifying the inequality problem—it is transforming our understanding both of the problem and how to approach it. Effectively addressing inequality today requires a paradigm shift in how we approach both inequality and the larger questions of development and fairness it is a part of: *we must now approach them as global problems within a global market society.* Given that the transnational space now resembles more closely what we think of as domestic space than it does our traditional accounts of the international context for inequality policy, the kinds of things we do in Western social welfare democracies at the local community level to ameliorate inequality and promote opportunity for everyone are closer to the heart of post-global "development" than to traditional international law and policy solutions, such as large multilateral structural adjustments and "development" policies.

In developed Western societies, efforts to reduce poverty, promote opportunity and address inequality—in short, the domestic equivalent of development (which has gone by many terms, most recently in the U.S. as "community development")—have entailed a sustained effort to make sure everyone gets the fullest possible benefits of that society, i.e., that we respect and support each member's aspirations for the best life possible within that society. This has involved a process of identifying and removing obstacles to both resources and social mobility, determining responsibilities and obligations, and building capacity (Opportunity Nation 2014; Chetty et al. 2014). It also means ensuring equal opportunity (meaning opportunities are not blocked by discrimination or other barriers considered unfair by that society) in both access to social resources, and participation in social institutions such as politics and the markets for labor, goods and services (Sen 1999).[25] In short, fulfilling the promise of development in local communities has meant ensuring *opportunity* and *fairness* for all in the context of a market society.

Insofar as globalization has collapsed the boundaries between the local and the global, then reimagining development in a post-national environment (and, with it, inequality policy) means reconstructing our paradigm so that artificial distinctions between opportunity and fairness for "Us", and what passes as "opportunity" and "fairness" for "Them," are eliminated. It means rejecting the view that national boundaries justify distinguishing pejoratively between "Our" aspirations and "Theirs", and foregoing facile excuses for failing to support aspirations transnationally in ways we expect our aspirations to be respected at home.

---

[24] See (UN Department of Economic and Social Affairs 2013), UN inequality poses serious threats to wellbeing of people at all levels of the income distribution; (The World Bank 2015), inequality one of three top challenges to development today. See generally (Piketty 2014; Stiglitz 2015; Anderson 1999).

[25] See (Bourguignon 2016, pp. 11, 15), citing the importance of eliminating all forms of discrimination for effectively addressing inequality problem; See also (Opportunity Nation 2014).

When viewed from this perspective, global inequality policy—and development policies generally—are incoherent. For example, we recognize in domestic community development that "place" is important to one's life prospects, so enabling both geographic and social mobility are important goals for local development (Opportunity Nation 2014). However, at the global level, we instead maintain tight restrictions on geographic and hence social mobility, hoping instead that if we send over trade and investment, others will develop "over there".[26] Regarding education, we acknowledge domestically that access to quality education, whether through geographical mobility or school reform, is critical to opportunity (Duncan and Murnane 2014). However, at the global level, International Monetary Fund (IMF) client states have traditionally been forced to reduce social spending on education in order to reach public budgetary targets (Rowden 2011). In domestic "development" we have seen a resurgence of interest in the diversity and importance of the "local", in the effectiveness of multiple smaller-scale, community-based development incentives and programs (Mander and Goldsmith 2000). Yet at the global level we have favored multilateral economic policies that reduce policy space for domestic variations and experiments in development policy, a clear case of the global overriding the local.[27] The bottom line is that "pre-global" distinctions between national and international social relations have allowed us to pursue inconsistent macro-level policies that enable growing inequality and result in neither development nor justice.

What should be done? What "global" policies can reduce domestic inequality and global inequality? What *truly* can be done globally? This depends on very complex causality issues, but at heart it is about comprehensively ensuring opportunity and fairness for all in a global market society. For IEL this means focusing first on institutions.

John Rawls has written famously that justice is the first virtue of institutions (Rawls 1971). By this he means that the fundamental question for institutional arrangements is whether or not they are just, i.e. whether the inequalities they create are justified (Rawls 1971).[28] However, for Rawls and for many others, while investigating the justice of institutional frameworks, or what Rawls calls the "basic structure," is a key task for political theory, it has been conceived of as a *domestic* inquiry.[29] Globalization has rendered such binary structures and assumptions unsustainable. By "institutions" we now must include both domestic institutions, such as public and private law, the political process and socioeconomic structures such as the market, which are well-understood to impact inequality as well as their international correlates, such as international law and international organizations, together with the global market and its international and domestic regulatory bodies—in short, all of the institutions and regulatory structures which affect inequality and its remediation at all levels.[30]

The paradigm shift this essay urges means that in order to address inequality effectively we should continue to work on global and local institutional reform, but in a new, coordinated fashion, recognizing that IEL institutions operate in a single global social and economic space.

For IEL this means first ensuring that the global economy itself promotes opportunity and fairness. We need to reform international economic rules and institutions where they exacerbate inequality, in areas such as trade and investment,[31] tax law (Benshalom 2009; Repetti 2008), IMF and World Bank lending (Garcia 2008), global finance (Buckley et al. 2016), resource and borrowing privileges

---

[26] See, e.g., (Stiglitz 2007), discussing the anomalies created by liberalizing capital flows while resisting freer movement by labor, especially unskilled labor.

[27] ((United Nations Conference on Trade and Development(UNCTAD) 2014)), hereinafter UNCTAD; (Gallagher 2011), WTO and US trade and investment regulation leave little room for policy space.

[28] The justifiability (or not) of inequality is also central to theological reflection on the problem of inequality (see footnote 18), for example within Catholic social thought. See, e.g., (Christiansen 1984) (surveying post-Vatican II Catholic social thought on inequality on the 20th anniversary of the Papal Encylical *Pacem in terris*).

[29] For Rawls, beyond national boundaries, different fairness norms apply. See (Rawls 2002; Maffetone 2011).

[30] In global justice theory these are referred to collectively as the "global basic structure." See (Garcia 2013a, p. 174) and sources cited therein; (Føllesdal 2008).

[31] See, e.g., (Garcia et al. 2015), discussing reform of investment treaty framework.

(Pogge 2010; Wenar 2008), and policies favoring multinational corporate immunity.[32] We also need to reform the rules by which global institutions operate through unequal governance structures, to enhance the voice of the members most burdened by development and inequality challenges and most affected by institutional policies (Torres 2010).

Going beyond this, we also need to ensure that IEL is reformed to support efforts to realize opportunity and fairness through our domestic institutions and policies. In IEL terms, this means protecting policy space for local measures aimed at ameliorating inequality.[33] IEL institutions should incorporate as a policy something like the principle of subsidiarity pioneered at the institutional level by the EU: if there are successful local policies, how can we protect their policy space, support similar policies and policy experimentation in other "locales", and scale them up for transnational or global application as appropriate? Some countries *have* been able to buck the trend of rising inequality, suggesting that domestic social and economic policies can play a crucial role in determining inequality trends (UN Department of Economic and Social Affairs 2013, p. 99). IEL institutions must ensure, at a minimum, that their policies support successful local efforts, so the multilateral level can work as partner, not overseer.[34]

5. Conclusions

Inequality problems raise a host of issues that have long been studied by a variety of disciplines, and addressed through a range of institutions, laws and policy strategies at local, international and now "global" levels. One common denominator has been that institutions matter, both global institutions (for their own policy efforts and for their impact on national policy efforts) and domestic institutions themselves. We are in danger of reaching levels of inequality not seen since before World War II, with serious consequences for all levels of society. Addressing inequality effectively today means a new understanding of how our efforts to work through global and domestic institutions, and in particular international economic law, are part of an integrated and comprehensive approach to promoting opportunity and fairness in a global market society.

Conflicts of Interest: The author declares no conflict of interest.

References

Aisch, Gregor, Adam Pearce, and Bryant Rousseau. 2016. How Far Is Europe Swinging to the Right? *The New York Times*, July 5. Available online: http://www.nytimes.com/interactive/2016/05/22/world/europe/europe-right-wing-austria-hungary.html (accessed on 15 April 2017).

Allee, Todd L., and Jamie E. Scalera. 2012. The Divergent Effects of Joining International Organizations: Trade Gains and the Rigors of WTO Accession. *International Organization* 66: 243–45. [CrossRef]

Anderson, Elizabeth. 1999. What is the Point of Equality? *Ethics* 109: 287–337. [CrossRef]

Ault, Hugh J., Wolfgang Schoen, and Stephen E. Shay. 2014. Base Erosion and Profit Shifting: A Roadmap for Reform. *Bulletin for International Taxation* 68: 275–79.

Benshalom, Ilan. 2009. The New Poor at Our Gates: Global Justice Implications for International Trade and Tax Law. *New York University Law Review* 85: 1–82.

Boas, Morten, and Benedicte Bull. 2010. *International Development*. Thousand Oaks: SAGE Publications Ltd.

---

[32] See, e.g., (Waddock 2008), surveying the emerging institutional infrastructure for ensuring responsible corporate activity in the face of formal regulatory gaps.

[33] See footnote 35.

[34] For example, the IMF has recently begun recommending that client governments implement policies to facilitate better access to education, improved health outcomes, stronger labor laws and redistributive social welfare policies to help raise the income share of the poor and the middle class irrespective of the economic development of a country. See (Dabla-Norris et al. 2015, p. 27; UN Department of Economic and Social Affairs 2013, pp. 103–5). However, it is important for the IMF to avoid past mistakes and recognize that such policies should be implemented in a manner cognizant of local needs and conditions, not as one-size-fits-all programming. See (Dabla-Norris et al. 2015, p. 28).

Bourguignon, Francois. 2016. Inequality and Globalization: How the Rich Get Richer as the Poor Catch up. *Foreign Affairs* 95: 11–15.

Buber, Martin. 2004. *I and Thou*. Translated by Ronald Gregor Smith. New York: Continuum.

Buckley, Ross P., Emilios Avgouleas, and Douglas W. Arner. 2016. *Reconceptualising Global Finance and Its Regulation*. New York: Cambridge University Press.

Carmody, Chi, Frank J. Garcia, and John Linarelli. 2012. *Global Justice and International Economic Law: Opportunities and Prospects*. New York: Cambridge University Press.

Chetty, Raj, Nathaniel Hendren, Patrick Kline, and Emmanuel Saez. 2014. Where Is the Land of Opportunity? The Geography of Intergenerational Mobility in the United States. Working Paper No. 19843, National Bureau of Economic Research Cambridge, MA, USA.

Chimni, B. S. 2007. The Past, Present and Future of International Law: A Critical Third World Approach. *Melbourne Journal of International Law* 8: 499–515.

Christiansen, Drew S. J. 1984. On Relative Equality: Catholic Egalitarianism After Vatican II. *Theological Studies* 45: 651–75. [CrossRef]

Credit Suisse. 2015. *Global Wealth Report 2015*. Zürich: Credit Suisse, pp. 15–21.

Duncan, Greg J., and Richard J. Murnane. 2014. *Restoring Opportunity: The Crisis of Inequality and the Challenge for American Education*. Cambridge: Harvard Education Press.

Dabla-Norris, Era, Kalpana Kochhar, Nujin Suphaphiphat, Frantisek Ricka, and Evridiki Tsounta. 2015. *Causes and Consequences of Income Inequality: A Global Perspective*. Washington: International Monetary Fund.

Føllesdal, Andreas. 2008. When Common Interests Are Not Common: Why the Global Basic Structure Should Be Democratic. *Indiana Journal of Global Legal Studies* 16: 585–604. [CrossRef]

Gallagher, Kevin P. 2011. Losing Control: Policy Space to Prevent and Mitigate Financial Crises in Trade and Investment Agreements. *Development Policy Review* 29: 387–413. [CrossRef]

Garcia, Frank J. 2003. *Trade, Inequality and Justice: Toward a Liberal Theory of Just Trade*. New York: Brill-Nijhoff.

Garcia, Frank J. 2006. Trade, Justice and Security. In *Trade as Guarantor of Peace, Liberty and Security? Critical, Empirical and Historical Perspectives*. Edited by Colin Picker, Constance Z. Wagner and Padideh Ala'i. Washington: The American Society of International Law.

Garcia, Frank J. 2008. Global Justice and the Bretton Woods Institutions. In *The Future of International Economic Law*. Edited by John Jackson and William J. Davey. New York: Oxford University Press.

Garcia, Frank J. 2013a. Between Cosmopolis and Community: Globalization and the Emerging Basis for Global Justice. *NYU Journal of International Law & Politics* 46: 1–53.

Garcia, Frank J. 2013b. *Global Justice and International Economic Law: Three Takes*. Cambridge: Cambridge University Press.

Garcia, Frank J. 2015. Capital in the Twenty-First Century. *Journal of International Law* 18: 188–97.

Garcia, Frank J. 2016a. Convergences: A Prospectus for Justice in a Global Market Society. *Manchester Journal of International Economic Law, Forthcoming* 13: 128–51.

Garcia, Frank J. 2016b. Development. In *Encyclopedia of International Economic Law, Forthcoming*. Edited by Krista Nadakavukaren Schefer and Thomas Cottier. Cheltenham: Edward Elgar Publishing.

Garcia, Frank J., Lindita Ciko, Apurv Gaurav, and Kirrin Hough. 2015. Reforming the International Investment Regime: Lessons from International Trade Law. *Journal of International Economic Law* 18: 861–92. [CrossRef]

Giddens, Anthony. 2000. The Globalizing of Modernity. In *The Global Transformation Reader*. Edited by Daniel Held and Anthony G. Mcgrew. Malden: Blackwell Publishing Inc.

Harvey, Fiona. 2015. Paris Climate Change Agreement: The world's Greatest Diplomatic Success. *The Guardian*, December 14. Available online: https://www.theguardian.com/environment/2015/dec/13/paris-climate-deal-cop-diplomacy-developing-united-nations (accessed on 15 April 2017).

Herman, Edward S. 1999. *The Triumph of the Market: Essays on Economics, Politics and the Media*. Boston: South End Press.

Hopkins, Anthony G. *Globalization in World History*. New York: W.W. Norton & Company.

James, Deborah. 2012. Who Should Run the Global Economy? *Al Jazeera*, April 23. Available online: http://www.aljazeera.com/indepth/opinion/2012/04/2012422104847102233.html (accessed on 15 April 2017).

Jones, Kent. 2010. *The Doha Blues: Institutional Crisis and Reform in the WTO*. Oxford: Oxford University Press, p. 45.

Keeley, Brian. 2015. *OECD Insights, Income Inequality: The Gap between Rich and Poor*. Paris: OECD Publishing, p. 103.

Kotz, David M., and Terrence McDonough. 2010. Global neoliberalism and the contemporary social structure of accumulation. In *Contemporary Capitalism and its Crises: Social Structure of Accumulation Theory for the 21st Century*. Edited by Terrence McDonough, Michael Reich and David M. Kotz. New York: Cambridge University Press.

Lakner, Christoph, and Branko Milanovich. 2013. Global Income Distribution: From the Fall of the Berlin Wall to the Great Recession. World Bank Policy Research Working Paper WPS6719, the World Bank, Washington, DC, USA.

Lloyd, Peter. 2010. Global economic integration. *Pacific Economic Review* 15: 71–86. [CrossRef]

Maffetone, Pietro. 2011. The Law of Peoples: Beyond Incoherence and Apology. *Journal of International Political Theory* 7: 190–211. [CrossRef]

Mander, Jerry, and Edward Goldsmith. 2000. *The Case against the Economy, and for a Turn toward the Local*, 2nd ed. New York: Earthscan.

Messner, Dirk. 2001. World Society—Structures and Trends. In *Global Trends and Global Governance*. Edited by Paul Kennedy, Dirk Messner and Franz Nuscheler. London: Pluto Press.

OECD. 2013a. *Base Erosion and Profit Shifting (BEPS)*. Paris: OECD.

OECD. 2013b. *Interconnected Economies: Benefitting From Global Value Chains*. Paris: OECD.

OECD. 2015. *OECD/G20 Base Erosion and Profit Shifting Project*. Paris: OECD.

Opportunity Nation. 2014. *Opportunity since 1970: A Historical Report*. Boston: Opportunity Nation. Available online: https://opportunitynation.org/history-of-opportunity/ (accessed on 15 April 2017).

Oxfam International. 2016. An Economy for the 1%: How Privilege and Power in the Economy Drive Extreme Inequality and How This Can Be Stopped. Available online: https://www.oxfam.org/sites/www.oxfam.org/files/file_attachments/bp210-economy-one-percent-tax-havens-180116-en_0.pdf (accessed on 15 April 2017).

Piketty, Thomas. 2014. *Capital in the Twenty-First Century*. Translated by Arthur Goldhammer. Cambridge: Belknap Press.

Pogge, Thomas. 2008. *World Poverty and Human Rights: Cosmopolitan Responsibilities and Reforms*, 2nd ed. Malden: Polity Press.

Pogge, Thomas. 2010. *Politics as Usual: What Lies Behind the Pro-Poor Rhetoric*. Cambridge: Belknap Press.

Prakash, Aseem, and Jeffrey A. Hart. 2000. Indicators of Economic Integration. *Global Governance* 6: 95–114.

Rawls, John. 1971. *A Theory of Justice*. Cambridge: Belknap Press, p. 3.

Rawls, John. 2002. *The Law of Peoples: With "The Idea of Public Reason Revisited"*, 4th ed. Cambridge: Harvard University Press.

Repetti, James R. 2008. Democracy and Opportunity: A New Paradigm in Tax Equity. *Vanderbilt Law Review* 61: 1129–86.

Rieger, Joerg. 2013. The Ethics of Wealth in a World of Economic Inequality: A Christian Perspective in a Buddhist-Christian Dialogue. *Buddhist-Christian Studies* 33: 153–62. [CrossRef]

Rolland, Sonia E. 2012. *Development at the WTO*. Oxford: Oxford University Press.

Rowden, Rick. 2011. *Impacts of IMF Policies on National Education Budgets and Teachers*. Brussels: Education International Research Institute.

Sassen, Saskia. 2008. *Territory, Authority, Rights: From Medieval to Global Assemblages*. Princeton: Princeton University Press.

Schlozman, Kay Lehman, Henry E. Brady, and Sidney Verba. 2016. Citizen Voice in the New Gilded Age: Megaphones for a Few-Whispers for the Rest. Unpublished manuscript. Microsoft Word file.

Sen, Amartya. 1999. *Development as Freedom*. New York: Random House, Inc., p. 9.

Beth A. Simmons, Frank Dobbin, and Geoffrey Garrett, eds. 2008. *The Global Diffusion of Markets and Democracy*. Cambridge: Cambridge University Press.

Slater, Don, and Fran Tonkiss. 2013. *Market Society: Market and Modern Social Theory*. Malden: Blackwell Publishers Inc.

Stiglitz, Joseph E. 2007. *Making Globalization Work*. New York: WW Norton & Company, pp. 88–90.

Stiglitz, Joseph E. 2015. The Great Divide: Unequal Societies and What We Can Do about Them. *International Labour Review* 154: 415–16.

The World Bank. 2015. *Development Goals in an Era of Demographic Change*. Washington: The World Bank.

The World Bank. 2016. *World Development Report 2016: Digital Dividends*. Washington: The World Bank.

The World Bank. 2017a. Foreign direct investment, net flows (% of GDP). Available online: http://data.worldbank. org/indicator/BX.KLT.DINV.WD.GD.ZS?end=2014&start=1970 (accessed on 15 July 2016).

The World Bank. 2017b. Foreign Direct Investment, Net Inflows (BoP, Current US$). Available online: http://data.worldbank.org/indicator/BX.KLT.DINV.CD.WD?end=2014&start=1970 (accessed on 15 July 2016).

The World Bank. 2017c. Trade (% of GDP). Available online: http://data.worldbank.org/indicator/NE.TRD. GNFS.ZS?start=1970 (accessed on 15 July 2016).

Torres, Hector. 2010. Reforming the International Monetary Fund—Why its Legitimacy is at Stake. *Journal of International Economic Law* 10: 443–60. [CrossRef]

United Nations Conference on Trade and Development (UNCTAD). 2014. *World Investment Report 2014*. Genève: United Nations Conference on Trade and Development (UNCTAD).

United Nations Conference on Trade and Development (UNCTAD). 2016. *World Investment Report 2016*. Genève: United Nations Conference on Trade and Development (UNCTAD).

UN Department of Economic and Social Affairs. 2013. *Inequality Matters: Report on the World Social Situation 2013*. New York: United Nations. Available online: http://www.un.org/esa/socdev/documents/reports/InequalityMatters.pdf (accessed 15 April 2017).

UN General Assembly. 1974. Resolution adopted by the General Assembly 3201 (S-VI): Declaration on the Establishment of a New International Economic Order. Available online: http://www.un-documents.net/s6r3201.htm (accessed on 15 April 2017).

Waddock, Sandra. 2008. Building a New Institutional Infrastructure for Corporate Responsibility. *The Academy of Management Perspectives* 22: 87–108. [CrossRef]

Wenar, Leif. 2008. Property Rights and the Resource Curse. *Philosophy & Public Affairs* 36: 2–32.

World Trade Organization. 2015. International Trade Statistics. Available online: https://www.wto.org/english/res_e/statis_e/its2015_e/its2015_e.pdf (accessed on 15 April 2017).

![religions](religions logo) MDPI

Article

The System Isn't Broken. It's Fixed

Micah Lott

Philosophy Department, Boston College, Stokes 245N, 21 Campanella Way, Chestnut Hill, MA 02467, USA; micah.lott@bc.edu

Academic Editors: Kenneth Himes and Kate Ward
Received: 7 February 2017; Accepted: 28 March 2017; Published: 5 April 2017

Abstract: This paper has two distinct and related aims. First, I attempt to clarify the oft-made claim that somehow the "system is fixed". What is meant by that charge and how is it distinct from other kinds of complaints with regard to economic inequality? Second, I attempt to show how important it is to understand what we are doing *together* as members of a (political) economy. Without a clear conception of our joint, collaborative active, it is difficult to have a fruitful discussion of economic justice. Throughout the paper, I borrow insights from the philosopher Elizabeth Anderson.

Keywords: egalitarianism; equality of opportunity; equality of outcome; John Rawls; joint cooperative activity; Elizabeth Anderson

1. The Complaint about Inequality

My title is a phrase that I first heard at a rally for campaign-finance reform. However, I think it also describes how many people feel about our economy—that it is "rigged" in favor of certain positions, or sectors, or individuals. The complaint here is that some people do much better than others, in material terms, *not* because of (a) effort or talent or contribution or anything that could be described as "merit," *nor* because of (b) luck or fortune or anything accidental or impossible to predict, but because of (c) the way the system is arranged—the way things have been set up to be. The complaint is not about vast differences in the luck of the draw. Rather the complaint is that the deck is stacked. Or to shift metaphors: the playing field is not level. The fix is in.

I think this is a complaint of the right shape when it comes to thinking about economic inequality[1]. So if we want to think clearly about inequality, we need to get clear on this *kind* of claim and what it presupposes. In particular, it presupposes that there is something we are doing together, in the sense of a joint, cooperative activity. It is only in the context of a game that we are already playing that it makes sense to complain about a stacked deck or an un-level playing field. And whether or not those complaints are justified depends on the nature of the game. Likewise, in the case of political economy, we need to first grasp the joint activity—the practice, or set of practices—that provides "the subject of justice", in Rawls' phrase[2].

Until we can (a) agree that there is something are we are doing together in this sense, and (b) arrive at an acceptable *conception* of our joint activity (or joint activities), we will not be able to understand or evaluate any claim that "the system is fixed". We will not have a sense of what "the system" is, and

---

[1] I do not mean that this is the only legitimate type of complaint about economic inequality. Rather I mean that this type of complaint makes sense, and that it is especially relevant to our situation—i.e., that it captures the core of the concern that many people have about the economic inequality in our society.

[2] For Rawls the subject of justice is the "basic structure" of a society. My point here is not to endorse Rawls's particular approach to the subject of justice, or his particular conception of the basic structure. However, I think Rawls was correct to insist that in thinking about socioeconomic justice we must get clear on whatever it is that we are doing together—our practices and institutions that provide the basis for claims about (in)justice. (Rawls 1971, pp. 7–11). See also (Young 2011, pp. 34–74).

what standards properly apply to it. However, if we can arrive at a conception of our joint activity, then we will have much of we need to understand and evaluate the relevant claims. So this is where the action is, in my view, when it comes to normative thinking about economic inequality. And yet, we face challenges at precisely this point. "The system" seems extremely hard to define, either vague or hopelessly complex. Moreover, there are ways in which the fundamentally cooperative character of our economic life is hidden from view, and easy to overlook.

In light of all this, my paper has two modest aims. In the next section, I try to spell out the complaint that "the system is fixed" and to distinguish it from other concerns about economic inequality. In the third section, I try to show both the importance and the difficulty of bringing into view what we are doing together—i.e., arriving at a proper conception of our joint activity. To do this, I will consider a recent essay by the philosopher Elizabeth Anderson.

2. Four Distinctions

Let us consider four distinctions that are important for our normative thinking about inequality. Taken together, these distinctions will bring the complaint about economic inequality into clearer focus. First, we can distinguish between:

(1) Concerns about equality per se, which are essentially relational in character. These are concerns about the similarities and differences in the way people are treated by others or by institutions, including differences in status, standing, and recognition.

(2) Concerns about *sufficiency*, which are about everyone having enough in some respect—e.g., enough for a flourishing life. These concerns are not essentially relational. Instead they are about the absolute position of certain people, such as the standard of living of the poor.

I accept that in many contexts, we should focus on absolute position rather than equality or inequality. However, that is not my concern here, because it is not the complaint of someone who says that "the system is fixed". That is a complaint about justice. And Aristotle was correct: justice is about *"to ison"*—the equal[3]. Justice is sensitive to the relationship between people in a way that looks to their relative positions, not merely their absolute positions. In this respect, considerations of justice are distinct from considerations of compassion or humanitarian concern.

This distinction is worth emphasizing, because in conversations about economic equality, some people want to shift the focus to sufficiency or poverty, as if equality per se is a distraction[4]. To such attempts to shift the conversation, I say: No. If someone complains that there is an injustice, then we have to take that claim at face value, and evaluate it. And if there *is* an injustice—if the deck is stacked—we cannot solve that problem by simply shifting the topic to sufficiency. That would be like telling someone, "Sure the deck is stacked, but your cards aren't *that* bad ... "

Second, we can distinguish between:

(1) Concern with equality of position *simpliciter* and *for its own sake*—a state of affairs in which everyone has the same amount of stuff, or is in the same position.

(2) Concern with equality in how one *treats* and *is treated* by others—that one's relationships embody equality of standing and mutual recognition; that no one is dominated by another, or simply has to accept their situation "and deal with it" because the will of someone else determines what happens to them.

---

3 "If, then, the unjust is unequal, the just is equal, which is in fact what is held to be the case by everyone, even without argument." (Aristotle 2011).

4 See, e.g., (Frankfurt 2015).

The focus of egalitarianism, as I understand it, is the second of these, not the first. It is a caricature of actual egalitarian thought to suppose otherwise. Egalitarians do not make a fetish of states of affairs in which everyone has equal stuff. Rather, they are concerned that everyone be treated as moral equals with an equal claim to respect, and that social and economic practices reflect this equality. Our interest in material equality flows from a deeper commitment to equal dignity[5].

The egalitarian concern with equal treatment and equal regard (rather than equality of position for its own sake) fits with a focus on joint activity. For our practices and institutions treat people in various ways, and they shape how individuals treat and are treated by others. This treatment includes expressing or embodying attitudes about the value or standing of the participants—what the practice "says", implicitly or explicitly, about the character, worth, status, etc., of various persons.

To be clear, the second distinction is *not* the same as yet a third distinction, between:

(1)   Equality of opportunity[6]
(2)   Equality of outcome

Egalitarians care about *both* of these kinds of equality, depending on the context. However, *neither* of these is about the value of equality of position *simpliciter* and for its own sake. Rather, depending on the context, equality of opportunity and/or equality of outcome can matter—if they do matter—because, given the shared activity among persons, their equal moral standing gives them a claim to equal opportunities and/or equal outcomes.[7]

Finally, we should distinguish two ways of understanding that idea that the system has been "fixed" or "rigged":

(1)   A (quasi)conspiracy theory view, which posits individuals who have intentionally rigged the system and are pulling the levers of power.
(2)   A human responsibility view, which holds simply that there are humanly created and maintained practices that are evaluable according to standards of justice (unlike naturally occurring phenomena).

I am interested in the second idea, not the first. The second idea is all we need to make sense of the claim that there is some injustice in the arrangement of our joint activity, or traceable to that arrangement.

With these four distinctions in mind, we can return to the idea that "the system is fixed", which I said is the kind of complaint we should focus on when it comes to economic inequality. We can now say that this complaint (a) embodies a concern with equality per se, rather than with sufficiency or absolute position, but (b) this concern is not based in valuing the equality of a material position for its own sake—rather, we are concerned with equality in the material realm because of a deeper commitment to the equal dignity of persons, and (c) the type of equality that matters remains to be seen—it might be *either* the equality of opportunity or the equality of outcome or both, and (d) all of this presupposes the reality of our joint, cooperative activity, not a conspiracy.

3. What Are We Doing Together?

In order to evaluate a complaint of this kind, we require some conception our joint, cooperative activity. In brief, what are we doing together? And who are "we" anyway?

Answering these questions involves two broad tasks, and these tasks correspond to two ways that we might disagree over how to characterize the activity.[8] Roughly speaking, the first task is to provide

---

[5]   For powerful statements of this point, see (Anderson 1999) and (Sheffler 2003).
[6]   A further important distinction is between formal equality of opportunity and fair equality of opportunity. See (Rawls 1971, Chp. II, sct. 14).
[7]   For further discussion, see (Scanlon 2003).
[8]   The line between these two tasks might not be a bright one. And in labeling one task "first", I am not saying that it must come first chronologically.

a *normative* characterization of the activity, by which I mean an account of the purpose of the activity and a normative conception of the participants. Aristotle, for example, argues against those who see a *polis* as a community organized merely for the sake of trade and mutual protection. To look at a *polis* that way reflects a failure to grasp the true purpose of a polis in fostering the happiness (*eudaimonia*) of the citizens (Aristotle 1998). Or take another example: In thinking about political life, should we conceive of all citizens as "free and equal, reasonable and rational"? Or should we conceive of the participants in civic activity in different terms, such as those that imply some natural hierarchies of rights and privileges?

A second task concerns what we can loosely call "matters of fact". Here the challenge is to figure out what is actually going on with the practice, or what has happened in the past, or is likely to happen in the future. We might agree on the normative characterization of the activity—the point of the practice and the normative conception of the participants—but disagree about what the participants are actually doing or experiencing. In the extreme case, we might disagree about whether a given practice even exists. On the other hand, we might agree on what is happening, but disagree about whether this amounts to failure or success in living up to the true purpose of the practice and the normative standing of the participants. So when it comes to thinking about our joint economic activity, we need both a normative characterization of what we are doing together and an accurate sense of what is actually going on.

Thus far I have been describing things at a rather abstract level. To make matters more concrete, I turn now to a recent essay by Elizabeth Anderson, "Equality and Freedom in the Workplace: Recovering Republican Insights". Anderson's essay, I believe, does a brilliant job of showing both (a) how our joint activity can be hidden from view, and (b) how bringing that activity into view can re-frame our normativity thinking about (in)equality.

Anderson begins by looking at various employment laws that aim to benefit workers and provide them with greater control—e.g., minimum wage laws, safety laws, union laws. Such laws, of course, are often favored by those who are worried about economic inequality. Indeed, they are frequently seen as a way to make our economic arrangements more just, or "less fixed". As Anderson notes, however, opponents of these laws object that they interfere with the liberty of employers and employees alike. If consenting adults are willing to sign a labor contract to work on different terms, who are we to interfere with their freedom by making it illegal to do so? Anderson notes that liberal egalitarians have a standard rejoinder to this free contract ideology. The rejoinder is that "unequal bargaining power between workers and employers makes the labor contract not truly voluntary" (Anderson 2015, p. 49)—we need some equality of the *starting point* to ensure *truly* free contracts. Understood this way, the disagreement is between parties who both value freedom, but who disagree over *when* a contract is truly free: "advocates of laissez-faire see attempts to secure equality of bargaining power as a threat to individual freedom. Liberal egalitarians see some level of equality as a prerequisite in individual freedom."(Anderson 2015, pp. 49–50).

Anderson argues, however, that both sides vastly overestimate the role of bargaining in labor contracts, and underestimate the role of the state. As she says:

> The typical worker, upon being hired for a job, is not given a chance to negotiate. Nor is she handed a contract detailing the terms of the deal. She is handed a uniform, or a mop, or a key to her office, and told when to show up. The critical terms are not even what is said, but what is left unspecified. The terms do not have to be spelled out, because they have been set not by a meeting of minds of the parties, but by a default baseline defined by corporate, property, and employment law that establishes the legal parameters for the constitution of capitalist firms. Negotiated labor contracts mostly make only minor modifications to a relationship whose normatively critical features have already been set by law independently of the will of both parties, much as prenuptial agreements make minor modifications on the marriage "contract" whose fundamental terms are set by law." (Anderson 2015, p. 50)

Why have both libertarians and liberal egalitarians overlooked this point? Because "they conflate capitalism with the market, and therefore imagine that the labor contract is the outcome of market orderings generated independently of the state."(Anderson 2015) This picture is wrong, however, because it leaves out the crucial role of capitalist firms in shaping the terms of labor. It also leaves out the essential role of the state in defining the structure, or constitution, of capitalist forms. What is distinctive of capitalism is not markets, but capitalist firms. And the "*labor contract is not properly seen as an exchange of commodities on the market, but as the way workers get incorporated under the governance of productive enterprises* [capitalist firms]. Employees are governed by their bosses. The general form of that government is determined by the laws of property, incorporation, and labor, not by contract."(Anderson 2015)

This means that the constitution of capitalist firms is rightly seen as a political creation. And in a democracy, this means that the constitution of firms is the result of *joint cooperative activity*. Such firms exist, and have their shape, only because of something that we, *qua* citizens, have done and are doing, in our making, enforcing, and following laws. Capitalist firms exist only because we—all of us—make and sustain them through our joint political activity. Politics makes the market.

It follows from this, Anderson argues, that the constitution of capitalist firms should be seen as a "public good", and hence properly subject to control by democratic processes and evaluation by democratic standards. And this makes a big difference for arguments about employment and labor laws concerning wages, safety, unions, and workplace democracy. To see the difference, consider this analogy: If we accept the standard framing of debates about labor and employment laws, then provisions to strengthen the position of workers will look like government interference in the market—like a fan running onto the field to catch a fly ball (Anderson 2015, pp. 40–51). The argument between libertarians and egalitarians is then over whether or not such interference is justified. However, that overlooks the real role of the state, which is making the rules of the game, and hence making it possible to play in the first place—i.e., in creating the distinctly capitalist markets that structure our economy. It overlooks, in other words, something we are *already doing together* qua citizens. Something which might have been taken as a *given*, and hence as a baseline from which to argue, is now seen as the *product* of our joint, cooperative activity. And bringing that joint activity into view dramatically shifts the terms of the debate in thinking about equality (and freedom).

4. Conclusions

In this essay, I have tried to do two things. First, I have attempted to understand a central complaint about economic inequality—to explore and refine the thought that "the system is fixed". Second, I have argued that to take this complaint seriously, we need to arrive at a characterization of our joint activity that is both normatively and descriptively correct. However, I have not argued for a particular characterization of our joint activity, beyond the basic notion of cooperation among persons equal in dignity. And I have not provided an account of the standards according to which our economic arrangements should be judged to be just or unjust. Nor have I said anything about the facts, about what is actually going on with us. Thus, while I have tried to provide some orientation for our thinking about economic inequality, all the real work remains to be done.

References

Anderson, Elizabeth. 1999. What is the Point of Equality? *Ethics* 109: 287–337. [CrossRef]
Anderson, Elizabeth. 2015. Equality and Freedom in the Workplace: Recovering Republican Insights. *Social Philosophy and Policy* 31: 48–69. [CrossRef]
Aristotle. 1998. *Politics III*. Translated by C. D. C. Reeve. Indianapolis: Hackett Publishing Company.
Aristotle. 2011. *Nicomachean Ethics: Book V*. Translated by Robert C. Bartlett, and Susan D. Collins. Chicago: University of Chicago Press, p. 95.
Frankfurt, Harry. 2015. *On Inequality*. Princeton: Princeton University Press.
Rawls, John. 1971. *Theory of Justice*. Cambridge: Harvard University Press.

Scanlon, Tim. 2003. The diversity of objections to inequality. In *The Difficulty of Tolerance*. Cambridge: Cambridge University Press, pp. 202–18.

Sheffler, Samuel. 2003. What is Egalitarianism? *Philosophy and Public Affairs* 31: 5–39. [CrossRef]

Young, Iris Marion. 2011. Structure as the Subject of Justice. In *Responsibility for Justice*. Oxford: Oxford University Press, pp. 34–74.

Article

Wealth, Well-Being, and the Danger of Having Too Much

Dustin Crummett

Department of Philosophy, University of Notre Dame, 100 Malloy Hall, Notre Dame, IN 46556, USA;
Dustin.R.Crummett.1@nd.edu

Academic Editors: Kate Ward and Kenneth Himes
Received: 5 February 2017; Accepted: 26 April 2017; Published: 8 May 2017

Abstract: It is impossible for an agent who is classically economically rational to have so much wealth that it is harmful for them, since such an agent would simply give away their excess wealth. Actual agents, vulnerable to akrasia and lacking full information, are not economically rational, but economists, ethicists and political philosophers have nonetheless mostly ignored the possibility that having too much might be harmful in some ways. I survey the major philosophical theories of well-being and draw on ethics and the social sciences to point out several ways in which, on the most plausible of these theories, having too much, relative to other members of one's society, might be harmful to oneself (for instance, by making it harder for one to have appropriate relationships with others, or by making it more likely than one will develop undesirable character traits). I argue that because egalitarian policies prevent these harms and provide the advantaged with other benefits (such as access to public goods which help rich and poor alike), egalitarian policies are not as harmful to the rich as is commonly supposed, and may even be helpful to them on balance. I close by discussing the practical implications of this.

Keywords: political philosophy; ethics; well-being; economic inequality; psychology

1. Introduction

In 2013, around the time the idea which later became this paper initially occurred to me, the twenty-five highest earning hedge fund managers in the United States together brought in about 24.3 billion dollars in personal income (Vardi 2014). Average median income for an American wage earner that year was estimated to be $28,031.02 (Social Security Administration 2013), which means that the twenty-five hedge fund managers collectively made as much as about 867,000 median wage earners (that's 34,376 workers apiece). Because much of their income derives from "management fees", which they receive regardless of how well their funds actually perform, managers can rake in tremendous amounts of money even when it's questionable whether they contribute anything to the economy, much less as much as thirty-five thousand average workers (Vardi 2014; Creswell 2011). An especially striking example of this is Steve Cohen, who made 2.3 billion dollars in 2013—the same year his firm paid 1.8 billion dollars in fines for insider trading, and despite the fact that his investments significantly underperformed the Dow Jones, NASDAQ, and S&P 500 indices (Vardi 2014; Rooney 2013). In fairness, though Cohen did worse than the indices, he did, apparently, "beat most other hedge fund managers" (Vardi 2014). The situation with regard to material inequality is hardly better if we look at wealth, rather than income; between them, the four-hundred richest Americans are worth about as much the bottom one-hundred ninety-four million (Frank 2015).

There are a lot of good reasons to be worried about this state of affairs and others like it. We might worry on behalf of the forty-seven million Americans who live in poverty (DeNavas-Walt and Proctor 2015). We might worry on behalf of American workers, who must deal with not only the hardship but also the insult of having had their wages stagnate or decline for decades while the rich grow ever richer (Greenstone and Looney 2012; Matthews 2012) We might worry on behalf of those in poverty in the developing world whose lives might have been drastically improved with the money that went to the managers. We might worry about our society, whose democratic character might be threatened by extreme material inequality (see (Stiglitz 2012)). We might even worry on general grounds of economic efficiency, which is not likely to be promoted by paying people billions of dollars for doing a bad job. However, it might not occur to us to worry that all this is bad for the hedge fund managers *themselves*. I want to argue here that perhaps it should.

Say that people who make, say, tens of millions of dollars or more per year, or who have many tens of millions of dollars or more in assets, and who mostly keep their money or spend it on goods or services for themselves, all while other people, and particularly other members of their own society, have *so* much less, are *living lives of vast wealth* (or, for short, are *vastly wealthy*). I intend this as a semi-technical definition. It's possible (though extremely unusual) to live a life of vast wealth without ever actually being *wealthy*, provided you spend your money fast enough. It's also possible to be extremely wealthy without living a life of vast wealth; the definition is meant to exclude people who make such sums and then, say, give most to the Gates Foundation, as well as people who use the bulk of their money in ways which, though not exactly *altruistic*, are nonetheless unusually productive from society's point of view (e.g., starting a business which produces something of great importance). I take no stand here about these groups of people here. I will also not attempt to figure out how well those who are wealthy, but don't reach the level of *vastly* wealthy, are doing. (Some of my arguments will apply to the merely *very* wealthy, but not all will).[1]

As for the effect of living lives of vast wealth, I consider two questions. The first question takes for granted that you live in a society basically like the present United States and asks what the effect on your well-being of living a life of vast wealth is likely to be, as compared to the effect of living, say, a comfortable middle-class life, or perhaps a merely *very* wealthy life. I argue that it's plausible that it will tend to be pretty bad for you, or at least not nearly as good as one might think. (I think this is true *especially*, but not exclusively, for rent-seekers who acquire their wealth in a way that's more or less unconnected from whether they're producing anything of social value). The second asks whether those who live lives of vast wealth would be better off in a more egalitarian society which discouraged or prevented them from living such lives. I argue that, because such a society would prevent them from experiencing the harms of that kind of life while also providing them with improved access to certain public goods, it's plausible that they would be better off. Both of these are questions in *ethics*: they have to do with what's good for the people in question. The consequences for social and political philosophy are not immediately obvious. For instance, we might think that the purpose of government is to ensure that people have the ability to live their lives as they see fit, regardless of whether those lives are good or bad for them and, in fact, without making any judgments about what's good or bad for people at all, and that attempting to prevent the wealthy from harming themselves by acquiring too much would be objectionably paternalistic. In the final section, I consider the social and political implications of our answers to the first two questions. Treating the fact that living a life of vast wealth is bad for one as a reason to implement egalitarian distributive policies may be objectionably paternalistic, though I argue that this is far from obvious. But even if it is objectionably paternalistic, I think the position I defend, if taken to heart, could play a useful role in developing and promulgating an attractive egalitarian ethos.

---

[1] Roughly speaking, the reason for focusing specifically on the *vastly* wealthy is that there clearly are *some* benefits of being very wealthy, and some reasons why it might be bad for one to be vastly wealthy, which don't apply to merely being very wealthy. My thought is that there are greatly decreasing marginal benefits involved in going from very to vastly wealthy, as well as additional harms, so that the case for vast wealth being overall harmful is easier to make than the one for being merely very wealthy. This leaves open the question of whether being very wealthy is overall good or bad for someone.

My fellow ethicists and political philosophers in the analytic tradition have mostly dismissed the possibility that, outside of special circumstances, having too much wealth might be seriously bad for you.[2] I think (Rawls 1999, p. 123)) is representative when, defending the claim that the parties in the original position would want to maximize their share of material resources, he writes:

> I have assumed throughout that the persons in the original position are rational. But I have also assumed that they do not know their conception of the good. This means that while they know that they have some rational plan of life, they do not know the details of this plan...How, then, can they decide which conceptions of justice are most to their advantage?...I postulate that they...assume that they normally prefer more primary social goods rather than less. Of course, it may turn out, once the veil of ignorance is removed, that some of them for religious or other reasons may not, in fact, want more of these goods. But from the standpoint of the original position, it is rational for the parties to suppose that they do want a larger share, since in any case they are not compelled to accept more if they do not wish to.

When Rawls talks about "advantage" here, he is speaking, not directly about one's well-being, but about one's ability to pursue one's rational plan of life. However, for Rawls, these are intimately related; see Part III of *A Theory of Justice*, which winds up endorsing a kind of desire-satisfaction view. (Ultimately, the things I say about the effects on our well-being of vast wealth according to desire satisfaction views should apply to Rawls' own view of our well-being, as well as to the question of whether vast wealth is helpful or harmful in our pursuit of our rational plan of life). Besides this, two things are notable about this passage. One is that Rawls apparently thinks that extreme wealth could frustrate our preferences only if we have unusual preferences, such as wanting to be a religious ascetic. The other is that he thinks that, even if having more wealth *would* frustrate our preferences, this wouldn't be very concerning, since we could just refuse it.

The first point will be a major target throughout the rest of this paper. As far as the second point is concerned, Rawls is relying on a standard conception of economic rationality according to which agents always have all the information relevant to satisfying their preferences and always pursue their preferences in the most efficient manner:

> The concept of rationality invoked here...is the standard one familiar in social theory. Thus in the usual way, a rational person is thought to have a coherent set of preferences between the options open to him. He ranks these options according to how well they further his purposes; he follows the plan which will satisfy more of his desires rather than less, and which has the greater chance of being successfully executed (Rawls 1999, pp. 123–24).

Assuming that well-being consists of satisfying one's preferences (see Section 2), agents who were like this usually couldn't be harmed by excess wealth. As long as no one forced the agent to take it, they could just decline any excess wealth, and if they wound up with a harmful level of wealth (say, by inheriting it as a child, or because their plans changed), then as long as there were no barriers to getting rid of it, they could just give it away. While the parties in the original position are stipulated to be economically rational, however, they are supposed to be the representatives of real human agents, who are not. Real humans do not always know which actions will best fulfill their preferences, and I will argue in Section 3 that, contrary to what many of us suppose, it's plausible that extreme wealth often tends to frustrate many of our most important preferences. Likewise, humans, being susceptible to *akrasia*—weakness of will—often act in ways which they *realize* will needlessly frustrate their preferences (see (Stroud 2014)). Furthermore, as I discuss in the next section, fulfilling your

---

2   Of course, there has been a great deal of discussion about economic inequality more broadly (see, e.g., Lamont and Favor (2013) for an overview). What philosophers have dismissed is the *specific* claim that too much money might be bad for you.

preferences may not always be good for you anyway. Of course, Rawls (as I explain in the final section) realized that actual human agents were not literally economically rational in the sense above; presumably, what he thought was that this conception was *close enough* to actual human behavior, while also being manageably simple, to justify the assumption for purposes of the original position. Part of what I hope to show here, however, is that, when it comes to the topic at hand, this may very well be false, and at any rate can't just be *assumed*.

Against the consensus, a few philosophers have considered the possibility that extreme wealth might be harmful. (Wolff (2015, pp. 212–13)) notes that a historically prominent egalitarian tradition does just that:

> ...there is an egalitarian tradition of questioning the value of material resources, and especially the culture of consumption. A good life is one of friendship, creation and appreciation of art and literature, development of creativity, and mutual support... This view, associated with William Morris and John Ruskin, is that material resources are a snare and a distraction...

And Harry Frankfurt, in his recent book *On Inequality*, writes that:

> In addition to the incidence of poverty, another part of our current economic disorder is that while many of our people have too little, quite a number of others have too much. The very rich have, indisputably, a great deal more than they need in order to live active, productive, and comfortable lives. In extracting from the economic wealth of the nation much more than they require in order to live well, those who are excessively affluent are guilty of a kind of economic gluttony...
>
> Apart from harmful psychological and moral effects upon the lives of the gluttons themselves, economic gluttony presents a ridiculous and disgusting spectacle. Taken together with the adjacent spectacle of a sizeable class of people who endure significant economic deprivation, and who are as a consequence more or less impotent, the general impression given by our economic arrangements is both ugly and morally offensive (Frankfurt 2015, pp. 3–5).

But neither Wolff nor Frankfurt does much to develop these thoughts; (Frankfurt 2015, 5, fn. 1) explicitly says that while the "moral and psychological problems arising from the fact that some people have too much are eminently worthy of study and analysis", he will (understandably) instead focus on the "more pressing phenomenon of people who have too little". I attempt to develop and defend the view here.

Furthermore, and perhaps surprisingly, neither Wolff nor Frankfurt takes these as reasons to be concerned about economic inequality *as such*. (Wolff (2015, pp. 212–13)) sympathetically glosses the view he discusses as being that, since material resources are a snare and a distraction, "...those who think that we must equalize resources are missing the point and falling into a form of fetishism." Wolff instead endorses *social* egalitarianism, which posits that people are owed a society in which they relate to others as equals, but that whatever material differences are compatible with this are fine. (Some social egalitarians think that very few material differences are compatible with this, so that social equality requires a substantial degree of economic inequality; see, e.g., (Scheffler 2015). But Wolff's comment about "fetishism" suggests that he doesn't think this). Meanwhile, Frankfurt thinks the problem is not *inequality*, exactly, but that some have so much while others don't have enough. The rest of his book argues that distributive justice has been achieved once everyone has *enough*, where "to say that someone has enough money means—more or less—that he is content, or that it is reasonable for him to be content, with having no more money than he actually has" (Frankfurt 2015, p. 47); past that point, concern because some have more than others "tends to distract [those concerned] from recognizing their most authentic ambitions, which are those that derive from the character of their own lives, and not those that are imposed on them by the conditions in which others happen to live"

(Frankfurt 2015, p. 89). My arguments will imply that those living lives of vast wealth are harmed *both* because they do so while others do not have enough *and* because they do so while having vastly more than the others members of their society, regardless of whether those others have enough. Exactly what this means for egalitarians will be discussed in Section 5.

In the next section, I survey the elements involved in the major philosophical accounts of well-being: hedonism, desire theory, objective list theory, and hybrid theories. In Section 3, I consider the impact of living a life of vast wealth on well-being, arguing that is probably bad (or least not as good as you might think) according to the most plausible versions of any of these theories. In Section 4, I consider the impact of egalitarian distributive policies upon the wealthy, arguing that those living lives of vast wealth would probably tend to be better off in societies which made it harder to do so. In Section 5, I discuss some of the implications for social and political philosophy of the earlier sections. Parts of my argument will be somewhat tentative. At times, I will appeal to empirical judgments which seem plausible to me but which it is hard to be sure about, and at times I will appeal to normative judgments which I don't have adequate space to defend here. Nonetheless, I hope to establish that there is a strong case in favor of my conclusions.

2. Accounts of Well-Being

Philosophers have discussed four major families of theories of *well-being*—of what, fundamentally, makes your life go well or poorly *for you* (see (Parfit 1984), Appendix I for a historically important overview, and (Crisp 2013) for a more recent one). *Hedonists* (e.g., (Crisp 2006)) think that well-being consists of pleasant phenomenal states (such as the pleasing warmth I feel when I rub the bellies of my cats, Apollo and Artemis) and that ill-being consists of nasty ones (such as the sharp pain I feel when Apollo decides he's had enough and scratches me). The more and better the nice experiences you have, the better your life is for you, and vice versa. *Desire theorists* (e.g., (Rawls 1999, chp. 7)) think that well-being consists in the satisfaction of one's desires, or of some subset of one's desires, while ill-being consists in their frustration. Generally, the more and stronger the relevant desires which you satisfy, and the fewer and weaker your relevant frustrated desires are, the better your life is for you.[3] Both hedonists and desire theorists are *subjectivists*, insofar as they think that whether something is good or bad fundamentally depends wholly, in one way or another, on my mental states.

By contrast, *objective list theorists* (e.g., (Griffin 1986)) think that, while pleasure or desire satisfaction may be components of our well-being, other states of affairs can also be intrinsically good or bad for us regardless of the attitudes or hedonic responses we have towards them.[4] There are many candidates for inclusion on the list, and objective list theorists need not claim to have identified all of the list's elements; Derek Parfit (Parfit 1984, p. 499) suggests as paradigmatic objective goods "moral goodness, rational activity, the development of one's abilities, having children and being a good parent, knowledge, and the awareness of true beauty" and as paradigmatic objective list evils "being betrayed, manipulated, slandered, deceived, being deprived of liberty or dignity, and enjoying either sadistic pleasure, or aesthetic pleasure in what is in fact ugly."

Finally, many philosophers (e.g., (Kagan 2009)) are attracted to the thought that there must be some sort of objective element to our well-being, but doubt that anything could be good *for us* while we remain totally cold to it (for a statement of this as a criticism of the objective list theory, see (Railton 1986, p. 9)). These *hybrid theorists* think, that for something to be good for us, it must be true *both* that we have some subjective response to something (such as enjoying it (Kagan 2009) or wanting it, e.g., (Lauinger 2013)) *and* that the thing in question has the right kind of objective value.

---

[3] There are variants of the desire theory which treat some attitude other than desires as important; Heathwood (2014, p. 202) suggests as candidates "favoring something, wanting it, caring about it, valuing it, believing it valuable, liking it, trying to get it, having it as a goal, being fond of it, being for it, having an interest in it, and the like." Nothing about which attitude we pick should make a big difference to my argument, so, for ease, I'll just continue speaking of "desires."

[4] For a similar approach, see James O'Sullivan's account of capabilities theory in his essay in the current volume.

(As Heathwood (2014, p. 207) puts the point, the hybrid theory suggests that "well-being consists in receiving things that (1) the subject has some pro-attitude toward... and that (2) have some value, or special status, independent of these attitudes. One's life goes better not simply when one gets what one wants or likes, but when one is wanting or liking, and getting, *the right things*.")[5] This partition of theories is not logically exhaustive, and the boundaries between them are not always precise,[6] but they give us a good sense of the major lines philosophers have pursued when thinking about well-being.

These theories can all agree that well-being consists in having one of, or some combination of, three things: nice hedonic states, desire satisfaction, and objective goods. Likewise, they agree that ill-being consists in having one of, or some combination of, three things: nasty hedonic states, desire frustration, and objective bads. My method in the next section, then, will be to consider what impact living a life of vast wealth might have on each of these putative components of well-being; we can then use our judgments about the impact on these putative components to determine what the impact will be according to whatever overall theory we endorse. I will argue that, by the metric of any of these components, living a life of vast wealth will probably tend to be bad (or at least only minimally good) for us, and accordingly that living such a life will not be a good bet, regardless of which theory we hold. I hope that what I say will be have fairly broad appeal, but at times I will appeal to points which seem plausible according to my own sympathies (which lie in the direction of an objective list or hybrid theory) but are controversial. Accordingly, I will first say a bit about my views on how these different components relate to well-being.

I think it's clear that hedonic states play *some* role in our well-being; that agony is intrinsically bad for us, for instance, seems about as clear to me as anything. On the other hand, I'm somewhat skeptical that desires are intrinsically important for well-being. The mere fact that I desire something does not seem to me to be the right sort of thing to *explain why* that thing's good for me; rather, I think I desire things because (among other reasons) I think that, for reasons other than the fact that I desire them, they would be good for me and therefore *worth* desiring. (This is a statement of what's often called the "direction of fit objection"—intuitively, I desire things because they're good for me, not the other way around). While it's often true that getting something I desire would be good for me, and would not be good for me if I did *not* desire that thing, I think the most plausible cases of that form can be explained by other considerations (for instance, the fact that getting what I want usually brings me enjoyment; see (Parfit and Scheffler 2011, pp. 65–70) for a series of arguments which can be adapted to support my view).[7] But my view is in the minority, so that it will be important to consider which is the most plausible way to flesh out a view on which desires are intrinsically important to our well-being. This turns out to be a complicated question.

We could hold that *any* time I have a desire and it is satisfied, this is intrinsically good for me. But this isn't plausible. At the very least, we should say that only things which I desire *in themselves*, rather than instrumentally, can contribute to my well-being. If I want a hat only because I think it will make me look cool, and I care about looking cool in and of itself, then what matters in itself is only looking cool. (If, for some reason, I can't get the hat, but I look cool for some other reason, the fact that I didn't get the hat wouldn't matter). I also think it is plausible that the only desires which intrinsically matter for me are those which I have *and would still have in some suitably idealized condition* (e.g., one where I was fully informed about the relevant matters, instrumentally rational, and mentally healthy. Exactly how to spell out the idealized condition in question is controversial, and I won't attempt to sort it out here). For instance, if I want to marry someone who is cheating on me but I wouldn't want

---

[5]   Hybrid theorists have a number of options about what constitutes *harm*; see Shelly Kagan's (as far as I know, unpublished) paper "What is Ill-being when Well-being is Enjoying the Good?"

[6]   E.g., Heathwood (2006) argues, I think implausibly, that the most credible versions of hedonism and the desire theory are actually the same theory.

[7]   The section is about desire theories of *reasons*, rather than well-being, but most of the suggestions have relevant analogues.

to if I knew the truth, then it seems plausible to think that fulfilling my goal of marrying that person won't be intrinsically good for me.

There is also a further question about the *scope* of the desires whose satisfaction or frustration might directly affect contribute to my well-being. Parfit 1984, p. 494) suggests that if I briefly meet a stranger, and altruistically form a desire that the stranger's disease be cured, it's implausible that the stranger's later being cured, unbeknownst to me, is good *for me*. The idea here would be that, for a desire to make a difference to *my* well-being, it must be *about my life* in some important way. However, people sympathetic to this view will often agree that *some* desires which are *largely* about things other than my own life can affect my well-being. Parfit himself (Parfit 1984, p. 495) suggests that the desire to be a successful parent is about your life in the relevant way, even though whether the desire is satisfied will depend largely on how the lives of other people (namely, your children) go. Heathwood (2014, p. 215) suggests that the desire theorist should expand the scope even further, allowing your desire that your favorite sports team win to intrinsically affect your well-being, even though, assuming you don't *play* for the team, this is about your life only in a very tenuous sense. I won't take a stance on which, exactly, is the most plausible way to draw the line is question. But I do think that, if desires intrinsically affect our well-being, desires such as those that I help, and not harm, my loved ones and my community will do so.

Finally, there are the objective goods. As my remarks have already indicated, I am convinced that there must at least be some objective *element* to well-being. Nozick (1974, pp. 42–45) asks us to imagine the experience machine, a virtual reality device capable of stimulating our brain so as to delude us into thinking that we are accomplishing great deeds, forming blissful relationships, and so on, all while we are really closed up in a machine somewhere. I do not think a life spent entirely in the experience machine would be *terrible* for you. (If I wanted to wreak terrible vengeance on my foe, putting him in the experience machine to experience intense but delusional ecstasy would not really be my first choice). But I (and Nozick) think it is clear that an otherwise similar life in which you *really* did those great things would be better for you; accordingly, merely having nice subjective experiences is not enough for an ideally fulfilled life. Desire theorists can avoid saying that someone in the experience machine has an ideal life, since many of their desires are actually unfulfilled. (What I desire, presumably, is to do great deeds, form blissful relationships, and so on, not *just* to *feel* like I am doing those things). But Rawls has us imagine a "grass-counter", whose only intrinsic desire is to "count blades of grass in various geometrically shaped areas such as park squares and well-trimmed lawns" (Rawls 1999, p. 379) and who then successfully does that a lot. We can say that he holds onto the desires after becoming fully informed, instrumentally rational, free of pathologies, and so on. Rawls is willing to bite the bullet and say that, if he gets to spend lots of time counting grass, the grass-counter's life is good for him. But I doubt many of us are tempted to envy him; his life seems to me at *most* as good as one in the experience machine, depending on how much he enjoys what he's doing. So merely getting what you desire, even if that is also accompanied by pleasure, is not enough for an ideal life, either. I think examples like these can undermine any purely subjective theory of well-being, showing that it makes a difference whether we are really engaged with things of objective value.

This, alone, doesn't tell us whether we should favor an objective list or hybrid theory of well-being. I am fairly sympathetic to thinking that certain things can *harm* us, whether or not we care about them. If you don't care about the fact that your child hates you, this may well make you *worse*, rather than better, off. I'm more sympathetic to the thought that even things of objective value can't be *good* for you if you're totally cold to them, though I'm uncertain. On the other hand, I do think that pleasure can be good for us, even if it's taken in something without objective value. For instance, I doubt there is anything objectively valuable about making toy airplanes dogfight, but if I enjoy doing that (which, in fact, I do,) doing that seems good for me. However, while I think pleasure can be good for me even if taken in something without objective value, I also think that the contribution pleasure ultimately makes to my well-being can be affected by the objective value of what the pleasure is taken in. So, for instance, if my pleasure was taken in something of objective value rather than in making the toy planes dogfight, maybe that would be better for me. Meanwhile, malicious pleasure taken in the suffering of some innocent stranger certainly seems less good for me than harmless pleasure taken in playing with the planes, if the former sort of pleasure is even intrinsically good for me at all.[8] For similar reasons, I think we should say that the intrinsic contribution to our well-being made by satisfying desires likewise varies with the objective value of the thing desired, if desire satisfaction makes an intrinsic contribution to our well-being.

I will not attempt to come up with any comprehensive list of objective goods; I have no such list. Instead, I will simply note what I think are some plausible candidates, as they become relevant. Of course, that there are objective elements to our well-being does *not* imply that there is any one, unique way of living which is best for people. Suppose, for instance, that appreciation of beauty isn't really my thing. There are plenty of other objectively valuable things with which to engage, and the fact that any plausible theory will put some at least some weight on what I desire or enjoy means that pursuing those will probably be better for me. Nonetheless, if something prevents me from fully engaging with a wide range of important objective goods, then it seems plausible that this will reduce my well-being, especially if they are things which people tend to enjoy or care a lot about.

3. Living a Life of Vast Wealth

3.1. Hedonic States

There are some saints who rejoice in physical hardship. For the rest of us, pleasant hedonic states tend to have material preconditions. For a pleasant life, one usually needs at least some food, shelter, clean water, and so on. Once one's physical needs are met, wealth can allow one to provide for one's loved ones, gain peace of mind through financial security, obtain better medical care and engage in pleasurable leisure activities and stimulating projects. But there will clearly be a point at which this levels off. Barring extenuating circumstances, a member of the upper middle class in a modern Western nation can easily enjoy a material standard of living that, in most respects, vastly exceeds that available to *literally* anyone in the world throughout the vast majority of human history. There is clearly some sort of limit to how much pleasure one can get from material goods, at least given a certain level of technological development: one's food can't be but so tasty, one's environment can't be but so temperate, one's pillows can't be but so comfortable, and one's gizmos can't fit but so many whirligigs. Consider Buffett (2010) statement regarding his decision to give away the vast majority of his fortune:

> More than 99% of my wealth will go to philanthropy during my lifetime or at death. Measured by dollars, this commitment is large. In a comparative sense, though, many individuals give more to others every day.

> Millions of people who regularly contribute to churches, schools, and other organizations thereby relinquish the use of funds that would otherwise benefit their own families. The dollars these people drop into a collection plate or give to United Way mean forgone movies, dinners out, or other personal pleasures. In contrast, my family and I will give up nothing we need or want by fulfilling this 99% pledge...

> This pledge will leave my lifestyle untouched and that of my children as well. They have already received significant sums for their personal use and will receive more in the future.

---

[8]   There are two ways to think about what's happening in these cases. One is to say that the value for me of the state of affairs *my experiencing pleasure* changes depending on what the pleasure is taken in. The other is to say that the value of the state of affairs *my experiencing pleasure* is constant regardless of what the pleasure is taken in, but that the value for me of the state of affairs *my experiencing pleasure in some innocent stranger's suffering* is less the sum of the values for me of the states of affairs *my experiencing pleasure* and *some innocent stranger suffering*. (For a relevant discussion, see (Dancy 2004, chp. 10)). This is a technical point without practical implications for us here. I think the latter view is correct, but will sometimes speak as if the former view is true, just because doing so is easier.

They live comfortable and productive lives. And I will continue to live in a manner that gives me everything that I could possibly want in life.

Empirical evidence suggests that the average American's *overall evaluation* of how well their life is going continues to improve into higher income levels (Kahneman and Deaton 2010). (This is what we would expect if they *believe* that having more money increases well-being, whether or not it does). However, their day-to-day evaluation of their emotional states—of "the frequency and intensity of experiences of joy, fascination, anxiety, sadness, anger, and affection that make one's life pleasant or unpleasant" (Kahneman and Deaton 2010, p. 16489)—stops increasing somewhere around the decidedly middle-class amount of $75,000 a year (Kahneman and Deaton 2010, p. 16489). Even up to this point, increased income seems to increase happiness primarily by making it easier to cope with life's misfortunes, rather than by, say, allowing one to buy nicer things. (That is to say, as one approaches $75,000, it's not so much that one's baseline level of happiness increases as it is that that the *decreases* in happiness caused by things like divorces or illnesses are less pronounced (Kahneman and Deaton 2010, p. 16489)).

These data do not focus on the *vastly* wealthy, however. One could speculate that perhaps emotional well-being begins increasing again after some threshold is reached. Maybe certain, extremely expensive things are just far more fun than any cheaper items. But I see no particular reason to think that's true. We could speculate, I think with at least as much intuitive plausibility, that vast wealth tends to add stress to one's life, and so to make one worse off by the standard of hedonic well-being. After all, one has more to keep track of and more to potentially lose. This is suggested by Buffett's remark that:

> Some material things make my life more enjoyable; many, however, would not. I like having an expensive private plane, but owning a half-dozen homes would be a burden. Too often, a vast collection of possessions ends up possessing its owner. The asset I most value, aside from health, is interesting, diverse, and long-standing friends.

Additionally, in some cases, there are fairly concrete reasons for thinking that, by the metric of hedonic well-being, one will be made worse off by vast wealth. For instance, I'll discuss in the next section the fact that extreme wealth may tend to have negative effects on one's personal relationships. A vast body of research (e.g., (Feeney and Collins 2015)) suggests that healthy relationships are an important component of emotional well-being. So, I think that, if anything, the evidence makes it more likely that there tends to be a *negative* impact on one's emotional well-being as income continues to increase.

Furthermore, if there are hedonic benefits that come with living a life of vast wealth, it's plausible to think that these will primarily come as a result of *comparative*, rather than absolute, advantages. That is to say, the pleasure will come as a result of favorably comparing the amount of money you have, or what you consume, to the amount of money you had or what you were consuming in the past, or to what the other people in your social circle have or consume. (see (Frank 2011)). If, as I suggested earlier, the contribution which pleasure makes to our well-being depends on what it's taken in, it's not clear to me that pleasure taken just in having material advantages over others will be of much benefit to us. Furthermore, implementing egalitarian distributive policies will likely leave many of these comparative advantages in place; unless the policies are *very* radical, they will allow some to be wealthier than others, and will allow people to become wealthier throughout the course of their lives. If the vastly wealthy benefit from these comparative advantages, the fact that many of them will be left in place, even as the absolute amount of wealth available to the vastly wealthy decreases, will help blunt whatever negative impact egalitarian distributive policies might have on them.

As far as I'm aware, then, there is no direct research on the usual hedonic impact of living a life of vast wealth, as opposed to living a comfortable upper-middle class life, or a merely very wealthy life. However, I think there no particular reason to expect it to be positive, and some reason to expect it be negative. By the metric of hedonic states, living a life of vast wealth at least doesn't seem to be a particularly smart bet. Further, to the extent that there are hedonic advantages from living a life of vast wealth, it seems plausible to think that many of them will not be severely negatively impacted by egalitarian distributive policies.

3.2. Desire Satisfaction and Objective Goods

People who believe in objective goods tend to think that they are the things we would desire for ourselves if we were fully informed, rational, mentally healthy, and so on. Meanwhile, desire theorists tend to think the things we would usually desire if fully informed, etc. are those on the objective list. This isn't a coincidence; part of the reason for adding the conditions about full information and the rest to the desire theory are to allow it to accommodate the common sense intuitions about what sorts of things are usually good for us which objectivists rely on in developing their lists of goods. (There is probably not any plausible way for the desire theorist to rule out, in principle, people like the grass-counter, whose desires are fixed on seemingly pointless and arbitrary things despite being fully informed, etc. But by adding idealization conditions, and by also claiming that most of us wouldn't want stuff like that if we met those conditions, desire theorists can say that their theory gives the intuitively correct answer as to what would be good for us in the vast majority of normal cases). Because of this tendency to agree, it will be convenient to discuss desire satisfaction and objective goods alongside one another. I will begin by discussing some possible ways in which living a life of vast wealth might be good for us by these measures, and will then discuss some ways in which it might be bad. Of course, there is no way to consider every possible benefit or harm which might result; instead, I'll simply note what occur to me as the major ones.

3.2.1. Possible Benefits

Some people pretty clearly desire vast wealth for its own sake. They want, for instance, to grow their already tremendous fortunes, not because there is any conceivable *use* for their money, but just because they desire more money. I'm not aware of any philosopher who has claimed that living a life of vast of wealth is *in itself* objectively valuable; on the contrary, objectivists have often asserted that money is *only* instrumentally valuable (see, e.g., I-II.Q2.A2 of the *Summa Theologica*). As for desire satisfaction, there are three things to be said. One is that if we think that the value of satisfying a desire varies with whether the thing desired is objectively valuable, then satisfying this desire does not seem likely to be very valuable. The second is that I doubt many people really would maintain this desire if fully informed, rational, and mentally healthy. This would mean realizing and internalizing the fact that this kind of life is (as I discussed above) not likely to improve one's emotional well-being and has the drawbacks I discuss below, and nonetheless holding onto the desire. This does not strike me as a typical reaction. The third point to make is that how strongly we intrinsically desire various levels of wealth is shaped by how much others in our society have, and how much we have right now. It may, then, again be the case that egalitarian distributive policies would not harm the vastly wealthy on this score, since their desires would adjust to be for levels of wealth which were achievable under the egalitarian scheme. (At least, this might be true for those *raised* under the egalitarian scheme; it may not be true for a vastly wealthy person as an egalitarian scheme is implemented). Similar remarks apply if someone desires, not an absolute amount of money, but just to have as much or more money than others.

Someone might also desire financial security for themselves and their loved ones, and someone might likewise think that providing our loved ones with such security can itself be an intrinsic good for us, even if we don't wind up needing it. This strikes me as fairly reasonable. However, while it's hard to say *precisely* how much financial security is enough, it seems safe to say that the vastly wealthy have achieved this level *many, many* times over. Someone with just nineteen million dollars has enough to give themselves a $75,000 annual stipend from 2017 until the USS Enterprise returns from the successful completion of the five-year voyage of exploration portrayed in *Star Trek: The Original*

Series.[9] Someone who, having that much—or even any significant fraction of that much—continued to pursue the accumulation of wealth for reasons of financial security would be carrying a reasonable precaution to a pathological degree.

Better candidates for benefits might involve things like aesthetic or cultural engagement. Vastly wealthy people can easily travel without the hassle most of us face, since they can do things like buying or renting private jets; they can feel at home in foreign countries, since they can literally own homes there; they can buy the originals of important works of art; and so on.[10] I can understand these things being candidates for objective goods, and I can understand finding them appealing even if you think they probably won't add much more pleasure to your life. In addition, there may be other good things which are part of such a lifestyle and which I haven't imagined. (Admittedly, never having lived that way, it might be hard for me to imagine all the perks). But these potential benefits must be balanced against the potential harms which I discuss next.

There are also some goods which are difficult for upper-middle class people to afford, but easily available to *both* very wealthy *and* vastly wealthy people. An anonymous referee suggests that I should count "having access to the most recent (and hence very expensive) medical care if one needs it" and "university education for all one's children's at the world's best universities, without putting your children in debt" as being among the benefits of vast wealth. Clearly, these sound appealing. However, they are also usually easily affordable for people who are "merely" multi-millionaires, without being vastly wealthy (in my semi-technical sense). If things like this outweigh whatever harms may be associated with being merely very wealthy, then this would be an argument for being very wealthy, but *not* for being vastly wealthy: one could have these benefits while avoiding those harms, discussed in Section 3.2.2, which apply to the very but not vastly wealthy. It would be fine for purposes of my argument if there is *some* much lower level of wealth at which vastly wealthy people would, *ceteris paribus*, tend to be much better off (or at least not much worse off,) though there is a further question about which level would be optimal.

3.2.2. Possible Harms

I think there are a number of ways in which living a life of vast wealth might be harmful by the metrics of desire satisfaction or objective goods. I will consider five here. Some of these only involve an increased statistical chance of some bad outcome obtaining, while others are more or less inherent to living a life of vast wealth in a way that makes them very difficult to avoid, at least in circumstances like ours. The first is that, in living a life of vast wealth, one is complicit in the perpetrating of inequalities which (it is plausible to think) have disastrous effects upon one's society. There is a strong case to be made that severe inequality in income and wealth hinders economic growth, weakens democratic institutions, erodes social trust, undermines the rule of law, and leads to a wide variety of poor social outcomes, such as worsened health and higher crimes rates (Stiglitz 2012; Wilkinson and Pickett 2010; Schlozman in the present volume). Even a very wealthy person who doesn't engage in the most flagrant behaviors driving this process—by, say, using their money to gain political influence—still contributes to this process to some degree by claiming wealth and income which might otherwise be more evenly divided. Likewise, they still benefit, in a way most of us find unsavory, from a state of affairs which is detrimental to society as a whole. The complicity in harm is especially pronounced when the money in question is gained through rent-seeking, since, in those cases, there is not any countervailing social benefit produced.

Most of us do not want to be complicit in bringing harm on our society or our communities. It's not just that we desire, on our community's behalf, that it not come to harm, though hopefully we do

---

9   Nineteen million dollars divided by seventy-five thousand dollars is 253.333..., meaning it could run from 2017 until a few months into 2271. The Enterprise's mission lasts from 2265–2270.
10 I'm grateful to Paul Weithman for pressing me on this point.

desire that; we also desire, *for ourselves,* that we not be the agents of that harm. (Suppose you learned that something bad had befallen your country; suppose you learned, further, that you were partly responsible for that bad thing. Wouldn't you feel even worse after learning the new information?) In addition, being complicit in this kind of harm seems like a plausible candidate for an objective bad. Accordingly, such complicity is likely to be bad for us by the metrics of desire satisfaction and objective considerations.

Second, extreme wealth seems to have a corrosive effect on one's character. Having a bad character is a plausible candidate for an objective bad, and most of us desire to have a good, and not a bad, character. Again, it isn't just that, from a disinterested moral perspective, we want everyone to be virtuous, and therefore want ourselves to be virtuous as well (though this may also be true). It's that we want, *for ourselves,* to be a certain kind of person. (Imagine the difference in your reaction from realizing that you possess a serious character flaw about which you had deceived yourself versus your reaction at merely learning that some stranger who you'd never met possessed that flaw). Thus, by either of the two metrics considered here, it seems plausible that being vicious will be bad for us.

Kate Ward has argued from a theological perspective that wealth grants the condition of hyperagency which can interfere with the pursuit of virtues like humility and justice (Ward 2016). There is also a substantial body of empirical work on more mundane vices which are associated with being rich. Despite having more to spare than poorer people and (due to the possibility of tax deductions) experiencing less of a financial marginal cost with each dollar they give, richer people tend to give a substantially lower percentage of their income to charity than poorer people; furthermore, when the rich *do* give, they are more likely to give to relatively morally trivial causes that primarily benefit themselves and other rich people, such as art museums, and less likely to give to organizations that actually help those in need (Independent Sector 2001; Stern 2013). These results are reflected in experimental situations, where lower class individuals are more generous to anonymous strangers (Piff et al. 2010). (It is true that, in recent years, hundreds of billionaires have pledged to give away half of their fortunes as part of an effort spearheaded by Bill Gates and Warren Buffett. But the substantial majority of signatories appear to enjoy the positive publicity without actually fulfilling the requirements of the pledge; see (Coffey 2015)).

Additionally, the wealthy score higher on personality tests intended to measure narcissism and a sense of entitlement (Piff 2013) and, at least in some experimental situations, appear to be less trusting (Piff et al. 2010). They exhibit significantly lower levels of compassion and are less empathetic to the point of being worse at reading other people's facial expressions (Kraus et al. 2012). Richer people are more likely to cut off other cars and pedestrians while driving, more likely to cheat in games with small monetary prizes (despite, obviously, needing the money less), and are more likely to withhold vital information from job candidates in mock interviews (Piff et al. 2013). Priming experimental subjects with feelings of chaos leads makes lower-class participants, relative to upper-class participants, more likely to want to participate in community building activities, while it makes upper-class participants relatively more likely to say that they would sacrifice communal ties for an increased salary and more likely to express agreement with statements like "I feel that money is the only thing I can really count on" and "I believe that time not spent making money is time wasted" (Piff et al. 2012). Additionally, there is good reason to think that these flaws are partly *caused by,* rather than merely correlated with, class, since merely increasing *feelings* of being wealthy in experimental subjects (by asking them to think about people who are poorer than they are) brings out many of the same anti-social behaviors as are found among those who are actually wealthy. For instance, subjects who are so primed tend to eat more candy from a supply they're told is intended for children participating in a later experiment (Piff et al. 2013) (that is, merely feeling wealthy *literally* makes you take candy from children!).

Furthermore, these vices and others may be exacerbated among those who live lives of vast wealth from the start. Willis (2013), part of the family that started the Georgia-Pacific corporation and now a psychotherapist who works with wealthy families, writes that she wiled away her youth because her wealthy upbringing left her lazy and without a drive to engage in meaningful work:

> The biggest curse of intergenerational wealth for me and many other people is the illusion that you don't have to do much with your life... My wandering 20s were an example of too much too soon. My parents wanted me to enjoy the freedom of youth. They meant for my financial ease to be a gift. Unfortunately, it didn't occur to me to do anything with my life...

> Recently, a client said to me, "When you're raised by rich people you're not taught to do anything." You're not taught to do practical things, because everything is done for you. It's a challenge to hone the skills you need to function outside of that setting.

> Many people who aren't wealthy think it would be great to not have to learn to do anything, or just to learn what one chooses. Perhaps they don't recognize the value of feeling confident and building a purposeful, meaningful life. The only way to get there is to tough out mistakes and failures. Though inheritors are given many things, no one is given a meaningful life. For that we all have to work.

Willis likewise writes that ingratitude is another "curse" of family wealth:

> Ingratitude. We all know what this looks like. It is the attitude of entitlement and arrogance. Ingratitude is insidious, based on fear and anger. It leads to low self-esteem, insecurity and the self-doubt that comes from never having become good at anything.

> When I was in my 20s, ingratitude ruled my life. Due to my lack of experience working with others, I thought everything had to be exactly the way I wanted it. Planning for my first wedding, at age 29, I threw a fit that there were no gardenias available in January. I was inconsolable. The florist provided some kind of white flowers, as close as they could come to the gardenias I coveted, and I was furious.

Of course, we could find many other stories to the same effect. The point here is not to romanticize poverty, which puts strains of its own on one's character. The point is instead that after one no longer faces the constant insecurity, or social stigma, or physical threats, or other factors which produce such strain, accumulating substantially *more* opens one up to the vices discussed above. From the perspective of well-being, this may be dangerous.

Third, living a life of vast wealth often has deleterious effects both on one's personal relationships and on one's relationship with the broader communities which one is a part of. Most of us value these relationships, and such relationships are plausible candidates for being objectively important, so, again, whether these relationships are healthy or dysfunctional may be important to our well-being. It's easy to see what sorts of what bad impacts developing the negative character traits just described might have on one's personal relationships. For instance, (Kraus et al. 2012, p. 559) argue that even among intimates such as romantic partners, the wealthy are significantly more likely to form what they call "exchange relationships"—in which "individuals seek to trade relationship benefits with partners (e.g., emotional support, responding to needs) for equal value, and they keep track of costs and benefits within their relationships"—and less likely to simply respond to the needs of their loved ones without trying to get something out of it.

Cohen (2009, pp. 5–6) contrasted the norms governing a camping trip—in which people willingly cooperate without trying to maximize their own advantage—with the exchange norms which govern market transactions:

> You could imagine a camping trip where everybody asserts her rights over the pieces of equipment, and the talents, that she brings, and where bargaining proceeds with respect to who is going to pay what to whom to be allowed, for example, to use a knife to peel the potatoes, and how much he is going to charge others for those now peeled potatoes that he bought in an unpeeled condition from another camper, and so on. You could base

a camping trip on the principles of market exchange and the strictly private ownership of shared facilities.

Now, most people would hate that.

Cohen goes on to argue that camping trip norms, rather than market norms, ought to govern the economy as a whole. *That* is supposed to be the controversial part of the argument; he plausibly supposes that no one would really want to run a camping trip as an exchange relationship. Yet the wealthy, whatever they want, are apparently more likely to form exchange relationships, not only on camping trips, but also everywhere else.

In concrete terms, these problems sometimes show up in the family lives of the extremely wealthy. Willis (2013) suggests that, within familial contexts, extreme wealth tends to lead to "too much financial focus:"

> This focus can be so big that families neglect human, intellectual and social capital in the family. As a result, there's no balance. Instead, the emphasis is on the dollars, the assets, the strategies and the money managers. Family meetings only cover financial concerns. Some of my wealthy clients have spent years looking for a way to bring up family communication, relationships, and effective parenting.

Indeed, there exists an entire industry of books by counselors and wealth advisors (e.g., (Willis 2012); (Collier 2012); (Lombardo 2012)) aimed wholly or largely at helping the extremely wealthy deal with the potential impact of wealth on their families. (One of these books (Lombardo 2012) has the unsettling subtitle "Why Rich Kids Hate Their Parents!") And many of the wealthy themselves seem to recognize the potential problem; one study focusing primarily on families with one hundred million dollars or more in assets, almost half of inheritors were "highly concerned" that their inheritance would negatively impact their personal relationships (Frank 2012a). (I am not aware of any data suggesting that this makes them noticeably more likely to turn down or give away their fortunes, however).

Many of us also value the relations we stand in with members of communities—churches, schools, cities, states, countries, religions, and so on—which stretch far beyond the group of people we directly interact with. (This is often especially evident after tragedies, where members of the affected community express a sense of kinship and solidarity with one another, even if the community is far too large for all of the people in it to have met). These sorts of relations can also be strained by living a life of vast wealth. In some cases, this is because, as mentioned above, living such a life involves active complicity in harming the community. But it can also be because living such a life cuts one off from certain shared experiences and struggles. As Cohen (2009, pp. 35–36) notes:

> We cannot enjoy full community, you and I, if you make and keep, say, ten times as much money as I do, because my life will then labor under challenges that you will never face, challenges that you could help me cope with, but do not, because you keep your money. To illustrate. I am rich, and I live an easy life, whereas you are poor... You have to ride the crowded bus every day, whereas I pass by you in my comfortable car. One day, however, I must take the bus, because my wife needs the car. I can reasonably complain about that to a fellow car driver, but not to you. I can't say to you: "It's awful that I have to take the bus today." There is a lack of community between us of just the sort that naturally obtains between me and the fellow car-driver. And it will show itself in many other ways, for we enjoy widely different powers to care for ourselves, to protect and care for our offspring, to avoid danger, and so on.[11]

We might quibble over the degree to which a difference in income of ten times will generate this lack of community. But if I make *tens of thousands of times* as much as my compatriots, it will be hard for me

---

[11] For more (in a very different context) on how shared adversity can deepen relationships, see (Ekstrom 2013), esp. p. 271.

to even *know about*, much less share in, the struggles of ordinary people. In an important way, I am alienated.[12]

Fourth, many religious traditions suggests that one's spiritual life is likely to be harmed by vast wealth. Christianity is my religion, and the only one I am really qualified to discuss, and this is certainly the view of the New Testament. Wealth is viewed as competing with God for one's affections, and as an impediment to being fully dedicated to carrying out God's will (e.g., Matthew 6:19–24). The New Testament goes as far as to promise apocalyptic judgment against the wealthy, sometimes in lurid terms (e.g., James 5:1–5). But even setting aside questions of *punishment*, nearly any religion views spiritual fulfillment as the best thing possible for a human being, and anything which prevents such fulfillment as to be avoided, even at great cost. If this is right, and if living a life of vast wealth is in tension with such fulfillment, then such a life will be a tragedy.

Fifth, it is possible that those living lives of vast wealth tend thereby to harm their loved ones, and especially their children, by facilitating their loved ones living lives of vast wealth. I've discussed a number of ways in which living such a life may be harmful, and have suggested that some of these harms may be particularly pronounced for those who are born into vast wealth. The vastly wealthy tend to promote their family members living such lives, both by leaving them inheritances and by providing them with plush living conditions, gifts, financial assistance, and so on. They thereby inflict these harms on those they care the most about. The wealthy actually tend to *share* the worry I discuss here, though it doesn't seem to reliably change their behavior. Survey data suggests that eighty-two percent of millionaires want their children to create their own wealth, (Frank 2013), and only thirty-two percent are convinced that their children are responsible enough to handle inheriting their fortunes (Frank 2012b). They nonetheless often leave their children substantial inheritances (Frank 2013), for understandable reasons. (For one thing, it could pretty awkward not to, though some form of akrasia may also play a part). More than four-fifths of millionaires say that raising their children well is their most important goal (Frank 2013), and doing so (and otherwise doing good, and not harm, to one's loved ones) is a plausible candidate for an objective good. This could, then, raise a serious threat to the well-being of those living lives of vast wealth.

My own judgment is that the possible harms surveyed in this section will tend to outweigh the possible benefits. The possible benefits of living a life of vast wealth seem to me to be things which are *nice* but *inessential*. Meanwhile, living such a life may threaten things, such as one's relationships with one's loved ones, community, and God, or one's ability to be a virtuous person, which are among the core constituents of well-being. Accordingly, from the perspective of desire satisfaction or objective goods, I think that living a life of vast wealth will tend to be bad, and perhaps *extremely* bad. But even if we disagree, it at least seems safe to say that, by these metrics, living such a life will tend not to be as good as one might think.

4. Egalitarian Societies

I'll now consider whether those inclined to live lives of vast wealth would do better under a more egalitarian economic scheme which made it prevented them from doing so harder for them to do so, or at least to do so to the same degree. There are several ways in which they might be harmed. First, if some people actually benefit from living lives of vast wealth, their achieving these benefits might be hampered by egalitarian distributive policies.[13] However, the argument of the last section provides two reasons for thinking we shouldn't be too worried about that. The first is that, if the previous sections are correct, living such a life is usually not good for you. The second is that, as I noted, some of the supposed benefits may result from having more than others, or more than one used to have, or

---

[12] Wealthy people also tend to be literally, physically separated from everyone else; see (Florida and Mellander 2015).

[13] For a review of one such policy, the Earned Income Tax Credit, see the essay by Quinn and Cahill in the present volume.

from meeting some socially conditioned standard of wealth, and these benefits (to the extent that they really are benefits) may be left largely intact by egalitarian policies.

Admittedly, there may well be some *short-term* subjective harms imposed upon the vastly wealthy by implementing egalitarian societies. They may be made unhappy by the facts of having their taxes raised, or of having less income than they used to have, or of needing to make some lifestyle adjustments; likewise, these things may frustrate some of their desires.[14] But I suspect that they would adjust, and that these subjective harms would be relatively short-lived. The top marginal tax rate in the United States in 1963 was ninety-one percent (Shiller 2012). Implementing a tax rate anywhere near that today would be unthinkable; even if something like that was somehow made law, the backlash would be tremendous. But I don't see much evidence that wealthy people are all that much happier about paying their taxes now than they were then, or that wealthy Americans are much happier about paying their taxes than are wealthy Europeans who live in countries with much higher tax rates. Given that they will have more than plenty either way, wealthy people seem to adjust to differing economic schemes. (By contrast, the poor do not seem to adapt to poverty (Clark et al. 2013)).[15]

We might also worry that egalitarian policies would prevent or discourage the vastly wealthy from doing things with their money other than keeping it or spending it on themselves, such as giving it to charity or devoting it to socially valuable forms of entrepreneurship. Insofar as these other things can be meaningful forms of engagement with things outside oneself, using money for these might more plausibly be thought to contribute positively to one's well-being. Remember that, at the beginning, I said I would take no stand on people who use most of their money for things like this. However, people living lives of vast wealth often use *some* of their money for things like this. It might be thought that, the less post-tax income and wealth they have, the greater the marginal cost (in terms of giving up stuff they want, or whatever) they perceive themselves to experience from charitable giving, so that higher tax rates would deter activities like this. If activities like this promote one's well-being, this might harm them. Further, insofar as these things produce more social value than whatever other people would have done with the money, we would lose out on the added social value these activities provide. However, economic policy can also provide forces which push in the other direction. For instance, if people are allowed to deduct charitable donations or entrepreneurial expenses from their taxes, then higher tax rates may *encourage* people to put their money towards these things, since the marginal economic cost of doing so would be lower (due to the attendant tax deductions being higher (see (Shiller 2012)). Of course, the net result will depend on the specifics of the case and the exact sort of egalitarian policies we have in mind. But the point is just that, even granting the presuppositions of this worry, it may not be as big a problem as it might at first appear.

On the other hand, there are a number of ways in which these people might be better off in a more egalitarian society. If I'm correct in thinking that living lives of vast wealth tends to be harmful, an egalitarian scheme would prevent those harms. But an egalitarian society might also promote public

---

[14] People are substantially more bothered by losing money they already have than by failing to gain additional money, as the literature on "loss aversion" in behavioral economics (e.g., (Kahneman et al. 1991)) has shown.

[15] The philosophical literature on "adaptive preferences" shows us that sometimes, the fact that someone will adjust to a hardship does not make things much better. If, say, a member of a marginalized group, believing that they will never gain basic rights, decides, sour-grapes style, that they don't want such rights anyway, or never aspires to having such rights to begin with, this doesn't seem to make the denial of basic rights any less harmful or any more morally justifiable. It might be thought that appealing to the fact that the vastly wealthy will adjust is objectionable in a way analogous to appealing to the fact that some members of marginalized may adjust. But the case for being worried about adaptive preferences is strongest when adapting one's preference involves giving up a desire for a basic constituent of well-being, or to something which forms a core part of one's identity. Being content with merely having *plenty* of money is hardly like this. So, for instance, Serene Khader (2011, p. 42), appealing to an objectivist understanding of well-being, suggests that adaptive preferences are problematic when they are "(1) preferences inconsistent with basic flourishing that are (2) formed under conditions unconducive to basic flourishing and (3) that we believe people might be persuaded to transform upon normative scrutiny of their preferences and exposure to conditions more conducive to flourishing." But learning to be content while living under the sort of economic scheme possessed by, say, the European social democracies does not meet any of these conditions. (If anything, if the argument of this paper is correct, the opposite is true!)

goods, or reduce social dysfunction, in ways which benefit everyone, including the very wealthy. The economist Robert H. Frank (2012c) suggests a thought experiment:

> Let's say that two societies differ only in their mixes of public and private spending. In one society, lower taxes on the wealthy allow them to drive very fine cars—say, $180,000 Bentleys. The streets and highways in this society, however, are riddled with foot-deep potholes. In the other society, the wealthy pay higher taxes that support well-maintained roads, but drive $120,000 BMWs...

> In which society would the wealthy be happier? Because product-quality improvements cost much more to achieve beyond some point, the absolute quality of a $180,000 car may be only slightly higher than one costing $120,000. Additionally, because not even the most sophisticated automotive suspensions can neutralize deep potholes, it's little wonder that most people think the BMW drivers would be happier, not to mention safer.

In fact, as noted earlier, concrete data shows that material inequality is associated with a wide range of social ills, from worsened health to higher crime (Wilkinson and Pickett 2010, chp. 4–12), and there is reason to think the relationship is at least partly causal (Wilkinson and Pickett 2010, pp. 190–96). These problems disproportionately affect the poor, but many also harm the rich, sometimes in surprising ways. For instance, increased material inequality seems to reduce health and life expectancy, not only for the poor, but also for the rich (Wilkinson and Pickett 2010, p. 84), perhaps for reasons having to do with status anxiety and reduced social trust (Wilkinson and Pickett 2010, chp. 3). Of course, there is plenty of room for further work here. But in light of these considerations, it seems plausible to me that those living lives of vast wealth would tend to be better off, and perhaps *much* better off, under a more egalitarian scheme.

5. Implications

If the argument of the last two sections is correct, then egalitarian economic policies might benefit, not only those at the bottom, but also many of those at the top. There is a further question about whether the government should treat this as a *reason to* implement the egalitarian economic policies. It might be claimed that this would be objectionably paternalistic, insofar as it would involve interfering, ostensibly for their own good, with what the vastly wealthy want to do. It might be claimed that the job of government is not to make people better off, but rather to (say) protect citizens' ability to pursue their own conceptions of the good without the government making judgments about whether their conception of the good is correct or whether they are pursuing it in an efficient way. This worry is strengthened by the fact that one of the considerations to which I appealed in explaining how vast wealth might be harmful was religious; if (as we should) we believe in a liberal society, then we believe that promoting religious goods is not a suitable goal for the government, and so believe that any case for paternalistic intervention would need to do without that consideration.

But keep in mind that it may well be that many of the vastly wealthy would largely agree with the *value* judgments I made above, and that they continue living lives of vast wealth due to empirical ignorance of the consequences, or failure to see the implications of what they know, or weakness of will. Paternalistic intervention in those cases would represent, not the imposition of an alien conception of the good, but rather an attempt to help the people in question better achieve their own aims. If any kind of paternalism is acceptable, it would be this (for what is probably the best defense of paternalism of this sort, see (Conly 2012)), though even that sort is extremely controversial (see some of the essays in (Coons and Weber 2013)). (However, it is worth noting that in our society there is very broad support for many policies which seem to be most naturally interpreted as involving this kind of paternalism, such as seat belt laws). (Rawls 1999, p. 218)) himself thought that the parties in the original position would be open to allowing paternalistic interventions which promote the rational preferences of those interfered with (though, as I mentioned earlier, he is primarily concerned about their rational plans of life, not their well-being *as such*):

It is...rational for them to protect themselves against their own irrational inclinations by consenting to a scheme of penalties that may give them a sufficient motive to avoid foolish actions and by accepting certain impositions designed to undo the unfortunate consequences of their imprudent behavior. For these cases the parties adopt principles stipulating when others are authorized to act in their behalf and to override their present wishes if necessary; and this they do recognizing that sometimes their capacity to act rationally for their good may fail, or be lacking altogether. Thus the principles of paternalism are those that the parties would acknowledge in the original position to protect themselves against the weakness and infirmities of their reason and will in society. Others are authorized and sometimes required to act on our behalf and to do what we would do for ourselves if we were rational, this authorization coming into effect only when we cannot look after our own good. Paternalistic decisions are to be guided by the individual's own settled preferences and interests insofar as they are not irrational, or failing a knowledge of these, by the theory of primary goods.

If my arguments about the implications of the desire satisfaction theory of well-being are correct, then the "settled preferences" of the vastly wealthy would in fact be promoted by egalitarian economic policies. Accordingly, if my arguments have succeeded, then the remark from Rawls which I quoted in the introduction is misguided: past a certain point, the parties in the original position should perhaps consider denying themselves more primary goods.

But apart from all this, it may be possible to take the arguments of earlier chapters as providing a *non-paternalistic* reason to implement egalitarian policies. Here's why: it may be that some vastly wealthy people would prefer, *ceteris paribus*, to live in a more economically egalitarian society, and that they would prefer this *for themselves*, not merely for disinterested reasons. Perhaps they feel this way due to some of the considerations mentioned in this paper. (Of course, they could always *move* to a society with more economic equality, but the fact that they don't doesn't show that they wouldn't, *ceteris paribus*, prefer to live in such a society, since might require them to give up a lot, such as connections to friends, family, and places they've grown to love). However, no vastly wealthy person can make our society an economically egalitarian one simply by relinquishing their own vast wealth. If they simply relinquished their own wealth, they would not experience the increased public goods mentioned in Section 4. Furthermore, recall that there were a number of times in Section 3 when I suggested that certain advantages of being vastly wealthy depended on how wealthy one was *relative* to other very wealthy people; any such advantages would be lost if the people in question gave up their vast wealth while others didn't. These factors mean it may turn out that there are vastly wealthy people who would be better off if *all* the vastly wealthy gave up their vast wealth, and who would prefer that they do so, but who will be rendered worse off if they, so to speak, unilaterally disarm. Enacting egalitarian economic policies to help *them* would not be paternalistic.[16] A rough analogy can be drawn with minimum wage laws. Opponents of such laws sometimes portray them as a kind of paternalism, saying that, if workers want to work for less than the minimum wage, they should be allowed to do so. A response is to say that workers will tend to be better off if *all* workers (perhaps because they are required by law) do not work unless they are paid the minimum wage, but that individual workers will suffer if they hold out for the minimum wage and all other workers do not, since they will simply not get jobs. The minimum wage would then not be a paternalistic policy, but a solution to a kind of coordination problem. It may well still hurt *some* workers, but the defender

---

[16] An anonymous referee for *Religions* suggests another interesting way in which this might work. I noted in Section 3.2.2 that the wealthy often given their children substantial inheritances, against their better judgment. Presumably, part of the reason for this is that social norms put strong pressure on them to do so. It's possible that certain egalitarian policies, like very high estate taxes, might remove this pressure by making it the case that rich people generally *can't* give their children very large inheritances. The fact that others can't do so would then be a benefit to those who don't want to, but are pressured into doing so.

of the minimum wage claims that this is an acceptable consequence. In the same way, an egalitarian might defend egalitarian economic policies, not as a kind of paternalism, but in order to help those vastly wealthy who reasonably prefer living in an economically egalitarian society. Of course, this does not, itself, tell us whether implementing an egalitarian economic policy in order to help those people would be justified. (If nothing else, perhaps it could be part of a case which also had other justifications). The point here has just been to point out that, *if* we take promoting the well-being of citizens as a proper role of government, there are non-paternalistic ways of taking the arguments of this chapter to support egalitarian economic policies.

But setting all that aside, *even if* the arguments of this chapter do not provide any kind of justification for implementing egalitarian economic policies, they nonetheless have interesting implications for egalitarian theory and practice. Here's one. Achieving a stable egalitarian society is not just a matter of working out which laws a just society would pass. It is also a matter of articulating attractive egalitarian norms and promoting those among the members of society. An egalitarian ethos is necessary if egalitarian laws are going to be passed and obeyed, and if people are going to treat one another as equals within the latitude granted by laws. And I think the arguments of the earlier sections can aid in developing and promulgating such an ethos.

In popular political discourse, those concerned about economic inequality are sometimes charged with promoting a "politics of envy"; the claim is that they cater to the unsavory jealousy of some for what the successful have. (For instance, Mitt Romney said as much during the (2012) presidential election Luhby (2012)). Egalitarian philosophers such as Dworkin (1980, p. 285) have sometimes played into this charge by suggesting that the criteria for whether an economic distribution is just is whether it is "envy-free", in the sense of being such that no one would prefer having someone else's bundle of resources rather than their own. Elizabeth Anderson has criticized this view, arguing both that it is "embarrassing for egalitarians" (Anderson 1999, p. 287) and that it is implausible and unattractive:

> If much recent academic work defending equality had been secretly penned by conservatives, could the results be any more embarrassing for egalitarians? Consider how much of this work leaves itself open to classic and devastating conservative criticisms. Ronald Dworkin defines equality as an "envy-free" distribution of resources. This feeds the suspicion that the motive behind egalitarian policies is mere envy....
>
> Envy's thought is "I want what you have." It is hard to see how such wants can generate obligations on the part of the envied. To even offer one's own envy as a reason to the envied to satisfy one's desire is profoundly disrespectful (Anderson 1999, pp. 287, 307).[17]

Anderson thinks that, instead of equality of resources of the sort defended by Dworkin, we should care fundamentally about social equality (or, as she calls it, "democratic equality"). And, like Jonathan Wolff, she thinks social equality with a fairly large degree of economic inequality; for instance, she rejects Rawls' difference principle as too "demanding" (Anderson 1999, p. 326).

But if my view is right, the standard-bearers of economic inequality, those living lives of vast wealth, are generally not in an enviable position. The reasonable attitude towards them, whatever it is, will be something complicated; their situation is at least partly their own doing, and has hurt the rest of society, but has also hurt them. If it became widely accepted that there were good arguments for this view, it would have several implications. One is that there would be an answer to the criticism that concern for economic inequality is driven by envy—namely, that, at least in the case of the vastly wealthy, people are not likely to be envious of them anyway, since their position is widely recognized

---

17 I think Anderson is actually unfair to Dworkin here. The envy test is a *test*; it is supposed to tell us that, when a distribution is envy free, it is just. That doesn't mean that the fact that the distribution is envy free is *why* it is just, or is the reason for aiming at that distribution, and, in fact, I think Dworkin would reject those claims. But this doesn't matter too much, since, if I am right, the envy test fails anyway

to be unenviable. We could thus respond to the anti-egalitarian argument without compromising our commitment to economic equality. A second is that egalitarian philosophers would not be tempted to make embarrassing pronouncements about eliminating envy, and could instead focus on developing and articulating more plausible and attractive justifications for their views. A third is that, to the extent that ordinary people actually *are* envious of those living lives of vast wealth, this might help convince them that living such lives is not something desirable. We would successfully combat envy after all, but by showing it to be misguided rather than by catering to it.

A fourth is that this view might help motivate those living lives of vast wealth to support egalitarianism, rather than impeding it in the pursuit of perceived self-interest. We all know that the very wealthy commonly use their wealth and status in order to protect their ability to lead lives of vast wealth. They use donations to curry favor with politicians, obtain favorable results from regulators using the prospects of cushy corporate jobs (the phenomenon known as "regulatory capture"), fund research that supports their agendas, and so on (see (Oreskes and Conway 2010); (Stiglitz 2012)). In doing these things, they harm the worst-off, exacerbate economic inequality, and corrode the integrity of our democratic institutions. Certain legal steps (such as campaign finance reform) might be able to alleviate some of these problems, but, in a tragic irony, it's difficult to get such measures implemented as long as the problem they're meant to address exists.

However, if a consensus formed that living a life of vast wealth wasn't really desirable anyway, the wealthy might naturally be less inclined to impede the proper functioning of government so as to promote their ability to live such lives. Roughly this point is made by Robert H. Frank when he writes:

> Although big-money donors are a diverse group, many of them want lower tax rates for themselves and less stringent regulations for their businesses—and they've been brilliantly effective in getting them. Their success has increased their incomes still further, allowing them to make even larger contributions and to demand even bigger favors. This vicious circle was strengthened considerably by the Supreme Court's decision in the Citizen's United Case. And so, each year, the possibility of new laws to curb money's influence appears to recede...
>
> Reformers castigate wealthy donors for supporting self-serving policies. But instead, the reformers could call attention to the evidence that the donors themselves would fare better, in purely practical terms, without the tax cuts and deregulation they've been promoting. You don't have to be a cynical economist to believe that the second strategy has brighter prospects (Frank 2012c).

Capitalism has proven extremely effective at harnessing the human inclination to look out for oneself. In doing so it has produced tremendous material prosperity, but also, very often, great economic inequality. However, if the arguments in earlier sections were to become widely endorsed, enlightened self-interest might be harnessed to *promote* economic equality, rather than hinder it.[18] Disseminating arguments like this might then be a useful component in the egalitarian toolbox. I am substantially less sanguine than Frank appears to be about the prospects of converting the wealthy *en masse*. (I'd be happy if we convinced anyone at all). But in an era of increasing inequality, I think we should take what we can get.

6. Conclusions

As mentioned earlier, I do not regard the argument I have presented here as decisive in their present forms. Many of the relevant issues deserve further study. However, I hope to have shown that there is a good case to be made for the conclusions that (1) vast wealth tends to be bad for people, or at least not nearly as good for them as one might think, (2) egalitarian economic policies would probably

---

[18] This way of putting the point was suggested by one of the referees for *Religions*.

tend to benefit vastly wealthy people on balance, and (3) these facts have interesting implications for egalitarian theory and practice.

Acknowledgments: I am grateful to many people for feedback on and discussions of various versions of this paper, including Paul Weithman, David Solomon, Marilie Coetsee, Sylwia Wilczewska, David Jost, Nathan Hershberger, the editors of this volume, participants at the "Growing Apart: the Implications of Economic Inequality" conference at Boston University, the taxi driver who took me to that conference, and two anonymous referees for *Religions*. I am also grateful to my cats, Artemis and Apollo, who did not provide feedback on the paper, but did inspire an example in Section 2, as well as providing emotional support and encouragement during the paper's writing.

Conflicts of Interest: The author declares no conflict of interest.

References

Anderson, Elizabeth. 1999. What is the Point of Equality? *Ethics* 109: 287–337. [CrossRef]

Buffett, Warren. 2010. My Philanthropic Pledge. Available online: Givingpledge.org (accessed on 2 September 2016).

Clark, Andrew E., Conchita D'Ambrosio, and Simone Ghislandi. 2013. Poverty and Well-being: Panel Evidence from Germany. Society for the Study of Economic Inequality Working Papers Series. Available online: http://www.ecineq.org/milano/WP/ECINEQ2013-291.pdf (accessed on 2 September 2016).

Coffey, Brendan. 2015. Pledge Aside, Dead Billionaires Don't Have to Give Away Half Their Fortune. Bloomberg. Available online: http://www.bloomberg.com/news/articles/2015-06-04/as-billionaires-bask-in-glow-of-pledge-giving-half-is-optional (accessed on 2 September 2016).

Cohen, Gerald Allan. 2009. *Why Not Socialism?* Princeton: Princeton University Press.

Collier, Charles. 2012. *Wealth in Families*, 3rd ed. Cambridge: President and Fellows of Harvard College.

Conly, Sarah. 2012. *Against Autonomy: Justifying Coercive Paternalism*. Cambridge: Cambridge University Press.

Christian Coons, and Michael Weber, eds. 2013. *Paternalism: Theory and Practice*. Cambridge: Cambridge University Press.

Creswell, Julie. 2011. Even Funds That Lagged Paid Richly. *New York Times*. Available online: http://www.nytimes.com/2011/04/01/business/01hedge.html (accessed on 26 August 2016).

Crisp, Roger. 2006. *Reasons and the Good*. Oxford: Oxford University Press.

Crisp, Roger. 2013. Well-Being. *Stanford Encyclopedia of Philosophy*. Available online: http://plato.stanford.edu/entries/well-being/ (accessed on 2 September 2016).

Dancy, Jonathan. 2004. *Ethics without Principles*. Oxford: Oxford University Press.

DeNavas-Walt, Carmen, and Bernadette D. Proctor. 2015. Income and Poverty in the United States: 2014. In *United States Census Bureau*. Available online: http://www.census.gov/library/publications/2015/demo/p60-252.html (accessed on 26 August 2016).

Dworkin, Ronald. 1980. What is Equality? Part 2: Equality of Resources. *Philosophy & Public Affairs* 10: 283–345.

Ekstrom, Laura. 2013. A Christian Theodicy. In *The Blackwell Companion to the Problem of Evil*. Edited by Justin P. McBrayer and Daniel Howard-Snyder. Malden: Wiley-Blackwell.

Feeney, Brooke C., and Nancy L. Collins. 2015. A New Look at Social Support: A Theoretical Perspective on Thriving Through Relationships. *Personality and Social Psychology Review* 19: 113–47. [CrossRef] [PubMed]

Florida, Richard, and Charlotta Mellander. 2015. Segregated City: The Geography of Economic Segregation in America's Metros. *Martin Prosperity Institute*. Available online: http://martinprosperity.org/content/segregated-city/ (accessed on 26 April 2017).

Frank, Robert. 2012a. Rich Kids Worry Money Will Strain Family Ties. *CNBC*. Available online: http://www.cnbc.com/id/47726433 (accessed on 2 September 2016).

Frank, Robert. 2012b. Millionaire Parents Say Their Kids Are Unfit to Inherit. *CNBC*. Available online: http://www.cnbc.com/id/47859258 (accessed on 2 September 2016).

Frank, Robert H. 2012c. When Low Taxes Don't Help the Rich. *The New York Times*. Available online: http://www.nytimes.com/2012/10/28/business/how-rich-political-donors-are-hurting-themselves.html (accessed on 2 September 2016).

Frank, Robert. 2013. Wealthy Don't Want to Spoil Kids, but Can't Help It. *CNBC*. Available online: http://www.cnbc.com/id/100367067 (accessed on 2 September 2016).

Frank, Robert. 2015. Top 20 Billionaires Worth as Much as Half of America. *CNBC*. Available online: http://www.cnbc.com/2015/12/04/top-20-billionaires-worth-as-much-as-half-of-america.html (accessed on 26 August 2016).

Frank, Robert H. 2011. *The Darwin Economy: Liberty, Competition, and the Common Good.* Princeton: Princeton University Press.

Frankfurt, Harry. 2015. *On Inequality.* Princeton: Princeton University Press.

Independent Sector. 2001. Giving & Volunteering in the United States: Findings from a National Survey. Available online: http://www.cpanda.org/pdfs/gv/GV01Report.pdf (accessed on 2 September 2016).

Greenstone, Michael, and Adam Looney. 2012. The Uncomfortable Truth about American Wages. *New York Times.* Available online: http://economix.blogs.nytimes.com/2012/10/22/the-uncomfortable-truth-about-american-wages/ (accessed on 26 August 2016).

Griffin, James. 1986. *Well-Being: Its Meaning, Measurement, and Moral Importance.* Oxford: Clarendon Press.

Heathwood, Chris. 2006. Desire Satisfactionism and Hedonism. *Philosophical Studies* 128: 539–63. [CrossRef]

Heathwood, Chris. 2014. Subjective Theories of Well-being. In *The Cambridge Companion to Utilitarianism.* Edited by Ben Eggleston and Dale E. Miller. Cambridge: Cambridge University Press.

Kagan, Shelly. 2009. Well-Being as Enjoying the Good. *Philosophical Perspectives* 23: 253–72. [CrossRef]

Kahneman, Daniel, and Angus Deaton. 2010. High Income Improves Evaluation of Life but not Emotional Well-Being. *Proceedings of the National Academy of Sciences of the United States of America* 103: 16489–93. [CrossRef] [PubMed]

Kahneman, Daniel, Jack L. Knetsch, and Richard H. Thaler. 1991. The Endowment Effect, Loss Aversion, and Status Quo Bias. *The Journal of Economic Perspectives* 5: 193–206. [CrossRef]

Khader, Serene J. 2011. *Adaptive Preferences and Women's Empowerment.* Oxford: Oxford University Press.

Kraus, Michael W., Paul K. Piff, Rodolfo Mendoza-Denton, Michelle L. Rheinschmidt, and Dacher Keltner. 2012. Social Class, Solipsism, and Contextualism: How the Rich are Different from the Poor. *Psychological Review* 119: 546–72.

Lamont, Julian, and Christi Favor. 2013. Distributive Justice. *Stanford Encyclopedia of Philosophy.* Available online: https://plato.stanford.edu/entries/justice-distributive/ (accessed on 26 April 2017).

Lauinger, William. 2013. The Missing Desires Objection to Hybrid Theories of Well-Being. *The Southern Journal of Philosophy* 51: 270–95. [CrossRef]

Lombardo, Franco. 2012. *The Great White Elephant: Why Rich Kids Hate Their Parents!* White Rock: Roper House Publishing.

Luhby, Tami. 2012. Romney: Income Inequality Is Just 'Envy'. *CNN.com.* Available online: http://money.cnn.com/2012/01/12/news/economy/romney_envy/ (accessed on 5 September 2016).

Matthews, Dylan. 2012. Wages Aren't Stagnating, They're Plummeting. *Washington Post.* Available online: http://www.washingtonpost.com/blogs/wonkblog/wp/2012/07/31/wages-arent-stagnating-theyre-plummeting/ (accessed on 14 December 2013).

Nozick, Robert. 1974. *Anarchy, State, and Utopia.* New York: Basic Books.

Oreskes, Naomi, and Erik M. Conway. 2010. *Merchants of Doubt: How a Handful of Scientists Obscured the Truth on Issues from Tobacco Smoke to Global Warming.* New York: Bloomsbury Press.

Parfit, Derek. 1984. *Reasons and Persons.* Oxford: Oxford University Press.

Parfit, Derek, and Samuel Scheffler. 2011. *On What Matters, Volume I.* Oxford: Oxford University Press.

Piff, Paul K. 2013. Wealth and the Inflated Self: Class, Entitlement, and Narcissism. *Personality and Social Psychology Bulletin* 40: 34–43. [CrossRef] [PubMed]

Piff, Paul K., Michael W. Kraus, Stèphane Cotè, Bonnie Hayden Cheng, and Dacher Keltner. 2010. Having Less, Giving More: The Influence of Social Class on Prosocial Behavior. *Journal of Personality and Social Psychology* 99: 771–84. [CrossRef] [PubMed]

Piff, Paul K., Daniel M. Stancato, Andres G. Martinez, Michael W. Kraus, and Dacher Keltner. 2012. Class, Chaos, and the Construction of Community. *Journal of Personality and Social Psychology* 103: 949–62. [CrossRef] [PubMed]

Piff, Paul K., Daniel M. Stancato, Stèphane Cotè, Rodolfo Mendoza-Denton, and Dacher Keltner. 2013. Higher Social Class Predicts Increased Unethical Behavior. *Proceedings of the National Academy of Sciences of the United States of America* 109: 4086–91. [CrossRef] [PubMed]

Rawls, John. 1999. *A Theory of Justice: Revised Edition.* Cambridge: Harvard University Press.

Railton, Peter. 1986. Facts and Values. *Philosophical Topics* 14: 5–31. [CrossRef]

Rooney, Ben. 2013. Stocks: 2013 Is One for the Books. *CNN.* Available online: http://buzz.money.cnn.com/2013/12/31/stocks-record-bull-market/ (accessed on 26 August 2016).

Scheffler, Samuel. 2015. The Practice of Equality. In *Social Equality: On What it Means to Be Equals*. Edited by Carina Fourie, Fabian Schuppert and Ivo Wallimann-Helmer. Oxford: Oxford University Press.

Shiller, Robert. 2012. High Taxes Needn't Discourage Philanthropy. *New York Times*. Available online: http://www.nytimes.com/2012/07/29/business/if-raising-top-tax-rates-encourage-charitable-giving.html?_r=0 (accessed on 2 September 2016).

Stiglitz, Joseph. 2012. *The Price of Inequality: How Today's Divided Society Endangers Our Future*. New York: W. W. Norton.

Stern, Ken. 2013. Why the Rich Don't Give to Charity. *The Atlantic*. Available online: http://www.theatlantic.com/magazine/archive/2013/04/why-the-rich-dont-give/309254/ (accessed on 2 September 2016).

Stroud, Sarah. 2014. Weakness of Will. *Stanford Encyclopedia of Philosophy*. Available online: https://plato.stanford.edu/entries/weakness-will/ (accessed on 26 April 2017).

Vardi, Nathan. 2014. The Twenty-Five Highest-Earning Hedge Fund Managers and Traders. *Forbes*. Available online: http://www.forbes.com/sites/nathanvardi/2014/02/26/the-highest-earning-hedge-fund-managers-and-traders/#212421af1984 (accessed on 26 August 2016).

Social Security Administration. 2013. Wage Statistics for 2013. Available online: https://www.ssa.gov/cgi-bin/netcomp.cgi?year=2013 (accessed on 26 August 2016).

Ward, Kate. 2016. Wealth, Poverty and Economic Inequality: A Christian Virtue Response. Available online: https://search.proquest.com/docview/1797412295?accountid=100 (accessed on 24 April 2017).

Wilkinson, Richard, and Kate Pickett. 2010. *The Spirit Level: Why Greater Equality Makes Societies Stronger*. New York: Bloomsbury Press.

Willis, Thayer Chatham. 2012. *Beyond Gold: True Wealth for Inheritors*. Portland: New Concord Press.

Willis, Thayer. 2013. Why Family Wealth Is a Curse. *Forbes*. Available online: http://www.forbes.com/sites/deborahljacobs/2013/03/01/why-family-wealth-is-a-curse/#439d9a537fc1 (accessed on 2 September 2016).

Wolff, Jonathan. 2015. Social Equality and Social Inequality. In *Social Equality: On What it Means to Be Equals*. Edited by Carina Fourie, Fabian Schuppert and Ivo Wallimann-Helmer. Oxford: Oxford University Press.

religions

MDPI

Article

Economic Inequality and the New School of American Economics

Stephen Leccese

History Department, 613 Dealy Hall, Fordham University, 441 E. Fordham Road, Bronx, NY 10458, USA; Stephen Leccese sleccese@fordham.edu

Academic Editors: Kate Ward and Kenneth Himes
Received: 4 February 2017; Accepted: 10 May 2017; Published: 24 May 2017

Abstract: This essay analyzes economic inequality in the Gilded Age, roughly from 1865 to 1900. It focuses specifically on a group of economists who identified working-class consumption as an economic stimulus, and accordingly advocated an increase in wages to bring this about. It is structured in three sections: first, it demonstrates how industrialization in the late-nineteenth century sparked social tensions, convincing observers that there was a crisis of inequality; second, it explains how these tensions produced a "New School" of economics who sought to alleviate these issues by changing economic doctrine; it concludes by noting how this New School exerted an influence on public policy in the Progressive Era. In their conception, economics should be redesigned to promote a more equal distribution of wealth. Therefore, higher wages would stimulate working-class consumption, which would stabilize the economy and overall alleviate class conflict. This story offers a unique way to view the development of consumerism and social reform in American history.

Keywords: economics; minimum wage; intellectual history; economic reform; Gilded Age; industrialization; consumption

1. Introduction

Economic inequality is not a new problem in America, nor are proposed solutions to the problem. Indeed, economic inequality was considered a serious issue in the past, particularly in America's Gilded Age—the period, roughly from the end of the Civil War to the turn of the twentieth century, when a rising wealth gap and conditions among the working class convinced contemporaries that they were facing a crisis of inequality. These conditions sparked a key intellectual change among a group of economists dubbed the "New School." These economists broke from economic traditions, and argued that the discipline of economics should focus on achieving a more equal distribution of wealth for the working class. The New School advanced several theories that altered economics, bu this essay focuses on their views towards wages, poverty, and consumption. Using their published work and archival materials, the essay demonstrates that in response to economic and class unrest in the 1870s and 1880s, the New Economists developed a new political economy focused on the working class. In their theories, consumer spending was the driving force of the modern economy, meaning wages and profits were not at odds with each other. Accordingly, they identified economic inequality as harmful to economic growth and social progress. Increasing the consumer base through wage growth and decreased working hours, these economists argued, would alleviate problems of economic instability and class strife that were associated with America's transition to industrial capitalism.

The New School economists were largely younger Americans who professionally came of age in the tumultuous 1870s and 1880s, when the economy experienced numerous recessions and there seemed to be a threat of open class warfare. Reformer Richard T. Ely described the New School's concerns most succinctly: "We saw a good deal of poverty on the one hand and a concentration of wealth on the other hand; and we did not feel that all was well with our country" (Ely 1977, p. 154). Ely and his colleagues considered economic analysis a tool of social reform. One of their many proposed reforms was increasing the consumer base by raising wages and leisure time for the working class. Such a viewpoint, however, put them in conflict with conventional American biases towards wages and consumption. The prevailing view on wages stated that employers could not raise workers' pay without cutting into their own profits. Furthermore, traditional American beliefs regarded thrift as an important moral value; unnecessary spending eroded republican virtue.[1] Therefore advocating increased spending, as the New School did, endangered the whole republican experiment according to this viewpoint. Such background is necessary to demonstrate the degree to which New School economists were challenging conventional wisdom.

This essay accordingly proceeds in three sections. The first describes how America's rapid industrialization after the Civil War led to social and economic unrest, convincing observers that they were facing a full-fledged crisis of inequality. The second section examines how that crisis of inequality sparked intellectual changes among economists. It notes how the New-School economists developed their ideas and differed from their primary intellectual opponents, the classical liberals. Finally, the essay concludes with a brief examination of how the New School came in contact with politicians and influenced progressive policy at the turn of the century.

2. The Problem of Inequality

When twenty-six-year-old Richard T. Ely returned from Europe in 1880, PhD in economics from the University of Heidelberg in hand, he was deeply disturbed by conditions in his home country. "On my return from Germany, after an absence of three years," he reminisced, "I became aware that our country was experiencing a crisis. The masses desired changes, not merely in surface phenomena, but in the very foundations of the social order" (Ely 1977, p. 66). "The masses" Ely referred to were the millions of wage earners that made up America's working class. Facing poor working and living conditions—explored in detail below—this working class grew increasingly restless, as the number of annual strikes exploded during the 1880s and 1890s. Ely and his colleagues—intellectuals and public servants including Francis A. Walker, John Bates Clark, Edwin Seligman, Henry Carter Adams, Carroll D. Wright, and George Gunton—were of the opinion that an imperfect distribution of wealth was to blame for this social dislocation. They accordingly focused their efforts on analyzing the so-called labor question in America, offering solutions focused on building the domestic market to alleviate economic inequality.

This perception of a crisis of inequality developed along with the Industrial Revolution. Beginning in England in the late eighteenth century,[2] exponential economic growth became the norm for industrializing countries (Piketty 2014, pp. 1–35). Vastly increased industrial production and availability of affordable consumer goods led several to declare an environment of abundance, in contrast to the preindustrial age of scarcity (Fox 1967, chp. 1). Indeed, during the second half of the nineteenth century, some of the largest fortunes in human history were accumulated among America's "robber barons," the captains of the new mass-production industries that took off after the Civil War. This rapid industrial and economic development allowed the United States to gain world power status in the early twentieth century.[3]

Despite unquestionable progress, however, this was in no way a time of equal wealth distribution. Those who worked for the robber barons often felt as if they were left out of this economic progress. As Thomas Piketty's statistics demonstrate, the Gilded Age saw a sharp increase in wealth inequality, more so than America had experienced in the past. In 1810, the richest 1% of Americans held about 25%

---

[1] For more on the connections between wealth and virtue, see Dustin Crummett's paper in this volume.

[2] For the factors that led to the British Industrial Revolution and the development of its consumer market, see (Allen 2009; McKendrick et al. 1984).

[3] For relative international development, see (Kennedy 1989).

of the wealth. Between 1870 and 1910, the years of rapid industrialization, that share increased from 31% to 45%, a jump of nearly 50% (Piketty 2014, p. 348). As a general trend, real wages increased steadily from 1860 to 1900 as general price deflation decreased the cost of living, a clear benefit to the working class.[4] Nonetheless, life for working families remained tenuous, mostly characterized by uncertainty. In a world with no welfare or unemployment insurance, job loss or workplace injury could land a family in the streets. Working-class women and children often had to work to supplement a father's income (Dubofsky 1996, pp. 18–30; McGerr 2010, pp. 13–20; Montgomery 1987).

Despite twelve-hour workdays, working class families rarely earned enough to accumulate much of a safety net. As Daniel Horowitz notes, an investigation in 1875 found that working families in Massachusetts spent up to 90% of their income on basic necessities (Horowitz 1985, chp. 1). With very little savings, lower class families suffered disproportionately in the regular periods of economic depression that struck the country from the 1870s until the turn of the century. When a depression hit, employers most often responded by either cutting wages or laying off workers in mass. (Montgomery 1987, pp. 60–62, 171–72).[5] Observers of the time saw this situation as the primary social issue of the day. It is no accident that the extremely popular Henry George titled his economic treatise *Progress and Poverty*, arguing that while "the previous century has been marked by a prodigious increase in wealth-producing power," those who did the productive work toiled in poverty (George 1879, pp. 1–2).

Left with few options, workers increasingly responded to their conditions with strikes. The late nineteenth century saw an explosion in the level of labor unrest: in 1881, when statistics were first kept, there were 477 strikes nationwide; just five years later in 1886 there were 1572; by 1901 there were 3012.[6] As statistics demonstrate, the majority of these strikes were related to wages and working conditions. Between 1881 and 1900, *Historical Statistics of the United States* lists three times more strikes due to "wages and working hours" than the next reason, "union organization."[7] Some of the largest and most famous strikes of the era were due to direct wage cuts. The Great Railroad Strike of 1877 and the Pullman Strike of 1894, for instance, came in response to multiple reductions to employee wages (Dubofsky 1996, pp. 45–54; Brands 1995, pp. 144–60).

While the working class' material condition was a concern, rising inequality had an equally troubling ideological impact on Americans. The rise of a permanent industrial working class contradicted the national vision that Americans had constructed for themselves. Crucial to that vision was independence and opportunity. Historians have identified a belief that wage labor was meant as a temporary condition for young men while they accumulated enough capital to start their own businesses. This belief was the cornerstone of antebellum free labor ideology (Rodgers 1974). Of course as Eric Foner demonstrates, free labor thought was very much a construction that did not fit reality for American workers. There was always a sizeable wage-laboring class in early America, and historians have noted high levels of poverty, especially in urban areas (Foner 1995, chp. 1; Nash 1986; Stansell 1987). Yet although the ideal did not quite fit the reality, free labor thought remained influential well into the Gilded Age. The labor unrest of the late-nineteenth century, however, demonstrated that free labor ideology had not produced the utopian conditions that Americans expected it to (Foner 1981, chp. 6). The loss of independence that resulted from permanent wage work challenged the vision Americans had crafted for themselves. Of course, as Olivier Zunz demonstrates, well-paid white collar work eventually helped Americans overcome their aversion to permanent wage labor (Zunz 1990, pp. 48–50). However during the transitional period in the Gilded Age, the increasing size of the working

---

4 See Tables 1 and 5 in (Porter 1980).
5 For a fictional yet revealing account of a working class family's plight, see (Sinclair 1906).
6 Table Ba4954–4964—Work stoppages, workers involved, average duration, and person-days idle: 1881–1998, *HSUS*.
7 Table Ba4965–4970—Work stoppages and workers involved, by major issue: 1881–1981, *HSUS*. The totals are 13, 919 strikes due to wages and hours, 4291 due to union organization, and 5588 classed as "other".

class coupled with labor unrest convinced contemporaries that they were facing a legitimate crisis of inequality.

3. Economic Responses

Amid instability in economics and social relations, it was plain for all to see that there were problems in American society. Naturally, contemporaries questioned what exactly was wrong. With rigid class formation, America seemed to have developed the very conditions that were supposed to be left behind in Europe, so observers were left scrambling for answers. People of diverse political persuasions and social backgrounds commented on the current state of affairs. There was general consensus that indeed there was a problem—in fact, most industrialized countries of this era struggled with the "social question," namely increasing poverty and class unrest (Fischer 1966). However, the suggested remedies for the problem proved a contentious argument among Americans. Opinions on what exactly had gone wrong had huge implications for the nature of economic inequality and how best to address it.

One response to the economic hard times was reactionary. A collection of economists, businessmen, and editors came to support classical liberalism and traditional economics. Liberal reformers like E.L. Godkin and William Graham Sumner believed that economic and social issues could be solved with a return to the values of classical economics, which they argued had been forgotten during the Civil War. Seeing a large tariff, taxes, and Reconstruction measures, liberals argued that the state needed to go back to its minimal antebellum role. Most importantly, the individual should remain the primary economic actor with no outside interference (Sproat 1968). With such biases, they stuck with the free labor view that low-paid wage labor was only a temporary condition meant for young men. In time, if they were frugal, they would be able to accumulate enough capital to start their own businesses and escape the wage system (Rodgers 1974). By this line of thinking, if one remained a poor wage laborer, then it must be due to some personal shortcoming. Indeed the most common complaints about workers were that they had no self-control and didn't know how to save their money. William Graham Sumner complained that reformers like the New School "gloss over all the faults of the classes in question, and they exaggerate their misfortunes and their virtues." Sumner represents the view that only individuals can pull themselves out of poverty through their own hard work (Sumner 1883, pp. 21–22). If workers lacked the necessary self-restraint, liberals argued, they should be instructed on proper etiquette rather than receive assistance from the state or charity (Sproat 1968, pp. 213–15). Overall, the classical liberals argued that if workers would only learn to save their money, economic problems could be alleviated.[8]

In making their arguments, the liberals were drawing heavily from classical political economy and American traditions. They were students of the English school of political economy and adhered to certain classical tenets like the wage-fund doctrine. Briefly, this doctrine asserts that labor is paid out of a fund built from the last production period. Capitalists take their profits from their previous production and earmark a certain amount to pay as wages in the next period. Wages therefore boiled down to a simple equation: wage-fund divided by number of laborers.[9] Since the wage-fund came out of a defined pool of capital, economists had traditionally viewed wages and profits as at odds with one another (Smith 2003, p. 94; Ricardo 1817, pp. 144–45; Mill 2001).

In addition to this influence from classical thinkers, liberals also drew from American traditions. Going back to Puritan tradition, thrift and hard work were key values for American society.[10]

---

[8] This is of course not to single out the liberals as evil for their views towards government action. With the rampant government corruption of the Gilded Age, liberals had concrete reasons to mistrust the state. They believed that indeed the best way to alleviate poverty was to stop government interference in the private and economic sphere.

[9] John Stuart Mill articulates this doctrine most clearly in (Mill 2001) For a more concise definition see (Cohen 2002; Currarino 2011).

[10] The classic analysis on work ethic remains (Weber 1930).

Accordingly, antebellum Americans held decidedly ambivalent views towards consumption and placed far greater value on productivity. This focus on thrift was not simply because Americans liked saving money; thrift was intimately tied to republican virtue. Americans decried consumption and luxury as harmful and even immoral. The bias among Americans was that European society had become corrupt through luxury. Attempting to avoid the problems of Europe, Americans placed a high value on republicanism, of which a large part was an independent, virtuous citizenry.[11] Luxury spending was thought to erode this individual virtue. By this logic, consumption and luxury endangered America's entire republican experiment (McCoy 1980). Popular writers like Amasa Walker wrote about the moral character of consumption. He distinguishes between money "spent" on luxuries and money "reproduced" when it is invested as capital. For Walker, "right consumption" was only useful insofar as it encouraged industry from a person, which is a key republican trait (Walker 1867). In sum, thrift meant much more for Americans than simple economic principles—it helped form the basis of the republican society they were trying to create.

While the liberals took their influence from these traditional ideals, the New School's inspiration came from what they considered a more modern source, the German Historical School. Throughout the 1870s and 1880s, Germany responded to the social problems of industrialization by building a proto-welfare state. Historical economists supported such measures through organizations like the *Verein für Sozialpolitik* (Association for Social Policy), which produced qualitative studies of social problems and recommended corrective legislation. (Grimmer-Solem 2003; Rodgers 1998; Schäfer 2000). A prevailing intellectual trend of the day was exchange between Germany and the United States, as American students travelled there and studied with key figures of the Historical School. With ideas from Germany, many of these students came back to the United States and became primary actors in the budding Progressive Movement (Rodgers 1998; Schäfer 2000).

With influence from Germany, the New School began developing new ideas about the economy and society. At the core of their creed was a rejection of the liberal view that society was merely a collection of individuals. Rather, as Richard Ely articulated, society was its own organism that had different needs than its individual parts (Ely 1889, p. 14). Since society was an organism, poverty among one class inhibited the development of the whole social body. Using this logic, the New School rejected the belief that wages and profits were at odds. Alleviating poverty and economic inequality would serve as an economic stimulus, as the working class could therefore have more disposable income. With better economic conditions, workers would have no reason to strike, leading to a peaceful and prosperous society.

The first American to address these issues was Francis A. Walker. Walker did not study abroad, but his work as a government statistician led him to similar conclusions that society was a complex organism (Dorfman 1949, pp. 101–3). Rather than despair over the shocking development of a permanent industrial working class, Walker made that working class an object of economic analysis in his 1876 work, *The Wages Question*. Seeing struggling laborers led Walker to conclude that mere subsistence wages are not efficient and lead to the degradation of labor. Poor food and housing will cause a decline in health, making workers unable to work as productively. Going further, Walker argues that consistent poverty destroys peoples' ambition. Therefore the threat of starvation is not a motivator, but a cause of overall moral and economic degradation (Walker 1876, pp. 84–88).

With this framework, Walker then moved on to attack the prevailing view on wages, the wage-fund doctrine. He found the wage-fund doctrine static and unrealistic. Employers do not consciously build a fund that they plan to dispense in the form of wages, he argued; rather, wages represent a purchase of labor power. Capitalists purchase labor as an investment to produce wealth. Therefore wages represent an advance payment, as the capitalist hopes to profit from his production

---

[11] For the various understandings of the qualities of republicanism and its importance in early America, see (Wood 1969; Shalhope 1982).

(Walker 1876, pp. 109–10; Walker 1875, pp. 102–3). By this new understanding, wages shouldn't be considered a static price that cannot rise, but rather something that should increase in value as the wealth produced rises.

Walker's penchant for challenging orthodoxy earned him a prestigious place among the emerging New School. The group advanced from a loose network of economists dissatisfied with the status quo to an organized force with the foundation of the American Economic Association in 1885, with Walker elected as its first president.[12] The group's primary architect, Richard Ely, deliberately modeled the group on the German *Verein für Sozialpolitik*, and all founding officers except Walker—Ely, John Bates Clark, Edwin Seligman, Edmund James, and Henry C. Adams—had studied in Germany.[13] There were many facets in the new theories that the New School advocated, but for the topic of economic inequality, it is most effective to analyze how the New School developed a new theory of wages to address poverty. For the New School, a primary economic issue was that mass production had become so efficient that goods were manufactured faster than they could be consumed. In America, the so-called under-consumption thesis can be traced back to the 1860s, when Commissioner of the Revenue David Wells noted that industrial production was outrunning population growth.[14] The idea that under-consumption was the cause of hard times grew from there. Labor leaders connected high wages to increased consumption from at least the early 1860s. Most notably Ira Steward of the eight-hour movement argued that working-class consumption would prove beneficial to the economy (Douglas 1932; Glickman 1997).[15] This opinion penetrated academic economics during the 1870s and 1880s. In what could be dubbed "the discovery of the consumer," the New School argued that problems of economic instability and inequality could be solved with a vastly expanded consumer base. Some contemporaries thought the need for consumers meant the US should expand overseas in search of markets. The New School argued that these new markets were available domestically, in the form of America's large working class. Rather than the liberals, who argued that workers needed to be taught self-control, these rebellious economists were of the opinion that the working class should be given the resources to consume *more*.[16]

To advance this theory, the New School had to break the notion that wages and profits were at odds with each other. Walker had already made strides against the wage-fund doctrine, but he still considered thrift an important individual virtue (Walker 1883, p. 73). Others pushed the argument further and argued that high wages and consumption were in fact *good* for business and economic prosperity. There are numerous intellectuals who fit into this mold. However for concise yet revealing examples, we can look to economists John Bates Clark and George Gunton. They both specifically use the well-being of the working class as their main object of analysis, making them a perfect fit for the theme of addressing economic inequality. Moderately influenced by socialist economics, Clark and Gunton overall argue that a poor working class was counterproductive for social stability and economic growth. It represented an untapped consumer market that if given the resources, would boost domestic consumption significantly.

John Bates Clark recognized that mass production had made an enlarged consumer base an economic necessity, and argued that the best way to achieve this was to ensure that "workers share in the benefits of civilization" (Clark to Seligman 1891). In attacking the wage-fund, Clark shows his socialist influence in pointing out that labor produces the wealth for the capitalist. Therefore, wages do not consist of a fund built by the capitalist and earmarked for wage payments, as the wage-fund dictates. Rather, wages represent labor's fair share in the production of wealth (Clark 1887, pp. 126–30).

---

[12] For background on the formation of the AEA, see (Furner 1975).

[13] (Ely to Seligman 1885; American Economic Association 1886).

[14] (New York Times 1869; Wells 1877).

[15] Steward did not produce much writing in his lifetime, but for his views see (Steward 1863; Steward 1868).

[16] For an explanation of how these issues of consumption were tied to economic citizenship, see (Currarino 2011).

Low wages do not represent a fair share of production because labor is therefore owed far more than it receives.

But Clark went further than simply demonstrating the injustice of low wages—he argued that raising the working class' condition was an economic stimulus. Paying workers as little as possible and allowing them no leisure time was an attempt to transform them into productive machines. Clark argues that this expectation hurts capitalists, ultimately, because "to make a man a machine is to make him anything but productive" (Clark 1887, p. 53). On the other hand, if workers are provided with leisure time and more spending power, they will use the opportunity for rest and relaxation. Not only will the increased consumption stimulate the economy, but capitalists will benefit from labor force that is more productive because it has restored its energy.

George Gunton even more forcefully argued that high wages were a benefit for everyone, expanding his analysis to envisioning a society centered on consumption. As a student of Ira Steward, Gunton pushed the theory of consumption to its logical end, essentially arguing that a consumerist society was the only way to achieve social stability. Gunton identified poverty as overall harmful to society, and argued that "social progress depended upon improving the material condition of the masses" (Gunton 1887, p. 23, 78). However, Gunton didn't advocate an abolition of capitalism to end inequality, as other radicals did. Instead he advocated a form of wealth redistribution that involved increasing the overall wealth of society. A way to bring this about was through an increase in consumption. In his view, the working class is so numerous that even a small increase in consumption would mean huge economic growth (Gunton 1891, p. 85). His theory essentially argued that all boats could rise equally in this new economic environment of abundance.

Key to Gunton's work was of course increasing wages. Gunton attacked the belief that high wages hurt profits. That line of thinking assumes that workers are only producers and not consumers as well. But as Gunton wrote, "consumption is the economic basis of production," and "the laborer is as important factor in the one as he is in the other" (Gunton 1887, pp. 30–31). Therefore, low wages only result in a limited market because the working class can only consume necessities. Ultimately, this hurts the capitalists, because it eliminates the consumer base and prevents the expansion of markets. Gunton argued that wages did not represent a cost, but an investment. Higher wages were a temporary expense that would provide capitalists with an expanded market for their goods. This investment would eventually return to them in the form of profits (Gunton 1887, p. 7).

According to the views of Clark, Gunton, and others, poverty and low wages were a social and economic handicap. They would not deny that there was significant economic growth in the late-nineteenth century—statistics make this clear, and the New School expressed wonder at the human progress that had produced such growth. Yet it was a "nervous prosperity," to use historian Albro Martin's phrase. For observers of the time, this growth seemed uneven, with serious depressions in 1873, 1882, and 1893, in addition to smaller panics.[17] Their argument was that long-term stability required a more even distribution of wealth. Such a measure would prevent depressions and improve the working class' standard of living, thereby resulting in a more peaceful society free of class strife.

4. The New School and Public Policy

Yet fascinating as this intellectual story is, the New School's efforts would mean little if they did not exert real-world influence. As history shows, indeed they did. The New School did not merely theorize about alleviating economic inequality. They also took active steps to influence public policy, and exercised an understated influence on progressive reform at the turn of the twentieth century.

As labor unrest intensified, the federal government realized the situation required closer study, rather than just usage of federal troops to crush strikes. A key figure in the development of state policy was New School member Carroll D. Wright. As a pioneer in the collection and assessment

---

[17]   See (Martin 1980).

of labor statistics in Massachusetts—it was his report in 1875 that uncovered the condition of that state's working families—he was the obvious choice to head the new federal Bureau of Labor Statistics, formed in 1884. His first report as Commissioner of Labor echoes the under-consumption thesis that his New-School colleagues subscribed to. Wright identifies the twin problems of overproduction and under-consumption as the cause of the general boom and bust cycle of the late 1800s. While writing that there is "no absolute remedy for depressions," Wright nonetheless makes suggestions that could alleviate the intensity and length of economic panics. Among his recommendations are increasing the purchasing power of laborers through the introduction of a stable currency, control of the labor supply by limiting contract labor, and a shortening of the work day. Wright theorized that such methods would increase the consuming power of the general public. This would enable the domestic market to absorb excess production (Wright 1968, pp. 290–93). Wright served as Commissioner of Labor for twenty years until 1905, and continued advocating his version of the under-consumption thesis (Leiby 1960, p. 136).

Wright was of course Commissioner of Labor when Theodore Roosevelt was making his name as the first progressive president, and Roosevelt considered him an important adviser. Wright was especially an influence on Roosevelt's decisions in arbitrating the 1902 Anthracite Coal Strike.[18] Roosevelt, however, was already well-acquainted with the New School by the time he became president. Several economists served as Roosevelt's advisers or confidantes when he was governor of New York from 1899 to 1900. At various points, George Gunton, Edwin Seligman, Richard Ely, and John Bates Clark advised Roosevelt on policy related to economics, labor, and big business (Chessman 1965; Hurwitz 1968).[19]

We can see the New School's influence in certain legislation that Roosevelt supported and passed. For instance, George Gunton was once asked in a lecture what legislation he would pass if given the opportunity, and he outlined three laws: First, a universal eight-hour law; second, a pension program to assure workers an income after retirement; and third, that children under 16 would not be permitted to work more than half-time. Gunton's reasoning was that protections like these would increase leisure time for workers to spend money, supporting his theory for a consumer society (Gunton 1897). Upon becoming governor, Roosevelt named Gunton his labor adviser and passed similar legislation, including an eight-hour law for public employees, regulation of child labor, and minimum wage increases for certain public and private sector employees (Hurwitz 1968, pp. 220–28). Such actions stand as an example that the New School was not satisfied with simply theorizing about social reform, but took active steps to influence policy. In Roosevelt, they found a political partner who was open to their suggestions on certain progressive legislation, particularly labor protections. Roosevelt incorporated their ideas into his platform as one of the most important policymakers of the Progressive Era.

5. Conclusions

While the previous investigation is far from comprehensive, it demonstrates clearly that economists of the New School identified economic inequality as harmful to social progress in Gilded-Age America. From their viewpoint, they saw class unrest and economic instability all around them, leading to fears that society was on the verge of revolution. The New School blamed shortcomings in classical economics for this condition, due to a focus on production and the capitalist middle class over the working class. In shifting their focus from production to distribution, the New School developed theories on how to ensure the working class benefited from industrialization. To solve the problem, they advocated a greater level of wage equality to stimulate working-class

---

[18] See examples of Wright and Roosevelt's correspondence in *Letters of Theodore Roosevelt* (Morrision 1951–54a).
[19] For instances where Roosevelt sought their advice and input, see *TR Letters* (Morrision 1951–54b, 1129, 1239).

consumption. This principle—increasing mass consumption—became key to adjusting economics to fit modern conditions, as the New School saw it.

In making these arguments, the New School offers a unique framework from which to view mass consumption. Historians often view consumerism as a development driven by business elites, who used advertising techniques to shape the American public into consumers (Ewen 1976; Leach 1994; McGovern 2009; Scanlon 1995). Yet as we've seen, advocates of consumerism were not always businessmen hoping to maximize profit. The New School economists conceived of consumption as a tool of social reform. They believed that by transforming the working class into consumers, America could achieve economic and social stability. We can further see how these theories were put into practice, as Theodore Roosevelt's New School advisers advocated protections for the working class through eight-hour laws and minimum wages. Exploring the New School therefore provides an enlightening, if unconventional, way to view social reform and how problems of economic inequality were addressed in the past.

Conflicts of Interest: The author declares no conflict of interest.

References

Allen, Robert C. 2009. *The British Industrial Revolution in Global Perspective*. New York: Cambridge University Press.

American Economic Association. 1886. List of Officers and Members. *Publications of the American Economic Association* 1: 40–46.

Brands, H.W. 1995. *The Reckless Decade: America in the 1890s*. New York: St. Martin's Press.

Chessman, Wallace G. 1965. *Governor Theodore Roosevelt: The Albany Apprenticeship, 1898–1900*. Cambridge: Harvard University Press.

Clark, John Bates. 1887. *The Philosophy of Wealth: Economic Principles Newly Formulated*, 2nd ed. Boston: Ginn.

John Bates Clark to Edwin Seligman, 30 May 1891, Folder 8, Box 1, Series 1: Correspondence, John Bates Clark Papers, Columbia University Rare Book and Manuscript Library, New York, NY.

Cohen, Nancy. 2002. *The Reconstruction of American Liberalism, 1865–1914*. Chapel Hill: University of North Carolina Press.

Currarino, Rosanne. 2011. *The Labor Question in America: Economic Democracy in the Gilded Age*. Urbana: University of Illinois Press.

Dorfman, Joseph. 1949. *The Economic Mind in American Civilization Vol. 3: 1865–1918*. New York: Viking Press.

Douglas, Dorothy. 1932. Ira Steward on Consumption and Unemployment. *Journal of Political Economy* 40: 532–43. [CrossRef]

Dubofsky, Melvyn. 1996. *Industrialism and the American Worker, 1865–1920*, 3rd ed. Wheeling: Harlan Davidson.

Ely, Richard T. 1889. *An Introduction to Political Economy*. New York: Chautauqua Press.

Ely, Richard T. 1977. *Ground under Our Feet: An Autobiography*. New York: Arno Press.

Richard T. Ely to Edwin Seligman, 23 June 1885, Box C9, Series 1: Correspondence, Edwin R.A. Seligman Papers, Columbia University Rare Book and Manuscript Library, New York, NY.

Ewen, Stuart. 1976. *Captains of Consciousness: Advertising and the Social Roots of the Consumer Culture*. New York: McGraw-Hill.

Fischer, Wolfram. 1966. Social Tensions at Early Stages of Industrialization. *Comparative Studies in Society and History* 9: 64–83. [CrossRef]

Foner, Eric. 1981. *Politics and Ideology in the Age of the Civil War*. New York: Oxford University Press.

Foner, Eric. 1995. *Free Soil, Free Labor, Free Men: The Ideology of the Republican Party before the Civil War*, 2nd ed. New York: Oxford University Press.

Furner, Mary O. 1975. *Advocacy and Objectivity: A Crisis in the Professionalization of American Social Science, 1865–1905*. Lexington: University Press of Kentucky.

Fox, Daniel M. 1967. *The Discovery of Abundance: Simon N. Patten and the Transformation of Social Theory*. Ann Arbor: University of Michigan Press.

George, Henry. 1879. *Progress and Poverty*. New York: Doubleday, Page and Co.

Glickman, Lawrence. 1997. Workers of the World, Consume: Ira Steward and the Origins of Labor Consumerism. *International Labor and Working-Class History* 52: 72–86. [CrossRef]

Grimmer-Solem, Erik. 2003. *The Rise of Historical Economics and Social Reform in Germany, 1864–1894*. New York: Clarendon Press.

Gunton, George. 1887. *Wealth and Progress*. New York: D. Appleton.

Gunton, George. 1891. *Principles of Social Economics*. New York: G.P. Putnam's Sons.

Gunton, George. 1897. "Our Economic Creed," *Lecture Bulletin of the Institute of Social Economics*.

Horowitz, Daniel. 1985. *The Morality of Spending: Attitudes toward the Consumer Society in America, 1875–1940*. Baltimore: Johns Hopkins University Press.

Hurwitz, Howard. 1968. *Theodore Roosevelt and Labor in New York State, 1880–1900*, 2nd ed. New York: AMS Press.

Kennedy, Paul. 1989. *The Rise and Fall of the Great Powers*. New York: Vintage.

Leach, William. 1994. *Land of Desire: Merchants, Power, and the Rise of a New American Culture*. New York: Vintage.

Leiby, James. 1960. *Carroll Wright and Labor Reform: The Origin of Labor Statistics*. Cambridge: Harvard University Press.

Martin, Albro. 1980. *Economy from Reconstruction to 1914*. Boston: Division of Research, Graduate School of Business Administration, Harvard University.

McCoy, Drew R. 1980. *The Elusive Republic: Political Economy in Jeffersonian America*. Chapel Hill: University of North Carolina Press.

McGerr, Michael. 2010. *A Fierce Discontent: The Rise and Fall of the Progressive Movement in America. 1870–1920*. New York: Free Press.

McGovern, Charles. 2009. *Sold American: Consumption and Citizenship, 1890–1945*. Chapel Hill: University of North Carolina Press.

McKendrick, Neil, John Brewer, and J.H. Plumb. 1984. *The Birth of a Consumer Society: Commercialization of Eighteenth Century England*. London: HarperCollins Publishers Ltd.

Mill, John Stuart. 2001. *Principles of Political Economy*. Kitchener: Batoche Books.

Montgomery, David. 1987. *The Fall of the House of Labor: The Workplace, the State, and American Labor Activism, 1865–1925*. New York: Cambridge University Press.

Elting Morrison, ed. 1951–54a. *Letters of Theodore Roosevelt*. Cambridge: Harvard University Press, vol. 1.

Elting Morrison, ed. 1951–54b. *Letters of Theodore Roosevelt*. Cambridge: Harvard University Press, vol. 2.

Nash, Gary B. 1986. *The Urban Crucible: The Northern Seaports and the Origins of the American Revolution*. Cambridge: Harvard University Press.

New York Times. 1869. Third Annual Report of Commissioner David A. Wells. *New York Times*, January 6.

Piketty, Thomas. 2014. *Capital in the Twenty-First Century*. Translated by Arthur Goldhammer. Cambridge: Belknap Press.

Porter, Glenn. 1980. Prices and Wages. In *Encyclopedia of American Economic History*. New York: Simon & Schuster Trade, pp. 234–44.

Ricardo, David. 1817. *On the Principles of Political Economy and Taxation*. London: J. M'Creery.

Rodgers, Daniel T. 1974. *The Work Ethic in Industrial America 1850–1920*. Chicago: University of Chicago Press.

Rodgers, Daniel T. 1998. *Atlantic Crossings: Social Politics in a Progressive Age*. Cambridge: Belknap Press.

Scanlon, Jennifer. 1995. *Inarticulate Longings: The Ladies' Home Journal, Gender, and the Promises of Consumer Culture*. New York: Routledge.

Schäfer, Axel R. 2000. *American Progressives and German Social Reform, 1875–1920: Social Ethics, Moral Control, and the Regulatory State in a Transatlantic Context*. Stuttgart: Franz Steiner Verlag.

Shalhope, Robert E. 1982. Republicanism and Early American Historiography. *William and Mary Quarterly* 39: 333–56. [CrossRef]

Sinclair, Upton. 1906. *The Jungle*. New York: Doubleday.

Smith, Adam. 2003. *The Wealth of Nations*. New York: Random House.

Sproat, John G. 1968. *"The Best Men": Liberal Reformers in the Gilded Age*. New York: Oxford University Press.

Stansell, Christine. 1987. *City of Women: Sex and Class in New York, 1789–1860*. Urbana: University of Illinois Press.

Steward, Ira. 1863. *The Eight Hour Movement: A Reduction of Hours is an Increase of Wages*. Boston: Boston Labor Reform Association.

Steward, Ira. 1868. *The Meaning of the Eight Hour Movement*. Boston: self-published.

Sumner, William Graham. 1883. *What Social Classes Owe To Each Other*. New York: Harper & Brothers.

Walker, Amasa. 1867. *The Science of Wealth*. Boston: Little Brown and company.

Walker, Francis Amasa. 1875. The Wage-Fund Theory. *North American Review* 120: 84–119.

Walker, Francis A. 1876. *The Wages Question.* New York: Henry Holt.

Walker, Francis A. 1883. *Political Economy.* New York: Henry Holt.

Wells, David Ames. 1877. How Shall the Nation Regain Prosperity? *North American Review* 125: 110–32.

Weber, Max. 1930. *The Protestant Ethic and the Spirit of Capitalism.* Translated by Talcott Parsons. New York: Scribner.

Wood, Gordon S. 1969. *The Creation of the American Republic, 1776–1787.* Chapel Hill: University of North Carolina Press.

Wright, Carroll D. 1968. *Industrial Depressions: The First Annual Report of the United States Commissioner of Labor.* New York: Augustus M. Kelly Publishers.

Zunz, Olivier. 1990. *Making America Corporate, 1870–1920.* Chicago: University of Chicago Press.

![religions logo] *religions*

MDPI

Article

Catholic Social Teaching on Building a Just Society: The Need for a Ceiling and a Floor

Kenneth Himes

Department of Theology, Boston College, 140 Commonwealth Avenue, Chestnut Hill, MA 02467, USA;
kenneth.himes@bc.edu

Academic Editors: Kate Ward and Roberto Cipriani
Received: 7 February 2017; Accepted: 22 March 2017; Published: 31 March 2017

Abstract: Msg. John A. Ryan was the leading voice for economic justice among American Catholics in the first half of the twentieth century. Although he was a champion of the proposal for a living wage to establish a minimum floor below which no worker might fall, Ryan gave little attention to whether there ought to be a ceiling to limit wealth among concentrated elites. I believe Ryan's natural law methodology hindered a fuller vision of economic justice when addressing inequality. Contemporary Catholic social teaching, shaped by documents like Vatican II's *Gaudium et spes*, has formulated a communitarian approach to justice that deals more adequately with the dangers of vast economic disparities. The essay concludes with a few ideas regarding how the post-conciliar outlook assists in rectifying the growing trend of economic inequality within American society.

Keywords: economic inequality; Catholic social teaching; John Ryan; living wage; *Gaudium et spes*; communitarianism; relative equality

1. Introduction

This presentation is an exercise in thinking about economic inequality from the perspective of Catholic social teaching (CST). In doing so, I will discuss the foremost thinker on economic ethics in the history of American Catholicism, Msgr. John A. Ryan, who wrote extensively on the issue of wage justice. Ryan provides an interesting case because he was deeply committed to worker justice throughout his long career, yet economic inequality was not a particular focus of his efforts. I will suggest why that is so, by discussing Ryan's natural law methodology within the Catholic social tradition that left him less troubled by inequality than he ought to have been. I will then propose that developments after Vatican II have led CST on economic justice to take more seriously the need to address inequality. In closing, I will comment upon the contribution that CST might make to our nation's discussion about the growing problem of significant economic inequality.[1]

The expression "Catholic social teaching" refers to a body of literature produced by hierarchical leaders in the Catholic church, popes or bishops, who have tried to address the political, economic, and social implications of Christian belief. How might the various teachings of the Catholic church shape

---

[1] This essay was written in tandem with several others that were first presented at a public conference on economic inequality at Boston College in April of 2016. Many of those other essays provide ample evidence of the pernicious effects of the economic inequality within American economic life. Having listened to the ideas of my seminar colleagues this year and having read the materials they each contributed to the seminar, I will not rehearse the evidence that significant economic inequality undermines democratic politics; effectively denies equality of opportunity in personal development; and has negative effects on housing, education, health and family life. Other essays in this issue make these points. Therefore, I encourage the reader to consult the essays by other seminar participants. See especially those of V. Chen, T. Dearing, F. Garcia, S. Kochuthara, J. Quinn and K. Cahill, K. Schlozman, M. Walsh and M. Theodorakakis, and K. Ward for arguments about various negative implications of our present social condition.

the way that believers respond to social issues? In particular, how does adherence to the Catholic tradition impact how one might think about economic inequality?

In 1891, Pope Leo XIII wrote a document entitled *Rerum novarum* (On the Condition of Labor), in which he presented what he saw as the primary social concern of the time, the "plight of the working class."[2] At the time, the ideology of free contract still had powerful support in the United States. There were none of the social policies of the modern welfare state in place: minimal wage laws, occupational safety regulations, child labor laws, or limitations on the length of the workday or workweek. There were no paid sick leaves, paid vacations or retirement pensions. The movement of organized labor was still in its infancy in the United States.

Leo's text is widely cited by scholars of CST as the beginning of formal papal social teaching.[3] In that encyclical, a circular letter sent to all Catholic bishops, Leo claimed belief in human dignity and the moral equality of persons to be foundational for a sound view of justice. Workers had a right to wages that would secure essential material goods sufficient to enable a frugal but decent lifestyle for the worker and dependents. At the same time, Leo did not explore the full possible implications of moral equality and equal dignity for social, political, and economic life. The pope, who was of aristocratic ancestry, had no strong objection to social hierarchy in society, oligarchic or monarchical political orders, nor dramatic wealth differentials in an economy.

Later popes memorialized Leo's encyclical with their own social teaching, often promulgated as anniversary celebrations of *Rerum novarum*.[4] These texts, along with additional encyclicals, apostolic letters, conciliar texts, and various other episcopal documents have developed the church's thinking about the meaning of moral equality and human dignity in such a manner that they have effectively moved Catholic teaching away from acquiescence of significant economic inequality toward what has been characterized as a "relative egalitarianism" when reflecting upon economic justice.[5]

2. John Ryan and a Living Wage

Among those inspired by Leo's encyclical was a young Minnesotan, John A. Ryan, who had decided to study for the priesthood and was in the seminary during the 1890s. Ryan's early interest in economic justice stemmed from reading the *Irish World* and the populist politics of Ignatius Donnelly, a member of the National Farmers' Alliance. Later, Ryan aligned with the more mainline Progressive movement. While in the seminary, he studied the work of the economist Richard Ely. When Ryan began doctoral studies in moral theology, he took economic courses, though they were not required, and studied John Hobson's theory of under-consumption for his dissertation on *A Living Wage*.

Rerum novarum was significant for Ryan as it affirmed the idea of state intervention in the economy. It also shaped his commitment to a natural law method that was only sparingly related to explicit theological commitments. What Ryan did was relate natural law ethics to Progressivism and in so doing built bridges between Progressives and American Catholics. For Progressives, he helped them to see that Catholic natural law thinking could be utilized to embrace social reform. For American Catholics, many of whom were Irish and German immigrants, Ryan helped them accept that state intervention could be a means to advance the cause of working class people rather than oppress them. This was no small matter for Irish Catholics experienced with British rule or German Catholics familiar with Bismarck's *Kulturkampf*. The key starting point for Ryan's economic ethics was the equal dignity

---

2   Leo XIII. *Rerum novarum*, #44 (as is customary with papal documents the number refers to the paragraph not page of the document).

3   See, for example, (O'Brien and Shannon 1995; Curran 2002).

4   Pius XI. *Quadragesimo anno* (1931); Pius XII. Pentecost Sermon (1941); John XXIII. *Mater et magistra* (1961); Paul VI. *Octogesima adveniens* (1971); John Paul II. *Laborem exercens* (1981) and *Centesimus annus* (1991).

5   (Christiansen 1984). Following Christiansen, the modifier "relative" is crucial to understand the Catholic viewpoint. The equality being sought is not an absolute leveling by which everyone receives the exact same benefit and shares the exact same burden. "*Rather, it points to a situation in which inequalities are held within a defined range set by moral limits.*" Those limits are set by the need to sustain and enhance "*the bonds uniting people to one another*" (pp. 653–54, italics in original).

of human beings based upon their common human nature as creatures of God, which he rightly saw as the starting point of CST.

Ryan has been called the foremost exponent of CST during both the Progressive Era and the New Deal years. His ambition was to extend democratic ideals to the economic order. From 1906, when he published his doctoral dissertation on the ethical demand for *A Living Wage*[6], until his death in 1945, Ryan was strikingly consistent in his arguments for what economic justice entailed. He further developed, but did not significantly depart from, the argument of his dissertation with the publication of his other major work, *Distributive Justice* in 1916.[7] Overall, Ryan published more than eighty books and pamphlets, along with numerous essays and speeches, as well as serving as ghostwriter for many statements by American Catholic bishops. This latter role was due to Ryan being the founding director of the Social Action Department of what was then called the National Catholic War Conference, later the National Catholic Welfare Conference, and eventually the U.S. Conference of Catholic Bishops. He remained in that role of director until his death almost thirty years later.

Key for Ryan's economic ethics was a belief in what CST has come to refer to as the universal destiny of goods.[8] For Ryan, the idea that the goods of creation exist to meet the basic needs of all people is based on three claims. First, early human history illustrates it with primitive communism in regard to land ownership and efforts to help the poor; second, the Christian faith long taught that every person has a right to a share in communal wealth necessary to maintain life; and, finally, human reason shows that persons have equal dignity and worth.

Ryan then argued in three moves for what he called a living wage as the minimum of justice: (1) the universal destiny of goods means all have an equal claim upon nature's bounty; (2) this inherent right of access to the earth's goods is conditioned upon useful labor; and (3) those in control of natural resources are obliged to provide access to such resources for all willing to work. Every worker had a right to a decent living stemming from his or her labor since this was the only way most workers could share in the goods of creation. A living wage should be a family living wage. Ryan assumed that there was a male wage earner who would receive the wage, thereby allowing the adult female to maintain the home and supervise the dependent children.

For Ryan's social ethics, the ultimate norm is human welfare and this is determined not speculatively, but by what actually happens to people when choosing one policy over another. This reflects Ryan's inductive and empirical side. The fundamental content in ethics is the meaning of the human person and that is explored in terms of personal rights grounded in human dignity. What legitimates any particular right is human welfare for every person has the duty of self-perfection or personal development.

A human being has rights to all things essential for reasonable development of the person consistent with the rights of others to essential things for their personal development. The state is natural (because persons are social) and necessary (because persons cannot develop apart from the state). The aim of the state is to promote the common good or public welfare. Ryan's "welfare theory" of the state is to safeguard all necessary rights as its primary role, with secondary functions of education, health, safety, charity, public works, morals, religion, and industrial regulation. Economic ethics is mainly about the proper distribution of worldly goods.

It is important to understand the distinction that Ryan made between human welfare, his preferred term, and social welfare, which he used to describe those reformers who advocated some form of social utilitarianism. The danger of social welfare as a norm is that it might conceivably be used to override the essential rights of individuals in the pursuit of overall societal benefit. Ryan, who was committed to the dignity of each individual, employed human welfare as his standard to make clear that, first and foremost, the essential rights of the individual were to be secured before considering

---

[6]   (Ryan 1906)

[7]   (Ryan 1916, 1927 rev., 1942 rev.)

[8]   "God intended the earth and all it contains for the use of every human being and people." Vatican II, *Gaudium et spes*, #69

societal goods. The focus was on the individual, and whether or not the person had the opportunity for his or her self-development. While fully supporting Ryan's commitment to the individual and his rejection of social utility as the foremost norm, I do want to suggest that Ryan's ideal of justice may be too intently concerned with provision of those goods essential for self-development to the neglect of other aspects of justice.

Ryan was strongly committed to equality when it came to a person's claim to the essential goods for self-perfection. However, the scope of that right to essential goods was narrowly drawn. Everyone had a right to a decent livelihood, and this was at the heart of Ryan's project from the time he wrote his dissertation. Once that entitlement was established, and Ryan was confident that a specific figure for a living wage could be determined, then inequality could occur due to a variety of factors including merit, effort, and greater capacity for development.[9] Ryan was not prepared to defend as a matter of justice any rights beyond the specific rights essential for the opportunity to develop. By being so specific about the right to the goods necessary for self-development, Ryan left little room for claims based on equality in his conception of justice. In his approach, the essential right to self-development was equal and absolute as well as specific. Justice required that society secure that for each person. Once that is achieved, however, Ryan was open to "presumptive rights to unequal shares of income and wealth."[10]

Ryan's moral theory of justice was based on his natural law method and belief in the equality of human dignity. From that commitment, he developed the claim about the absolute and equal right of every person to those goods necessary for self-development. The subject of economics played no role in Ryan's theory to this point. Where economics does enter in is when the topic becomes how to ensure that the essential right is protected. For Ryan, living in the modern industrial society of twentieth century America, economics determined that the best means of securing the right to self-development was to guarantee a living family wage for every worker.

Ryan's economic training led him to conclude that, although economic factors did not impinge on the philosophical determination of the existence of a right to self-development, such factors did impinge on his approach to justice in two other ways. First, the reality of a modern market system made the payment to a worker of a family living wage the crucial and most common way of ensuring each individual's personal development. Second, economic factors like productivity, efficiency, scarcity, and effort all played into his conclusion that economic inequality was necessary to attain human welfare on a long-term basis, that is, "a society's long-run provision for the means essential for individuals' self-development."[11]

Ryan does not avoid "the question of indefinitely large profits." In accordance with the analysis above, he concludes that "as a general rule, business men who face conditions of active competition have a right to all the profits that they can get, so long as they use fair business methods." Among those fair methods is the payment of a family living wage, as well as honesty in dealing with buyers and sellers. "When those conditions are fulfilled, the freedom to take indefinitely large profits is justified by the canon of human welfare."[12]

Although Ryan accepted capitalism, in principle, he never supported what he called 'historical' capitalism, the economic system that actually emerged in the United States. For Ryan, the system of historical capitalism as found in the U.S. embodied a set of interlocking principles that were unacceptable. Politically, there was opposition to any state intervention in the economy; economically,

9   (Ryan 1906, p. 75).
10 (Beckley 1992, p. 140). Beckley's analysis of Ryan's theory of justice is the best treatment of which I am aware. His conclusion that Ryan does not give as much weight to equality as he might have is similar to mine. Throughout this section my presentation has been informed by Beckley's work.
11 (Ibid. p. 148).
12 (Ryan 1916, 1927 rev., 1942 rev., p. 255).

there was the conviction that unlimited production automatically translated into unlimited markets and full employment; and, ethically, there was an extreme individualistic reading of property rights.

During the Progressive era, Ryan saw three flaws in the economic order: inadequate remuneration for workers, excessive income for a small minority, and narrow distribution of capital ownership. The disproportion of income growth between rich and poor between 1900 and 1929 was especially problematic for Ryan, for if workers had insufficient income, they could not stimulate demand. Lacking demand, there would be a downturn in production meant to expand supply, which would lead to layoffs and increased unemployment. Loss of wages would only further reduce demand so the economy becomes entrapped in a depression. This is what Ryan believed led to the great economic collapse in 1929. It is important to note that Ryan's concern about excessive inequality was not a moral argument, but an economic one. Unless workers had sufficient income they could not stimulate economic growth through demand. Barring that level of inequality, however, which would be remedied by a living wage, Ryan had no further criticism of "indefinitely large profits."

As a remedy to the historic capitalism he experienced, Ryan argued the case for a living wage through state regulation and legislation that, in effect, built a floor below which no one ought to be allowed to sink. This was a significant development in American Catholic social thought and in the political sensibilities of many immigrant Catholics. Today, however, few beyond the most committed social Darwinists or Ayn Rand disciples would oppose the idea of a floor below which a decent society ought not let a person fall

3. Post-Conciliar Catholic Social Teaching and Relative Egalitarianism

The more interesting ethical question, to my mind, when addressing inequality is not whether there is a floor beneath which none should fall (that is widely acknowledged among Christian ethicists), but is there a ceiling above which none should rise? John Ryan's economic ethic made the case clearly and cogently that a living wage ensuring the essential goods needed for personal self-development was a right that must be secured. In this section of my essay, I would like to discuss why Ryan failed to argue for a ceiling and not just a floor when addressing economic inequality. I believe one major reason is that Ryan was so committed to a natural law methodology that he gave little attention to a biblical and theological approach, which might promote a more communitarian perspective on economic justice that gives greater weight to the ills of inequality.

The movement toward a more biblical and theological methodology in CST was profoundly influenced by the event of Vatican II. The development in CST inspired by the Council can be illustrated by the "Pastoral Constitution on the Church in the Modern World" (*Gaudium et spes*) and its communitarian perspective. This perspective can be found in four elements of the Pastoral Constitution's message.

First, the understanding of the human person in the document can be described as relational. In one place, the text cites Jesus' prayer in John 17, 21–2 where he prayed to his Father, "that all may be one . . . as we are one. The document goes on to claim that this prayer "implied a certain likeness between the union of the divine Persons, and in the union of God's children in truth and charity."[13] The bishops maintain that "having been created in the image of God . . . all people are called to one and the same goal, namely, God himself." Love of God and love of one's neighbor cannot be separated, and is the first and greatest commandment. "To people growing daily more dependent on one another, and to a world becoming more unified every day, this truth proves to be of a paramount importance." The council fathers state that, "social life is not something added on to the person," but is necessary for human flourishing.[14] "[T]hrough dealings with others, through reciprocal duties, and through

---

[13] Vatican II, *Gaudium et spes*, #24.
[14] Ibid. #25.

fraternal dialogue people develop all their gifts and are able to rise to their destiny."[15] Consequently, the Pastoral Constitution proclaims, "by their innermost nature human persons are social beings, and unless they related themselves to others they can neither live nor develop their potential."[16]

Once the social nature of the person is clearly asserted, the second element of the perspective is addressed, namely that community is the social ideal. For "God did not create the person for life in isolation, but for the formation of social unity."[17] Rather God, "from the beginning of salvation history...has chosen people not just as individuals but as members of a certain community."[18] Thus, "the will to play one's role in common endeavors should be everywhere encouraged."[19] It is this firm conviction about the centrality of communal life for human development that undergirds the theme of the universal destiny of goods: "God intended the earth and all that it contains for the use of every human being and people."[20] This demands that "attention must always be paid to the universal purpose for which created goods are meant" no matter the "diverse and changeable" patterns of private ownership that exist.[21] This communitarian perspective provides the context not only for proper understanding of property rights but all genuine human rights. "For the protection of personal rights is a necessary condition for the active participation of citizens, whether as individuals or collectively, in the life and government of the state."[22] Indeed, politics can be understood as the art of enabling wider and wiser participation in community. "It is in full accord with human nature that juridical-political structures should, with ever better success and without any discrimination, afford all their citizens the chance to participate freely and actively in establishing the constitutional bases of a political community, governing the state, determining the scope and purposes of various institutions, and choosing leaders."[23] Of course, the entire aim of political life is to promote and protect the common good; "the political community exists for that common good in which the community finds its full justification and meaning."[24]

The third element of the communitarian perspective articulated by Vatican II is its linkage with the ecclesiology of the council. As the bishops wrote, "Everything we have said about the dignity of the human person, and about the human community and the profound meaning of human activity lays the foundation for the relationship between the Church and the world."[25] In *Lumen gentium*, the Dogmatic Constitution of the Church, there is the statement that the church is a sacrament of the unity of humankind. The bishops quote themselves in *Gaudium et spes* when they say, "For the promotion of unity belongs to the innermost nature of the church, since she is, 'by her relationship with Christ, both a sacramental sign and an instrument of intimate union with God and of the unity of all humankind.'"[26] They saw in this text an affirmation that the church's task is the fostering of unity and a common life among people.

Finally, the fourth element constituting the communitarian perspective is the centrality of solidarity in CST. The council fathers begin with the observation that "One of the salient features of the modern world is the growing interdependence of persons one on the other."[27] While technical progress in communication, trade, travel, and other advances have promoted this interdependence, the genuine dialogue sought "does not reach its perfection on the level of technical progress, but on the deeper

---

[15] Ibid.
[16] Ibid. #12.
[17] Ibid. #31.
[18] Ibid.
[19] Ibid.
[20] Ibid. #69.
[21] Ibid.
[22] Ibid. #73.
[23] Ibid. #75.
[24] Ibid. #74.
[25] Ibid. #40.
[26] Vatican II, *Gaudium et spes*, #42 quoting *Lumen gentium*, #1.
[27] Ibid. #23

level of interpersonal relationship."[28] This understanding paved the way for the later claim of John Paul II that "*interdependence*, sensed as a *system determining* relationships in the contemporary world, in its economic, cultural, political, and religious elements," must be "accepted as a *moral category*. When independence becomes recognized in this way, the correlative response as a moral and social attitude, as a 'virtue,' is *solidarity*."[29] For John Paul, it was crucial that, "Interdependence must be transformed into *solidarity*."[30] To convey the more interpersonal dimension of solidarity compared to the empirical fact of interdependence, the pope employed the image of the interdependent other "as a sharer, on a par with ourselves, in the banquet of life to which all are equally invited by God."[31]

The solidaristic ethic emerging out of the communitarian perspective gives greater emphasis to the importance of equality than the pre-conciliar natural law methodology employed by Ryan. As the bishops wrote, "although rightful differences exist between people, the equal dignity of persons demands that a more humane and just condition of life be brought about. For excessive economic and social differences between the members of the one human family or population groups cause scandal, and militate against social justice, equity, the dignity of the human person, as well as social and international peace."[32]

The theological vision of humanity as one family and the church as a sacrament (i.e., an external or material symbol that makes visible an internal or spiritual reality) of that unity serves as a backdrop to the ethic espoused in CST. The theological theme of the communion of humankind has its counterpart in an ethical principle of solidarity. This principle generates moral norms regulating the political and economic framework espoused in CST. Solidarity serves as the ethical expression of the "deep theory" that generates recent CST.[33]

By the expression "deep theory," I refer to the taken-for-granted understanding of justice in an ethical theory. It is "the tacit intuition or vision that undergirds a conception of justice."[34] When the Catholic imagination envisions a just society, it depicts a situation in which humans exist in right relationship to one another. Within the Catholic imagination, the human good is related to the experience of communities that practice mutual respect and honor, forgiveness and love. Consequently, the Catholic understanding of justice demands the creation of genuine community where belonging, respect, friendship, forgiveness, and love are essential to human well-being. These are goods not readily captured by the language of rights and duties. Instead, they are better understood as conditions required for the establishment and flourishing of human community. Central to the theory of justice in modern CST is the recognition that human dignity can be realized and protected only in community.[35]

In summary, Vatican II affirmed human solidarity as a major theme and goal of a Catholic social ethic. The goal became solidarity and relative equality became the normative principle: the regular use of public policies, including "redistribution, to redress significant differences between groups is necessary to preserve and foster community."[36] As noted earlier, "relative" means inequalities are held within a defined range set by moral limits. The desired goal is community that sustains and enhances bonds that unite people.[37]

---

[28] Ibid.
[29] John Paul II, *Sollicitudo rei socialis* (On Social Concern), #38. Italics in original.
[30] Ibid. #39. Italics in original.
[31] Ibid.
[32] *Gaudium et spes*, #29.
[33] See (Christiansen 1984, p. 658)
[34] (Ibid. p. 668).
[35] (USCCB 1986, #14)
[36] (Christiansen 1984, p. 653)
[37] See, note 5.

4. The Breakdown of Solidarity due to Inequality

Yet today, as in the past, wealth and power can provide significant opportunities for people to isolate themselves from one another, to secede from our common life. More than one observer has cited the trend of people losing interest in public goods while using private means to avoid the harm stemming from the decay of public life. While it is true that many wealthy still rely on public monies in a variety of ways—for example, private jets require a whole network of publicly financed air traffic control and airports—nonetheless, it is also true that there is a growing disengagement with public life.

It is clear that the very rich have been pulling away from the rest of American society. The empirical data show that the share of income going to the top 1%, the top 5%, and top 10% have all grown far more than the lower half of the population. The top 1% now receive more than 20% of total household income. The top 20% gets almost half of all income. The share of total income that goes to the wealthiest quintile is higher than at any time since 1929, just before the great stock market crash.

The process of secession of the top one-fifth of high earners from the rest of American society is a gradual one and takes a variety of forms. Many wealthy people now live in residential enclaves that employ private companies for security, trash collection, even road maintenance, while nearby municipalities are too financially strapped to provide such services adequately. Privileged children attend private schools, summer camps, and other activities available only to those who can pay for the entrance fees. As public parks and playgrounds deteriorate, there is a proliferation of private health clubs, golf clubs, tennis clubs, and every other type of recreational association in which the costs are shared by members. It is not hard to detect in the animosity towards taxation a lost sense of solidarity whereby citizens contributed to public services and goods that may or may not have been directly beneficial to them.

Patterns of public benevolence also illustrate the tendency of the successful to secede from the larger society. The charity of the affluent does not go mainly to social welfare programs for the poor. Instead, most philanthropy of the wealthy is directed to the places and institutions that entertain, inspire, cure, or educate wealthy Americans—art museums, opera houses, theaters, orchestras, ballet companies, private hospitals, and elite universities. Corporate philanthropy follows the same self-serving pattern. For some time now, corporate giving to primary and secondary education has been less than the amount host communities grant businesses through tax breaks and subsidies.

CST recognizes that the appeal to solidarity may not be heard by those who can successfully isolate themselves from the experience of interdependence with the poor. Hence, the point in CST that solidarity must be understood as more than an acknowledgement of empirical interdependence. Instead, it is a moral imperative generated by a communitarian outlook that challenges liberal individualism. Like other moral imperatives, it calls for conversion; it asks for change in the way we have structured our social order. Solidarity must be a conscious choice of people who seek ways of improving the good of all, if a commitment to the common good demands that some place limits on their own desires or stated interests that should be done. CST argues not from enlightened self-interest but from a theological claim about the unity of the human family and the moral obligations that arise from a vision of the community of persons.

Whereas John Ryan, along with other pre-conciliar social theorists, endorsed distributive justice that provided a minimum for all, the relative egalitarianism of a theologically informed CST demonstrates greater sensitivity to how huge disparities in wealth and income create and perpetuate divisions that prevent the building up of a shared common life. Solidarity as a commitment to truly care for the well-being of the other is a countermeasure to the secession of the successful that is a result of the yawning gaps between rich and poor. Given the residential patterns of many Americans, the one thing neighbors have in common is income levels and this is what constitutes the false notion of community for Americans. It leads to what Robert Bellah once called "lifestyle enclaves."[38]

John Ryan's focus on natural law reasoning prevented him from integrating the sort of theological themes into his social ethic that later CST has developed. As a result, his argument for a living wage, as important as it was, left his political program with a floor but no ceiling. Today, we must move beyond Ryan's approach. I believe an economic ethic informed by CST requires that we set a ceiling as well as establish a floor when we address the inequality of wealth accumulation and annual income.

5. What Might the Christian Community Do?

I close this reflection by suggesting some ways for the ecclesial community to move forward in the pursuit of economic justice.

First, we must acknowledge that two types of structures are at work in any culture: ideological and operational. Operational structures refer to the *patterns of behaviour* that make up our social world, e.g., zoning laws, tax systems, international trade agreements, health care systems, monetary and banking policies. These are operational structures. Ideological structures refer to *patterns of belief*, the configuration of values that make up our social understanding. Operational structures are wrong when the ideological structure implicit in them and supportive of them offends human dignity. Ideological structures demean persons when values other than human dignity become the organizing and dominating values of a society.

Part of the task in promoting social change is to analyze the values of a culture so as to awaken different moral sensibilities, calling forth new images of what might constitute human fulfillment. To bring about change on the operational level, there is the need to complement or even precede it by transformation on the ideological level. Therefore, if the Christian community is to be effective in bringing about social change, a dual focus is necessary, addressing both types of structure: operational and ideological. However, although the community of faith must act where it can on the operational structures of a society, its real strength is to foster and tutor the moral imagination so as to combat the ideological structures that undergird and inspire operational structures denigrating human persons.

The prevailing view of economic policy making is that people are essentially self-interested rather than altruistic and behave the same way whether they are buying a car or voting on a public referendum. Personal preferences are not significantly affected by politics or moral norms but driven more by self-interest. The public good is simply the sum of individual preferences. Society is working effectively whenever people's preferences can be satisfied without making other people worse off. Usually, market exchanges suffice for improving society this way.

Such a policy approach does not take ideas seriously. It does not inquire into our ideas about what is ethically good for society, nor does the economic approach see the utility of debating the relative merits of differing conceptions of the good society. The prevailing view shortchanges the role that normative visions can play in shaping what people want and expect from government, their fellow citizens, and themselves. Furthermore, the dominant approach disregards the importance of public deliberation for refining and revising normative visions.

CST suggests that ideas about what is good for society ought to occupy a more prominent place in public life. The responsibility of those who deal with public policy is not reducible to identifying what people want for themselves and then to go about implementing the most efficient means to satisfy these wants. Instead, CST suggests that the Christian community ought to provide alternative visions of what is desirable and possible, to stimulate deliberation about them, to provoke an examination of a culture's assumptions and values, and thereby deepen society's self-understanding.

---

[38] (Bellah et al 1985, pp. 71–75). A thoughtful reviewer of this paper raised the question of whether my real objection is to the lack of solidarity in American society rather than economic inequality. While I agree that inequality can be distinguished from the question of solidarity, I think in practice, and as documented by several of the empirical papers in the first part of this issue, vast economic inequality inevitably breeds a breakdown in solidarity.

Many of the important policy initiatives in recent decades cannot be explained by the prevailing view of public policy. The civil rights laws of the 1960s, the movements of public health, consumer safety, and environmental protection in the 1970s—these policies were not motivated mainly by individuals seeking to satisfy selfish preferences. People supported these initiatives largely because they thought it would be good for American society. In addition, public support for these initiatives has not been stable and unchanging, since public support has grown and evolved as people engaged the ideas and values underlying various policy proposals.

It is also true that some of the most accomplished government leaders are those men and women who purposefully craft visions of what is desirable and possible for society to do. Rather than simply giving voice to already existing public wants, the true art of political leadership has been to give voice to half-known, half-articulated hopes and dreams that people have for their society. If that is true, then there is more room for the influence of CST than is sometimes thought. There was a time when child labor in factories and mills was widely accepted in this country—and then it was not. There was a time when cigarette smoking was widespread and unquestioned in public places—and then it was not. How does the unthinkable become thinkable? How does the conventional wisdom become unconventional? Or vice versa?

Adherents of CST have an obligation to at least raise the topic of whether the solution to huge inequality requires more than putting in place floors for those at the bottom. Supporters of CST ought to raise the issue of putting in place ceilings to prevent some to rise too high above the rest. Of course, it is not only ideas, but ideas translated into policies that are necessary to move our nation in the right direction.

Let me close with four brief policy ideas that are worth discussing as illustrations of how the construction of a ceiling in order to restrain inequality might be built.

1. Move toward a higher top personal income tax rate by revising the present top rate of 39.6% for those making $415,000 or more, to several additional stages of 45% for those making more than $750,00, 50% for those making more than $1.25 million, and 55% for those making more than $2 million.
2. Create different and higher rates of annual taxation on non-earned income, i.e., investment returns, once it rises above a certain threshold, say $50,000 of non-earned income annually.
3. Establish higher inheritance taxes. This might be along the line of Atkinson's Lifetime Capital Receipts Tax (with a spousal exemption). Choose a tax-exempt ceiling, say $100,000 in gifts over the course of a lifetime. After that figure, every gift is taxed starting at 20% with a progressive rate as the amount increases over a lifetime. The tax is on the receiver of the benefit not the giver. That might encourage givers to spread their wealth around, giving it to more people who have little inheritance rather than a favored few who gather the bulk of it.
4. Develop a new tax on corporations that exceed a certain highest/lowest pay ratio; for example, 100–1 when comparing top compensation to median compensation in each corporation—or, less coercively, require an annual public listing of pay ratios in every company in order to promote a voluntary effort at a more equal distribution of a company's assets.[39]

These are merely policy ideas cited for the sake of illustration. I do not mean to endorse or recommend any of them without further examination. Rather, I mention them in order to provoke conversation about the goal of implementing a ceiling as well as a floor when we think about economic inequality. I do not think the policy discussion can or should go forward until we have done the work of public discourse that expands our moral and political imaginations beyond the conventional wisdom about what is a good society. U.S. citizens should consider alternative formulations of what a

---

[39] The above proposals are just a few that I have adapted from (Atkinson 2015).

good and just society might look like. In that project, I think CST and the Catholic community have a useful role to play in advocating relative equality as integral to economic justice.

Conflicts of Interest: The author declares no conflict of interest.

References

Atkinson, Anthony. 2015. *Inequality: What Can Be Done?* Cambridge: Harvard University Press.

Beckley, Harlan. 1992. *Passion for Justice*. Louisville: Westminster/John Knox Press, p. 140.

Bellah, Robert, Richard Madsen, William M. Sullivan, Ann Swidler, and Steven M. Tipton. 1985. *Habits of the Heart*. Berkeley: University of California Press.

Christiansen, Drew. 1984. On Relative Equality. *Theological Studies* 45: 651–75. [CrossRef]

Curran, Charles. 2002. *Catholic Social Teaching 1891-Present*. Washington: Georgetown University Press.

O'Brien, David, and Thomas Shannon. 1995. *Catholic Social Teaching: The Documentary Heritage*. Maryknoll: Orbis Books.

Ryan, John. 1906. *A Living Wage: Its Ethical and Economic Aspects*. New York: Macmillan Company.

Ryan, John. 1916. *Distributive Justice*. New York: Macmillan Company, 1927 rev., 1942 rev.

United States Catholic Bishops. 1986. Economic Justice for All: Pastoral Letter on Catholic Social Teaching and the U.S. Economy. Available online: http://www.usccb.org/upload/economic_justice_for_all.pdf (accessed on 29 March 2017).

religions

MDPI

Article

The Economic and Ethical Implications of Living Wages

Joyce Ann Konigsburg

Duquesne University, 600 Forbes Ave, Pittsburgh, PA 15282, USA; konigsburgj@duq.edu

Academic Editors: Kate Ward and Kenneth Himes
Received: 9 March 2017; Accepted: 14 April 2017; Published: 20 April 2017

Abstract: Although rhetoric about wages and jobs often emphasizes the effects of globalization, questions remain as to whether United States workers are paid adequately to sustain a reasonable standard of living. One solution is to implement a living wage, which is accurate and specific to a local economy but more computationally complex than a one-size-fits-all minimum wage. When considered economically, a living wage has the potential to increase business and production costs as well as lower profits and cause job loss. From ethical viewpoints articulated in Catholic social thought, sustainable wages enhance human dignity by supporting human agency, encouraging creativity, and permitting contributions to the common good. This article explores whether the positive ethical outcomes of implementing a living wage outweigh any possibly negative, unintended economic results.

Keywords: economic inequality; social justice; interdisciplinary studies; living wages; just wages; economic implications; ethical implications

1. Introduction

Although it debuted in the late 1970's, Italian playwright Dario Fo's working-class farce, translated as "They Don't Pay? We Can't Pay!" or more emphatically "We Won't Pay! We Won't Pay!" captures the timeless struggle between employer profits and employee wages. In the story, an economic downturn forces a factory to reduce workers' wages while at the same time rent is due and prices at the local market soar. Frustrated and desperate, women shoppers loot the store, stealing food for their tables. They hide the items under coats, appearing to be pregnant in order to fool their husbands and the police. Slapstick adventures ensue. Yet the play raises serious ethical issues regarding human rights, dignity, and survival in unjust economic conditions. Of fundamental concern is whether workers in the United States are paid adequately to support a reasonable standard of living and accumulate long-term wealth. From ethical viewpoints articulated in Catholic social thought, sustainable wages enhance human dignity by supporting human agency, encouraging creativity, and permitting contributions to the common good. They also enable greater economic, community, and political participation, thereby promoting justice. One solution to inadequate compensation is the notion of a living wage, which frequently differs from legislated national minimum wage amounts. Because a living wage reflects specific local economic conditions, it more accurately meets a worker's basic needs in a particular area. The ultimate question regarding living wage proposals is whether the positive ethical effects of reducing wage inadequacy and its resultant poverty are economically sustainable.

2. Living Wage Definition

Local living wage ordinances comprise multiple types of benefits that affect various categories of employees. By definition, a living wage enables a person to support oneself and one's family without government assistance. As a result, workers contribute to society by paying taxes, by acquiring wealth for long-term goals, and by spending their income locally, which stimulates economic development, often in the neediest communities. (See Stephen Leccese's work in this volume on historical views of workers' wages and spending in the economy.) Unlike a one-size-fits-all minimum wage floor, living wages are tailored to the local economy and its standard of living, which makes the wage more accurate but involves a more complex calculation and definition. A living wage calculator estimates an hourly wage for a 40-hour workweek that affords one head-of-household (with various combinations that comprise a family) the means to live in a certain area. The Austin-Round Rock, Texas area, for example, calculates an income based on costs of shelter, taxes, and utilities at fair market housing rates [1]. Additionally, the wage includes per person food allowances from the USDA's Thrifty Food Plan tables, average medical insurance prices across age groups, budgets for clothing, personal items, and transportation from consumer expenditure surveys, along with a small budget allocation for long-term expenses and savings.

3. Economic Implications of a Living Wage

One advantage to local living wage ordinances is their flexibility and customization to a specific community's economic conditions. Businessmen such as Henry Ford and Edward Filene understood that paying reasonable wages was sound business policy; the practice expands a laborer's purchasing power and enables him or her to buy the company's products ([2], p. 5). A rise in aggregate demand stimulates the economy, especially since "low-wage workers are more apt to spend earnings locally, circulating money back into local economies" ([2], p. 6). Thus, "increasing the economic self-sufficiency of workers enhances business productivity and opens new markets, while also reducing poverty, strengthening communities, and shrinking the demand for government assistance to low-income families" ([2], p. 7). These positive multiplier effects help rebuild lives and strengthen local economies.

Increasing worker pay above the poverty line to a living wage not only helps families escape the stigma of poverty, it also reduces reliance on government welfare programs. Many workers and their families receive public assistance because their employers do not pay enough to meet the employee's basic needs ([3], p. 5). Rather than encourage businesses to compensate employees appropriately, the government, through taxpayers, subsidizes businesses that pay low wages. The government also loses revenue from income and social security taxes when businesses pay minimal wages, rather than higher living wages in some areas [4]. A living wage must be sufficient to support a person without government subsidies; otherwise, it "could increase cash earnings only at the expense of other forms of income, changing the composition but not the amount of income" [5]. As incomes increase, workers reduce their reliance on government assistance. Living wage earners are able to pay their taxes, contribute to social security, and save for emergencies as well as their own retirement. In doing so, some of the living wages costs affecting business owners and consumers are offset by gains to small businesses and individual taxpayers at federal and local levels.

Not only do workers and taxpayers benefit from living wages, business owners profit in a variety of ways. The efficiency wage hypothesis suggests, "the productivity of a firm's employees increases as their wage is increased, at least over an economically relevant part of its [wage] range" ([6], p. 848). With less absenteeism, and lower turnover, the estimated cost savings for companies "could be as high as 20 to 25 percent of their total living wage costs" ([7], p. 19). For instance, the owner of travel agency, Idyll, Ltd., concedes "the trade-off for paying decent wages is lower immediate profits, but adds that his costs would be up in other areas (recruitment and training) if he 'skimped on employee pay'" ([2], p. 17). In Los Angeles for example, security screeners had a high turnover rate of 94.7 percent before the living wage, but their turnover rate dropped to just 18.7 percent when earnings increased from $6.45 to $10.00 an hour ([8], pp. 10, 54). Reduced employee attrition lowers recruiting and training costs while cultivating an experienced workforce. Furthermore, satisfied clients generate repeat business with less marketing and sales effort, which yields higher profit margins and added benefits ([8], pp. 9–10). Because living wage ordinances prevent government contract bidders from undercutting wages or benefits, service quality becomes a key differentiator among competitors ([9], pp. 21–23). To summarize, employee loyalty as well as proficiency results in higher product quality, efficiency, and consistent customer service, all of which are in the self-interest of company managers and owners.

Most economic models predict that higher wages result in greater production costs. Rising production costs increase prices for goods, which reduce product demand until the supply and demand curves reach a new equilibrium point. Demand elasticity however may not be as strong an economic influence since "a living wage stimulates the overall demand for goods and services in the economy and can result in job growth" [4]. Likewise, standard economic efficiency theories argue that increasing wages drives less efficient employers out of business or causes layoffs. In these situations, "employers may find ways to offset the increased labor costs for low-wage labor by reducing costs in other dimensions" ([10], p. 32) such as improving processes, utilizing technology, or using labor more effectively. As a result, employers expect greater productivity from workers, so, it is logical for "some [job] substitutions to occur, both by educational credentials and age, though, the magnitude of such substitutions is likely to be modest" ([7], p. 33). Most labor layoff/substitution occurs at living wage ordinance boundaries, either by area or by business-type, because better skilled people earning between minimum and living wage apply and are hired for comparable living wage jobs. Although job substitution does not alter the goal of paying workers livable wages, it does affect who earns the higher wage.

Neoclassical economic theory also predicts greater unemployment when wages increase. Living wages potentially cause unintended effects, especially "if employers need to raise the wages of other workers to maintain a wage hierarchy within the firm, [then] the ripple effect can cause even greater employment losses" ([11], p. 14). However, it is difficult to determine the extent of these losses. An Economic Policy Institute study in 1998 concluded that "after four years in force, the Baltimore living wage increase did not result in any discernible job loss" ([2], p. 10). In fact, research by Card and Krueger corroborate studies by Neumark and Wascher that living wage or "higher minimum wage mandates do not behave in the manner predicted by competitive models and that average firm employment does not decline but may in fact increase slightly following minimum wage increases" ([9], p. 6). The unemployed often fill positions that the formerly underemployed no longer need to make ends meet. When asked what a worker was going to do with the extra money after Alexandria, VA passed its living wage ordinance, he replied, "Quit my third job!" ([12], p. 26). Evidence reveals that employment rates hold relatively steady if the coverage area or wage increases are modest.

Implementing living wages may prompt businesses to relocate operations to more favorable, cost-effective locations. Economically, "firms should be drawn to low-wage areas, causing job growth to be highest where pay is lowest, as long as all other things—taxes, public services, rents, access to customers and so forth—are equal" ([13], p. 6). However, several factors go into a decision to relocate. The issues include labor and production costs, customer base, business type, labor supply, and the area economy. Sometimes a location has intrinsic value, such as waterfront, views, or proximity to sports arenas or convention centers, which complicates the decision. Existing companies ultimately must decide whether the marginal benefits of relocation are greater than the costs of relocation in addition to living wage cost increases.

Whether a business relocates, absorbs expenses, or raises prices depends on factors such as the cost increase percentage, the firm's competition, and the product's demand elasticity. If production costs increase one to two percent, companies may decide to absorb expenses rather than risk losing business ([9], p. 24). Likewise, some effects of raising prices are minimal. At the San Francisco airport, for example, passing higher employee compensation costs to consumers results in an increase of $1.42 per passenger ([8], pp. 9, 49). With living wage ordinances, it is easier for local firms competing for similar business to raise their prices since their competitors face similar cost increases. Yet increasing prices in global markets is problematic because competitors are not subject to local living wage rules.

4. Ethical Implications of a Living Wage

The economic implications of a living wage address whether wages can be increased but not whether wages should be increased. Evaluating the ethical implications of a living wage involves what it does for and to the people and how people subsequently participate in the economy ([14], para. 1, 13). Hence, according to Catholic social teaching a living wage is ethical if it upholds human rights and dignity, supports the common good, enables participation, creates right relationships, and secures economic justice for all stakeholders.

The Christian principle of human dignity states that each human being is sacred and holy because a person is a child of God; made in God's image. Dignity comes from God, not from one's livelihood, salary, or bank account totals. Although humans possess the talents and skills necessary to build wealth through labor, merely possessing wealth hinders one's ultimate goal of eternal life; instead, wealth must be used justly ([15], para. 22, 34–35). God therefore calls humanity to co-create, to transform the earth through work, which is good and thus enhances human dignity ([16], para. 9, 25). Work entails more than a fair income; it encourages people to grow and develop by sharing in the responsibility and creativity of the labor process. A worker offers labor in return for sustenance and a share in God's creation, so a laborer has a natural right to a wage that sustains a person and his or her children, one that adequately addresses one's essential needs ([15], para. 9, 32, 61–63). In the Catholic tradition, economic institutions are to serve workers rather than exploit them ([14], para. 13, 28). Employers promote human dignity by respecting workers, considering their well-being, protecting religious freedom and property, besides paying them what they are justly due ([15], para. 31–32). With just (living) wages for just work, employers as well as employees contribute to the common good.

Humans are by nature social beings; they find their identity and full development by participating in community. Work is one form of interrelated participation with others. Consequently, the employee, employer, and consumer all have duties within the economic order. The employee's duty is to contribute value to a company's product in return for a wage as well as "contributing to the common good, according to his [sic] own abilities and the needs of others" ([17], para. 30). Economist Milton Friedman asserts the social responsibility of business is "to use its resources and engage in activities designed to increase its profits" ([18], p. 1). However, Catholic social teaching views business as a particular group of people striving to satisfy their basic needs in service to society in general ([19], para. 35). An employer's duty is to provide just wages to all workers since "to exercise pressure for the sake of gain, upon the indigent and destitute, and to make one's profit out of the need of another, is condemned by all laws, human and divine" ([15], para. 17). Early in the twentieth century, employers believed they had a moral responsibility to pay their workers a living wage and those "who paid less than a living were viewed as harming not only their workers' health and morals but the health of the community as well" ([20], pp. 216–17). Without living wages, people must meet their basic needs by working longer hours, sometimes at multiple workplaces, which leaves little time for family, faith, or civic activities.

Consumer decisions also directly influence wages; yet few shoppers consider their roles in supporting living wages. Too frequently, "people want cheaper shoes and most do not care who makes them" ([21], p. 417). Many people claim invincible ignorance since they seldom ponder what businesses must do to offer low prices and still make a profit. Commerce, along a global supply chain, entails an interrelated dependence among persons, states, and various socio-economic institutions, all of which Pope John Paul II refers to as indirect employers ([16], para. 17). Consequently, high wages and low prices often conflict because paying living wages along the entire supply chain quickly gets complicated and expensive [22]. But John Ryan argues that the consumer "is morally bound to pay such prices for goods as will enable all business men [sic] to obtain a decent livelihood" ([23], p. 362). By purchasing items from ethical firms paying adequate wages, consumers take moral responsibility for their buying behaviors; their product choices reflect their cultural values ([19], para. 36). Furthermore, consumers should choose ethical investments so that present and future capital eventually benefits individuals along with the common good.

Critical ethical indicators of society's economic health include its wealth production as well as its income distribution. (See Kenneth Himes' work in this volume on John Ryan regarding wage ceilings and floors.) In 1965, the average American CEO-to-worker pay ratio was 20-to-1; but 50 years later, the ratio was 303-to-1 ([24], pp. 2, 6). The principle of solidarity suggests, "when ratios of compensation between highest and lowest paid workers in a firm become too great; there is a loss of unity and reciprocity" ([25], p. 14). If a society values individualism rather than solidarity, then it creates a Darwinian survival-of-the-fittest attitude rather than a community of persons working toward the common good. Consequently, the result is income inequality. Excessive inequality hinders a community's ability to solve problems or achieve common objectives; societies grow more slowly and have more trouble adjusting to changes than those with equitable distributions of wealth and income ([26], p. 15). (See Kate Ward's work in this volume on inequality and the virtue of hospitality.) One's inability to keep pace with rising costs while observing others' incomes increase rapidly, causes discord, strife, violence for society and violates a value of fairness and societal cooperation [27]. Reassuringly, wealth distribution is a social scheme, so it is open to improvement. Catholic social teaching supports just distribution of income through the stewardship of low-interest loans, such as micro-loans, which allow low-income people to start small business, buy homes, and better themselves through hard work ([14], para. 265, 274–79). Moreover, profit sharing, stock ownership, and pension/retirement programs also effectively distribute business capital to workers ([14], para. 300). Trade and labor unions likewise contribute to equable income distribution when they collectively negotiate of behalf of workers without harming vulnerable members of society or the common good ([14], para. 106). Equitable income distribution promotes workplace harmony in addition to a just economy.

Another vital component to sustaining community is the inclusion and participation of all citizens in its economy. Because the current economic system requires wealth in order to participate, from a Catholic social thought perspective, it would be judged an unjust failure. The inability to participate in political or economic activity is the ultimate injustice toward a person and rectifying it is the highest social priority ([14], para. 77, 91). Rectifying this injustice requires a preferential option for the poor, which calls for greater solidarity with and among the underprivileged in economic and political decisions, especially regarding employment and wages ([14], para. 88). By promoting the common good, "human dignity of all is realized when people gain the power to work together to improve their lives, strengthen their families, and contribute to society" ([14], para. 91) since basic justice calls for economic participation through employment and property ownership. Nevertheless, to participate fully in the economy and obtain property, people require an adequate flow of income that enables long-term accumulated wealth. Eventually, amassed wealth provides insurance for emergencies plus collateral for business loans, mortgages, or capital purchases. A living wage therefore establishes economic justice ([28], p. 69). In addition to a living wage, workers require adequate health care, job and old age security, healthy working conditions, and periodic rest for rejuvenation ([14], para. 103). Solidarity interconnects all people worldwide; nevertheless, global markets create intense competition for inexpensive labor. However, respect for worker's rights and dignity must direct appropriate living wage solutions for each nation's and the world's economies ([16], para. 17). Behaving ethically and responsibly dissuades unfair business competition that takes advantage of impoverished workers who must compete against each other for low-paying jobs.

Wealth accumulation creates private property for workers. According to Catholic social teaching, the right to private property is sacred and represents wages in a different form ([15], para. 4, 35). Ownership, however, equates to stewardship of goods originally meant for all, thus, private property has a social dimension; the state has the duty to prevent people from abusing private property rights and harming the common good ([14] para. 114–15). As a result, philosophical debates ensue over whether government has the authority to regulate the price of labor. One side of the argument appeals to workers' rights, dignity, and justice, while the other side claims regulations are a form of coercion, which violates their property rights ([29], pp. 156–60). The first argument appeals to notions of social and economic justice, which utilize moral principles to create economic institutions that distribute wealth, property, and opportunities within society that benefits the whole society. In terms of commutative justice, which involves justice between two individuals or entities, those arguing against wage regulation perceive it to be unfair to businesses. Instead, they favor market forces for setting wages; yet, what is referred to as the free market is not free at all because government agencies often manipulate interest rates and other economic indicators while granting businesses billions of dollars in subsidies, tax breaks, and other forms of corporate welfare in the name of economic growth ([3], pp. 12–15). Both viewpoints concede that wages enabling people to live above the poverty line are a noble goal, as long as it respects the rights of both employer and employee through free negotiation. Nevertheless, a delicate balance exists between economic justice and fiscal prudence that influences government action. If the government establishes living wage regulations without creating economic and social structures to support it, then many individual employers cannot unilaterally pay wages above the market wage; they will be unable to compete. Competitors utilizing inexpensive overseas labor or other cost cutting supply-chain mechanisms force other firms to cut wages, lay off workers, relocate abroad, or close.

The broad role of government is to promote security, encourage prosperity, and provide protection for all citizens. For example, the United States government has a history of setting job quality standards, which include minimum wage laws, overtime requirements, prohibitions against child labor, occupational safety and health standards, family and medical leave, and now living wage ordinances. However, the State is not expected to resolve every social problem. In Catholic social teaching, the principle of subsidiarity claims that the most local levels of governance are more appropriate for determining responsibilities and making decisions within communities since the individual, the family, and society are all prior to the State ([14], para. 99). According to this principle, the business community is the proper level of subsidiary to establish living wage amounts and regulations. If companies ignore their duty or are unable to sustain their business at just wage rates, then the State has a duty to protect its citizens, especially the vulnerable ones. Government regulation frequently causes tension between conflicting viewpoints regarding commutative and social justice. What appears to be coercion or a violation of property rights to businesses may in fact be State intervention to benefit society. By legislating living wages, the State imposes the stewardship function on businesses to share their wealth in a just manner that benefits the common good.

Two primary components of economic justice entail the right to work and the right to a just wage. For a living wage to be considered just, it must sustain worker and family expenses with enough income to acquire long-term wealth. A fair wage also includes a benefits package and skills training. In a just worker-employer relationship, "an employer must recognize that employees 'surrender' their time and energy and so they cannot use it for another purpose" ([30], pp. 10–11), thereby requiring a living wage in return. Furthermore, the free consent of both parties is necessary. If workers agree to low wages under duress, then the arrangement is unjust and invalid ([15], para. 61, 63). For businesses, profits are an essential, legitimate goal, but not at the expense of paying unjust wages. As President Franklin D. Roosevelt said, "No business that depends for existence on paying less than living wages has any right to continue in this country" ([31], p. 14). Worker rights take precedence, so laborers should be paid a living wage prior to determining business profits. On the one hand, "it would be unjust to demand excessive wages, which a business cannot pay without its ruin and consequent calamity to the workers" ([32], para. 72). On the other hand, businesses are not to use this principle of feasibility to act inefficiently or to supplement low wage rates with government programs.

5. Conclusions

In Catholic social thought, businesses have the moral responsibility to act as stewards of a company's property and profits and to establish right relationships with their employees by paying them just wages. The economic benefits from paying living wages are increased productivity, quality, innovation, and morale, all of which contribute to greater profits. Failing to do so, the government has an obligation to protect society, especially the poorest workers, and to ensure the common good for all.

Ethical consumer choices also maintain solidarity and a healthy economic order for all stakeholders. However, a living wage involves more than increasing a person's hourly rate of pay. In adding value to finished products, a worker establishes the right to a living wage. The act of escaping poverty then sustaining a livelihood without government subsidies restores human dignity and builds wealth. With security and wealth, workers participate in family, economic, and political activities, thereby contributing to the common good. Consequently, the notion of living wages is sustainable economically and supportable ethically.

Conflicts of Interest: The author declares no conflict of interest.

References

1. Amy K. Glasmeier. "Living Wage Calculation for Austin-Round Rock, TX." *Massachusetts Institute of Technology Living Wage Calculator.* Available online: http://livingwage.mit.edu/metros/12420 (accessed on 15 February 2017).
2. Karen Kraut, Scott Klinger, and Chuck Collins. *Choosing the High Road: Businesses that Pay a Living Wage and Prosper.* Boston: Responsible Wealth, 2000.
3. Carol Zabin, Arindrajit Dube, and Ken Jacobs. *The Hidden Public Costs of Low-Wage Jobs in California.* Berkley: The National Economic Development and Law Center, University of California, Berkley, 2004.
4. Ralph Scharnau. "American Workers Deserve Enactment of U.S. Living Wage; Congressional Pay Goes up, But the Federal Minimum Has Not Risen Since 1997." *Dubuque Telegraph Herald*, 7 August 2005.
5. Craig Garthwaite. "'Living Wage' Laws Don't Help Low-Income Families." *Budget & Tax News*, 1 September 2005.
6. James M. Malcomson. "Unemployment and the Efficiency Wage Hypothesis." *The Economic Journal* 91 (1981): 848–66. [CrossRef]
7. Robert Pollin. "Evaluating Living Wage Laws in the United States: Good Intentions and Economic Reality in Conflict? " *Journal of Strategic Contracting and Negotiation* 19 (2005): 3–24. [CrossRef]
8. Michael Reich, Peter Hall, and Ken Jacobs. *Living Wages and Economic Performance: The San Francisco Airport Model.* Berkeley: Institute of Industrial Relations, 2003.
9. Mark Brenner. *The Economic Impact of Living Wage Ordinances.* Amherst: Political Economy Research Institute, 2003.
10. David Neumark. "Living Wages: Protection for or Protection from Low-Wage Workers? " *Industrial and Labor Relations Review* 58 (2004): 27–51. [CrossRef]
11. Madeline Zavodny. "Reexamining the Minimum Wage." In *Southwest Economy.* Dallas: Federal Reserve Bank of Dallas, 1996, pp. 12–15.
12. Bobbi Murray. "Living Wage Comes of Age." *The Nation* 273 (2001): 24–27.
13. Lori L. Taylor. "The Border: Is It Really a Low Wage Area? " In *Monograph.* Dallas: Federal Reserve Bank of Dallas, 2001, pp. 6–8.
14. National Conference of Catholic Bishops. "Economic Justice for All: On Catholic Social Teaching and the U.S. Economy." In *Catholic Social Teaching: The Documentary Heritage.* Edited by David J. O'Brien and Thomas Shannon. Maryknoll: Orbis Books, 1992, pp. 572–680.
15. Leo, XIII. "Rerum Novarum (The Condition of Labor)." In *Catholic Social Teaching: The Documentary Heritage.* Edited by David J. O'Brien and Thomas Shannon. Maryknoll: Orbis Books, 1992, pp. 12–39.
16. John Paul, II. "Laborem Exercens (On Human Work)." In *Catholic Social Teaching: The Documentary Heritage.* Edited by David J. O'Brien and Thomas Shannon. Maryknoll: Orbis Books, 1992, pp. 350–92.
17. Paul, VI. "Gaudium et Spes (Pastoral Constitution on the Church in the Modern World)." In *Catholic Social Teaching: The Documentary Heritage.* Edited by David J. O'Brien and Thomas Shannon. Maryknoll: Orbis Books, 1992, pp. 164–237.
18. Anonymous. "Doing Well by Doing Good." *The Economist* 355 (2000): 65–67.
19. John Paul, II. "Centesimus Annus (On the Hundredth Anniversary of Rerum Novarum)." In *Catholic Social Teaching: The Documentary Heritage.* Edited by David J. O'Brien and Thomas Shannon. Maryknoll: Orbis Books, 1992, pp. 437–88.
20. Deborah M. Figart, Ellen Mutari, and Marilyn Power. *Living Wages, Equal Wages: Gender and Labor Market Policies in the United States.* New York: Routledge, 2002.

21. Andrei Shleifer. "Does Competition Destroy Ethical Behavior? " *AEA Papers and Proceedings* 94 (2004): 414–18. [CrossRef]
22. Andrew Muras. "Duties of the Consumer." *Religion and Liberty* 13 (2003): 10–12.
23. John A. Ryan. *Distributive Justice: The Right and Wrong of Our Present Distribution of Wealth*. New York: Macmillan, 1916.
24. Lawrence Mishel, and Alyssa Davis. "Top CEOs Make 300 Times More than Typical Workers: Pay Growth Surpasses Stock Gains and Wage Growth of Top 0.1 Percent." *Economic Policy Institute Issue Brief*, 21 June 2015, #399.
25. Patricia Ann Lamoureux. "Is a Living Wage a Just Wage? " *America, the National Catholic Weekly* 184 (2001): 12–15.
26. Austin Equity Commission. *Improving the Odds, Building a Comprehensive Opportunity Structure for Austin*. Austin: Austin Equity Commission, 2001.
27. Bob Brownstein. "Is It Ethical to Shop at Wal-Mart? " Paper presented at the Ethics at Noon Conference, Santa Clara University Markkula Center for Applied Ethics, Santa Clara, CA, USA, 12 April 2004.
28. Lawrence B. Glickman. *A Living Wage: American Workers and the Making of Consumer Society*. Ithaca: Cornell University Press, 1997.
29. Helen Alford, and Michael J. Naughton. *Managing as if Faith Mattered: Christian Social Principles in the Modern Organization*. Notre Dame: University of Notre Dame Press, 2001.
30. Michael J. Naughton. "A Theology of Fair Pay." *Regent Business Review* 15 (2005): 9–14.
31. Richard Freeman. "Fighting for Other Folk's Wages: The Logic and Illogic of Living Wage Campaigns." *Industrial Relations* 44 (2005). 14–31.
32. Pius, XI. "Quadragesimo Anno (After Forty Years)." In *Catholic Social Teaching: The Documentary Heritage*. Edited by David J. O'Brien and Thomas Shannon. Maryknoll: Orbis Books, 1992, pp. 40–80.

![religions logo] *religions*

MDPI

Article

Jesuit and Feminist Hospitality: Pope Francis' Virtue Response to Inequality

Kate Ward

Theology Department, Marquette University, Milwaukee, WI 53233, USA; katharine.ward@marquette.edu;
Tel.: +1-414-288-3737

Academic Editors: Kenneth Himes and Roberto Cipriani
Received: 3 February 2017; Accepted: 5 April 2017; Published: 19 April 2017

Abstract: Pope Francis is the first Jesuit pope and has made economic inequality a theme of his pontificate. This article shows that Pope Francis diagnoses economic inequality as both a structural problem and a problem of virtue, and that the virtue he calls for in response is what James F. Keenan, SJ has called Jesuit hospitality. Reviewing contemporary theological work on hospitality, I show that Francis' Jesuit hospitality shares many features with hospitality as described by feminist theologians. Namely, it is risky, takes place across difference, acknowledges the marginality of both host and guest, and promises mutual benefit to each party. Francis' account of the spiritual practice of encounter provides a concrete vision of Jesuit hospitality in action. This article contributes to existing literature on the uniquely Jesuit nature of Francis' theology and to work showing the resonance of his intellectual standpoint with feminist approaches. It proposes a Christian virtue response to the pressing contemporary problem of economic inequality.

Keywords: inequality; virtue; hospitality; Jesuit; Pope Francis; feminism

1. Introduction

In today's globalized, unequal world, 2.2 billion people live on less than $2 U.S. per day while 62 individuals own as much wealth as the poorest half of the world [1]. This and other shocking statistics have made economic inequality an issue of urgent concern for scholars, policy makers and religious leaders. Pope Francis spoke out strongly on the issue in his 2013 apostolic exhortation, *Evangelii Gaudium*, which links the harmful reality of extreme economic inequality with the church's evangelical mission [2]. Francis insists that economic inequality excludes many people from society as those with privilege withdraw from common life and turn inward. Scholars across disciplines confirm this insight [3–5].

In the first section of this essay, I review Francis' description of the problem of inequality in *Evangelii Gaudium*, showing how his diagnosis of inequality's damage affirms and goes beyond the insights of social scientists to show inequality as a virtue problem. In the essay's second section, I review recent scholarship on the virtue of hospitality, demonstrating how feminist scholars insist that hospitality is risky, mutual, marginal, and takes place across difference. In the third section, I argue that Francis' virtue perspective on inequality presumes the virtue James F. Keenan, SJ calls Jesuit hospitality as a solution, while Francis deepens our understanding of that virtue by proposing his own spiritual practice of encounter. I draw this work together to argue that the virtue of hospitality, understood in Jesuit and feminist keys, can help us respond to extreme economic inequality in our time. This research makes two contributions: it proposes a Christian virtue response to the pressing contemporary problem of economic inequality, and it details an aspect of Francis' theology, particularly as Jesuit, that is heretofore little appreciated.

2. Inequality as a Virtue Problem

Not many years ago, I would have felt it necessary to make the case that economic inequality should be discussed as a problem distinct from poverty; that it had related, but distinct causes, impacts, and solutions. Today, however, as attested by the work of many authors in this volume, it is widely understood that extreme economic inequality threatens the well-being of societies and the individuals within them, and that some of these harms would remain even if extreme poverty were sufficiently addressed. For example, inequality limits political voice [4]. It correlates with serious social problems including crime, incarceration, drug abuse, poor health, and early death, and affects all members of society, not just the poorest, on these measures [5]. Inequality harms social mobility [6], which has negative psychological and social impacts for unemployed people [3]. Evidence continues to mount that inequality is a problem distinct from poverty and should be treated as such.

Pope Francis certainly concurs with the insights of social scientists about inequality's harms, but he adds a nuance: he diagnoses inequality as a virtue problem. The virtue approach to understanding the moral life asks what qualities we need to develop to make us truly human, and how we can develop them in our own lives ([7], p. 23). Francis explores the impact of inequality on the virtues, or qualities, persons are able to develop throughout their lives, and finds that inequality causes exclusion, threatening our ability to become fully human, flourishing beings in community with one another. First I will show how Francis takes up the impact of inequality on societal structures and the common good, and then turn to his analysis of its effect on personal virtue.

For Francis, the worst effect of widespread inequality is exclusion. He writes this: "It is no longer simply about exploitation and oppression, but something new. Exclusion ultimately has to do with what it means to be a part of the society in which we live; those excluded are no longer society's underside or its fringes or its disenfranchised—they are no longer even a part of it" ([2], p. 53). Inclusion demands societies prioritize "education, access to health care, and above all employment [in] free, creative, participatory and mutually supportive labour" ([2], p. 192). This is a rich and detailed view of what inclusion looks like—it is not mere subsistence, nor mere access to consumer goods, but full participation in those goods that members of society create through their life together.

Francis ratifies the findings of public health scholars by noting that when people are excluded from society, the result is often violence.[1] He says: "When a society [...] is willing to leave a part of itself on the fringes, no political programmes or resources spent on law enforcement or surveillance systems can indefinitely guarantee tranquility" ([2], p. 59). When he says "When a society is *willing* to leave part of itself on the fringes," Francis clearly insists that people are not excluded by inequality because of their own individual failings. Rather, allowing some to be excluded from life by the economy is a choice, an act of will on the part of society, and a society can choose to shape things differently.[2]

Pope Francis is very clear on the fact that inequality is not natural or inevitable. Rather, it is created by human choices and can be changed. He says, "Some people continue to defend trickle-down theories which assume that economic growth, encouraged by a free market, will inevitably succeed in bringing about greater justice and inclusiveness in the world." And he calls this view an "opinion, which has never been confirmed by the facts" ([2], p. 54). He decries "ideologies which defend the absolute autonomy of the marketplace," ([2], p. 56) and says "No to a financial system which rules rather than serves" ([2], p. 57). Human dignity should be absolute, but the current financial system sees money and power as absolute and human dignity as relative (ibid.)

Thus far, the perspective of *Evangelii Gaudium* on the harmful aspects of inequality sounds similar to the critiques offered by thinkers in the secular realm. Inequality harms the common good when

---

[1] Social scientists concur that violence in society rises with inequality: see ([5], pp. 140–41).

[2] Pope Francis' writings are notable for his broad reliance on the statements of bishops from all around the world. *Evangelii Gaudium* includes quotes from bishops' groups on six continents, like this statement from the bishops of Brazil: "We know that there is enough food for everyone and that hunger is the result of a poor distribution of goods and income" ([2], p. 191). Hunger is not inevitable, and neither is inequality. Both are products of human choice.

it excludes people from the basic needs of life; when it keeps them from meaningful work and from participation in society; and when it leads to violence [3–5]. Inequality is a structural problem, it was created by human choice, and it can be changed. While it's certainly valuable that Pope Francis adds the impact of his global stature to these critiques, in fact his most unique contribution lies elsewhere. The unique word that Pope Francis has to say on inequality is that it's a virtue problem. Not only is it a symptom of certain moral failings in societies, it helps cause moral failings and make them worse, interfering with the development of virtues like solidarity, compassion, and justice.

Francis eloquently describes the way that global inequalities help keep people who are comfortable from experiencing solidarity with the suffering poor. He says:

> To sustain a lifestyle which excludes others, or to sustain enthusiasm for that selfish ideal, a globalization of indifference has developed. Almost without being aware of it, we end up being incapable of feeling compassion at the outcry of the poor, weeping for other people's pain, and feeling a need to help them. [...] The culture of prosperity deadens us; we are thrilled if the market offers us something new to purchase. In the meantime all those lives stunted for lack of opportunity seem a mere spectacle; they fail to move us ([2], p. 54).

It's important to note here that Francis acknowledges the mutual relationship between the virtue of a person and the society a person lives in and helps to create. At one time we might have said that social sin is simply a manifestation of the sum of individual sins—for example, that because many people lack temperance, societies display consumerism.[3] Francis is saying something more complex, describing a vicious circle. The globalization of indifference helps to shape indifferent persons, whose actions, or rather failure to act, expand the culture of indifference. The globalization of indifference impedes persons from developing and exercising the virtues of compassion, solidarity and justice.

The argument that unequal societies impede virtue is relatively new in theology. Although Pope Francis is its best-known exponent, the argument is not unique to him. I want to briefly call attention to a few other theologians who have made similar points. (Very much in line with theologians' concerns, philosopher Dustin Crummett, in this volume, shows how vast wealth can impede well-being from an objective list or hybrid, rather than a virtue, theory of well-being [11].)

An instantly memorable account of how inequality in society impedes virtue comes from the Nigerian theologian Olubiyi Adeniyi Adewale in his essay on the parable of Lazarus and the rich man (Luke 16:19–31). As Luke's Gospel tells us, Lazarus was a beggar who received no help from a rich man, until they both died and the rich man came to regret his hard-heartedness.

In Lazarus' time on earth, the only help he received was from "dogs [who] came and licked his sores." Adewale says that in African belief, the saliva of dogs can be helpful for healing, and Jews in Jesus' time believed this as well. So the dogs who licked Lazarus' sores were helping him—but the rich man, of course did not help him at all. Adewale argues that the rich man thus failed to be human. Blinded by his own love for money, he reveals himself as less human than the dogs [12].

Adewale compares Christians in wealthy societies to the rich man in the parable. Thanks to globalized media, he says, "like the biblical Lazarus, the poor in Africa have been laid at the gate of the rich brethren of the developed countries [...] Unfortunately, to date, a large percentage of the believers in the developed countries seem to have decided not to "see" their covenant brethren in distress" ([12], p. 40). The wealth of Christians in developed countries interferes with their development of the virtues of compassion and justice.

U.S. theologians have also addressed the link between virtue or vice and inequality. In 2008, Bryan Massingale wrote that in the U.S., individualism, consumerism and racism create a unique type of "cultured indifference" to the poor [13]. This is similar to Pope Francis' suggestion that the

---

[3] That no theologian would describe the relationship between social sin and personal virtue so simplistically today is thanks to the great work of many theologians who explain it more thoughtfully. See for example [8–10].

"globalization of indifference" shapes our response to those in poverty. David Cloutier's work on luxury [14,15] and Julie Hanlon Rubio's family ethics of consumption [16] also point in this direction. When Cloutier warns against luxury and Rubio promotes tithing, they are not just thinking of the funds that could be redirected to address poverty, although that is part of their concern. They also suggest that spending lavishly, even if one can afford it, may promote vice and that we can help ourselves develop virtues like compassion and solidarity by living more moderately.

Following Francis and other theologians, we could understand economic inequality, and our position within unequal societies by virtue of wealth or poverty, as a type of moral luck. In virtue ethics, moral luck indicates acknowledgement that due to life circumstances beyond our control, we are not all equally positioned to pursue virtue ([7], pp. 29–30; see also [17]). Rubio acknowledges this when she notes that a typical middle-class lifestyle leaves many Christian parents wanting something "more" and "deeper" for themselves and their children, and counsels virtuous practice as a solution ([16], pp. 191–92). Cloutier does the same when he shows how the positional nature of certain economic goods encourages the vice of luxury ([15], pp. 160–66), and Francis when he insists that inequality encourages moral deadness ([2], p. 54). That is all I will say about that now, simply to acknowledge that the notion that life circumstances shape our pursuit of virtue, sometimes for the worse, is a notion growing in acceptance in Christian virtue ethics.

While Francis recognizes the economic and social factors that create and sustain inequality, there is no clearer evidence of the fact that he recognizes inequality as a virtue problem than his proposed solution: the virtuous practice of encounter. His description of the practice of encounter helps us read Francis' theology particularly as Jesuit.[4]

In *Evangelii Gaudium* and other writings, as well as by example through his actions, Francis calls Christians to be "the church which goes forth" ([2], p. 24). "Going forth," "going out of ourselves," is one of the most common phrases in *Evangelii Gaudium*. Francis' description of encounter clearly evokes the virtue James F. Keenan, a Jesuit like Francis, has called "Jesuit hospitality" [19]. Before introducing the notion of Jesuit hospitality and showing how Francis' theology of encounter relies on this virtue, I will review recent scholarship on hospitality to show how this virtue has evolved, in the understanding of contemporary feminist theologians, to a virtue that crosses boundaries of difference, accepts risk, embraces marginality of both host and guest, produces mutual benefit for both host and guest, and ably meets the demands of a world of deep inequality.

3. Hospitality in a Feminist Key

By far the most in-depth and interesting recent work on the virtue of hospitality comes from authors with implicit or explicit feminist commitments. No surprise there, as attention to embodiment, quotidian life, and activity traditionally gendered as feminine are among the feminist intellectual commitments that urge attention to this most vexed of virtues. Many begin by rejecting traditional mischaracterizations of the virtue. Feminist authors universally denounce visions of hospitality as "cozy" and "sentimental," what Letty Russell associates with "tea and crumpets" ([20], p. 19) and "terminal niceness" ([20], p. 80). For Russell, hospitality is also practiced in a way that "deforms" it from its purpose when "it is practiced as a way of caring for so called 'inferior people' by those who are more advantaged and able to prove their superiority by being 'generous,'" a model of hospitality Russell criticizes with the term 'lady bountiful.' ([20], pp. 80–81).[5] Elizabeth Newman blasts "Disney World hospitality" which paints God's realm as a magic kingdom of ease, free from challenge ([21], p. 24).

---

[4]   Pope Francis has often acknowledged the deep influence of Ignatian spirituality on his life and thought, and many commentators observe this in everything from the language he uses to instruct the Curia to his personal humility ([18], pp. 414–17).

[5]   Feminists have long remarked that certain qualities or behaviors are subject to criticism in women but not in men, leading to the existence of gendered insults that have no equivalent for men. "Lady bountiful" appears to be one of these.

In contrast to all these notions, scholars today insist, hospitality is a risky virtue.[6] It involves risk to both guest and host, places host and guest in touch with their own status of marginality, and forces hosts to confront the limits of their own ability to pursue virtue and do the right thing. Since hospitality by definition is practiced across boundaries of difference, it forces host and guest to acknowledge and embrace their own differences rather than attempting to erase them. As we begin to see why hospitality is the virtue that economic inequality demands, let us examine feminist visions of hospitality in more detail.

3.1. Difference

Christian understandings of hospitality are informed by its practice in ancient Middle Eastern and Greco-Roman contexts, where hospitality was understood as an important condition of encounters across group boundaries. For Biblical scholar Laurie Brink, Jesus' encounters with the Syro-Phoenician woman (Mark 7:24–30) and the Samaritan woman at the well (John 4) reveal that "we are always the other encountering the other," sometimes host and sometimes guest ([23], p. 19). In each of these exchanges, both Jesus and his interlocutor were transformed by their encounter. For Jessica Wrobleski, hospitality simultaneously requires and deconstructs boundaries between host and guest ([24], p. 75). Letty Russell similarly notes that difference is a precondition for hospitality: "Hospitality is the practice of God's welcome by reaching across difference to participate in God's actions bringing justice and healing to our world in crisis" ([20], p. 19).

These scholars insist that hospitality occurs in spaces where difference exists between host and guest. By offering and accepting hospitality, host and guest acknowledge their own differences and say Yes to encountering one another despite them.[7] Hospitality thus insists on encountering the other as she is, in her particularity, resisting any easy erasure of deeply felt distinctions of identity. Thus Letty Russell describes hospitality as "unity without uniformity" ([20], p. 80).

3.2. Risk

In the ancient context and in our contemporary understanding, difference often signals danger. By describing hospitality as risky, today's feminist theologians acknowledge that difference is commonly perceived as dangerous, without necessarily validating the view of the dangerous other.

Jewish theological ethicist Laurie Zoloth notes that Jewish, Muslim and Christian scriptures praise the "risky hospitality" practiced by Joseph in Genesis when he welcomed the brothers who had formerly threatened to kill him. Risky hospitality is practiced across a relationship of asymmetry, giving to those who "do not deserve it" and "cannot bless you" ([25], p. 384). Zoloth reminds us that risky hospitality will be necessary to welcome refugees when climate change decimates food supplies. Ilsup Ahn agrees that hospitality should be free from consideration of recompense, arguing that to keep an offer of hospitality from becoming a "gift" that incurs an "invisible debt" on the part of the guest, hosts must remember their own indebtedness to God ([26], pp. 259–60).[8]

Many scholars draw attention to risk by deploying Jacques Derrida's coinage of "hostipitality," which reminds us that *hospitality* takes place in spaces where *hostility* could potentially have occurred instead (e.g., [24], p. 31). One such scholar, John Blevins, uses queer theory's call to subvert norms

---

[6] My use of "risky" to describe hospitality is indebted to Laurie Zoloth, as I explain further on. Feminist sociologist Megan Moodie has an interesting, different perspective on risk, which she argues is gendered masculine (as in the valorization of risk in financial investing) in contrast to feminine-gendered "peril" which is not chosen [22].

[7] My use of "despite" here is not intended to eliminate the possibility that host and guest could offer and accept hospitality while *celebrating* their differences. Rather, I intend to signal the view of difference as negative that underlay ancient understandings of hospitality and that too frequently remains today.

[8] Kelly S. Johnson's comments on the title of her book *The Fear of Beggars* are relevant here and elsewhere: "Facing beggars, we fear poverty, we fear conflict, we fear drowning in the demands that may arise if we open ourselves to the needs of others, we fear the entanglements of gratitude [...] Yet, many of us also fear that refusing to be family to the poor is refusing membership in the body of Christ, which is the greatest danger of all." ([27], p. 5).

to describe "queer hospitality" as that hospitality that aims to subvert norms despite ever present risk of violence [28]. Jessica Wrobleski describes how the practice of hospitality in the Biblical context (as throughout much of the ancient world, and today in many formerly colonized countries) offered hospitality to a stranger *before* asking for an account of the stranger's identity and purposes. This acknowledges both the stranger's potential vulnerability and her potential power, as she might be a human enemy or a divine messenger in disguise, sent to judge the host ([24], pp. 15–16; see also [29]). Hospitality in its ancient sense and in contemporary understanding involves clear risk to the host.

Wrobleski's book on the limits of hospitality notes that as humans are finite, so our hospitality must have limits. To navigate these limits justly, it helps to understand hospitality as risky by nature. We must ask, when do those limits on hospitality arise from the legitimate desire of a host to offer her guests safety and when do we place unjust limits on our own hospitality under the guise of safety ([24], p. 20)? Wrobleski warns, "The legitimate need for safety can become so exaggerated that it builds walls of suspicion and hostility in place of limits of hospitality [...] While a measure of security is necessary for the creation of safe and friendly spaces, making the need for security absolute can also become idolatrous" ([24], p. 104). In our practice of hospitality, we also must attend to potential injustices that may undergird our own safety and comfort. In situations of inequality, including racial and economic inequality, Wrobleski notes, one source of *unjust* limits to our hospitality is the fact that security for some comes at the cost of danger and plunder from others ([24], pp. 100–1). Reclaiming a view of hospitality as a risky virtue allows us to pursue a practice of hospitality that refuses to prioritize an idolatrous view of our own safety over others' basic justice.

3.3. Marginality

It is relatively common to note that Christian hospitality deals with marginality in the persons of guests. For example, Letty Russell finds that "welcome of and advocacy for the marginalized" is a key component of God's hospitality in the Christian Scriptures. The Hebrew people are challenged in Exodus to welcome the stranger because they themselves were once strangers (Ex 23:9), she elaborates, rescued from their outsider status by God's hospitality ([20], p. 83).

Christine Pohl moves marginality in hospitality to a more prominent role by noting that Christian hospitality is often motivated or inspired by the *host's* own experience of being marginalized ([30], p. 121). In fact, hospitality requires hosts with experience on the margins:

> The normative practice of hospitality, which in addition to providing food and shelter to strangers also includes recognition, community, and the possibility of transcending social difference, requires hosts who are in some way marginal to prevailing social structures and meanings. Without this marginal dimension, the relation between hosts and guests often serves the more conservative function of reinforcing existing social relations and hierarchies ([30], p. 124).

The emphasis on the marginality of host in hospitality relationships is reinforced throughout the Christian tradition, Pohl finds, beginning with Jesus' own marginality. Wealthy women in the early church who wished to emulate Jesus' practice of hospitality "created [their own] marginality" by giving away their wealth in order to travel and minister to those in need ([30], p. 127). This strategy of creating marginality in order to provide hospitality was retrieved throughout Christian history by groups including early Methodists and the Salvation Army ([30], pp. 132–33). Pohl argues that to truly practice hospitality today, Christians may need to "cultivate a constructive marginality" by seeking out friendship and community with those very different from them ([30], p. 124).

3.4. Mutuality

A fourth and final feature of hospitality through feminist lenses is its mutuality. Feminist theologians insist that hospitality can describe an exchange that brings benefit to those on each side. As Wrobleski writes, "the best experiences of hospitality are often those in which guests take on some of the roles of hosts and hosts also experience the presence of their guests as refreshment and gift" ([24], p. 73). Russell concurs: "Hospitality is a two-way street of mutual ministry where we often exchange roles and learn the most from those whom we considered 'different' or 'other'" ([20], p. 20). Her criticism of the "lady bountiful" model of hospitality which establishes the host's superiority over her needy guest stems in part from the error of the view that hospitality could be present when only one party derives benefit. Meghan Clark concurs, finding that the experience of accepting hospitality from poor women in a global service encounter enabled the recognition of equal human dignity that is required for true solidarity ([31], pp. 133–35).[9]

Hospitality in feminist understanding is a risky, mutual, marginal practice across difference. It is clear how the contemporary world of globalized economic inequality demands such a virtue. Hospitality in a feminist key shares many features with the virtue James F. Keenan, SJ calls Jesuit hospitality, to which I now turn.

4. Jesuit Hospitality

Much has been written about how Francis' Jesuit vocation influences his theology, spirituality, and public actions and writings [18,33]. Neglected to date is the clear influence of the Jesuit charism on Francis' approach to inequality in *Evangelii Gaudium*. Francis diagnoses inequality as a virtue problem for which he prescribes encounter at the margins. His work immediately calls to mind the virtue James F. Keenan calls Jesuit hospitality.

Drawing on the writings of Ignatius and his early followers, Keenan finds that Jesuit identity has always been understood primarily in terms of its apostolic mission.[10] Jesuit hospitality, then, is that hospitality that goes out and meets people on the road where they are. Keenan says that Jesuit priests, and all those who participate in their ministries, are "missioned to the marginalized" ([19], p. 235). "Jesuit identity," Keenan says, "is found in journeying towards those for whom nobody is caring" ([19], p. 237). Pedro Arrupe, SJ, then Superior General of the Society of Jesus, described Jesuit identity in a similar way when he founded the Jesuit Refugee Service. Arrupe noted that since the perilous situation of refugees is by definition global and constantly in flux, the Jesuit charisms of "availability and universality" rooted in St. Ignatius' plan for the Order particularly invite Jesuits to the service of those displaced throughout the world [34]. Keenan invokes this paradigmatic Jesuit ministry when he says that "the model for Jesuit hospitality is the refugee camp [...] Inasmuch as we go out to the whole world we are called especially to those who find no dwelling place in this world" ([19], p. 240).

Compare this to Francis' perspective in *Evangelii Gaudium*. He says, "All of us are asked to obey [God]'s call to go forth from our own comfort zone in order to reach all the "peripheries" in need of the light of the Gospel" ([2], p. 20.) Elsewhere he says, "The drive to go forth and give, to go out from ourselves, to keep pressing forward in the sowing of the good seed, remains ever present" ([2], p. 21). *Amoris Laetitia*, Francis' apostolic exhortation on family life, might seem like an obvious place to present a vision of hospitality in situ, where a family welcomes others into their own home. Yet even here Francis encourages families to be open to life "by going forth and spreading life by caring for others and seeking their happiness. This openness finds particular expression in hospitality" ([35], p. 324). Far from comfortably settling down into their own insular community, even families are called to

---

[9]   Chris Vogt also notes that hospitality and solidarity require each other in his treatment of virtues for fostering the common good. In contrast with solidarity, which governs thought and takes the structures of society as its focus, hospitality is a virtue that governs action and focuses primarily on interpersonal relations ([32], p. 401).

[10]   By pairing Jesuit hospitality and feminist perspectives on hospitality, I do not mean to suggest that the perspectives are mutually exclusive. Indeed, Keenan identifies as a feminist and many of the feminist scholars I cite are counted as "Jesuits" in Keenan's thought, because they teach at universities in the Jesuit charism. Rather, I hope to show that these schools of thought that may seem to have separate roots overlap in fruitful ways.

practice a hospitality of "going forth."[11] Francis urges those who lead lives of comfort out to the margins, even as he acknowledges how much that journey can challenge us.

Probably one of the most quoted statements from *Evangelii Gaudium* is this: "I prefer a Church which is bruised, hurting and dirty because it has been out on the streets, rather than a Church which is unhealthy from being confined and from clinging to its own security" ([2], p. 49). Hospitality "out on the streets" is Jesuit hospitality *par excellence*.

Certainly, Jesuit hospitality does not stop when one goes out and meets others out on the road; the quality and character of these marginal meetings is crucial. Francis concretizes and specifies what the practice of Jesuit hospitality looks like as his writings develop a vision of the spiritual practice of encounter. Profounder and more rich than simply being in the same place at the same time, encounter happens when we meet the other where they are. Francis uses the word in *Amoris Laetitia* to describe the first meeting of Adam and Eve, the initial recognition of a companion to relieve human solitude ([35], pp. 12–13). In *Laudato Si'*, he describes "true wisdom" as the result of "generous encounter between persons" ([37], p. 47), urges that cities be planned with an eye to opportunities for "encounter and mutual assistance" ([37], p. 150), and bemoans the limits social media has placed on genuine encounter ([37], p. 49). Encounter clearly must be interpreted in a concrete, embodied way.

Encounter for Francis happens when we are unselfishly open. In fact, the word "open" occurs more than fifty times in *Evangelii Gaudium*. Francis says, "To go out of ourselves and to join others is healthy for us. To be self-enclosed is to taste the bitter poison of immanence, and humanity will be worse for every selfish choice we make" ([2], p. 87). Augustine's definition of sin as being *incurvatus in se* is clearly behind this language.

Encounter is a human activity, and humans who are obsessed with wealth, who are swayed by the values of the market, are closed off to it. Francis says,

> Many try to escape from others and take refuge in the comfort of their privacy [...] Meanwhile, the Gospel tells us constantly to run the risk of a face-to-face encounter with others, with their physical presence which challenges us, with their pain and their pleas, with their joy which infects us in our close and continuous interaction ([2], p. 88).

Married people, he notes in *Amoris Laetitia*, experience the pain and joy of their partner on a daily basis and thus have a particular call to "foster a culture of encounter" ([35], p. 183).

Encounter is about paying attention to the one in front of you, Francis insists. "What the Holy Spirit mobilizes is not an unruly activism, but [a loving] attentiveness which considers the other "in a certain sense as one with ourselves." [...] Only on the basis of this real and sincere closeness can we properly accompany the poor on their path of liberation" ([2], p. 199). Recall here how feminist theologians insist that hospitality acknowledges and welcomes difference without flattening it.

For Francis, inequality causes and is caused by failures of virtue. The solution is a journey to the margins followed by a spiritual practice of encounter, giving loving attention across difference. Keenan helps us understand how Francis' response to inequality can be seen as Jesuit hospitality. I hope I have shown how much it also shares with hospitality in a feminist key.[12] Like the hospitality called for by Brink, Russell, Pohl, Wrobleski and others, Francis' Jesuit hospitality is risky, mutual, and

---

[11] Perhaps Francis was inspired in these reflections by his encounters with Latino/a family practices in the Argentine context. As Nichole Flores notes, "The Latina/o practice of extended communal family promotes solidarity by strengthening the larger community." ([36], p. 69).

[12] This is not the first work to note Francis' consonance with feminist perspectives. Christine Firer Hinze notes how Francis and feminists both strive to link local communities in "an inclusive community of justice and care" while respecting the local rootedness and particular cultures of each community ([38], p. 53). Megan McCabe has noted his expressed appreciation for the contributions of feminism in *Amoris Laetitia* [39]. Neither scholar asks or answers whether Pope Francis should be considered a feminist, which would require a far broader evaluation of his actions and statements on women and gender, and neither do I. Noting the consonance between his theological approach and feminist approaches helps us better understand and appreciate both.

takes place at the margins and across difference. It is a challenging, concrete solution to the virtue problem of economic inequality.

5. Conclusions

I have shown how Pope Francis addresses the issue of economic inequality as both a problem of social structures and a problem of virtue. Francis' insistence on the spiritual practice of encounter deepens our understanding of the possibilities of hospitality in both Jesuit and feminist keys. I would like to close with a few more thoughts on practicing the risky virtue of hospitality particularly directed at those most likely to read this—people who are relatively economically comfortable, though not members of the global richest one percent. Francis' description of encounter at the margins is clearly aimed at such people, urging them to go to the margins and encounter people who are poor—a practice of encounter that clearly demands risky, mutual hospitality, and which is clearly called for by our unequal world. But Joerg Rieger and Kwok Pui Lan, in their book inspired by the Occupy movement, add a demand, noting that people who would consider themselves "middle-class" in the U.S. context are better positioned than many for encounters with the global superrich. They propose reaching out to the wealthy, who benefit from global inequality, in a confrontational practice similar to that of Biblical prophecy [40]. In a similar vein, Letty Russell notes the possibility of practicing hospitality as an "outsider within" ([20], p. 21). When thinking about the practice of hospitality in response to inequality, we should prioritize hospitality at the margins, without forgetting opportunities for risky, marginal encounters with those who benefit from global inequality and who desperately need to hear Pope Francis' message of inclusion.

"Hospitality and gestures of solidarity cannot change unjust social systems," writes Christine Pohl, "but they are a dimension of the transformation process, as important for those with power as for those without it" ([30], p. 135). For Pope Francis, as we've seen, inequality is not simply a problem of unjust social systems. It is also a problem of virtue—both an indicator of virtue deficits in society, and a factor which contributes to their formation. Francis' solution, to risk an encounter at the margins, embodies the practice of the virtue of hospitality in a Jesuit and feminist key. This is the virtue demanded by our unequal world.

Acknowledgments: The author would like to thank the Theologian in Residence Program (Fort Collins, CO, USA) for an invitation to speak on Pope Francis and economic inequality in 2014–2015. An earlier version of this paper was presented at the College Theology Society 2015 annual meeting in Portland, OR, USA; the author thanks those in attendance for helpful comments. Thanks also to the two anonymous reviewers for *Religions* for their insightful feedback.

Conflicts of Interest: The author declares no conflict of interest.

References

1. Deborah Hardoon, Sophia Ayele, and Ricardo Fuentes-Nieva. "An Economy for the 1%." *OXFAM*. Available online: http://oxf.am/Znhx (accessed on 18 January 2016).
2. Pope Francis. "Evangelii Gaudium: Apostolic Exhortation on The Proclamation of The Gospel in Today's World." *Vatican.va*, 24 November 2013. Available online: https://w2.vatican.va/content/francesco/en/apost_exhortations/documents/papa-francesco_esortazione-ap_20131124_evangelii-gaudium.html (accessed on 15 August 2014).
3. Victor Tan Chen. "An Economy of Grace." *Religions* 8 (2017): article 43. [CrossRef]
4. Kay Lehman Schlozman. "Growing Economic Inequality and Its (Partially) Political Roots." *Religions* 8 (2017): under review.
5. Richard G. Wilkinson, and Kate Pickett. *The Spirit Level: Why Greater Equality Makes Societies Stronger*. New York: Bloomsbury Press, 2010.
6. Timothy M. Smeeding, Markus Jäntii, and Robert Erikson. *Persistence, Privilege, and Parenting: The Comparative Study of Intergenerational Mobility*. New York: Russell Sage Foundation, 2011.
7. Joseph J. Kotva. *The Christian Case for Virtue Ethics*. Washington: Georgetown University Press, 1996.
8. Daniel J. Daly. "Structures of Virtue and Vice." *New Blackfriars* 92 (2011): 341–57. [CrossRef]

9. Kenneth R. Himes. "Social Sin and the Role of the Individual." *Annual of the Society of Christian Ethics* 6 (1986): 183–218.
10. Jamie T. Phelps. "Joy Came in The Morning Risking Death for Resurrection: Confronting the Evil of Social Sin and Socially Sinful Structures." In *A Troubling in My Soul: Womanist Perspectives on Evil and Suffering*. Edited by Emilie Maureen Townes. Maryknoll: Orbis Books, 1993, pp. 48–64.
11. Dustin Crummett. "Wealth, Well-being, and the Danger of Having too Much." *Religions* 8 (2017): under review.
12. Olubiyi Adeniyi Adewale. "An Afro-Sociological Application of the Parable of the Rich Man and Lazarus (Luke 16:19–31)." *Black Theology: An International Journal* 4 (2006): 27–43. [CrossRef]
13. Bryan N. Massingale. "The Scandal of Poverty: 'Cultured Indifference' and the Option for the Poor Post-Katrina." *Journal of Religion & Society* 4 (2008): 55–72. Available online: http://moses.creighton.edu/jrs/2008/2008-29.pdf (accessed on 15 August 2014).
14. David M. Cloutier. "The Problem of Luxury in the Christian Life." *Journal of the Society of Christian Ethics* 32 (2012): 3–20. [CrossRef]
15. David M. Cloutier. *The Vice of Luxury: Economic Excess in a Consumer Age*. Washington: Georgetown University Press, 2016.
16. Julie Hanlon Rubio. *Family Ethics: Practices for Christians*. Washington: Georgetown University Press, 2010.
17. Lisa Tessman. *Burdened Virtues: Virtue Ethics for Liberatory Struggles*. New York: Oxford University Press, 2005.
18. Paul Vallely. *Pope Francis: The Struggle for the Soul of Catholicism*, rev. and expand. 2nd ed. London: Bloomsbury Continuum, 2015.
19. James F. Keenan. "Jesuit Hospitality? " In *Promise Renewed: Jesuit Higher Education for a New Millennium*. Edited by Martin R. Tripole. Chicago: Jesuit Way, 1999, pp. 230–44.
20. Letty M. Russell. *Just Hospitality: God's Welcome in a World of Difference*. Edited by J. Shannon Clarkson and Kate M. Ott. Louisville: Westminster John Knox Press, 2009.
21. Elizabeth Newman. *Untamed Hospitality: Welcoming God and Other Strangers*. Grand Rapids: Brazos Press, 2007.
22. Megan Moodie. "Microfinance and the Gender of Risk: The Case of Kiva.org." *Signs: Journal of Women in Culture & Society* 38 (2013): 279–302.
23. Laurie Brink, OP. "In Search of the Biblical Foundations of Prophetic Dialogue: Engaging a Hermeneutics of Otherness." *Missiology* 41 (2013): 9–21. [CrossRef]
24. Jessica Wrobleski. *The Limits of Hospitality*. Collegeville: Liturgical Press, 2012.
25. Laurie Zoloth. "Risky Hospitality: Ordinal Ethics and the Duties of Abundance." *Journal of the American Academy of Religion* 83 (2015): 373–87. [CrossRef]
26. Ilsup Ahn. "Economy of 'Invisible Debt' and Ethics of 'Radical Hospitality': Toward a Paradigm Change of Hospitality from 'Gift' to 'Forgiveness'." *Journal of Religious Ethics* 38 (2010): 243–67. [CrossRef]
27. Kelly S. Johnson. *The Fear of Beggars: Stewardship and Poverty in Christian Ethics*. Grand Rapids: William B. Eerdmans, 2007.
28. John Blevins. "Hospitality is a Queer Thing." *Journal of Pastoral Theology* 19 (2009): 104–17. [CrossRef]
29. Julius Mutugi Gathogo. "African Hospitality: Is It Compatible with the Ideal of Christ's Hospitality? Part 2." *Churchman* 120 (2006): 145–57.
30. Christine D. Pohl. "Hospitality from the Edge: The Significance of Marginality in the Practice of Welcome." *The Annual of the Society of Christian Ethics* 15 (1995): 121–36.
31. Meghan J. Clark. *The Vision of Catholic Social Thought: The Virtue of Solidarity and the Praxis of Human Rights*. Minneapolis: Fortress Press, 2014.
32. Christopher P. Vogt. "Fostering a Catholic Commitment to the Common Good: An Approach Rooted in Virtue Ethics." *Theological Studies* 68 (2007): 394–417. [CrossRef]
33. Chris Lowney. *Pope Francis: Why He Leads the Way He Leads: Lessons from the First Jesuit Pope*. Chicago: Loyola Press, 2013.
34. Pedro Arrupe, SJ. "The Society of Jesus and the Refugee Problem: Letter of Father Pedro Arrupe to all Jesuit Major Superiors." 14 November 1980. Available online: http://jrsusa.org/Assets/Sections/Downloads/ArrupeLetter.pdf (accessed on 29 March 2017).
35. Pope Francis. "Amoris Laetitia: On Love in the Family." *Vatican.va*, 19 March 2016. Available online: http://w2.vatican.va/content/dam/francesco/pdf/apost_exhortations/documents/papa-francesco_esortazione-ap_20160319_amoris-laetitia_en.pdf (accessed on 15 October 2016).

36. Nichole M. Flores. "Latina/o Families: Solidarity and the Common Good." *Journal of the Society of Christian Ethics* 33 (2013): 57–72. [CrossRef]

37. Pope Francis. "Laudato Si': On Care for Our Common Home." *Vatican.va*, 24 May 2015. Available online: http://w2.vatican.va/content/francesco/en/encyclicals/documents/papa-francesco_20150524_enciclica-laudato-si.html (accessed on 1 October 2016).

38. Christine Firer Hinze. *Glass Ceilings and Dirt Floors: Women, Work, and the Global Economy*. 2014 Madeleva Lecture in Spirituality. New York: Paulist Press, 2015.

39. Megan K. McCabe. "Francis, Family, and Feminism." *America Magazine*, 8 April 2016. Available online: http://www.americamagazine.org/issue/article/francis-family-and-feminism (accessed on 20 October 2016).

40. Joerg Rieger, and Kwok Pui-lan. *Occupy Religion: Theology of the Multitude*. Plymouth: Rowman & Littlefield Publishers, 2013.

religions

MDPI

Article

Twenty First Century Global Goal-Setting Addressing Global Inequality: An Interdisciplinary Ethical Analysis

James P. O'Sullivan

Social Ethics, Saint Joseph's University, Philadelphia, PA 19131, USA; josulliv@sju.edu

Academic Editors: Kate Ward and Kenneth Himes
Received: 3 February 2017; Accepted: 10 March 2017; Published: 28 March 2017

Abstract: This paper employs an interdisciplinary ethical analysis to evaluate how global inequality has been addressed by recent so-called "global goal-setting" initiatives. It seeks to contextualize these initiatives within theoretical paradigms of human rights and human development, and to utilize these paradigms in evaluating the successes and shortcomings of the goal-setting initiatives. It concludes that while these initiatives have achieved some success in addressing global inequality, much still remains to be done.

Keywords: human rights; human development; Catholic Social Teaching; sustainable development; global inequality; global poverty

1. Introduction

This paper will focus on how the Millennium Development Goals (MDGs) and their successors, the Sustainable Development Goals (SDGs), have attempted to address global inequality, both within and between countries, and in a variety of overlapping arenas, from economic inequality to gender equality. Utilizing the joint ethical analysis of Catholic Social Teaching (CST) and rights-based approaches to development, it contends that both of these "global goal-setting" initiatives fall short of adequately addressing the issue of inequality. It goes about this task by first articulating what is entailed in a joint vision of CST and a rights-based ethical perspective on development. Subsequently, it turns first to the MDGs and the ways in which they failed to adequately address inequality and then to the SDGs, addressing both their improvements and remaining short-comings. It concludes that while this latest global goal setting initiative contains significant advances in addressing inequality, several serious issues remain from a CST and right-based perspective regarding both the structure of the goals and the means to achieving them.

At the outset it can be said that the interdisciplinary perspective being utilized in this analysis entails, at base, the view that development properly understood goes beyond economic development to instead seek opportunities for realization of human aspirations and fundamental human capacities. In particular, the view from which we will operate suggests that development is to be understood, at least at minimum, as the participatory realization of the full and interrelated spectrum of human rights. In other words, development should be understood as fostering participation in all sectors of society, of securing human rights in the social, economic and political spheres of life. Further, development properly understood should take into account the process by which these fundamental requirements or rights—both social and economic and civil and political—must be fostered in ways sensitive to their interactions between one another, and in a manner that is necessarily participatory.

If this all sounds a bit abstract, we will further delineate this perspective in terms of our specific concerns, namely, global goal-setting and how these global projects interact with inequality. To be clear, though, we are working with an overarching vision of human development and human rights—something that can be found in both Catholic and secular thought and policy in various arenas—and we are applying this perspective to these initiatives to see how they live up to or fall short in addressing inequality.

2. Catholic Social Teaching, Human Rights, Capabilities and Human Development

It is important to first delve further into these significantly overlapping visions of the ends and means of development. We begin this task with Catholic Social Teaching (CST). Although not a monolithic body, CST has a certain organic unity based on an enduring commitment of the Church to certain basic values. The "official" or magisterial teaching (what were are calling CST) is that which emanates from the papacy, certain universal councils of bishops, or regional conferences of bishops. Regarding global poverty specifically, this teaching speaks in terms of "authentic" or "integral" human development, a concept which has evolved over the years and has now become codified in consistent magisterial teaching. In initial magisterial articulations on addressing global poverty through development, the focus was on economic development with little nuance, as with John XXIII's encyclical *Mater et Magistra*. However, with *Populorum Progressio*, Pope Paul VI gave a framework for the shape of genuine human development. This seminal 1967 document clearly delineates the "aspirations" of seeking to "do more, know more and have more in order to be more" and promulgates a vision of development "not limited to mere economic growth" but rather dedicated to the promotion of "every man and of the whole man" ([1], no. 6). This vision has been consistently reaffirmed at several levels of magisterial teaching, most recently in Benedict XVI's 2009 encyclical *Caritas in Veritate*. Therein the now Pontiff Emeritus explains that development has the goal of "rescuing people, first and foremost, from hunger, deprivation, endemic diseases and illiteracy", and further, fostering all peoples' "active participation, on equal terms, in the international economic progress", their "evolution into educated societies marked by solidarity", and their enjoyment and participation in "democratic regimes capable of ensuring freedom and peace" ([2], no. 21). Thus the Catholic concept of authentic/integral human development has as its end the greater realization of human wellbeing and flourishing.

This aim is further articulated in CST through the closely related understanding of human rights. In his seminal 1963 social encyclical *Pacem in Terris*, Pope John XXIII systematically outlined a full range of human rights stemming from inherent human dignity and necessary for the protection of such dignity. In many ways echoing the United Nations Universal Declaration of Human Rights, this range or spectrum includes both the civil and political rights to freedom of speech, worship, and assembly as well as social and economic rights to life, food, clothing, shelter, rest, medical care, and basic education and all other "necessary social services" [3]. More recently, the US Catholic bishops in their classic 1986 pastoral letter *Economic Justice for All* enumerate the link between justice and human rights. The bishops reaffirm the full spectrum of rights named in *Pacem in Terris* and explain that CST "spells out the basic demands of justice in greater detail in the human rights of every person" [4]. These fundamental rights are "prerequisites for a dignified life in community", are "bestowed on human beings by God and grounded in the nature and dignity of human persons" and are thus "not created by society", though society does have "a duty to secure and protect them" ([4], no. 79). In sum, then, the bishops assert that "fundamental personal rights- civil and political as well as social and economic- state the minimum conditions for social institutions that respect human dignity, social solidarity, and justice" ([4], no. 80).

Achieving the task of securing the full range of human rights through authentic human development will, as the American bishops explain, "make demands on *all* members of society, on all private sector institutions, and on government" ([4], no. 83). Thus from the perspective of CST, the full spectrum of human rights are interconnected and indivisible, and the promotion and protection of all these rights is a prime goal of authentic human development and an essential task of the whole of society, necessarily including, though not limited to, the state. Indeed, the participation of people is both the end and a necessary means in achieving development. As John Paul II explains, development is "most appropriately accomplished in the dedication of each people to its own development" ([5], no. 44).

Moreover, this task will include both the dismantling of entrenched structural and institutional obstacles to development and the reordering of society in a way that guarantees all persons the ability to participate actively in the economic, political, and cultural life of society ([4], no. 78).

But this task does not fall solely on domestic society, as CST also insists upon responsibilities for both rich and poor nations and stresses the need to realize authentic human development through genuine cooperation among all peoples. Indeed, the documents of CST are replete with calls for cooperation and "mutual assistance" between the various actors engaged in development, from wealthy governments, developing governments, nongovernmental organizations (NGOs), and the private sector. Pope John Paul II clearly expounds the need for cooperation in his encyclical *Sollicitudo Rei Socialis*, declaring that collaboration for human development "is in fact a duty of *all towards all*, and it must be shared" by all parts of the world ([5], no. 32).

We can now turn to the relation of CST to the "capabilities" or human development approach as articulated by both economist/philosopher Amartya Sen and political and classical philosopher Martha Nussbaum, as well as to the public policy that has been heavily influenced by such thinking. Before delving into the comparison it is helpful to briefly outline this approach and to clarify its various articulations and instantiations in public policy.

In brief, the capabilities approach is a theoretical paradigm that starts with the question: "What are people actually able to be and to do?" It can be helpfully understood as a "necessary counter theory" to development economics approaches which focus on economic growth (measured in GDP), or utility (measured in satisfaction of preferences), or equality of resources (as exemplified by John Rawls and consisting of a sort of egalitarian version of the GDP approach). There are different versions and emphasizes of the capabilities approach (we will return to these briefly below), but as Martha Nussbaum points out, it may still be treated "as a single, relatively unified approach to a set of questions about both quality of life and basic justice" [6]. The end of development for this approach is enhancing "capabilities" or substantial freedoms to achieve certain "functionings", and it is closely allied with the international human rights movement. Both movements recognize that all people have certain entitlements by virtue of their humanity and that it is a basic duty of society to respect and support these entitlements. Both Sen and Nussbaum acknowledge this common ground, as well as the common ground between the content of capabilities and the full spectrum of human rights found in the Universal Declaration—although Nussbaum is more explicit in enumerating certain capabilities and in making the link between them and Declaration rights.

The capabilities approach, combined with the more general paradigm of human development as propounded by thinkers such as Paul Streeten and Mahbub ul Haq, has had considerable influence on global policy making [7]. Indeed, the approach has become official policy of the United Nation Development Program (UNDP). Again, we must note that more nuance is involved than can be elucidated here; there are in fact several different ways of relating human rights to human development operative in the UNDP, the so-called "social justice" and "holistic approach" among them [8]. But although significant nuances exist, it is at the same time true that the similarities between the capabilities approach and other ways of speaking about human development are much more pronounced than any differences. Human rights as articulated in the various international declarations, covenants, etc., are not in competition with capabilities; there is, in fact, a strong link between them (as noted above), and they are both utilized in conjunction in development policy. Thus as the UNDP *Human Development Report* (HDR) explains, "human development shares a common vision with human rights" with the goal of both being "human freedom" and the two ideas "mutually reinforcing" [9]. Further, both of the global initiatives with which we are concerned in this paper, the MDGs and SDGs, are clearly shaped by both human development and human rights.

The similarities abound between the capabilities and human development approach—in both its theoretical and practical policy dimensions—and CST on human development and international justice. At base, both models of human development move far beyond a vision of economic development alone to a vision of human welfare and flourishing as the goal of development. This flourishing is elucidated by both the secular and Catholic concepts—at least partially—in terms of human rights. And, importantly, it is the full spectrum of rights that is emphasized in both: the protection, fulfillment, and promotion of *all* human rights. Significantly absent, then, is any bifurcation and juxtaposition of social-economic and civil-political rights. Thus, in short, the overall aims are quite similar: enabling people to be and do more in all the diverse spheres of human existence.

Further, in the various policies that are influenced by the secular approach, one can also see the manifestation of Catholic ideas of solidarity and concern for the least well off. Indeed, policies such as the MDGs call for a mode of poverty reduction and human development which represents many of CST's calls to greater unity, cooperation, shared responsibility and solidarity among all peoples. The Millennium Declaration launching the MDGs also made clear that there was a "motivating concern for the poor" and a duty "to all the worlds people, especially the most vulnerable" [10]. This clearly fits with the Catholic conception of "the preferential option for the poor". Thus, both CST and policies influenced by the capabilities/human development approach emphasize the values of equality, freedom, participation, nondiscrimination, and shared responsibility.

3. Millennium Development Goals (MDGs) and Sustainable Development Goal (SDGs)

It is important to explicate a bit more background on the global goal-setting initiatives themselves. The MDGs arose out of the milieu of late 20th century reevaluation of development economics and policy, particularly under the auspices of the United Nations. Systematic attempts to eliminate global poverty and underdevelopment go back many decades, but during the 1980s the early convergence of the human rights and development arenas became overshadowed as did the role for the United Nations in shaping development policy—in particular by the so-called Washington Consensus and the a neo-liberal model of growth entailing reduction in public expenditures and a decreased focus on poverty itself. The 1990s, however, saw the flowering of an era in which "human development" and capabilities began to guide significant elements of global development policy, particularly with the advent of the United Nations Development Program (UNDP), as well as the return of UN Summitry and UN prominence in setting the development agenda.

The immediate context of the MDGs was the 2000 United Nations Millennium Summit, the largest ever gathering of heads of state seeking to define a common vision for the 21st Century development agenda. This summit produced the United Nations Millennium Declaration, wherein all countries of the world, both "rich and poor", committed to doing all they could to eradicate poverty, promote human dignity and rights, and achieve peace, democracy, and environmental sustainability ([10], p. 1). The MDGs were the concrete set of objectives meant to launch this commitment.

The goals were as follows: (1) Eradicate Extreme Hunger and Poverty; (2) Achieve Universal Primary Education; (3) Promote Gender Equality and Empower Women; (4) Reduce Child Mortality; (5) Improve Maternal Health; (6) Combat HIV/AIDS, Malaria, and other diseases; (7) Ensure Environmental Sustainability; (8) Develop a Global Partnership for Development. These goals were further broken down into 18 targets and 52 indicators (and subsequent to a 2005 UN Summit, this was expanded to 21 targets and 60 indicators) ([11], p. 55).

The record of these goals from a rights-based and CST perspective is decidedly mixed. On one hand, as the Issues Brief from the United Nations inter-agency Technical Support Team (TST) summarizes, they have certainly had some success in highlighting "key development and human rights issues such as poverty and food, gender equality, health, education, water and sanitation, housing, and a global partnership for development" ([12], p. 1)[1]. Further, as the UNDP 2003 HDR extolls, they did indeed go far beyond focusing on economic growth and instead placed "human well-being and poverty reduction at the center of global development" and were linked to the "economic, social, and

---

[1] The Issues Brief was drafted by OHCR, UNICEF, UN Women, UNDP, and UNEP with comments from the following agencies: UNESCO, UNAIDS, World Bank, EOSG Rule of Law Unit, PBSO, ILO, UN-DESA, UNFPA, and ISOAA.

cultural rights enumerated in the Universal Declaration of Human Rights". They can therefore be said to be "building blocks of human development" and human rights and expressions of ideals with considerable moral force ([10], p. 28).

However, extensive evaluations undertaken by independent scholars, non-governmental organizations, and various UN bodies reveal much that is lacking from a human rights and CST perspective[2]. Basically, progress on the goals was "uneven within and across countries" and gaps exist "in what the goals set out to achieve, as well as in the way progress has been measured". Further, the overall focus of the MDGs on a "narrow and somewhat unbalanced set of goals failed to reflect the full ambition of the Millennium Declaration and its commitment to the Universal Declaration of Human Rights" ([12], p. 1). Thus from a rights-based perspective there are deficiencies in both vision and execution.

We can focus on the problems in how the MDGs addressed inequality both within and between countries. In the view of a wide variety of consultations, the MDGs' focus on "halfway" targets and on average progress has meant that—to quote the UN's Technical Support Team's amalgam analysis—"the poorest families, and most deprived and marginalized groups, including minorities, migrants, and indigenous peoples, have been left behind, even if the goals may be met in the aggregate at the national or global level" ([12], p. 4). This is true first of all regarding income and economic growth. The proportion of people living in extreme poverty has indeed been halved at a global level, however, much of these gains have occurred in China and India where the gains were driven largely by "aggregate gains through economic growth policies" that were "based upon policies that pre-dated the MDGs", and in many cases many people in those countries are not better off than they were 15 years ago [14]. In much of the rest of the world, as the Catholic Aid Agency, CAFOD, points out, the wellbeing of many poor people has deteriorated as a result of factors beyond their control, such as environmental degradation, economic crises, and rapid changes in crop prices [15]. And even though poverty has been reduced in many nations, inequality has continued to persist and widen in many more; indeed, inequality increased in the majority of countries [16].

This is a problem first of all because there are complex interactions between inequality, poverty and social stability, and the relationship between inequality, growth, and social stability was left largely unexamined by the MDG's agenda. In short, growth must be shared and put to use in building institutions that foster participation and opportunity for all people in the nation. Social stability depends on this, and it is a vital moral imperative of development as human rights, besides. The failure to focus on employment is a major element of this lacuna. But, as Mac Darrow, American University law professor and UN human rights specialist argues, the larger issue is that the "actual economic and social policies through which states have purportedly pursued the MDGs still appear overwhelmingly to be circumscribed within a long discredited neo-liberal economic growth model" [14].

Now, to be sure, economic growth within a country is an important element for achieving poverty reduction, but examining the *quality of growth* is essential from a rights-based and CST perspective. Inclusive and equitable growth that creates decent work should be of utmost importance, as should ensuring the quality of work through labor standards, and social protection for the losers in the process of growth, economic expansion, and concomitant creative destruction[3]. Given the lack of focus on equitable and inclusive growth, we can see, for instance, that while Sub-Saharan Africa has experienced declining poverty rates, it is still extremely vulnerable to shocks that could rapidly erode even the small gains that were made [17]. The MDGs simply failed to capture the problem of the most vulnerable whose rights need to be protected in the process of growth within countries [18]. Moreover, inequality and lack of participation have been shown to be directly related to increased social insecurity, unrest

---

[2]   For an early and definitive statement on the deficiencies in both the development and human rights community with regard to the Goals see [13].The paper was originally produced for the Millennium Project Task Force on Poverty and Economic Development and later revised for academic publication.

[3]   See Victor Tan Chen's work on the psychological impacts of unemployment on laid-off autoworkers in the present volume.

and violent conflict [19]. In short, then, again drawing on Mac Darrow, growth "cannot continue as the dominant policy objective as an end unto itself, without sufficient concern for its complex and contingent theoretical and empirical relationships with inequality" nor without sufficient appreciation of the "reverse causal relationship between social investments and growth" [14].

And in terms of fostering economic growth itself, Goal 8 on fostering a partnership, including improvements in aid, trade, and debt policies, failed to live up to the pledges made or the necessary improvements to achieve the goals. This is clearly a central failure, not in terms of the plan, but in terms of the action necessary to see it achieved. As we will see, there are reasons to fear whether this shortcoming will be remedied in the SDGs.

Beyond economic growth and inequality, there was also a failure in the MDGS to properly address inequalities regarding discrimination and gender. First of all, the issue of discriminatory practices, in particular regarding disability and social protection, failed to even make the list of goals and targets. The issue of gender equality did appear as Goal 3; however, progress here was tracked through only three indicators: education, employment, and political representation. Surely these are important elements of achieving gender equality, but as the TST Issues Brief argues, they leave out "crucial aspects of gender-specific discrimination such as violence against women, gender-based wage discrimination, women's disproportionate share of unpaid care work, sexual and reproductive health and rights, women's limited asset and property ownership, and unequal participation in decision-making at all levels" ([12], p. 2). Overall, then, as the United Nations Development Group's (UNDG) Inequalities Consultation revealed, by "not devoting sufficient attention to inequalities, the MDGs may have exacerbated the relative neglect of marginalized groups and contributed to widening social and economic inequalities" ([12], p. 1).

The successors to the MDGs, the SDGs, came out of wide consultation during which time many of the above noted concerns of human rights were taken into account. They are far wider in scope than their predecessors, and include an impressive—perhaps even daunting—list of key elements of global basic social justice and care for the Earth. They are as follows:

(1) End poverty in all its forms, everywhere; (2) End hunger, achieve food security and improved nutrition, and promote sustainable agriculture; (3) Ensure healthy lives and promote wellbeing for all at all ages; (4) Ensure inclusive and equitable quality education and promote lifelong learning opportunities for all; (5) Achieve gender equality and empower all women and girls; (6) Ensure availability and sustainable management of water and sanitation for all; (7) Ensure access to affordable, reliable, sustainable and modern energy for all; (8) Promote sustained, inclusive and sustainable economic growth, full and productive employment, and decent work for all; (9) Build resilient infrastructure, promote inclusive and sustainable industrialization, and foster innovation; (10) Reduce inequality within and among countries; (11) Make cities and human settlements inclusive, safe, resilient and sustainable; (12) Ensure sustainable consumption and production patterns; (13) Take urgent action to combat climate change and its impacts; (14) Conserve and sustainably use the oceans, seas and marine resources for sustainable development; (15) Protect, restore and promote sustainable use of terrestrial ecosystems, sustainably manage forests, combat desertification and halt and reverse land degradation, and halt biodiversity loss; (16) Promote peaceful and inclusive societies for sustainable development, provide access to justice for all and build effective, accountable and inclusive institutions at all levels; (17) Strengthen the means of implementation and revitalize the global partnership for sustainable development.

It suffices to say that the SDGs continue and expand the scope of the social and economic end of the spectrum of human rights also covered by the MDGs, but also expand the focus to key civil and political rights—including targets to enact and enforce non-discriminatory laws and to foster transparent, participatory and representative government at various levels. They therefore get at the important element of the interdependency of rights.

More specifically for our focus in this paper, they also go far in responding to the call from both states and civil society to specifically address inequalities within and between countries. Two of the

Goals explicitly address inequality: Goal 5 on gender and Goal 10 on economic inequality within and between countries and also on exclusion (social, economic and political) and discrimination. Other goals and targets include important language on equal and universal access to healthcare, education, energy, and housing, and on tackling gender disparities. These elements all reflect the key human rights principles of non-discrimination and equality [20]. They also address a key complaint against the MDGs as was seen above, namely that the aggregate process often came at the cost of neglecting the most hard-to reach groups. Therefore, the greater disaggregation of data between and within countries, along with a specific focus on the marginalized and poorest, are important advances from a rights based and human development perspective. Further, it is important to highlight that international inequality is also addressed in a more robust global partnership. This partnership includes very high targets for development assistance, and an integrated framework that looks to connect multiple areas of finance, trade, and public-private partnerships (we will return to this below).

Nevertheless, issues still remain regarding just how far the goals go in addressing inequality. First, although Goal 10 importantly targets inequality directly in several arenas and looks to disaggregation of data, there are problems in the way such disaggregation actually plays out across a variety of categories within various countries. As the HCHR (High Commissioner for Human Rights) argues, "combatting discrimination and inequalities requires disaggregation of data across a range of categories" but in the SDGs agenda "disaggregation by these categories would be subject to a decision on whether such characteristics are deemed *'relevant in the national context'*" ([21], p. 4). Data on how various segments of the population are faring is essential from a rights based and RTD perspective, regardless of the country's particular social norms or situations. Thus, as [profession]? Thomas Pogge and Mitu Sengupta argue, in addition to having its own goal, the "concern to avoid excessive inequality should also be integrated into the other goals" and "indicators used to monitor targets should be disaggregated by relevant categories such as gender, race, ethnicity, religion, and geographical area". In short, "no target should be considered achieved until it has been met for all relevant segments of a population" [22] in each country, and this criterion should apply to every country on earth.

Regarding *income inequality* in particular, at both the national and international level, the SDGs do not address the problem of what can be called "regulatory capture" and structures that tilt growth toward the wealthy and ultimately harm, or at least fail to benefit, the poor. In particular, as several commentators have pointed out, the "distribution of future growth is heavily influenced by the design of national and economic rules and practices" and because this is well known, "such rules and practices are heavily contested by various interested parties, such as industry associations, corporations, banks, hedge funds, and unions, all of which expend substantial efforts on lobbying for rules favorable to themselves". Even in "broadly democratic countries, the poorer segments of the population are often politically marginalized when their share of national household income is small," and thus "the social rules tend to disfavor these segments, causing them to fall farther and farther behind in income, health education, and social acceptance" ([22], p. 582). This vicious cycle is yet another example of the importance of the interdependence of rights and the need for a focus on economic rules—both national and global—to keep inequality within certain bounds; the SDGs do not go far enough in propounding such rules, or in recognizing the challenge of inequality. Indeed, there is a lack of ambition in the primary target, 10.1, to "progressively achieve and sustain income growth of the bottom 40 percent of the population at a rate higher than the national average". As Pogge and Sengupta argue, in light of "how enormous inequality has become, globally and in most countries, at the very least the demand should be that the income share of the poorest 40 percent will be substantially higher at the end of the period than at its beginning". Suitable measures for this would be necessary, for instance utilizing the Palma Ratio—the income share of a population's richest 10 percent divided by that of its poorest 40 percent ([22], p. 583).

Finally, it is essential to say something about the issues of financing, accountability and follow-through on the Goals, which were all major problems in the MDGs and are potentially still so in the SDGs. These issues are all directly related to the prospect of adequately addressing inequality.

As noted above, MDG 8 set out to form a robust global partnership, and as one prominent development analyst has argued, in so doing it is "arguably the most significant development since the International Covenant on Economic, Social, and Cultural Rights because it takes the idea of international state obligations beyond a statement of principle to list specific policy areas of required action: trade, aid, debt relief, and technology transfer" [23][4]. However, there has been a failure to actually establish a truly global partnership which necessarily must involve the overlapping and multifaceted arenas of aid, trade, debt, and global corporations. Part of the problem is that commitments in particular to official development assistance (ODA) that were made with the MDGs were not followed through upon, but other issues arise from a *lack of sufficient commitments being made in the first place*. Basically, there was insufficient attention to structural injustice in the current international and intergovernmental system and the concomitant need for reform and building-up of better global governance as well as to the role of private actors and international corporations in the global order. Ultimately, then, structural issues of global governance and true international and global accountability, partnership, and justice were not adequately addressed.

The SDGs contain significant improvements toward realizing international and national accountability and follow-through on the goals. First, they shift focus on accountability, declaring the ultimate accountability to be of states to their citizens, and as the HCHR points out, this represents an historic shift away from the 'donor-beneficiary' paradigm. The text also specifically identifies accountability as the purpose of the follow-up and review arrangements and highlights the important role of parliaments "in ensuring accountability for effective implementation" ([21], p. 5). Second, they are also still fully aware of the necessity of global solidarity and international accountability at various levels. As noted above, Goal 17—strengthening the means of implementation and revitalizing the global partnership— is certainly more comprehensive than was MDG 8, containing nineteen targets on issues such as finance, technology, trade, data monitoring, and accountability in all these arenas. Thus, SDG 17 has moved beyond MDG 8 and closer toward the more encompassing "Monterrey Consensus"[5]. The Third International Conference on Financing for Development held in Addis Adaba, Ethiopia in July 2015 also made important advances in promoting the global partnership for development [24]. Importantly, it recognized the complex and interweaving role of various players in achieving adequate financing, and the need for increased ODA, as well as new sources of aid was central. In particular, the private sector received greater focus, as did alternative sources of funding, and increased tax revenues from developing nations. The Conference also corrected a large omission in the Monterrey Consensus by looking to environmental issues and the impact of climate change on development.

Despite these advances, however, the key defect of MDG 8 also mars SDG 17: international accountability to the pledges made and the making of necessary commitments to structural change are both severely lacking. Thomas Pogge and Mitu Sengupta summarize the deficiency forcefully: "The world's most powerful agents—affluent states, international organizations, and multinational

---

[4] The targets are as follows: (8.A) to "develop further an open, rule-based, predictable, non-discriminatory trading and financial system"; (8.B) to "address the needs of the least developed countries," through such measures as tariff-free and quota-free access of least developed countries' exports, expanding debt relief and cancelling official bilateral debt, and "more generous Official Development Assistance (ODA) for countries committed to poverty reduction"; (8.C) addresses the "special needs of landlocked developing countries and small island developing states"; (8.D) deals with debt sustainability; (8.E) seeks to ensure access to affordable essential drugs in developing countries; (8.F) deals with the availability of information and communications technology.

[5] This emerged from the 2002 United Nations International Conference on Financing for Development in Monterrey, Mexico between heads of state and top ministers from world governments, heads of the IMF, the World Bank, and the WTO, and prominent leaders from the realms of business and civil society. The consensus became a major reference point for international development cooperation and a major milestone toward greater achievement of Goal 8. It covered six key policy priorities: (1.) Mobilizing domestic financial resources for development (including addressing issues of governance and corruption); (2.) Mobilizing private international resources, including foreign direct investment and other private flows; (3.) International trade as an engine for development; (4.) Increasing international financial and technical cooperation (in particular ODA); (5.) External Debt; (6.) Addressing systemic issues: enhancing the coherence and consistency of the international monetary, financial, and trading systems.

enterprises—will once again be shielded from any concrete responsibilities for achieving the development goals when, given their wealth and influence, they ought to be taking the lead in providing the needed resources and in implementing systemic institutional reforms addressing the root causes of poverty" [22]. Thus it remains to be seen whether commitments to multifaceted assistance and structural change in the global system will be followed through upon.

4. Conclusions

This paper has sought to give a portrait and interdisciplinary evaluation of how inequality has been addressed within the evolving framework of global goal-setting initiatives for achieving human rights and human development. It first detailed the overlapping ethical frameworks of human rights and development in CST and secular rights-based approaches to development. It then provided a background for global goal-setting initiatives before turning to the ways they can be evaluated in particular looking to the issue of inequality, both within and between countries. This analysis concluded that while it is true that the SDGs make significant improvements over the MDGS from a rights-based and CST perspective, there is much that could still be improved in the SDGs both in terms of their structure and in the accountability and follow through necessary to see them come to fruition.

Conflicts of Interest: The author declares no conflict of interest.

Abbreviations

CST	Catholic Social Teaching
MDGs	Millennium Development Goals
ODA	Official Development Assistance
RTD	Right to Development
SDGs	Sustainable Development Goals
TST	United Nations Interagency Technical Support Team
UNDG	United Nations Development Group
UNDP	United Nations Development Program

References and Notes

1. Pope Paul VI. "Populorum Progressio." In *Catholic Social Though: The Documentary Heritage*. Edited by David J. O'Brien and Thomas A. Shannon. New York: Maryknoll, 1992.
2. Pope Benedict XVI. "Caritas in Veritate." Available online: http://www.vatican.va/holy_father/benedict_xvi/encyclicals/documents/hf_ben-xvi_enc_20090629_caritas-in-veritate_en.html (accessed on 11 October 2016).
3. Pope John XXIII. "Pacem in Terris." In *Catholic Social Thought: The Documentary Heritage*. Edited by David J. O'Brien and Thomas A. Shannon. New York: Maryknoll, 1992.
4. U.S. Catholic Bishops. "Economic Justice for All." In *Catholic Social Thought: The Documentary Heritage*. Edited by David J. O'Brien and Thomas A. Shannon. New York: Maryknoll, 1992.
5. Pope John Paul II. "Sollicitudo Rei Socialis." In *Catholic Social Teaching: the Documentary Heritage*. Edited by David J. O'Brien and Thomas A. Shannon. New York: Maryknoll, 1992, pp. 395–436.
6. Martha Nussbaum. *Creating Capabilities*. Cambridge: Belknap Harvard, 2011.
7. See further for other human development approaches, Mahbub Ul Haq. *Reflections on Human Development*. New York: Oxford University Press, 1995.
8. Stephen P. Marks. "The Human Rights Framework for Development: Seven Approaches." Working paper, Francois-Xavier Bagnoud Center for Health and Human Rights, Harvard School of Public Health, Boston, MA, USA, 2003.
9. United Nations Development Program. *Human Development Report 2001*. New York: Oxford University Press, 2001, p. 9.
10. United Nations Development Program. *Human Development Report 2003: MDGs among Nations to End Poverty*. New York: Oxford University Press, 2003.

11. The original goals are enumerated in United Nations Secretary General. *Report of the Secretary General: Road Map towards the Implementation of the Millennium Declaration*. New York: United Nations, 2001. Available online: http://www.un.org/documents/ga/docs.56/a56326.pdf (accessed on 16 October 2016).

12. United Nations Technical Support Team. "Technical Support Team Issues Brief: 'Human Rights Including the Right to Development.' Available online: https://sustainabledevelopment.un.org/content/documents/2391TST%20Human%20Rights%20Issues%20Brief_FINAL.pdf (accessed on 17 November 2015).

13. Philip Alston. "Ships Passing in the Night: The Current State of the Human Rights and Development Debate seen through the Lens of the Millennium Development Goals." *Human Rights Quarterly* 27 (2005): 755–829. [CrossRef]

14. Mac Darrow. "The Millennium Development Goals: Milestones or Millstones? Human Rights Priorities for the Post-2015 Development Agenda." *Yale Human Rights and Development Law Journal* 15 (2012): 55–177.

15. Mark Tran. "Wellbeing of the Poor Has Deteriorated Over the Past 15 Years, Says Cafod." *The Guardian*, 29 July 2013.

16. Jan Vandermoortele. "The MDG Conundrum: Meeting the Targets without Missing the Point." *Development Policy Review* 27 (2009): 355–71. [CrossRef]

17. United Nations. "A Life of Dignity for All: Accelerating Progress toward the MDGs." 26 July 2013. Available online: http://daccess-dds-ny.un.org/doc/UNDOC/GEN/N13/409/32/PDF/N1340932.pdf?OpenElement (accessed on 11 November 2015).

18. Sakiko Fukuda-Parr, and Desmond McNeill. "Post 2015: A New Era of Accountability." Available online: https://unstats.un.org/unsd/statcoms/statcom_2015/seminars/post-2015/docs/Panel%201.3_FukudaParr%20.pdf (accessed on 10 January 2016).

19. World Bank. *World Bank Development Report 2011: "Conflict, Security, and Development"*. Washington: World Bank, 2011, vol. 30, pp. 75–76, which shows a causal relationship between group-based inequalities and violent conflict.

20. Steven Jensen, Allison Corkery, and Kate Donald. "Briefing Paper." Available online: http://www.humanrights.dk/files/media/dokumenter/udgivelser/research/nhri_briefingpaper_may2015.pdf (accessed on 11 June 2015).

21. Office of the High Commissioner for Human Rights. "Open Letter." Available online: http://www.ohchr.org/Documents/Issues/MDGs/Post2015/OpenLetter27July2015.pdf (accessed on 11 November 2015).

22. Thomas Pogge, and Mitu Sengupta. "The Sustainable Development Goals (SDGS) As Drafted: Nice Idea, Poor Execution." *Washington International Law Journal* 24 (2015): 571–709.

23. Sakiko Fukuda-Parr. "A Right to Development Critique of Millennium Development Goal 8." In *Realizing the Right to Development*. New York: UN Human Rights Commission, 2013, p. 202.

24. "Third International Conference 'Financing for Development'." Available online: http://www.un.org/esa/ffd/ffd3/conference.html (accessed on 20 March 2017).

![religions logo] *religions*

MDPI

Article

Economic Inequality: An Ethical Response

Shaji George Kochuthara

Department of Moral Theology, Faculty of Theology, Dharmaram Vidya Kshetram, Bangalore 560029, India;
kochuthshaji@gmail.com

Received: 3 July 2017; Accepted: 26 July 2017; Published: 4 August 2017

Abstract: This essay will inquire into the nature of economic inequality from the perspectives of Catholic social teaching and that of a theologian living and working in a developing country. My initial comments will discuss inequality within the context of economic globalization and the neo-liberal paradigm that dominates it. After commenting on the way that development is seen within that paradigm, I will show the impact upon the poor that has occurred as a result of neo-liberal economic policies in nations such as India. Following this exposition of what development according to the neo-liberal model looks like, I will offer another perspective on development drawn from the insights of Catholic social teaching. From that perspective, the importance of solidarity and its influence in shaping a more just and humane approach to development will be considered. The essay will conclude with a number of policy proposals that move away from the present and inadequate view of development to one inspired by a concern for solidarity with the least well off in our world.

Keywords: inequality; neo-liberal economics; globalization; development; Thomas Pogge; poverty; Catholic social teaching; solidarity; agriculture

1. Introduction

In general, inequality is natural. Human beings are different and unequal in intellectual capacity, physical strength, physical features, artistic capabilities, talents, social skills and so on. So, is it not natural that more hardworking and more efficient people become richer than others?

But, is the problem so simple? Is the economic inequality that exists in the world so natural and hence to be accepted as it is? Or, at least sometimes, should we hold that the economic inequality is human-made, and hence can be and has to be challenged and changed? And, does this inequality become an evil? If it does, when?

I am trying to explore answers to these questions, not as an economist, but in light of Catholic Social Teaching. Moreover, I shall approach the issue of economic inequality from the perspective of developing countries. Some of the examples given will be from India. But, similar cases can be found in various countries and regions. Most of my reflections will be in the context of globalization and the neo-liberal economic model that it promotes. I am not the proponent or opponent of any particular economic theory or economic model. However, I shall describe some of the developments in countries like India, so as to understand whether the present economic model is resulting in the marginalization and exclusion of people, individuals, sections and groups of society.

2. Development, Inequality and Poverty

There is no doubt that we need economic development. As Pope Paul VI has told, "Development is the new name for peace."[1] This development, if it has to ensure peace, should be accessible to all.

---

[1] This particular phrase is in fact the subheading given to paragraph numbers 76–77.

If only a few people are able to enjoy the fruits of development, leaving others in poverty, it will result in the dissatisfaction and unhappiness of those who are denied the benefits of development, and it will adversely affect peace within the nation and among nations. Already in his 1967 encyclical Pope Paul VI warned how inequality can threaten peace: "Extreme disparity between nations in economic, social and educational levels provokes jealousy and discord, often putting peace in jeopardy" (Paul 1967, para. 76–77). This is all the more true today, as the inequality is on the rise, not only among nations but also between the rich and the poor within the same nation.

Today, globalization and neo-liberalism are presented as the only models for development. Hence, to understand the problem of inequality, it is necessary to critically evaluate the achievements of globalization in reducing inequality and thus bringing about real development for all. Any form of resistance to this model is presented as anti-developmental. In general, in India, neo-liberalism is welcomed by the elite and the corporate sector, especially by those who are employed in IT, management and allied sectors, whereas many of those employed in agriculture, the poor and those working for social welfare are its opponents. It is difficult to define globalization. Globalization is often defined as the removal of barriers to free trade and the closer integration of national economies. In his book *Globalization and Its Discontents*, ex World Bank economist Joseph Stiglitz defines it as the removal of barriers to free trade and the closer integration of national economies. Stiglitz believes that globalisation can be a good thing but his career in one of the global institutions has also shown him first-hand the devastating effects these institutions' policies can have on poor people in developing countries (Stiglitz 2002, p. ix). Many do not consider globalization as a mere economic phenomenon though it may be the most visible dimension. Globalization is also a social, cultural and political phenomenon. N.R. Narayana Murthy, the co-founder and executive chairman of Infosys, in a lecture given at the Nani A. Palkhivala Trust in Mumbai, defines globalization at two levels:

> "At the macro level, it is about frictionless flow of capital, services, goods and labour across the globe. It is also about global sharing of ideas, knowledge and culture. It is about creating a shared concern and plan for global issues like poverty, AIDS and environment...At the microeconomic or firm level, it is about sourcing capital from where it is cheapest, sourcing talent from where it is best available, producing where it is most efficient and selling where the markets are, without being constrained by national boundaries" (Murthy 2007, p. 14).

Narayana Murthy defends globalization and in the same lecture he argues out why globalization is a necessity for development in India (Murthy 2007, pp. 14–20). But, as already pointed out, many others in India may not agree with his views. Considering globalization as the cause of all the problems in this world seems to be overly pessimistic. But, presenting globalization as a panacea for all the problems is too optimistic. However, it is pertinent to consider whether globalization, which claims to bring about real development, has managed to reduce inequality, and thus to make development more accessible to the less privileged and the marginalized.

In his paper, "Transcending the Washington View of Development," (Pogge 2013, pp. 73–101). Thomas Pogge shows how the official poverty statistics issued by the World Bank regarding the schedule towards achieving the first Millennium Development Goal (MDG1) which claims that poverty has been reduced, does not reflect the reality. According to him, on the contrary, poverty and undernourishment has only increased. He also says that in the last twenty-one years since the end of the Cold War, roughly 380 million people died from poverty-related causes. "Despite all of the proclaimed ideals, our seemingly lofty declarations, poverty and its concomitant human rights deprivations persist on a massive scale. They persist even while global average income is increasing and the world on the whole is doing quite well." Pogge holds that the enormous extent of the disparities that have built up during the globalization period in the distribution of global household income is responsible for this. In 2005, the top 5% of the world's population received 46.36% of the global household income, the next 20% almost the same proportion (that is, the top quarter had 90.34% of the global household income), whereas the other three quarters together had only 9.66%; the poorest quarter had only 0.78%. Pogge argues that only the richest 5% has gained in the globalization period (Pogge 2013, pp. 84–86).

3. Poverty, Rich-Poor Divide and the Rhetoric over Development

After independence (1947), India had adopted a semi-socialist economic policy. In 1991, a new economic policy of liberalization was adopted, giving more freedom for economic activity and imparting global linkage, leading to privatization and globalization. The positive effects of this new policy are seen in the increase in GDP growth rate, foreign direct investment, foreign exchange and outsourcing. Despite the after effects of the recession, growth rate in India was above 7% in 2015. Today, India is often presented as one of the growing economic powers. It is a member of the G 20, a member of BRICS (acronym for an association of five major emerging national economies, namely, Brazil, Russia, India, China and South Africa). Besides, it is predicted that by 2030 India may become the second largest economy in the world and by 2050 the largest. Among the 100 richest of the world, there are already many Indians.

While being proud of such achievements, we cannot ignore the growing rate of unemployment, widening disparities, neglect of agriculture and widespread poverty (Tyagi n.d.). The percentage of people living below poverty line may give an idea of the continuing poverty and growing disparity. Like many developed and developing countries that try to hide or ignore poverty within their own countries, it seems that India also has started to deny poverty within India, perhaps considering it as a shame, or to show that the economic policy being adopted is a success. We cannot ignore the burning truth that 33% of the world's poor live in India. According to the Reserve Bank of India statistics, the percentage of those below the poverty line was 35.97 in 1993–1994, 26.10 in 1999–2000 (Reserve Bank of India 2011).[2] However, according to a 2005 World Bank estimate, 41.6% of the total Indian population falls below the international poverty line of US$ 1.25 a day (Chen and Ravallion 2010, 1588). Recently, the criterion to define the poverty line resulted in a heated debate. The Indian Planning Commission's affidavit to the Supreme Court of India states that adjusting for inflation, the poverty line for an urban person is Rs 32.5 per day per person and for a rural person it is Rs 29.3 per day per person *[1 US$ = 65 Indian Rupees]*. This raised an outcry from many, since the said amount is not sufficient even for a single meal for even one person. Anyone who knows the price of pulses, cereals and vegetables would find this amount to determine the poverty line absurd. Even based on these poverty lines, the Planning Commission estimates that there are 407.4 million people below the poverty line in 2010–2011 (Parikh 2011). This is another indication of the attempts by governments and their agencies to show that poverty is reduced, even denying the basic facts. That is, instead of reducing poverty, they try to bring down the poverty line, and thus to claim that their policies have been successful! Whatever be the criterion for calculation, it is also evident that besides those living under the poverty line, many people live just above the poverty line. Moreover, we need to take into account the opinions that more than 70% of the people in India are poor (Singh 2015).

Poverty existed in India even before the introduction of neo-liberalism and globalization. But, what is pertinent is that the growth in GDP in the recent decades, an argument in favour of neo-liberal economy and development, is not reflected in the life of a good number of people. This points to the widening gap between the poor and the rich. On average, the poorest 10 per cent of Indians live on just Rs. 16 per day to survive whereas the richest 10 per cent spend Rs. 255 per day (NDTV 2012). Similarly, the claim that the present developmental policies create more jobs is not accepted by many. It is pointed out that in recent years the number of unemployed persons has increased (Kumar 2013).

---

[2] We may be confused by the statistics provided by different agencies. I have to acknowledge that the statistical data provided by different agencies do not agree with each other, and the criterion for deciding the poverty line is varied and confusing.

Can we agree at least on this? The economic status of the poor has not improved with neo-liberalism; even otherwise their life was not better. Today, as the result of the new economic policies, a number of rich people have become richer, many middle class people have become richer. So, what is wrong? Unfortunately, that is not the situation. Not only those living in extreme poverty, but others as well, are affected by the neo-liberal economic system. Imbalances and inequality in development make the poor poorer. The cost of living has sharply shot up as many people have found jobs in new sectors and their income has considerably increased. Take for example, the city of Bangalore, which is known as the IT hub of India. In the last 20 years, the population of Bangalore has grown three or four times—from 3 million to more than 12 million.[3] With the boom of the IT sector, hundreds of thousands of people have found jobs in software companies and BPO which offer them good salaries. A couple of million people are employed in public sectors, service sectors like education, etc.; the real estate business also thrives in the city. But, a good number of people are employed in low-income sectors, or many do not have a secure job or any job at all. There are hundreds of thousands of people who earn more than Rupees 50,000 or even 200,000 per month [*There are surely people who earn more than 1 million rupees per month*]. But, in the same city, there are hundreds of thousands of people who earn just 5000 or even below 2000 Rupees per month. Often that is the income for the whole family. Their income has not increased proportionately with the development. But, with the economic boom in the city, food, housing, education, healthcare and anything and everything have become very costly. For example, one single room apartment, with 12 × 12 room or 144 sq ft costs at least Rs. 5000 to 7000 or more per month; five to six people may share it; or it may be the house for an entire family. Besides, they will have to pay for water, electricity and other maintenance expenses of that apartment. In short, the so-called development has not improved the life of the poor; rather, their life is rendered more miserable. Even the lower middle class suffer. Today, even if a family of three persons earn Rs. 20,000 a month, it has become almost impossible for them to have a decent life in the city. It is not primarily because of inflation, but due to inequality.

In the beginning, many people in countries like India were apprehensive (and are still) that neo-liberalism is a form of economic colonialism, aimed at plundering the wealth of developing and poor nations in the guise of development. People in developed countries were rather enthusiastic about it, especially as it opened up new markets and job opportunities for them. But, years after its introduction, a good number of people in the developed countries do not seem to be so enthusiastic about it, especially since the economic recession. Millions of people in the developed countries have lost their jobs as many firms shifted their production units and offices to other countries where labour is cheap. To be added to this are millions of jobs outsourced to other countries. Does it mean that people in those countries benefit? But, we need to keep in mind that the primary intention of these companies is not the benefit of those nations, instead their own profit. Often, the multinational groups enter into deals with the local governments, to get their own terms accepted and to evade tax payments. Thus, though many people in the developing or poor countries benefit, the profit that the multinational firms make have increased enormously and this growth is without any solidarity with anyone anywhere, since they are not accountable to anyone either in their home countries or in the countries where they have opened their units. As a result, the development is largely the development of big firms, or the development of a few. There are those who obtain new jobs and better payment, but society as a whole is kept away from the benefits of development. This lack of the sense of solidarity reinforces inequalities, injustice, exploitation and subsequently poverty and suffering.

One of the major premises of the Washington Consensus is that 'freeing up' of markets promotes economic growth by attracting international investors. Foreign businesses are supposed to bring with them technical expertise and access to foreign markets and financial sources, thus creating new

---

[3] Though the official statistics may give it as 9 million, it is pointed out that including the suburbs which are practically part of the city, the population is more than 12 million. Some also say that considering the population Bangalore is already the third largest city in India.

employment opportunities. However, there is a flipside of this, namely, large global corporations often destroy local competition and home-grown industries. For example, Coca-Cola and Pepsi have wiped out many local soft drink manufacturers all over the world. If competition is the only norm, the small-scale industries and firms do not succeed, rather they are annihilated. This only adds to the number of poor, though the accumulation of wealth by the big firms will appear in the increase of the GDP.

4. Agricultural Sectors

Agricultural sectors in India have suffered a lot due to new economic policies. The agricultural land of small farmers has been taken to create Special Economic Zones (SEZ), without giving them sufficient compensation and without rehabilitating them. In many places, farmers have protested, but in most cases they have failed before the unholy alliance of politicians, bureaucrats and multinationals. Only in some places like Nandigram[4] in West Bengal and Plachimada[5] in Kerala the farmers could succeed in the agitation against the big companies. Since special subsidies for agriculture are reduced or removed, often to fulfil the conditions set by international organisations like World Trade Organization and International Monetary Fund, many are unable to continue farming. Take for example, the thousands of farmers who committed suicide in the last few years. It is said that in the state of Gujarat alone, the state which is often presented as the model of development, more than 16,000 farmers committed suicide in the last 10 years (Sarabhai 2011, p. 98). It may be paradoxical that the present prime minister of India, Narendara Modi, was the chief minister of Gujarat for over a decade, and he won the national election presenting the developments in Gujarat during his rule as the proof of his efficiency and as the model of development he would be able to achieve for the whole of India. Many recent studies show that the so-called development in Gujarat during Modi's rule was at the cost of granting special rights to the big companies, even denying basic facilities to farmers and the poor. In 2016, according to the data available until the month of May, 454 farmer suicides took place in Marathwada, one of the five regions of the state of Maharashtra (Kakodkari 2016). In Maharashtra too from 2014, the Bharatiya Janata Party is in power, and the Add to this the thousands of farmers who committed suicide in other states in India! The rate of suicide of farmers is on the rise, especially in the recent years and months. The picture is very grim when we also understand that in spite of the development in Industrial and IT sectors, the majority of Indians—70%—still depend of agriculture for their livelihood. I do not think that the situation will

---

[4]   At Nandigram in West Bengal, the Communist Party of India Marxist (CPIM) led government decided to expropriate 10,000 acres (40 km^2) of land from the farmers for a Special Economic Zone (SEZ) to be developed by the Indonesian based Salim Group for industrialization. This was opposed by the farmers and this led to widespread violence and killing and rape of many by the police and allegedly by the CPIM party workers in March 2007. Finally the government was forced to abandon the project. It may be paradoxical that the CPIM, who claims to be protectors of farmers, acted against the farmers and let loose violence on them. Eventually, the CPIM which ruled West Bengal for about three decades, lost the assembly election in 2011.

[5]   The Coke bottling plant set up in March 2000 began drawing over five hundred thousand litres of water from the wells on its premises each day. This resulted in the drastic depletion of water levels resulting in crop failure in the locality and thus inviting protests of the locals and environmental activists alike. Besides the depletion of water, the waste material from the factory caused serious problems for the health of the people. It took some more time for all the concerned including the *gram panchayat* (= elected body of local administration) to comprehend the gravity of the situation and to take actions. The plant was producing one litre of Cola from four litres of water leaving behind 2.7 litres of wastewater and solid wastes. The groundwater of the village got heavily polluted as solid wastes containing hazardous chromium, cadmium, lead, etc., caused severe health problems to the villagers. Moreover, the company distributed the solid wastes to the farmers as fertilizers, thus harming the farmland too. The campaign was quite spontaneous attracting world-wide attention and resulting in the temporary shutdown of the plant in March 2004. However, the legal battle and the struggle continued demanding compensation for the victims. In the beginning no political parties were involved in the struggle, though when the movement took momentum, many political parties got involved. However, it remained as a struggle led by the local people. The struggle was led by local people like Mayilamma, an illiterate adivasi woman, and C.K. Janu, another adivasi woman. They became both symbols of resistance against the corporate giant. On 30 April 2010, a high-power committee set up by the Government of Kerala indicted the Hindustan Coca Cola Beverages Private Limited for causing incalculable harm to the ecology and the people of Plachimada, assessing the overall cost of the damage at 2.16 billion rupees.

change drastically even if another party comes to power, unless the economic policy itself changes. Suicide is not a solution, but what drives the farmers to this extreme step? One of the justifications often given for inequality is that it is natural that hardworking people become richer. That may be true. But, what about these farmers who work hard from early morning until late in the evening and still do not manage to get back even what they spend? Is it the lack of hard work or the unjust economic system and market forces behind inequality? Thus, the economic policies and the market-driven economy lead to further exclusion and marginalization of farmers.

For many indigenous peoples, their culture is closely connected to their land. It has become a trend in many parts of the world, including India, to take away, often forcefully, the land belonging to indigenous people and the farmers. They do not have the power and tactics to resist the collaborated work of business groups and governments. In India, thousands of hectares of land in the mountains and forests, that was actually the home of Tribals and other indigenous people was snatched away from them for mining and for establishing huge industries, often using even the military and the police forces. Taking away their land means not only that they are robbed of their livelihood, but they are totally uprooted from their habitat and culture. Once they lose their land, they feel that they belong nowhere. In most cases, they were not given adequate compensation or land in other places to settle down, leaving them homeless and landless. It is said that the main reason behind the rise of violent revolutionary groups such as Naxals in many parts of India is this injustice done to the indigenous people. We cannot justify violence; but we cannot justify such injustice done to the poor and the weaker sections of the society, often authorised by the governments and officials to unlawfully help the powerful big business groups. Such an economic model and development that consider profit as the ultimate goal lead to the marginalization and alienation of the indigenous people. In turn, the human community loses the richness of their cultural heritage. Moreover, those people are alienated from society, and in many cases they may become part of violent and revolutionary movements, threatening peace and harmony in the society.

5. Neo-Liberalism, Corruption and Inequality

Corruption is not the invention of globalization. But, neo-liberal economy has given new faces to corruption. A study published in November 2010 by Global Financial Integrity (GFI), an international advocacy group, says that corruption in India has increased considerably after liberalization. According to its report, between 2002 and 2006, the loss to the government due to corruption was 16 billion dollars per year (Pinto 2011, p. 85). Why does this happen? An economic model, in which profit is the only value, becomes an economy without ethics. Profit, even at the denial of justice, becomes the only ethics. Such an economic system is disastrous, and will not lead to real development. As Arundhati Roy points out: "Twenty years ago, when the era of 'liberalisation, privatisation and globalisation' descended on us, we were told that public sector units and public infrastructure needed to be privatised because they were corrupt and inefficient...Now that nearly everything has been privatised...we find that corruption has grown exponentially..." (Roy 2011). For example, from 2006 to 2011, the Government of India wrote off corporate income tax worth 3749 billion Rupees (Desrochers 2011, pp. 155–56)[6]. At the same time, farmers or other poor people who fail to repay even one instalment of the loan taken, have to face legal procedures! When privileges are granted to the rich at the cost of the life of the poor, it becomes a clear case of injustice. This also means widening the gap between the rich and the poor, because the public funds available will be so much less.

---

[6]   *The Hindu*, 10 July 2011, 5.

6. Development and Inequality: An Ethical Evaluation in Light of Catholic Social Teaching (CST)[7]

6.1. Basic Principles of CST

There are a few key themes in CST, which can be said to be its foundation. In order to understand CST's approach to social and economic issues, it is necessary to understand these basic premises.[8] The limited scope of this paper does not permit an elaborate discussion on all these principles. We shall highlight only a few of these foundational principles which are relevant for our discussion on economic inequality.

1. *The Dignity of Every Person:* CST holds that every human person has a unique and sacred dignity. This dignity is not something acquired by one's effort, or granted by those in authority, but based on the truth that every person is created in the image and likeness of God (Gen 1:27). For CST, this implies that human development cannot be understood only in terms of economic development, but includes social, cultural, political and spiritual aspects of human person. That is, any government or system dominated by the concern of economic development alone is against authentic human development. The notion of the dignity of every person implies the equality of all human beings. Based on this, CST stands for a just sharing of social status, political power and economic resources. The concept of human rights basically derives from the equal dignity of all human beings.

2. *Solidarity:* CST is founded on the conviction that all of us belong to one human family, and hence we have the obligation to promote the rights and development of all people, irrespective of national boundaries. In particular, wealthy nations and wealthy persons have a greater obligation to promote the development of poorer nations and people. Dignity and intrinsic worth of persons cannot be understood in terms of an individualistic right in isolation, but only in the context of the obligations to human community as a whole.

3. *Family:* Family occupies an important place in CST. Family is the primary cell of the society and the 'domestic Church.' Hence CST criticises economic and social conditions that disturb family life (Second Vatican Council 1965, para 47).

4. *Private Property:* CST defends the right to private ownership of property. However, this is not an absolute and unconditional right. As *Populorum Progressio* says, "Private property does not constitute for anyone an absolute and unconditional right. No one is justified in keeping for his exclusive use what he does not need, when others lack necessities" (Paul 1967, para. 23). This is re-affirmed by John Paul II: "The goods of this world are equally meant for all. The right to private property is valid and necessary, but it does not nullify the value of this principle. Private property, in fact, is under a social mortgage" (John 1987, para. 42).

5. *Option for the Poor:* Rights of all human beings are to be ensured. At the same time, CST shows a special option for the poor, because the dignity and rights of the poor are often ignored and abused. This preferential option is rooted in the biblical concept of justice, namely, God has a preferential love and concern for the poor, the marginalized and the suffering. CST is also aware of the structures of sin which continue to keep the poor as poor or make their condition worse.

6. *Care of Creation:* CST has directly addressed this issue only in recent decades, but there is a growing concern over this, realizing its urgency, as it is evident from the encyclical letter of Pope Francis, *Laudato Si'* (Francis 2015). Human beings are called to be co-creators. They have to depend on the

---

[7] From the beginning of Christian history we find social teaching as an integral part of its teaching. However, usually 'Catholic Social Teaching' refers to the developing body of official Catholic social teaching beginning with *Rerum Novarum* (1891) of Pope Leo XIII (Leo 1891).

[8] For a detailed presentation of the foundational principles of CST, see (Massaro 2012; Deberri et al. 2003, pp. 18–34). The following paragraphs highlighting some of the foundational principles of CST are mainly based on these books

natural resources for their sustenance. But, this should be done respecting the ecological balance, not destroying it with selfishness and greed.

In the following sections, we shall discuss some of these in more detail.

6.2. Christian Vision of Wealth and Private Property

According to the Christian vision wealth is God's gift. Christianity is not against private property; it considers private property as integral to human freedom and dignity. However, as already mentioned above, in the Christian vision wealth ultimately belongs to all human beings; it should be shared in such a way that everyone should have sufficient wealth available for her/his well-being. While respecting and defending the right to private property, Christianity is clear that hoarding of wealth in the hands of a few, denying even the basic rights and needs of others is evil and sinful. Right to private property may naturally imply the possibility of economic inequality. However, inequality can become evil and sinful under various circumstances. As *Gaudium et Spes*, the Pastoral Constitution of the Second Vatican Council has clearly affirmed, "For excessive economic and social differences between the members of the one human family or population groups cause scandal, and militate against social justice, equity, the dignity of the human person, as well as social and international peace" (Second Vatican Council 1965, para. 29). Economic inequality becomes evil and sinful:

- If it denies the basic rights and well-being of others
- If persons, groups and sections of society are marginalised
- If wealth is not shared, especially with the needy
- If equal opportunities are denied, especially to the poor and weaker sections of the society
- If wealth is acquired violating the basic principles of justice and solidarity with others
- If inequality leads to conflicts in the society
- If profit instead of human persons becomes the centre of economic activity
- If wealth is acquired causing harm to nature, which belongs to all, including the generations to come

6.3. Globalization, Neo-Liberalism and Economic Solidarity

Thomas Pogge shows an inherent defect in the path neo-liberalism has taken which has led to such a dramatic rise in inequality, both internationally and intra-nationally. Globalization involves competitive systems, such as global economy and financial markets, politics and international relations, courts, etc. According to Pogge, "the fundamental flaw in the modern global economy is that the richest agents have both the ability and the incentives to invest extensive resources into regulatory capture in order to gain an ever increasing share of the social product for themselves." A complex set of supranational laws and regulations is an essential part of globalization. These regulations are often created by intergovernmental negotiations, practically by governments of the richest countries, large multinational corporations and banks, very rich individuals and the elites of the most powerful developing countries. It is a process which is undemocratic, intransparent, excluding the general public and a majority of the weaker governments. Hence Pogge says that, "It should not be surprising that the past seventeen years of globalization have led to income polarization as the rich minority capture ever more influence over supranational negotiations, further marginalizing the poorer majority of humanity." This income polarization happens not only internationally, but also intra-nationally (Pogge 2013, pp. 85–93).

All these make clear that free trade alone is not enough to ensure social justice. "The economy needs ethics in order to function correctly—not any ethics whatsoever, but an ethics which is people-oriented." (Benedict 2015, para. 45) The World Commission on the Social Dimension of Globalization underscores that the governance of globalization must be based on universally shared values and respect for human rights. It acknowledges that, "Globalization has developed in an ethical vacuum, where market success and failure have tended to become the ultimate standard of behaviour..." (World Commission on the Social Dimension of World Commission on the Social Dimension of Globalization 2004, no. 37, p. 7). Any economic system and developmental programmes should recognise the "centrality of the human person." (Benedict 2015, para. 47). Only if the economic system is based on the principle of solidarity, it will ensure justice and real distribution of wealth. Otherwise, it will only intensify and perpetuate injustice on the global level. "Solidarity is the awareness of a common humanity and global citizenship and the voluntary acceptance of the responsibilities which go with it. It is the conscious commitment to redress inequalities both within and between countries. It is based on recognition that in an interdependent world, poverty or oppression anywhere is a threat to prosperity and stability everywhere" (World Commission on the Social Dimension of World Commission on the Social Dimension of Globalization 2004, no. 41, p. 8).

Pope John Paul II has repeatedly said that, "peace for all of us comes from the justice of each of us." (John 1998) Development becomes real development only when it is sought in solidarity, which is an authentic moral virtue. Solidarity implies that there is a shared responsibility to assist countries and people excluded from or disadvantaged.

The Kingdom of God, the central message of Jesus Christ, envisions a human society that lives in solidarity, a human society that lives as a family where God is the Father of all and all, as children of the same Father, are brothers and sisters. As Pope Benedict XVI says in *Caritas in Veritate*, "The development of peoples depends, above all, on a recognition that the human race is a single family working together in true communion, not simply a group of subjects who happen to live side by side." (Benedict 2015, para. 53) Competitiveness and profit should not alienate the market from the solidarity with the human family. Only a "civilization of love" can ensure this (Benedict 2015, para. 33). This demands a genuine sense of sharing. "Solidarity is achieved by seeing to it that all human beings share in the available goods as a whole."[9] Seeing economic policies today, and the widening gap between the rich and poor nations and the rich and the poor within the same country, we may feel that the 'Kingdom of God' vision is only a utopian idea, an ideal that has no reality sense. We may find the Kingdom vision far removed from the actual situation today, but we continue to believe in its transforming power, and we continue to work towards it with hope.

6.4. Solidarity with the Environment

An important aspect of solidarity is the solidarity with the nature.[10] Often, the multinational companies which manage to influence and even dictate government policies easily ignore the havoc done to ecology and future generations. Rapid growth of the economy, which is the demand and need of the market, requires rapid and major expansion of infrastructure and resource extraction. To be added to this is the encouragement of wasteful consumption, especially by the rich, without which the present model of the market cannot survive. This results in projects and processes with negative consequences for the ecology. Liberalization of trade has led to rapid increase in exploitation of natural resources to earn foreign exchange, which has serious consequences for the traditional livelihoods and ecological balance in different regions. Norms to safeguard the ecology are sacrificed to make a 'friendly' climate for investment. Thomas Pogge points out that "wealthy countries contribute disproportionately to global pollution and yet they are allowed to enjoy the benefits of their polluting

---

[9] Oscar Andres Cardinal Rodriguez M. "The Catholic Church and the Globalization of Solidarity" (Rodriguez 2003, 4).

[10] Here I do not intend to discuss in detail how human beings should relate with nature, namely, nature as independently existing for itself, or nature as existing for human beings. For example, some of the Indian traditions treat nature as existing for itself, seeing the manifestation of God in everything, or nature as an extension of God, an approach which has been often called pantheistic. "Deep Ecology" in contemporary approaches to Ecological and Environmental philosophy has similar view of nature, though not with reference to God. A detailed discussion on this seems to be beyond the scope of this essay. Here the main concern is to ensure sustainable development, considering the needs of the present generation as well as those of the future generations. However, a completely anthropo-centric approach considering nature as existing only to be used by human beings may lead to 'exploiting it as much as possible'. Instead, what is needed is a relationship of mutuality.

activities without compensating the poor who bear the brunt of the hazards of pollution." The poor are more vulnerable to health risks and dangers of climate change wrought by pollution. According to a Global Humanitarian Forum report, climate change causes $125 billion in economic losses annually and 300,000 deaths, of which 99% are in less developed countries. (Pogge 2013, p. 93) Pope Francis has been a relentless advocate of the poor. In his encyclical, *Laudato Si: On Care of Our Common Home*, he explains how the question of the care of the environment and care of the poor are interrelated: "In fact, the deterioration of the environment and of society affects the most vulnerable people on the planet: 'Both everyday experience and scientific research show that the gravest effects of all attacks on the environment are suffered by the poorest.' For example, the depletion of fishing reserves especially hurts small fishing communities without the means to replace those resources; water pollution particularly affects the poor who cannot buy bottled water; and rises in the sea level mainly affect impoverished coastal populations who have nowhere else to go. The impact of present imbalances is also seen in the premature death of many of the poor, in conflicts sparked by the shortage of resources, and in any number of other problems which are insufficiently represented on global agendas" (Francis 2015, para. 48).

Solidarity requires that the developed nations, who are more responsible for the ecological damage bear in a proportionate manner the duty to compensate the damage done. *Laudato Si'* has something important to say in this regard: "Inequity affects not only individuals but entire countries; it compels us to consider an ethics of international relations. A true "ecological debt" exists, particularly between the global north and south, connected to commercial imbalances with effects on the environment, and the disproportionate use of natural resources by certain countries over long periods of time" (Francis 2015, para. 51).

7. Economic Development in Solidarity: A Few Proposals

Naturally, one may doubt: Will CST make any change? Is it realistic? Is it practical? Is it not too ideological? Such questions may not look so irrelevant. But, we have to consider the fact that the Church is not a political power, and it does not try to impose its teaching with the force of law. It does not legislate like a civil government or like international bodies such as UNO. Moreover, " … the Church does not propose economic and political systems or programs, nor does she show preference for one or the other, provided that human dignity is properly respected and promoted..." (John 1987, para. 41) Rather, CST is invitational, as the Christian message itself is. CST, first of all, invites persons to a new awareness and to act, in their personal and social life, based on that new awareness. This may be considered by some people as a limitation of CST. But, this can be also considered as a strength of CST, in the sense that, CST calls for a conversion of heart and social and economic changes emanating that conversion. It is also to be noted that CST is not addressed only to the Catholics, but to all people of good will. This implies that CST believes that people of good will listen to its voice, and though slowly, real socio-economic changes will happen, leading humanity to a better life. Based on this conviction, and based on our discussion, let us consider some of the concrete proposals for creating a more just world, though the ways and means of expressing solidarity may be varied, depending on the particular context and needs. Let me list below some of the proposals given by experts and world leaders in this regard:[11]

1. Goods are to be shared without excluding anyone, without some hoarding them depriving others of the right to own them. This is one of the basic principles to ensure solidarity both in the international and intra-national levels. This is especially to be ensured in the case of fossil fuels and other non-renewable energy sources.

---

[11] Here mainly we refer to some of the proposals given by Pope John Paul II (John 1998), Oscar Andres Cardinal Rodriguez M. (Rodriguez 2003, "The Catholic Church and the Globalization of Solidarity") and Thomas Pogge (Pogge 2013). Please note that these or similar suggestions have been given by many experts and world leaders.

2. International organisations should ensure just prices in trade. Multinational and big companies manage to arbitrarily determine the prices of agricultural products and natural resources. Often, the poor farmers become the victims of this unjust system, making them poorer. On an international level, subsidies are to be granted on essential goods to poor nations.

3. Affirmative action to support weaker sections of the society is necessary to build up a more egalitarian society. Poor sections within the nation are to be offered special subsidies. India, for example, had the system of granting subsidies to the poor and the middle class. Since the introduction of the neo-liberalism, a number of subsidies were cut, especially under the pressure of IMF, WTO, etc. It is claimed that subsidy system slows down the economic growth. However, it is paradoxical that to save big national and multinational companies, big amounts are written off. Often, the loss to the economy in writing off the debt of the multi-million companies is much more than the subsidies granted to the poor. Preferential choice for the poor is an essential element of solidarity.

4. Specially to be mentioned is the obligation of the developed/industrialized countries to help the poorest. This is essential to bring down inequality at the international level. In most cases, this is a demand of justice of restitution, that is, a compensation for unjustifiable exploitation that many poor countries had to undergo in the past. Without generous assistance, many such countries are unable to develop, as they still do not have the basic facilities and infrastructure. However, this assistance should not be on conditions which enslave them further.

5. External debt of the poor nations: Besides being backward, most of the poor nations are over-burdened by huge external debts which hinder their development. This is particularly true in the case of many African countries. Moreover, these debts often compel them to accept exploitative conditions by rich nations and multi-national corporations, resulting in further underdevelopment. Unless rich nations are willing to cancel the debt of the poor nations (or at least to write off a considerable amount of it), it will be impossible for these nations to find the path of development (Makwana 2006).

6. Patent regulations, which control the production of essential goods and their prices are to be reconsidered.[12] This is acutely felt in the case of life-saving and essential medicines. While respecting the right of the inventor and producer for just profit, patent regulations should become sensitive to the needs of the people, especially of the poor. The historic ruling given by the Supreme Court of India, rejecting the petition by Novartis, and allowing the domestic companies to continue to make copycat versions of the drug Gleevec (Glivec), gives new hopes to the poor. Whereas Gleevec may cost $70,000 a year, the Indian generic versions cost less than $2,500 a year.[13] Evidently, such steps may be resisted by the multi-national corporations. But, they are necessary steps not to exclude the poor and the less privileged from the benefits of development.

7. Banking and credit system have to become more accessible to the poor at affordable interest rates. Otherwise, their financial condition will be affected further and they will be marginalised from the benefits of economic progress.

8. Governments and NGOs should work together to ensure sustainable development, respecting the ecological conditions of the regions concerned. More investment should be made in developing

---

[12] To understand the extent to which patent regulations are misused for business motives, it is enough to consider the dispute over the patent for turmeric, a traditional spice and medicine used in India for thousands of years: http://www1.american.edu/ted/turmeric.htm. Another example would be the dispute on patent for neemtree, a medicinal tree: http://www1.american.edu/TED/neemtree.htm. There were also attempts to obtain patent for Basmati rice and such traditional crops.

[13] (Harris and Thomas 2013; Selvaraj 2013). Thomas Pogge's article referred to above will be very helpful regarding the patent regulations regarding drugs.

alternative energy sources. As mentioned above, though the harm done to ecology affects all, it is the poor who are affected more by the damage done to ecology.

9. An economic system where the multinational companies are accountable—either in their home country or where they set up their units—to the society should be developed. Terms and conditions for investment should not be decided unilaterally by those companies, but with the involvement of the state and the society.

10. Although the concept of Corporate Social Responsibility [CSR] is accepted in principle, there is a lack of clarity regarding its implementation. At the national and international levels, there should be clear understanding of the percentage of profit that the business firms invest in CSR. Investing this especially in education and healthcare is vital to bringing down inequality.

11. Special care should be taken to make education, including higher education, equitable and affordable. The upward movement of the poor and the middleclass depends to a great extent on education. If the fees are too high, they are practically excluded from the process of development, widening further the rich-poor gap.

12. Works of charity, though may not be accepted as a long-term solution by many, is a necessary way of expressing solidarity with the poor. The poor and the hungry will not be able to survive until economic equality is achieved and all have sufficient to survive. So, to deny charity to the hungry and those who live in utter misery and poverty on an ideological basis is equal to denying them the right to live.

13. In the private sector companies, there is often a huge difference between the payment for the employees in the highest ranks and those in the lowest ranks. Is it possible to decide upon the maximum difference in the salaries and benefits received by those in the topmost ranks and lowest ranks within the same firm, as well as in the same country?

Some of the above proposals refer to policies in the relationship among nations so that poorer nations may receive a more equitable and just share of the wealth, while others speak about policies to be implemented within the nation so that more just and equitable distribution of wealth may be ensured. International policies are also very important for the poor, since the burden of unjust policies more heavily falls on the poor.

8. Concluding Remarks

Addressing the new Vatican ambassadors in May 2013, Pope Francis said: "While the income of a minority is increasing exponentially, that of the majority is crumbling. This imbalance results from ideologies which uphold the absolute autonomy of markets and financial speculation, and thus deny the right of control to States, which are charged with providing for the common good. A new, invisible and at times virtual, tyranny is established, one which unilaterally and irremediably imposes its own laws and rules."

Economic prosperity, if it does not ensure justice to all, will not lead to long-lasting peace, well-being, and development in the world. Those who are denied justice and even a minimum means of life will rise against the powerful who deny them justice and oppress them in different ways. A number of revolutions and people's movements in the history of the human society clearly show this. Hence, development in solidarity is necessary for peace and harmony in this world. Ensuring justice is not merely to satisfy some legal requirements, or to avoid wars and conflicts. It comes out of the conviction that all people on earth basically form one single human community, that everyone is related to everyone else and everyone is responsible for the well-being of all. This concept of justice is fundamentally rooted in love and solidarity with all people on earth.

Conflicts of Interest: The author declares no conflict of interest.

References

Benedict, XVII. 2015. *Caritas in Veritate.* Available online: http://w2.vatican.va/content/benedict-xvi/en/encyclicals/documents/hf_ben-xvi_enc_20051225_deus-caritas-est.html (accessed on 30 June 2017).

Chen, Shaouha, and Martin Ravallion. 2010. The Developing World Is Poorer Than We Thought, but No Less Successful in the Fight against Poverty. *The Quarterly Journal of Economics*, 1577–1625. Available online: http://siteresources.worldbank.org/DEC/Resources/DevelopingworldispoorerQJE.pdf (accessed on 1 August 2017).

Deberri, Edward P., James E. Hug, Peter J. Henriot, and Michael J. Schultheis. 2003. *Catholic Social Teaching: Our Best Kept Secret*, 4th ed. New York: Orbis Books, pp. 18–34.

Desrochers, John. 2011. The State of India. *Integral Liberation* 15: 155–56.

Francis, Pope. 2015. *Laudato Si'. On Care for Our Common Home.* Available online: http://w2.vatican.va/content/francesco/en/encyclicals/documents/papa-francesco_20150524_enciclica-laudato-si.pdf (accessed on 30 June 2017).

Harris, Gardiner, and Katie Thomas. 2013. Low-Cost Drugs in Poor Nations Get a Lift in Indian Court. *New York Times.* April 1. Available online: http://www.nytimes.com/2013/04/02/business/global/top-court-in-india-rejects-novartis-drug-patent.html?pagewanted=all&_r=0 (accessed on 30 January 2015).

John, Paul, II. 1987. *Sollicitudo Rei Socialis.* Available online: http://w2.vatican.va/content/john-paul-ii/en/encyclicals/documents/hf_jp-ii_enc_30121987_sollicitudo-rei-socialis.html (accessed on 30 January 2016).

John, Paul, II. 1998. From the Justice of Each Comes Peace for All. Message of His Holiness Pope John Paul II for the Celebration of the World Day of Peace. January 1. Available online: http://www.vatican.va/holy_father/john_paul_ii/messages/peace/documents/hf_jp-ii_mes_08121997_xxxi-world-day-for-peace_en.html (accessed on 30 January 2016).

Kakodkari, Priyanka. 2016. Marathwada Farmer Suicides at 454, 22% Higher Than in 2015. *The Times of India.* May 28. Available online: http://timesofindia.indiatimes.com/india/Marathwada-farmer-suicides-at-454-22-higher-than-in-2015/articleshow/52473945.cms (accessed on 31 January 2016).

Kumar, N. D. Shiva. 2013. Unemployment Rate Increases in India. *The Times of India.* June 23. Available online: http://articles.timesofindia.indiatimes.com/2013-06-23/india/40146190_1_urban-india-urban-women-rural-women (accessed on 31 January 2016).

Leo, III. 1891. *Rerum Novarum.* Available online: http://w2.vatican.va/content/leo-xiii/en/encyclicals/documents/hf_l-xiii_enc_15051891_rerum-novarum.html (accessed on 25 January 2016).

Makwana, Rajesh. 2006. Cancelling Third World Debt. Share the World's Resources. Available online: http://www.stwr.org/aid-debt-development/cancelling-third-world-debt.html (accessed on 30 January 2016).

Massaro, S. J. Thomas. 2012. *Living Justice: Catholic Social Teaching in Action.* Lanham: Rowman and Littlefield Publishers.

Murthy, N. R. Narayana. 2007. *Making Globalization Work for India.* Mumbai: Nani A. Palkhivala Memorial Trust.

NDTV. 2012. Inequality Gap beween Rich and Poor Widens. Reported by Ketki Angre, and Haribans Sharma. Edited by Abhinav Bhatt. Available online: http://www.ndtv.com/india-news/inequality-gap-between-rich-and-poor-widens-495260 (accessed on 30 January 2016).

Parikh, Kirit. 2011. The Poverty Line Debate. *Hindustan Times.* Available online: http://www.hindustantimes.com/News-Feed/ColumnsOthers/The-poverty-line-debate/Article1-752547.aspx (accessed on 2 April 2012).

Paul, VI. 1967. *Populorum Progressio.* Available online: http://w2.vatican.va/content/paul-vi/en/encyclicals/documents/hf_p-vi_enc_26031967_populorum.html (accessed on 20 January 2016).

Pinto, Melwyn. 2011. Have We Failed Democracy in India? *Integral Liberation* 15: 85.

Pogge, Thomas. 2013. Transcending the Washington View of Development. In *Towards a Strong Global Economic System: Revealing the Logic of Gratuitousness in the Market Economy.* Edited by Saju Chackalackal. Bangalore: Dharmaram Publications.

Reserve Bank of India. 2011. Table 162: Number and Percentage of Population below Poverty Line. Available online: http://www.rbi.org.in/scripts/PublicationsView.aspx?id=13750 (accessed on 2 February 2016).

Rodriguez, Oscar Andres Cardinal M. 2003. The Catholic Church and the Globalization of Solidarity. Address to Caritas Internationalis, Vatican, July 7.

Roy, Arundhati. 2011. When Corruption is Viewed Fuzzily. *The Indian Express*. April 30. Available online: http://www.indianexpress.com/news/-when-corruption-is-viewed-fuzzily-/783688/0 (accessed on 2 February 2016).

Sarabhai, Mallika. 2011. Modi and His Mayajaal. *The Week*, October 30.

Second Vatican Council. 1965. *Gaudium et Spes*. Available online: http://www.vatican.va/archive/hist_councils/ii_vatican_council/documents/vat-ii_const_19651207_gaudium-et-spes_en.html (accessed on 1 February 2016).

Selvaraj, Sakthivel. 2013. Patent Justice. *The Hindu*. April 7. Available online: http://www.thehindu.com/news/national/patent-justice/article4588895.ece (accessed on 2 February 2016).

Singh, Rani. 2015. '70% of India's People are Still Poor,' Says Writer Harsh Mander. May 31. Available online: https://www.forbes.com/sites/ranisingh/2015/05/31/70-per-cent-of-indias-people-are-still-poor-says-writer-harsh-mander/#5ec3268619b7 (accessed on 1 August 2017).

Stiglitz, Joseph. 2002. *Globalization and Its Discontents*. London: Penguin Books.

Tyagi, Supreti. n.d. New Economic Policy-1991. Available online: http://www.scribd.com/doc/13709734/New-Economic-Policy-1991 (accessed on 2 February 2016).

World Commission on the Social Dimension of Globalization. 2004. *A Fair Globalization: Creating Opportunities for All*. Geneva: ILO Publications.

MDPI

St. Alban-Anlage 66

4052 Basel

Switzerland

Tel. +41 61 683 77 34

Fax +41 61 302 89 18

www.mdpi.com

Religions Editorial Office

E-mail: religions@mdpi.com

www.mdpi.com/journal/religions

www.ingramcontent.com/pod-product-compliance
Lightning Source LLC
Chambersburg PA
CBHW051314020426
42333CB00028B/3337